CROSSING BORDERS
IN LITERACY AND SCIENCE INSTRUCTION

**PERSPECTIVES ON THEORY
AND PRACTICE**

E. WENDY SAUL
UNIVERSITY OF MISSOURI–ST. LOUIS
ST. LOUIS, MISSOURI, USA

EDITOR

D1314514

**INTERNATIONAL
Reading Association**
800 BARKSDALE ROAD, PO BOX 8139
NEWARK, DE 19714-8139, USA
www.reading.org

NATIONAL SCIENCE TEACHERS ASSOCIATION
1840 WILSON BOULEVARD
ARLINGTON, VA 22201-3000, USA
www.nsta.org

The International Reading Association attempts, through its publications, to provide a forum for a wide spectrum of opinions on reading. This policy permits divergent viewpoints without implying the endorsement of the Association.

Director of Publications   Joan M. Irwin
Editorial Director, Books and Special Projects   Matthew W. Baker
Managing Editor   Shannon Benner
Permissions Editor   Janet S. Parrack
Acquisitions and Communications Coordinator   Corinne M. Mooney
Associate Editor, Books and Special Projects   Sara J. Murphy
Assistant Editor   Charlene M. Nichols
Administrative Assistant   Michele Jester
Senior Editorial Assistant   Tyanna L. Collins
Production Department Manager   Iona Muscella
Supervisor, Electronic Publishing   Anette Schütz
Senior Electronic Publishing Specialist   Cheryl J. Strum
Electronic Publishing Specialist   R. Lynn Harrison
Proofreader   Elizabeth C. Hunt

Project Editor   Shannon Benner

Production Assistance   Wendy A. Mazur, composition; Peggy Mason, proofreading

Cover Design   eurēka

Copyright 2004 by the International Reading Association, Inc.
All rights reserved. No part of this publication may be reproduced or transmitted in any form or by any means, electronic or mechanical, including photocopy, or any information storage and retrieval system, without permission from the publisher.

Web addresses in this book were correct as of the publication date but may have become inactive or otherwise modified since that time. If you notice a deactivated or changed Web address, please e-mail books@reading.org with the words "Website Update" in the subject line. In your message, specify the Web link, the book title, and the page number on which the link appears.

Library of Congress Cataloging-in-Publication Data
Crossing borders in literacy and science instruction : perspectives on theory and practice / E. Wendy Saul, editor.
     p. cm.
Includes bibliographical references and indexes.
  ISBN 0-87207-519-2
  1. Science--Study and teaching (Elementary). 2. Children's literature in science education. 3. Language experience approach in education.   I. Saul, Wendy.   II. International Reading Association.   III. National Science Teachers Association.
  LB1585.C68 2004
  372.3'5--dc22
                                                                                          2003023378

Contents

Acknowledgments

The development of this volume was supported by the National Science Foundation under grant number 9912078. Any opinions, findings, conclusions, or recommendations expressed are those of the authors and do not necessarily reflect the views of the National Science Foundation.

I thank Donna Dieckman, Donna Neutze, and Jill Hutchison for their continuing and intelligent guidance of the Elementary Science Integration Projects (ESIP). Sutton Stokes, research assistant and journalist, deserves special mention for his careful attention to the manuscripts that compose this volume. Shannon Benner, managing editor at the International Reading Association, has negotiated a massive amount of material with wit, patience, and competence and I thank her especially for her efforts.

EWS

Contributors

Donna E. Alvermann
Distinguished Research Professor
  of Reading Education
University of Georgia
Athens, Georgia, USA

Linda Baker
Professor of Psychology
University of Maryland,
  Baltimore County
Baltimore, Maryland, USA

Anne Barry
Elementary School Teacher
Jungman Elementary School
Chicago, Illinois, USA

Elizabeth B. Bernhardt
Professor of German Studies
Stanford University
Stanford, California, USA

Carol A. Donovan
Associate Professor of
  Interdisciplinary Teacher
  Education
University of Alabama
Tuscaloosa, Alabama, USA

Mariam Jean Dreher
Professor of Education
University of Maryland,
  College Park
College Park, Maryland, USA

Hubert M. Dyasi
Director, the Workshop Center
City College, City University
  of New York
New York, New York, USA

Rebecca E. Dyasi
Associate Professor of Education
Long Island University
Brooklyn, New York, USA

Allan Feldman
Professor of Science and Teacher
  Education
University of Massachusetts–
  Amherst
Amherst, Massachusetts, USA

Danielle J. Ford
Assistant Professor of Science
  Education
University of Delaware
Newark, Delaware, USA

James Paul Gee
Tashia Morgridge Professor
  of Reading
University of Wisconsin–Madison
Madison, Wisconsin, USA

Barbara J. Guzzetti
Professor of Language and Literacy
Arizona State University
Tempe, Arizona, USA

Brian Hand
Professor of Science Education
Iowa State University
Ames, Iowa, USA

William G. Holliday
Professor of Science Education
University of Maryland,
    College Park
College Park, Maryland, USA

Michael L. Kamil
Professor of Education
Stanford University
Stanford, California, USA

Michael P. Klentschy
Superintendent of Schools
El Centro School District
El Centro, California, USA

Jay L. Lemke
Professor of Educational Studies
University of Michigan
Ann Arbor, Michigan, USA

Shirley J. Magnusson
Senior Research Associate
    in Science Education
University of Michigan
Ann Arbor, Michigan, USA

Elizabeth Molina-De La Torre
Science Director
El Centro Elementary School
    District
El Centro, California, USA

Annemarie Sullivan Palincsar
Jean and Charles Walgreen
    Professor of Reading and Literacy
University of Michigan
Ann Arbor, Michigan, USA

Christine C. Pappas
Professor of Language and Literacy
University of Illinois at Chicago
Chicago, Illinois, USA

Harold Pratt
President
Educational Consultants, Inc.
Littleton, Colorado, USA

Norby Pratt
Vice President
Educational Consultants, Inc.
Littleton, Colorado, USA

Jeanne Reardon
Retired Educator
Montgomery County Public Schools
Rockville, Maryland, USA

Amy Rife
Elementary School Teacher
Alexander Hamilton Elementary
    School
Chicago, Illinois, USA

Wolff-Michael Roth
Lansdowne Professor of Applied
    Cognitive Science
University of Victoria
Victoria, British Columbia, Canada

E. Wendy Saul
Allen B. and Helen S. Shopmaker
   Professor of Education
University of Missouri–St. Louis
St. Louis, Missouri, USA

Cynthia Shanahan
Professor of Education
University of Illinois at Chicago
Chicago, Illinois, USA

Laura B. Smolkin
Associate Professor of Elementary
   Education
University of Virginia
Charlottesville, Virginia, USA

Maria Varelas
Associate Professor of Science
   Education
University of Illinois at Chicago
Chicago, Illinois, USA

Anita N. Voelker
Instructor of Education
Messiah College
Grantham, Pennsylvania, USA

Carolyn S. Wallace
Associate Professor of Science
   Education
University of Georgia
Athens, Georgia, USA

Robert E. Yager
Professor of Science Education
University of Iowa
Iowa City, Iowa, USA

Eun-Mi Yang
Graduate Student, Science
   Education
Iowa State University
Ames, Iowa, USA

Larry D. Yore
University of Victoria Distinguished
   Professor of Science Education
University of Victoria
Victoria, British Columbia, Canada

Introduction

E. WENDY SAUL

Illa Podendorf, science educator and children's book author, was working with two students, trying to teach them to observe more closely. She had placed two turtles of similar size and with similar markings in a pan and asked the children how they could tell the turtles apart. "That's easy," announced one of the children. "Just name them."

The obvious links between language and science that this child's answer implies—the idea that for him, naming was synonymous with knowing, that through a name one might capture the complexity and gestalt of "difference," and that a feeling of power in science is fueled by identification—are merely part of the complex relationship between these subjects. What worries me, however, is that we in the field of education are looking to connect literacy and science instruction by using methods that are almost as simple as those suggested by Ms. Podendorf's student. This book, in contrast, seeks to help readers create a more nuanced discussion of the topic.

Although there is little debate that an important connection exists between language and science, until recently the conversation about how students might best learn about either subject or what standards should be employed to judge sound educational practice took place largely in isolated professional organizations—the International Reading Association (IRA) and the National Council of Teachers of English (NCTE) in the case of literacy, and the National Science Teachers Association (NSTA) and the American Association for the Advancement of Science (AAAS) in the case of science. But there is an obvious danger in such partitioning.

In *The Myth of the Machine*, Lewis Mumford (1966) recognized the problem such separations might cause and proposed that we consider a special office, that of the generalist, whose job it is to look for overall patterns or discrepancies:

> The generalist brings together widely separated fields, prudently fenced off by specialists, into a larger common area, visible only from the air. Only by forfeiting the detail can the overall pattern be seen, and once that pattern is visible, new details unseen by even the most thorough and competent field workers digging through the buried strata, may become visible. The generalist's competence lies not in unearthing new evidence, but in putting together authentic fragments that are accidentally, or sometimes arbitrarily, separated, because

specialists tend to abide too rigorously by a gentlemen's agreement not to invade each other's territory. (p. 8)

Each chapter in this volume may not individually aspire to a generalist's perspective, but in the aggregate these pieces offer readers an overview of the work taking place in different intellectual communities. Herein you will find pieces from linguists considering the special languages of science; from science educators commenting on the work of literacy educators; from reading, writing, and children's literature specialists who embed in their work differing notions of the relationship between science text and science learning; and from teacher educators eager to see teachers as responsible for helping children achieve in both literacy and science.

Specific questions emerge: How does knowledge in one area help learners succeed (or fail) in the other? What can teachers and teacher educators do to create classroom situations that make literacy–science connections possible or more robust? What kinds of science discourse invite the naïve but interested student to engage, ask questions, doubt, and wonder? And how important are literacy–science connections anyway? In a situation in which teachers are struggling to teach basic decoding and memorization, what role does science play?

To help answer these and other questions, the National Science Foundation (NSF) funded a conference titled Crossing Borders: Connecting Science and Literacy, which was held in 2001 at the University of Maryland, Baltimore County. As one looks at the contributions that are based on presentations from this conference, one sees areas of agreement and disagreement, differing emphases and gaps. All the contributors agree, for instance, that the connections between language and science are important, but clearly, certain authors privilege knowledge garnered from one area over knowledge from the other. Should students begin by doing science and bring in literacy later as a way of communicating what they have learned? Or does it happen the other way around—that priority must be given to language use (reading, writing, and talking), with science becoming one more forum for using these basic skills? Perhaps the language–science connection finally happens only in context, where connections seem natural and necessary. And what if the primary style of discourse of certain children gives them easy access to this "science language" while others are discouraged from, or find themselves unable to use, the talk generally accepted as science-appropriate? Answers to questions such as these might well transform teaching practices.

Research to Inform Practice?

In an ideal world, researchers would study particular practices and look at large-scale trends, then policymakers and teachers could base their educational decisions on the work of these researchers. But education is a messy enterprise, and generalizing to practice is neither neatly nor easily done. From what data is the analysis conceived and from what analysis are new insights, products, or recommendations born? Even in a field such as science, in which the "controls" are more available and the criteria for peer review is better established, the ideal often is not realized.

Let's consider an example from medicine. Several years ago my physician (along with thousands of others) felt confident in recommending the use of hormone replacement therapy (HRT), even for those women without debilitating symptoms of menopause. Doctors assured patients that virtually all the studies strongly indicated that HRT appeared to protect the heart and ward off osteoporosis. Several years later, we have found that the earlier studies were wrong. I am not suggesting here that the scientist-authors of these early reports were in any way fraudulent in their claims or that physicians who recommended HRT were misinterpreting the findings in the literature. Rather, my assertion is that science is essentially about continuing to dig and revise and build and reconfigure. That is both the fun and frustration of the enterprise.

Surely we wish to make decisions based on the best science available, but in so doing, we in education must remember, and remind our colleagues, that educational research is both messy and imperfect. The contributions presented here need to be viewed in that context. If something proposed in these pages results in unexpected side effects that are as problematic (or more so) than the original problem the intervention sought to address, it does not make sense to persist with a plan based on that research. In looking at the recommendations supported by this volume, we also need to remember that studies of many seemingly excellent practices are not addressed in these pages.

But there are certain givens and ideas that most—if not all—of the contributors to this book see as important for teachers and teacher educators to consider as they go about trying to foster better language and better science study.

Navigating Science

Science clearly is more than isolated bits of information, although "information" is somehow central to an understanding of science. People who successfully find their way in science are able to tie together the bits of information at their disposal so that the information makes sense and, similar to adventurers in the woods, they can trace their footsteps, learn to follow someone else's tracks, and perhaps decide to go it on their own and try a different way. Good questions are what enable people who are good at science to progress and anticipate what might come next. Sometimes, ideas are confirmed as science-literate people talk or read; at other times, science people find themselves surprised, doubtful, or just plain curious. The authors of *Science for All Americans* (Rutherford & Ahlgren, 1990) refer to this ability to put information into some reasonable order as the ability to create science stories. The best science, in written or oral form, makes these science stories come alive. And the best teachers are aware of these story lines and seek to help students anticipate and reflect.

Equitable Access to Science

As we peruse those seated at the science table—people identified as professional scientists or those who can talk knowledgeably about topics of scientific interest—we notice that many are missing. Although NSF statistics suggest that increasingly large numbers of women are entering science-related fields (technology still lags far behind), the proportions of blacks and Hispanics in science, when considered in relation to their overall numbers in U.S. society, remain abysmally low (see the Division of Science Resources Statistics website: www.nsf.gov/sbe/srs/stats.htm). I believe that there is general agreement among the authors represented here that people in the United States need to do more to promote and ensure everyone's access to science. Sometimes explicitly and sometimes implicitly, the chapter authors ask how language is implicated in the understanding of, access to, and teaching of science.

Troubling Instruction

Elementary school teachers in Maryland, for example, are being asked to spend the entire morning on literacy instruction and most of the afternoon on math, leaving 20 minutes (or less) per day for science. As William G. Holliday noted in public conversation at the Crossing Borders conference (August 25, 2001), science is moving rapidly from a close fourth place after reading, writing, and arithmetic to a distant fourth.

But you might ask, Could not or should not literacy and science be taught together? Would not a child who has had experience using a thermometer be better equipped to read a piece on how the instrument works? Or, viewing the issue from the other side, would not a child interested in collecting rocks be well served by reading, writing, and talking about the source of that interest? Although logic might lead us to the obvious "yes," the prescribed materials in use in most schools at the present time allow for little such curricular integration.

And although the literacy community welcomes more expository text into the mix of reading selections, educators from the science community express a significant worry. Their fear, and a well-deserved fear it is, is that information in science textbooks or trade literature will be viewed as science rather than as *descriptions* of science. Will the hands-on aspect of science be ignored or forgotten? Will educators assuming the generalist's perch understand the nature of science and the importance of claims, evidence, and warranties? Are literacy educators willing to give up time now devoted to comprehension activities and assign it instead to the investigation of materials and processes?

To understand the dangers of this merger, look closely at the advertising strategies used by developers of science-related readers. This volume encourages teachers to critique rather than accept resources presented to them, to ask questions such as, Is completing crossword puzzles that include science vocabulary really a good way of teaching either science or literacy? Does a children's book with glossy photos and obscure text that is written to meet readability requirements actually contribute to, rather than dispel, scientific misconceptions? Does simply reading aloud a work of fiction that includes an animal character (e.g., *The Very Hungry Caterpillar* [Carle, 1987]) actually prompt students to explore their world more carefully and systematically? Educators need to think more expansively using the generalist's perspective. How might a given activity invite students' use of different media? Does it promote critical and creative thinking? When a truly effective literacy–science connection is created in the classroom, both the literacy and the science work undertaken by students makes sense in terms of both disciplines. Neither is subsumed under the other.

Material Resources

Although a number of the chapters in this book focus on one learning resource—such as hands-on materials, books, the Internet, illustrations, or talk—contributors agree that students need experience with a variety of sources and that, to date, schools have been rather limited in terms of the sources made available to young people. Jay L. Lemke (chapter 2) describes a wide variety of communication modalities used by scientists—words, mathematical notations, diagrams, gestures, and digital images—noting that science is best viewed as a multimodal, hybrid language. Teachers would do well to look around their classrooms and consider what resources are available. What opportunities do students have for expanding their knowledge? Are there resources to support multiple approaches to the same subject or problem? Does a discussion of books, for instance, include a careful look at the ways in which an author uses diagrams? Does work on the Internet allow for the kind of browsing that those with a reluctant curiosity might enjoy?

As Donna E. Alvermann notes in chapter 12,

> A pedagogy of multiliteracies broadens the meaning of text and relates textual reading to oral, aural, visual, tactile, and digital modes of learning as well as to the social skills necessary for communicating and collaborating while engaged in such learning. It also draws from the literature on critical literacy, and especially on "the critical literacy skills required for assessing, selecting, and rejecting information on the basis of group-negotiated criteria relevant to the problem and the situated community of practice-learners" (Luke, 2002, p. 142).

One caveat: The authors represented in this volume are clear in differentiating between *science literacy*—what someone who has a basic familiarity with science content and processes knows and is able to do—and the *literacy–science connection*—how an understanding of text (defined broadly) might support and be supported by an understanding of science knowledge. (For more on this topic, see Robert E. Yager's chapter 5.) Any evaluation of resources must keep this distinction in mind.

Teachers Make a Difference

In the past few years, a new version of "teacher-proof" materials has come into vogue, complete with scripted dialogues designed to promote particular sequences of conversation and repetition. The implication, of course, is that teachers are wanting both intellectually and in terms of pedagogical expertise. In contrast to that view, the authors represented in this volume have great respect for teachers. They value teachers' knowledge and believe that it is in context—in the classroom—that the success of any practice is finally tested.

Since their inception, AAAS, IRA, NCTE, and NSTA—the organizations dedicated to research and excellent practice in literacy or science—have worked hard to make the case for excellence in their respective fields. Interestingly, the practices each organization advocates have much in common: a valuing of student engagement, an attempt to theorize from both experimental and naturalistic studies, an appreciation of cultural diversity and differences in home language, and an effort to teach for understanding. But perhaps most important, these organizations value teacher knowledge and expertise. Although there is considerable disagreement about where and how the seeds of educational reform are most fruitfully sown, it is clear that teachers can and do affect the quality of education.

An Overview of This Collection

This collection is not intended to offer a blueprint for the learning of science-related language; rather it is intended to provoke thought and represent the variety of research efforts related to language–science connections taking place in education circles today. This volume includes quasi-theoretical pieces that help us to think differently about how language in general and the specific discourse of science work together. Seemingly, such chapters would offer little in the way of advice about what to do tomorrow in class, but they do cause readers to think seriously about their own beliefs and look more closely, and perhaps more systematically, at the ways in which children draw from or reject particular linguistic or cultural moves.

The book also includes literature reviews of sorts, targeted at helping readers understand trends in the literature. These meta-analyses provide readers with a good sense of what has been done, what has been agreed on, and where to look for more information on topics of particular interest. These chapters also prove useful when one needs to argue for or against a particular practice.

In addition, the book includes a number of naturalistic studies that take place in the field and offer a glimpse of teachers whose practices seem exemplary or very close to it. Although some readers may wish to comb the chapters herein for strategies worth emulating, it also is important to read carefully the analyses presented—what the researcher or observer sees happening and the ways in which those insights may coincide with or differ from the reader's own perceptions of the events described. Even when authors are willing to make direct connections between their findings and large-scale practice, my hope is that readers will question and further examine the ideas presented by asking themselves, Is this what I believe—what I value?

Some chapters look at particular interventions and ask what happens when specific materials or practices are used to foster language–science connections. Still other chapters included here advocate for particular practices. In neither case should the reader simply assume that there is total agreement about the practices or positions proposed; again, the ideas are offered for discussion and reflection. The hope on all counts is that in the collection of materials and in the juxtaposition of ideas, readers will find new ways of understanding and doing their work. My more personal hope is that as practitioners begin forging connections between language and science study and examining the results of their work, they will change the questions being asked and, perhaps, even the way research is being done.

Final Thoughts

Surely there are more patterns that a generalist might notice and an educator might learn from. But Mumford (1966) also cautions,

> Even when [the generalist] seems on the verge of completing an emerging pattern, he must not surreptitiously chip a piece to make it fit, as in a jigsaw puzzle, nor yet must he manufacture any of the pieces in order to fill out the design—although he of course may look in unlikely places for them. He must likewise be ready to scrap any piece of evidence, no matter however he may cherish it, as soon as one of his specialist colleagues discovers that it is suspect or that it does not fit into the particular environment or the particular time sequence under discussion. When not enough parts exist, the generalist must wait until competent authorities find or fabricate them. (p. 8)

The patterns we notice also need to be placed on the larger mosaic of educational reform. At present, the lion's share of both time and money is being spent on literacy education in general and reading in particular. And when literacy occupies the lion's share of the academic school day, science educators become interested in how they might recapture some of the time they have lost to drills and stories. Similarly, when science funding is high and the political winds blow favorably toward nature study or technology study, for instance, literacy educators begin looking hard for science biographies and science poems to complement hands-on units and attempt to incorporate strategies that give more attention to the ways in which literacy can support work across the disciplines. My hope is that this book gives readers some new and interesting ways to think about this balance between language and science study and to reflect on what is in the best interest of students. Consider these chapters as conversations to be enlivened by other voices— by your own voice. The contributions have been arranged to promote real talk and genuine curiosity.

Author Note

In addition to this book, follow-up efforts to examine the links between language and science also have resulted in at least two "white papers" forthcoming in *Reading Research Quarterly* ("New Directions in Language and Science Education Research") and the *Journal of Research in Science Teaching* ("Message From the 'Island Group': What Is Literacy in Science Literacy?" 2003).

REFERENCES

Luke, C. (2002). Re-crafting media and ICT literacies. In D.E. Alvermann (Ed.), *Adolescents and literacies in a digital world* (pp. 132–146). New York: Peter Lang.

Mumford, L. (1966) *The myth of the machine: Technics and human development*. New York: Harcourt, Brace.

Rutherford, F.J., & Ahlgren, A. (1990). *Science for all Americans* (American Association for the Advancement of Science Project 2061). New York: Oxford University Press.

CHILDREN'S LITERATURE REFERENCE

Carle, E. (1987). *The very hungry caterpillar*. New York: Philomel.

DESCRIBING
THE LANGUAGES
OF SCIENCE

The three chapters in this section by linguists James Paul Gee, Jay L. Lemke, and Wolff-Michael Roth all cause us to ask some fundamental, philosophical questions about the languages of science: What does it mean to be able to talk or write or read science? What are the markers of competence, and where do we look for signs that students are moving in that direction?

Gee's chapter, "Language in the Science Classroom: Academic Social Languages as the Heart of School-Based Literacy," asks us to consider how language enables or forwards scientific thinking and the presentation of scientific data. Academic languages—and science is surely one of them—must be learned. To help students acquire academic language, teachers need to remain cognizant of and sensitive to the various languages (discourses) and dispositions and cultural suppositions (Discourses) that students bring to school. Instruction also should focus on providing useful bridges between various discourse/Discourse communities. How might this be done? What curricular moves might invite students to find links between what they view as their natural discourses/Discourses and the discourses/Discourses used in the scientific community? And what might teachers do to make the journey easier and less threatening for those students trekking across wildly foreign terrain?

Lemke, a linguist with a background in theoretical physics, uses his chapter, "The Literacies of Science," to raise questions about the literacies of science—why they are what they are. In so doing he asks educators to attend to the literacy practices of working scientists, to the way scientists use multiple strategies to describe and explain their work. Teachers who limit literacy-related science instruction to reading, writing, and talking are in fact missing a significant portion of science communication. Lemke concludes by asking for an expanded conversation about the languages of science, one that takes into account gender and cultural identities and social relationships, and that attends to discourses and opportunities outside the normal purview of the school. This conversation needs to invite a critique of current practices as well as a replication of them.

Roth, author of "Gestures: The Leading Edge in Literacy Development," asks readers to expand their definition of language and to consider the uses of hand and body movements as students try to incorporate new information into their world. Again, there is important advice for teachers embedded in this study. Roth encourages teachers to watch closely—not just listen and read—as students try to explain or describe scientific phenomena. Would it make sense to encourage students to revisit experiences through gesture, for example? And similarly, Roth asserts that when teachers seek to explain or answer questions, they need to think about how their own use of gesture might be employed to greatest effect.

Together these chapters situate the conversation about language–science connections in a broad intellectual landscape.

CHAPTER 1

Language in the Science Classroom: Academic Social Languages as the Heart of School-Based Literacy

JAMES PAUL GEE

There are different "ways with printed words" embedded in different social and cultural groups, institutions, and social practices. Literacy, in that sense, takes multiple forms. Furthermore, literacy, viewed in terms of the different sorts of social practices in which it is embedded, is almost always integrally involved with oral language and ways of acting, interacting, and thinking, and not just reading and writing (see Barton, 1994; Gee, 1996; Street, 1995, for overviews of this approach to literacy). In regard to schooling, I would argue that schools need to focus on the acquisition of academic language within specific social practices and not on literacy as a general thing or as only reading and writing. In school, especially as one moves beyond the first couple years, reading and writing are (or most certainly should be) fully embedded in and integrated with learning, using, and talking about specific content.

No domain represents academic sorts of language better than science. Science makes demands on students to use language—oral and printed—as well as other symbol systems that epitomize the types of representational systems and practices that students need to master for higher levels of school success. In addition, these languages and representational systems are at the heart of living in and thinking critically about modern societies.

Although I also construe language as integrally involved with identities and social practices, this chapter argues for a set of claims about the connections between language and science learning. (The connections, however, are the same for all school subjects.) In much of science education, language is pushed into the background or ignored, while thinking or doing are brought into the foreground as if these tasks had little to do with language. I think that these "foreground" activities have much to do with language, however. Each of my claims in this chapter implies a particular property that science instruction ought to have, although little work in science instruction that I am aware of speaks directly to these properties.

Academic Language and the Social Language Code

First claim: Success in school is primarily contingent on learners' willingness and ability to cope with academic language.

In the recent debates over early reading, the alphabetic code has been given pride of place (National Institute of Child Health and Human Development, 2000; Snow, Burns, & Griffin 1998; see Gee, 1999a, for discussion). However, more children fail in school, in the long run, because they cannot cope with "academic language" than because they cannot decode print. Academic language is related to a family of languages that I will call *social languages*. English, similar to any human language, is not a single language but is composed of a myriad of different "social languages," some of which are forms of academic language (Gee, 1996, 1999b).

A social language is a way of using language to enact a particular socially situated identity and carry out a particular socially situated activity. For example, there are ways of speaking and acting like a (specific type of) doctor, street gang member, postmodern literary critic, football fanatic, neoliberal economist, working-class male, adaptationist biologist, and so forth, through an endless array of identities. Often, of course, we can recognize a particular socially situated kind of person engaged in a characteristic sort of activity through his or her use of a given social language without our actually being able to enact that kind of person or carry out that activity. We can be producers or consumers of particular social languages, or we can be both.

Recognizing a particular social language is also a matter of a code. Let us call it the *social language code*. Different patterns or correlations of grammatical elements (at the levels of phonology and graphology, morphology, words, syntax, discourse relations, and pragmatics) are associated with or map to particular social languages (specific styles of oral or written language or both) associated with specific socially situated identities and activities. So, here the code is not between sounds and letters but between grammatical patterns and styles of language (and their associated identities and activities).

Let me give an example. The following section of text comes from a school science textbook (Martin, 1990):

> The destruction of a land surface by the combined effects of abrasion and removal of weathered material by transporting agents is called erosion.... The production of rock waste by mechanical processes and chemical changes is called weathering. (p. 93)

A whole bevy of correlated grammatical features (i.e., features that hang together or pattern together in oral language or written texts or both) mark these sentences as part of a distinctive social language or style of language (in this case, academic). Some of these features are "heavy subjects" (e.g., long phrases such as "the production of rock waste by mechanical processes and chemical changes"); processes and actions named by nouns or nominalizations rather than verbs (e.g., "production"); passive main verbs ("is called"); passives inside nominalizations (e.g., "production by mechanical means"); modifiers that have more content than the nouns they modify (e.g., "transporting agents"); and complex embedding (e.g., "weathered material by transporting agents" is a nominalization embedded inside "the combined effects of...," and this more complex nominalization is embedded inside a yet larger nominalization, "the destruction of...").

This style of language also incorporates a great many distinctive discourse markers, that is, linguistic features that characterize larger stretches of text and give them unity and coherence as a certain type of text or "genre." For example, the genre here is explanatory definition, and it is characterized by classificatory language of a certain sort. Such language leads adept readers to form a classificatory scheme in their heads, something similar to this: "There are two kinds of change, erosion and weathering, and two kinds of weathering, mechanical and chemical."

Academic social languages constitute a large family of related (but, of course, different) social languages. Academic social languages are not primarily associated with subject areas as extensive as whole disciplines but with particular forms of intellectual inquiry that are sometimes subdomains of a discipline but that, especially today, often cross disciplinary boundaries. For example, different sorts of biologists talk, write, and act in different ways, and in some cases they share these ways more closely with some people outside biology (e.g., certain types of physicists) than they do with some other biologists. The same can be said of almost any other discipline.

Acquisition and Identity: Lifeworld vs. Specialist Worlds

Second claim: To acquire an academic social language, students must be willing to accept certain losses and see the acquisition of the academic social language as a gain.

When one acquires an academic social language—most especially a language associated with science—there are both significant losses and significant gains (Halliday & Martin, 1993). For example, consider the two sentences below. The first is in the social language of the "lifeworld," and the second is in an academic social language. (By the lifeworld, I mean that domain in which we speak and act as "ordinary," everyday, nonspecialist people. Of course, different social and cultural groups have different lifeworlds and different lifeworld social languages, although such lifeworld languages do share a good many features that cause linguists to refer to them collectively as *vernacular language*.)

1. Hornworms sure vary a lot in how well they grow.
2. Hornworm growth exhibits a significant amount of variation.

The subject of a sentence names what a sentence is about (its topic) and (when it comes first in the sentence) the perspective from which we are viewing the claims that we want to make (the sentence's "theme"). The lifeworld sentence above (sentence 1) is about hornworms (little, green worms) and launches off from the topic of the hornworm. The presence of the word *sure* helps to make the subject (hornworms) seem like a thing with which we are empathizing. The specialist sentence (sentence 2) is not about hornworms but about a trait or feature of hornworms (in particular, one that can be quantified) and launches off from this perspective. The hornworm seems to "disappear" from the sentence.

The lifeworld sentence involves dynamic processes (changes) named by verbs (*vary* and *grow*). People tend to care a good deal about changes and transformations, especially in things with which they empathize such as the hornworms in sentence 1. The specialist sentence, on the other hand, turns these dynamic processes into abstract things (*variation* and *growth*). The dynamic changes from sentence 1 disappear. Also, the lifeworld sentence has a verb with content (*vary*), but the specialist one has a verb of appearance (*exhibit*), which is a class of verbs similar to copulas (copulas are linking verbs, such as *to be*, that do not have much contentful meaning) and are not as deep or rich in content as verbs such as *vary*. Such copulas and verbs of appearance are basically just ways to relate things to each other (in this case, abstract things).

The lifeworld sentence has a quantity term (*how well*) that is not just about amount or degree but also is "telically evaluative," if I may coin a term. *How well* is about a quantity that is evaluates in terms of a telos, or end point, germane to the hornworm, that is, in terms of a point of good, proper, or full growth toward which hornworms are meant to progress. Some hornworms reach the telos, and others fall short. The specialist sentence replaces this telically evaluative term with a more precise measurement term that is "Discourse evaluative" (*significant amount*). (I use the term *Discourse* with a capital *D* for any distinctive culture or community of practice, such as biologists, associated with certain ways with words, deeds, and values; I use the term *discourse* with a little *d* simply for connected stretches of talk or written text.) *Significant amount* is about a quantity that is evaluated in terms of the goals, procedures, and even the telos of a Discourse (here a type of biology), not a hornworm. (By a Discourse, I mean any characteristic set of ways of combining words, deeds, and values so as to enact a particular type of socially recognizable identity, such as that of a certain type of biologist or a certain type of street gang member; see Gee, 1996). It is a particular area of biology that determines what is significant and what is not. All our hornworms could be stunted or otherwise untypical of well-grown hornworms (well-grown from a lifeworld, nonspecialist perspective) and still display a significant amount of variation in their sizes.

This last difference is related to another one: The lifeworld sentence contains an appreciative marker (*sure*), and the specialist sentence leaves out such markers. The appreciative marker communicates the attitude, interest, and even values of the speaker or writer. Attitude, interest, and values, in this sense, are left out of the specialist sentence.

So, when one has to leave the lifeworld way of speaking to acquire and then use the specialist language, some things are lost—concrete things such as hornworms and empathy for them; changes and transformations as dynamic, ongoing processes; and telos and appreciation. Some things gained are abstract ideas and relations among them; traits and the quantification and categorization of traits; and evaluation from within a specialized domain. The crucial question is, Why would someone—most especially a child in school—accept these losses?

My view is that people will accept this loss only if they see the gain *as a gain*. So, a crucial question in science education ought to be, What would make someone see acquiring a scientific social language as a gain? Social languages are tied to socially situated identities and activities, as we have seen. People can see a new social language as a gain only if they recognize and understand the sorts of socially situated identities and activities that use the social language, if they value these identities and activities or at least understand why they are valued, and if they believe they (will) have real access to these identities and activities or at least (will) have access to meaningful versions of them.

Thus, acquisition of a social language is heavily tied at the outset to identity issues. It is tied to the learner's willingness and trust to leave (for a time and place) the lifeworld and participate in another identity, one that, for anyone, represents a certain loss. For some people, it represents a more significant loss in terms of a disassociation from, and even opposition to, their lifeworlds because their lifeworlds are not the type of middle-class ones that historically have built up a sense of shared interests and values with some academic specialist domains.

Situated Meaning

Third claim: One does not know what a social language means in any sense that is useful for action unless one can situate the meanings of the social language's words and phrases in terms of embodied experiences.

Recent debates over reading have pointed out that although one's first (native) oral language is acquired by immersion in practice (socialization as part of a social group that uses that language), literacy often requires some degree of overt instruction (see Gee, 1994, for discussion). So, what about the acquisition of an academic social language? The language of adaptationist biology, for example, is no one's native language. Are academic social languages acquired largely through immersion in practice, or do they require a good deal of overt instruction as well? In reality—given that scientists tend to ignore language as a relevant factor—many a scientist has picked up a scientific social language through immersion in practice, with little or no overt instruction in the language.

Although I advocate overt instruction in academic social languages, both in the midst of practice and outside it, what I want to point out here is this: Social languages can be understood in two different ways, either as being largely verbal or as being situated. One can understand a piece of a scientific social language largely as a set of verbal definitions or rather general meanings for words and phrases and, in turn, one can relate words and phrases to each other in terms of these definitions or general meanings and general knowledge about grammatical patterns in the language. However, such an understanding is not all that useful when one has to engage in any activity using a specialist language.

Words and phrases in use in any social language, including lifeworld social languages, not only have relatively general meanings (which basically define the range of possible more-specific meanings a word can take on in actual contexts of use) but also have situated meanings. Words and phrases are associated with different situated meanings in different contexts, social languages, and Discourses. For example, consider what happens in your head when I say, "The coffee spilled; get a mop," versus "The coffee spilled; get a broom," versus "The coffee spilled; can you restack it?" In each case, you actively assemble a different situated meaning for the word *coffee* (as liquid, grains, or containers).

Let me develop a bit more what I mean by saying that "meanings" are assembled on the spot (and for the spot, so to speak). In the context of the lifeworld, if we are asked a question such as "How far does the light go?" while staring at a lamp, we are likely to answer something such as "Only as far as I can see the light illuminating the area near the lamp." In this case, we assemble a meaning for *light* that is something similar to "an illuminated region." In the context of physical science, on the other hand, we would answer the question quite differently and assemble a different meaning. In the case of physics, a number of different assemblies could be associated with *light*, one of which is *rays* (lines of light) that travel indefinitely far and can reflect off surfaces. In terms of this assembly, we would answer the question by saying, "The light travels forever unless it reflects off a surface." Of course, other assemblies for *light* exist in yet other Discourses. For example, in the context of theater, *light* is associated with things such as lighting effects. Further, new assemblies can and do arise as Discourses change and interact or as new situations arise.

Situated meanings are, crucially, rooted in embodied experience—one has to "see" the meaning as a pattern extracted from the concrete data of one's experience (Barsalou, 1999a, 1999b). To do so, one must have had a lot of practice with experiences that trigger the pattern. Situated meanings are not definitions. If one cannot situate the meaning of a word or phrase, then one has only a verbal meaning for the word or phrase. Such verbal meanings, although they can facilitate the passing of certain sorts of tests, are of limited value when language has to be put to use within activities.

Recent work in cognitive psychology has further developed this notion of "situatedness" (long taken for granted in work on pragmatics). Consider, for instance, the following two quotes:

1. "Comprehension is grounded in perceptual simulations that prepare agents for situated action." (Barsalou, 1999a, p. 77)
2. "To a particular person, the meaning of an object, event, or sentence is what that person can do with the object, event, or sentence." (Glenberg, 1997, p. 3)

These quotes are from a "family" of related viewpoints (e.g., Barsalou, 1999a, 1999b; Brown, Collins, & Dugid, 1989; Clark, 1997; Engeström, Miettinen, & Punamäki, 1999; Gee, 1992; Glenberg, 1997; Glenberg & Robertson, 1999; Hutchins, 1996; Latour, 1999; Lave, 1996; Lave & Wenger, 1991; Wenger, 1998; Wertsch, 1998). Although differences exist among the family members (alternative theories about situated cognition), they share the viewpoint that situated meaning in language is not an abstract propositional representation that resembles a verbal language. Rather, meaning in language is tied to people's experiences of situated action in the material and social world. Furthermore, these experiences (perceptions, feelings, actions, and interactions) are stored in the brain not in terms of propositions or language but in something similar to dynamic images tied to perceptions both of the world and of one's own body, internal states, and feelings: "Increasing evidence suggests that perceptual simulation is indeed central to comprehension" (Barsalou, 1999a, p. 74).

It is almost as if we videotape our experiences as we are having them, create a library of such videotapes, and edit them to make some prototypical tapes or a set of typical instances, but we stand ever ready to add new tapes to our library, re-edit the tapes based on new experiences, or draw from the library less typical tapes when the need arises. As we face new situations or new texts, we run our tape—perhaps a prototypical one, a set of typical ones, a set of contrasting ones, or a less typical one—in order to apply our old experiences to our new experience and to aid us in making, editing, and storing the videotape that will capture this new experience; integrating it into our library; and allowing us to make sense of it (both while we are having the experience and afterward).

These mental videotapes are what we think with and through. They are what we use to give meaning to our experiences in the world. They are what we use to give meaning to words and sentences. But they are not language or created in language (not even in propositions). Furthermore, because they are representations of experiences (including feelings, attitudes, embodied positions, and various sorts of "foregroundings" and "backgroundings" of attention), they are not just information or facts. Rather, they are value-laden, perspective-taking "movies in the mind." Of course, talking about videotapes in the mind is a metaphor that, like all metaphors, is incorrect if pushed too far (see Barsalou, 1999b, for how the metaphor can be spelled out in more realistic terms in regard to how the brain functions).

On this account, too, the meaning of a word (the way in which we give it meaning in a particular context) is not different than the meaning of an experience, object, or tool in the world (i.e., in terms of the way in which we give the experience, object, or tool meaning):

> The meaning of the glass to you, at that particular moment, is in terms of the actions available. The meaning of the glass changes when different constraints on action are combined. For example, in a noisy room, the glass may become a mechanism for capturing attention (by tapping it with a spoon), rather than a mechanism for quenching thirst. (Glenberg, 1997, p. 41)

Although Glenberg is talking about the meaning of a glass as an object in one's specific experience of the world at a given time and place, he could just as well be talking about the meaning of the word *glass* in one's specific experience of a piece of talk or written text at a given time and place. The meaning of the word *glass* in a given piece of talk or text would be given by running a mental simulation (a videotape) of how the glass fits into courses of action being built up in the "theaters" of our minds. These courses of action are based on how we understand all the other words and events in the world that surround the word *glass* as we read it: "The embodied models constructed to understand language are the same as those that underlie comprehension of the natural environment" (Glenberg, 1997, p. 17).

However, I want to state one important caution here. Much of the work in cognitive psychology stresses that the experiences in which situated meanings are rooted are ones we have had as embodied perceivers of, and actors in, the material world. However, situated meanings are also, importantly, rooted in experiences we have had as participants in specific rhetorical practices and activities, which are themselves a form of embodied engagement with the world. Consider, for example, the following sentence from a high school student's first and second drafts of a paper on albinism (the two drafts were separated by a good deal of work on the part of the teacher).

> First Draft: Then to let people know there are different types of Albinism, I will tell and explain all this.
>
> Second Draft: Finally, to let people know there are different types of Albinism, I will name and describe several.

In the first draft, the student appears to have formed situated meanings for *tell* and *explain* that have to do with telling a story and explicating the big picture ("all this") through that story. This is, as one might assume, an activity the student has experienced a great many times in his lifeworld. Unfortunately, in the sort of academic writing in which the student engaged for his or her paper, the phrase "different types of Albinism" requires a meaning situated in quite a different way, one inconsistent with how the student has situated the meanings of *tell* and *explain*.

Someone who has undertaken to classify things in academic Discourses of certain types would not be tempted to use *tell* and *explain* as this student has done. They would know that these words are not used in this way in, for example, a biological text, though they may very well not be able to say why this is so. Knowing such things is part of knowing the practice of these sorts of academic Discourses. (Note that *tell* and *explain* have other situated meanings in terms of which they could occur with the phrase "different types of Albinism"—for example, a teacher could write on a student essay, "You first need to tell your readers what the different types of Albinism are and then to explain how these types are distinguished.")

On the other hand, one can readily situate meanings for *name* and *describe* that are more consistent with the appropriate situated meaning for "different types of Albinism" (although one can situate inappropriate ones, of course, as in "Scientists name different types of Albinism differently"). To situate the most appropriate meanings for given words, one needs to have experienced certain acts of classification within certain sorts of Discourses.

I should note, as well, that even the student's second version is not quite right in terms of many academic Discourses' ways of classifying: *people* is wrong, and *name* is just a bit off; something similar to "There are different types of Albinism. Below, I list several of these and describe them" would have been better yet. This example, simple as it is, tells us how subtle a process situating meaning can be.

When anyone is trying to speak or write, or listen or read, within a given social language within a given Discourse, the crucial question becomes, What sorts of experiences (if any)—in terms of embodied practices and activities, including textual, conversational, and rhetorical ones—has this person had that can anchor the situated meanings of the words and phrases of this social language? Otherwise, one is stuck with merely a general and verbal understanding (the sort that, unfortunately, often is rewarded in school anyway).

Language Acquisition and Perspective Taking

Fourth claim: Language acquisition must involve access to and simulations of the perspectives of more advanced users of the language as these are used in practice.

My previous remarks on situated meaning argue that embodied experiences in the world and the active assembly of meaning based on these experiences are the foundation of meaning-in-use in language. However, I believe a strong case can be made that social interaction and dialogue of a certain sort also are crucial to the acquisition of any social language whatsoever. Consider, in this regard, the following idea from Tomasello's book *The Cultural Origins of Human Cognition* (2000):

> The perspectival nature of linguistic symbols, and the use of linguistic symbols in discourse interaction in which different perspectives are explicitly contrasted and shared, provide the raw material out of which the children of all cultures construct the flexible and multi-perspectival—perhaps even dialogical—cognitive representations that give human cognition much of its awesome and unique power. (p. 163)

Let's briefly analyze what this means. From the point of view of Tomasello's model, the words and grammar of a human language exist to allow people to take and communicate alternative perspectives on experience (see also Hanks, 1995). That is, words and grammar exist to give people alternative ways to view one and the same state of affairs. Language is not about conveying neutral or "objective" information; rather, it is about communicating perspectives on experience and action in the world, often in contrast to alternative and competing perspectives: "We may then say that linguistic symbols are social conventions for inducing others to construe, or take a perspective on, some experiential situation" (Tomasello, 2000, p. 118).

Let me give a couple examples of what it means when I say that words and grammar are not primarily about giving and getting information but, rather, about giving and getting different perspectives on experience. First, I visit Microsoft's web site: Is it selling its products, marketing them, or underpricing them against the competition? Are products I can download from the site without paying money for them free, are they being exchanged for my having bought other Microsoft products (e.g., Windows), or are there strings attached? Note how metaphors (such as *strings attached*) add greatly to, and are a central part of, the perspective taking that we can do. If I say, "Microsoft's new operating system is loaded with bugs," I take a perspective in which Microsoft is less agentive and responsible than if I use the grammatical construction "Microsoft has loaded its new operating system with bugs."

Here is another example: Do I say that a child who is using multiple cues to give meaning to a written text (i.e., using some decoding along with picture and context cues) is reading, or do I say (as some of the prophonics people do) that he or she is not really reading but is engaged in emergent literacy? (For prophonics people, the child is only really reading when he or she is decoding all the words in the text and is not using nondecoding cues for word recognition.) In this case, contending camps actually argue over what perspective on experience the terms *reading* or *really reading* ought to name. In the end, the point is that no wording is ever neutral or "just the facts." All wordings—given the very nature of language—are perspectives on experience that exist alongside competing perspectives in the grammar of the language and in actual social interactions.

How do children learn how words and grammar line up to express particular perspectives on experience? Interactive, interpersonal dialogue with more advanced peers and adults appears to be crucial. In such dialogue, children come to see, from time to time, that others have taken a different perspective on what is being talked about than they themselves have. At a certain developmental level, children have the capacity to distance themselves from their own perspectives and (internally) simulate the perspective the other person is taking, thereby coming to see how words and grammar express those perspectives (in contrast to the way in which different words and grammatical constructions express competing perspectives).

Later, in other interactions, or in thinking to him- or herself, the child can rerun such simulations and imitate the perspective taking that the more advanced peer or adult has done by using certain sorts of words and grammar. Through such simulations and imitative learning, children learn to use the symbolic means that other persons have used to share intentions with them: "In imitatively learning linguistic symbols from other persons in this way, I internalize not only their communicative intention (their intention to get me to share their perspective), but also the specific perspective they have actually taken" (Tomasello, 2000, p. 128).

Tomasello (2000) also points out—in line with our previous discussion that the world and texts are assigned meanings in the same way—that children come to use objects in the world as symbols at the same time (or with just a bit of a time lag) as they come to use linguistic symbols as perspective-taking devices on the world. Furthermore, children learn to use objects as symbols (to assign them different meanings that encode specific perspectives in different contexts) in the same way they learn to use linguistic symbols. In both cases, a child simulates in his or her head, and later imitates with his or her words and deeds, the perspectives his or her interlocutor must be taking on a given situation by using certain words and certain forms of grammar or by treating certain objects in certain ways. Thus, meaning for words, grammar, and objects comes from interactive, interpersonal dialogue: "Human symbols [are] inherently social, intersubjective, and perspectival" (Tomasello, 2000, p. 131).

Now, one might argue that Tomasello's work is germane only to the acquisition of one's native language early in life. But having this belief would mean missing one of the important points of work such as that of Tomasello and Hanks. A crucial point they are making, to my mind, is that grammar by its very nature, regardless of the social language within which it is used, is a perspective-taking device, learned in part by the human capacity to run simulations of experience (even from someone else's perspective) in our heads.

Science and Lifeworld Language

Fifth claim: Lifeworld language is problematic for science.

Many educators argue that the way to solve the identity issues with which I started this chapter (e.g., how do we get children to "buy into" the situated identity associated with a given academic Discourse?) is to allow and encourage them to use their everyday lifeworld (vernacular) languages for science talk. In my view, this idea comports poorly with everything I have said previously. However, the issue remains: Why can't we marry science to lifeworld languages? I believe there are good reasons to encourage children, even early on, to marry scientific activities with scientific ways of using words rather than with lifeworld languages, although lifeworld languages are obviously the starting point for the acquisition of any later social language, as Vygotsky (1978) pointed out. To make this argument, I want to work through one example based on the data discussed at greater length in Gee (1997) (see Rosebery, Warren, & Conant, n.d., for a deeper discussion of the relevant issues). In this example, a group of students in an elementary classroom have been discussing the question, What makes rust? They have developed a set of questions about rust such as, Does ordinary water cause rust? Does rain water cause rust? Does paint protect against rust? Do other things besides metal get rusty? To help answer these questions, the children have placed a number of metal and nonmetal objects in water to examine what does or does not get rusty, and to investigate a variety of other questions. In the following excerpt, the children have taken a metal bottle cap and a plastic plate out of the water. The cap had been sitting on the plate. They discuss the cap and plate. Similar to all interactive language, their language is replete with deictics (point words such as *like* and *that* or *he* and *she*). I have placed explanatory material in brackets to make clear what they are referring to.

Elizabeth: Do you think plastic would get rusty?

Philip: No 'cause we've got this [plastic plate here, and it is not rusty]—maybe [it would get rusty] if something metal was on this [plastic plate].

Jill: It [the plastic plate] will get old [and old things get rusty].

Philip: [If it were old and got rusty, then] Metal got on it like [it got on] this plastic plate.

Jill: Cuz like the bottle cap where the rust is from, the rust got off the metal [bottle cap] and went onto the plate.

Philip: But without the metal on top of the plastic [plate], you would never get, it [the plate] probably wouldn't ever get rusty.

Jill: You wouldn't get marks.

Elizabeth: Why these marks here [on the plastic plate]?

Jill: Because the rust comes off the things, and it goes onto there, and it stays.

Philip: And the rust gots nowhere to go, so it goes on the plate.

Jill: But if we didn't put the metal things on there [on the plate], it wouldn't be all rusty.

Philip: And if we didn't put the water on there [on the metal bottle cap, on the plastic cap, on the plate combination, or on the plate?—it is hard to tell which Philip is referring to], it wouldn't be all rusty.

Jill points out that rust comes off rusty metal things, such as the bottle cap, and leaves marks on other things such as the plastic plate on which the bottle cap was sitting. Later, she points out that if the rusty metal bottle cap had not been placed on the plastic plate, the plate would not be "all rusty." Philip formulates his last contribution above as a direct "copy" (such copying patterns are common in everyday vernacular speech) of Jill's immediately preceding contribution, pointing out that if water had not been placed on the metal bottle cap (and the plate on which it is sitting), then it would not be "all rusty."

This whole excerpt is typical of everyday language, and, in fact, reflects both the strength and the weakness of such language. In everyday language, when we are trying to make sense of a problematic situation, we use patterns and associations, and repetitions and parallelism—what might loosely be called "poetic" devices—to construct (or, as here, to coconstruct) a design that makes sense. Much everyday talk shares this feature with poetry, myth, and storytelling, regardless of what genre it formally is in. Far from intending to denigrate this approach to sense making, I have celebrated it elsewhere (see Gee, 1991) and have no doubt that it has given rise to some of human beings' deepest insights into the human condition. But everyday language is not how the Discourses of the sciences operate; in fact, although these Discourses most certainly grew out of this method of sense making, they developed partly in overt opposition to it (Bazerman, 1988).

Everyday language allows for juxtapositions of images and themes in the creation of patterns (such as "it wouldn't be all rusty"), and, as I have just stated, this sort of juxtaposition is very often an extremely powerful device in its own right. But from the perspective of scientific Discourse, it can create a symmetry that is misleading and obscures important underlying differences (e.g., the underlying reality behind a plastic plate that is all rusty and the one behind a metal cap that is all rusty). Unfortunately, in science it often is this obscured, underlying level that is crucial.

The children's everyday language in the excerpt obfuscates what we will see is a crucial distinction, and it also obscures the underlying mechanisms (here, cause and effect) that are the heart and soul of physical science. Jill's and Philip's parallel constructions—in particular, their uses of "all rusty" and "if we didn't put...on, it wouldn't be..."—obscure the fact that these two linguistic devices mean (or could mean) two very different things here. Rusty metal things cause things such as plastic plates to "be all rusty" (namely, by physical contact) in a quite different way than water causes metal things to "be all rusty" (namely, by a chemical reaction). Further, the plastic plate and the metal bottle cap are "all rusty" in two crucially different senses—that is, crucial for scientific Discourse, although not necessarily for everyday Discourse, which is content to pattern them together through the phrase "all rusty." In Jill's statement, *all rusty* means (or could mean) *covered in rust*, but in Philip's statement it means (or could mean) *a surface that has become rusted*. In other words, the distinction between having rust (a state) and having rusted (a process) is ignored.

It is typical for everyday language to obscure the details of causal, or other systematic, relations among things in favor of rather general and vague relations such as "all rusty" or "put on." Everyday language, in creating patterns and associations, is less careful about differences and underlying systematic relations, although these are crucial to science. Again, I do not intend to denigrate everyday language. The very weaknesses I am pointing to here are, in other contexts, sources of great power. Everyday language is much better, in fact, than the language of science in making integrative connections across domains (e.g., light as a psycho-social-physical element in which we bathe).

Conversation and Expanded Language

Sixth claim: A face-to-face conversational framework is problematic for the acquisition of scientific academic language.

Very often, even when classrooms import a form of a scientific social language into their discussions, they keep this talk in the typical style of interactive conversation among peers. In face-to-face conversations, both in the lifeworld and in science, people tend to use truncated language. That is, they use deictics, vague references, and ambiguous structures that are resolved by the shared knowledge the interlocutors have of what they are talking about and the context they share in their face-to-face encounter. This framework is fine for people who share a good deal of knowledge, know a lot about what they are talking about, and have mastered the social language in which they are communicating. However, such a framework is problematic for people trying to acquire a new social language. Such beginners cannot see the expanded forms of the social language used in overt ways that make public what they mean. The deictics, vague references, and ambiguous structures typical of face-to-face conversations hide meanings from these beginners and also hide the beginners' own meanings from more advanced peers and teachers who could otherwise scaffold their acquisition of the social language. Yet it is the expanded form of the language that ultimately underlies the meanings that people express and that appears in the sorts of writing and monologues that very often are the basis of evaluation in the schools.

Let me give one example, which is based on data taken from Rosebery, Puttick, and Bodwell (1996). The following discussion occurred in a second-grade classroom. Three girls in the class had designed an experiment to test how much light plants needed to grow well. They had raised fast-growing plants under different light conditions, including a dark closet, an environment that caused these plants to grow tall but with a sickly white color and very droopy leaves. The girls had given a report to their class and were engaged in a whole-class discussion. I have placed explanatory material in brackets to indicate what certain deictic and vague expressions mean (an ellipsis [...] represents material left out; this material was spoken by the teacher or other students in order to designate the next speaker):

Teacher: ...does anybody have any idea about why those [pale plants grown in the closet] might be that color [i.e., not green]?

Karen: Because, um, that's in the dark and it doesn't get any light maybe.

Girl: It does get a little light.

Girl: It gets the teeniest bit.

Aleisha: I think it's that color because it doesn't get that much light, and, it—it has—and plants grow with light, so.

Michael: Well, I think these are—there are these special rays in light that make it turn green and it's not getting those rays, so it won't turn green. Like a laser and a light beam are almost the sa—are almost different—I mean they are different kinds of light. So, maybe there's this kind of light in the air that maybe we can't see, but maybe the plants need it maybe to turn green.

Anna: I think, um, the rays, um, gives the plant food, and um, they, like, store the food in the leaves and cotyledon, and the food, like, makes it turn green? And stuff.

Michael: Yeah, that sounds like an idea behind my idea.

Will: Um, maybe it's not the light. Maybe it's heat...

Go: Maybe, um, light has something to make plants green, but in the closet it gets—it gets just a little air—little light, so it has, it doesn't has enough—enough things to make green. So, hmm, that stem can't get green.

The teacher's question "Does anybody have any idea about why those might be that color?" requires the children to know which plants he is indicating by the word *those*. Although this is not a problem because he is gesturing to the plants, the deictic reference coupled with the vague reference "that color" makes this sentence radically ambiguous. Does the teacher mean "Does anybody have any idea why the tall, droopy, sickly white plants are not green?" or does he mean "Does anybody have any idea why the tall, droopy, sickly white plants are white?" These are two different questions.

The girls' experiment has answered one of these questions ("Why are these plants not green?") with the first and most probable interpretation. Their answer would be something similar to, "Because plants require light to grow green [and greenness is a criterion the girls had agreed upon earlier as the test of healthy plants], these plants are not green because they did not get enough light." This is the most probable interpretation, but because the girls have just given a report that answers this question, it is rather paradoxical from a pragmatic viewpoint to ask this question. Why would someone ask, Does anybody have an idea? when three people have just presented such an idea? Of course, in typical teacher style, this teacher is merely trying to open up a whole-class "sense making" discussion in which all viewpoints will be heard. The second question—Why are these plants white?—has not been answered by the girls' experimental work, because, for all they know, sickly plants could be purple, blue, or any other color.

When Aleisha says "I think it's that color because it doesn't get that much light, and, it—it has—and plants grow with light, so," she probably is answering the first question, but another problem arises here. Aleisha's claim can have two quite different epistemological footings. It could be a commonsense lifeworld claim ("Everyone knows light makes plants grow"), or it could be an empirical claim based on the report the girls have given and the experimental work they have done. Of course, it is one of the points of this school's whole curriculum to get children to understand that, in a scientific Discourse of the sort being used in the class, people must make claims with the second, and not the first, epistemological footing.

Another ambiguity is at play in this discussion, and it centers around what the task is taken to be. Are the children supposed to be redoing descriptively what the girls have already, in a sense, done—namely, to state the connection between plant health and light and the grounds for it (this is what Aleisha and Go appear to be doing)? Or are they supposed to take the results of the girls' work for granted (light makes plants grow healthier) and explain the connection between light and plant health (this is what Michael and Anna appear to be doing)? There is even a third option: Perhaps they are supposed to try to challenge the control conditions of the girls' experiments (this is what Karen and Will appear to be doing).

The danger in this type of discussion (which, of course, also has many good features) is that "the rich can get richer and the poor, poorer." Children who can understand which interpretations are pragmatically most appropriate, anticipate what epistemological footing is called for, and expand the language into fuller forms are simultaneously learning and practicing science and scientific ways with words. Children who cannot perform these tasks as easily may simply end up being confused.

I certainly do not advocate abolishing face-to-face conversation as a vehicle for classroom discussions. But I think the conversations need to be supplemented with discussions in which children are asked to take longer turns, expand their language, and make clear their reasoning and its connections to what others have said. In such "monodialogical discussions," students also need to be scaffolded overtly in how they use and think about scientific social languages, interpretations, and arguments. For example, things like epistemological footing or the contrasting situated meanings of everyday words and the same-sounding words in a scientific social language need to be overtly discussed.

I believe, further, that learners also require expanded texts—displaying the fuller forms of the social language they are to acquire—placed in the midst of practice and discussion, not just assigned as reading outside these contexts. Finally, students need to have "reading lessons" on such expanded texts, during which people more expert than the students model how they read such texts and engage the students in overt discussion about the language and genre conventions of such texts and how these conventions arise from history and relate to current practices.

REFERENCES

Barsalou, L.W. (1999a). Language comprehension: Archival memory or preparation for situated action. *Discourse Processes, 28*, 61–80.

Barsalou, L.W. (1999b). Perceptual symbol systems. *Behavioral and Brain Sciences, 22*(4), 577–660.

Barton, D. (1994). *Literacy: An introduction to the ecology of written language.* Oxford, UK: Blackwell.

Bazerman, C. (1988). *Shaping written knowledge: The genre and activity of the experimental article in science.* Madison, WI: University of Wisconsin Press.

Brown, A.L., Collins, A., & Dugid, P. (1989). Situated cognition and the culture of learning. *Educational Researcher, 18*, 32–42.

Clark, A. (1997). *Being there: Putting brain, body, and world together again.* Cambridge, MA: MIT Press.

Engeström, Y., Miettinen, R., & Punamäki, R.-L. (Eds.). (1999). *Perspectives on activity theory.* Cambridge, UK: Cambridge University Press.

Gee, J.P. (1991). Memory and myth: A perspective on narrative. In A. McCabe (Ed.), *Developing narrative structure* (pp. 1–25). Hillsdale, NJ: Erlbaum.

Gee, J.P. (1992). *The social mind: Language, ideology, and social practice.* Westport, CT: Bergin & Garvey.

Gee, J.P. (1994). First language acquisition as a guide for theories of learning and pedagogy. *Linguistics and Education, 6*, 331–354.

Gee, J.P. (1996). *Social linguistics and literacies: Ideology in discourses* (2nd ed.). London: Taylor & Francis.

Gee, J.P. (1999a). *An introduction to discourse analysis: Theory and method.* London: Routledge.

Gee, J.P. (1999b). Reading and the new literacy studies: Reframing the National Academy of Sciences report on reading. *Journal of Literacy Research, 31*(3), 355–374.

Glenberg, A.M. (1997). What is memory for? *Behavioral and Brain Sciences, 20*, 1–19.

Glenberg, A.M., & Robertson, D.A. (1999). Indexical understanding of instructions. *Discourse Processes, 28*, 1–26.

Halliday, M.A.K., & Martin, J.R. (1993). *Writing science: Literacy and discursive power.* Pittsburgh, PA: University of Pittsburgh Press.

Hanks, W.F. (1995). *Language and communicative practices.* Boulder, CO: Westview.

Hutchins, E. (1995). *Cognition in the wild.* Cambridge, MA: MIT Press.

Latour, B. (1999). *Pandora's hope: Essays on the reality of science studies.* Cambridge, MA: Harvard University Press.

Lave, J. (1996). Teaching, as learning, in practice. *Mind, Culture, and Activity, 3*(3), 149–164.

Lave, J., & Wenger, E. (1991). *Situated learning: Legitimate peripheral participation.* New York: Cambridge University Press.

Martin, J.R. (1990). Literacy in science: Learning to handle text as technology. In F. Christie (Ed.), *Literacy for a changing world* (pp. 79–117). Camberwell, VIC, Australia: Australian Council for Educational Research.

National Institute of Child Health and Human Development. (2000). *Report of the National Reading Panel. Teaching children to read: An evidence-based assessment of the scientific research literature on reading and its implications for reading instruction* (NIH Publication No. 00-4769). Washington, DC: U.S. Government Printing Office.

Rosebery, A.S., Puttick, G.M., & Bodwell, M.B. (1996). *How much light does a plant need? Questions, data, and theories in a second-grade classroom.* Portsmouth, NH: Heinemann.

Rosebery, A.S., Warren, B., & Conant, F.R. (n.d.). *Appropriating scientific discourse: Findings from language minority classrooms* [Technical paper]. Cambridge, MA: TERC. Available: www.terc.edu/TEMPLATE/publications

Snow, C.E., Burns, M.S., & Griffin, P. (Eds.). (1998). *Preventing reading difficulties in young children.* Washington, DC: National Academy Press.

Street, B.V. (1995). *Social literacies: Critical approaches to literacy development, ethnography, and education.* Reading, MA: Addison-Wesley Higher Education.

Tomasello, M. (2000). *The cultural origins of human cognition.* Cambridge, MA: Harvard University Press.

Vygotsky, L.S. (1978). *Mind in society: The development of higher psychological processes* (M. Cole, V. John-Steiner, S. Scribner, & E. Souberman, Eds. and Trans.). Cambridge, MA: Harvard University Press. (Original work published 1934)

Wenger, E. (1998). *Communities of practice: Learning, meaning, and identity.* Cambridge, UK: Cambridge University Press.

Wertsch, J.V. (1998). *Mind as action.* Oxford, UK: Oxford University Press.

CHAPTER 2

The Literacies of Science

JAY L. LEMKE

One starting point for a dialogue between people in literacy education and science education is the way in which science uses multiple literacies. Literacy education usually begins with an emphasis on language and texts—how they are made and what they mean. Science education begins with questions about how things happen in the world. We might imagine a scientist studying literacy to be a bit like an ethnographer. An ethnographer of science and its literacies will encounter other scientists making and using texts but will look at the properties of texts only in relation to how they function in meaningful social and cultural activity.

What would our ethnographer see? Backs of envelopes with incomplete sketches, isolated words, a few lines of mathematical symbols, some arrows and question marks. Meticulous notebooks full of dates, columns, headings, and numbers. Shelves of textbooks, treatises, and handbooks. Piles of offprints, preprints, reprints, and printouts. People talking while jotting down formulas or sketching diagrams on whatever is at hand: a blackboard or whiteboard, a pad of paper, the back of an envelope, a napkin. People entering numbers in notebooks while adjusting dials and tilting their heads at funny angles. People sitting silently at computer screens filled with numbers, graphs, and bizarre visual displays, making little notes on pads of paper. And once in a great while, someone sitting at a keyboard and creating complete sentences of English, neatly arranged into paragraphs and separated by lines of mathematical symbols, tables of numbers, graphs of crooked lines, diagrams of apparatus, or more unusual visual displays.

Scientists often say that mathematics is the language of science, but it would be closer to the whole truth to say that the language of science is a unique hybrid: It is natural language as linguists define it, extended by the meaning repertoire of mathematics (the set of possible meanings that can be made with mathematical symbols and the conventions for interpreting them), contextualized by visual representations of many sorts, and embedded in a language (or, more properly, a semiotic) of meaningful, specialized actions afforded by the technological environments in which science is done. The texts of science are not written in any natural language studied by linguists. They are written in as much of this hybrid meaning-making system as can be presented on paper or animated on a computer screen.

Why? Is the use of these other semiotic media just a convenience, or is it a shortcut? Could we conduct science entirely with words? Not begging the question by counting every mathematical expression as some sort of word, the answer, pretty clearly, is no. And herein lies the heart of what I believe science has to say to literacy: Some meanings cannot be made with natural language, and natural language itself is an artificial notion, detached for academic and disciplinary reasons from the whole of embodied human communication. Human beings always do make meanings that go beyond the limitations of natural languages. Our biology and our survival in a material environment require us to do so. The *world* makes meanings that go beyond what natural language can say: Our proteins and cells and their membranes do, organisms of other species do, ecosystems do, and cosmology does. Science is the great enterprise of paying attention to the kinds of meanings that require us to go beyond natural language. Its weakness is that it sometimes has become so preoccupied with these meanings that it has forgotten that it also does use natural language, but natural language is not a tool whose properties it knows how to take into account. Science also sometimes excessively idealizes the systems it studies, never more so than when it forgets to take into account that scientists, as human beings themselves, are necessarily a part of every system of which we can have human knowledge.

I want to raise some questions here about the literacies of science and why they are what they are. I want to encourage science educators not only to study how teachers and students read, write, and talk science but also to learn more about how and why scientists do so, and to share with colleagues in literacy education the unique insights into the nature of literacy practices and literate texts that come from the perspective of science.

Meaning by Kind and Meaning by Degree

The whole of meaning—the whole of communication—is an evolved human capacity for survival in a physical and biological world. The whole of communication includes gestures and posture, facial expressions, mime, non-verbal vocalizations, drawings, and a great deal more. What can you communicate with a gesture that you cannot say in words? What can you represent with a drawing or a map that cannot be said? Even speech itself is more than just language: we vary the timbre and pacing of our voices and the sharpness and force of our articulation in ways that convey emotion, mood, health, seriousness, importance, urgency, surprise, doubt, need, desire, and a host of other core human meanings essential to social cohesion and group survival. In all these cases, we make meaning into a matter of degree.

Before the mathematics of a continuum (the infinity of points on a line), before any understanding of real numbers (e.g., 3.14159268 or *pi*), there was geometry—lengths and areas, ratios of lengths and areas, angles, and the Pythagorean irrational lengths (e.g., one side of a triangle that is square root of 2 inches long). Verbal mathematics began with the whole numbers, but visual mathematics never was limited to discrete values (one versus two versus three) and whole-number ratios ($\frac{1}{2}$, $\frac{2}{3}$, $\frac{5}{6}$, etc.). Verbal language was extended early on first from the whole numbers to unit fractions ($\frac{1}{2}$, $\frac{1}{3}$, $\frac{1}{4}$, $\frac{1}{5}$, etc.) and then to multiples of unit fractions, but only visual displays really could convey the holistic meaning of a nonsimple ratio (e.g., $\frac{7}{13}$). Visual displays can freeze into place what from time immemorial has been a function of bodily gesture and posture. How low do you bow? How firmly do you shake hands? How wide do you open your eyes? How soon do you respond? How close do you stand? At what angle do you raise your arm to point?

There are no names in natural language for all the angles from acute to obtuse. There is hardly any way in formal verbal language to express subtle differences of degree or ratio. There is no way to describe the shape of a mountain, cloud, or face or to describe precisely the twists and turns of a winding path. There are no words to distinguish degrees of speed or trajectories of motion. There are no words for *all* the intervals of time that matter in life. We can say "three seconds" or "three millennia" but without mathematics we cannot say 1.3758 seconds or 358,000,000,000 years, and even words like *seconds* and *millennia* (or *billions*) come to us from very old mathematics. There are not nearly enough words for all the degrees of certainty and doubt, importance and urgency, unexpectedness and surprise, or need and desire that matter to us. Why?

Linguistics does understand one part of human communication—not all of speech, nor even all of writing, but the ways in which discrete words combine to make vast numbers of possible meanings (yet always a finite number of them) and the ways in which discrete words are distinguished from one another by being composed of discrete classes of sounds. An infinite continuum of possible vocal articulations exists, but every linguistic community divides it arbitrarily into a relatively small number (less than 100, usually) of discrete sound zones. Speakers learn to keep away from the fuzzy borders between zones. Words are distinguished from other words not by subtle acoustic degrees of difference but by systematic contrasts between sounds in different zones—for example, *pat* or *pot* or *pit*, *pat* or *bat* or *fat*, or *pat* or *pad* or *pack*. Words do not blend into one another; they do not form a continuum, and neither do the meanings that natural language enables us to make with combinations of words. Every phrase, clause, and sentence stands in systematic contrast with a very large number of other related phrases, clauses, and sentences—for example, *a big man*, *a little man*, *a big dog*, *one big man*, or *the big man*. In grammar, a verb can be present or past tense, but there is no continuum or degree of tenses in between. We can speak in first person or third person, but there is no intermediate continuum of modes of address.

Natural language does have some resources for expressing matters of degree, but they are only discrete points of reference in the continuum (e.g., words such as *small*, *little*, *tiny*, *microscopic*, and *infinitesimal*). Natural language recognizes that not all things come in discrete, countable units—for example, one dog, two dogs, or three dogs. We can have one jar of water or two, but not two waters (except metaphorically for two bodies of water), and water is the sort of thing that can fill a jar to any possible degree. Named units of measure came historically long before the concept of measure, which in turn could not exist before the expression of arbitrary fractions of a unit. The concept of an amphora (big jug) of wine (one amphora, seven amphoras) came before the concept that any amount of wine could be measured as some number of amphora units (e.g., .85 amphoras, 123 and $7/16$ amphoras, etc.). The concept of a "unit of measure" is difficult even for many students today, once we take it beyond common phrases in natural language. It is not even a concept shared in all cultures (Verran, 2001). Of course, people measured things and recognized the concepts of length, weight, area, volume, and so on. It was the measurement of real objects that led to the need for unit fractions and multiples of unit fractions. It was the comparison of such measures that led to non-simple ratios, and the most basic natural comparison was the geometric angle. Natural language was extended to speak of fractions, and the arithmetic of the closed ring of rational numbers began (all whole numbers and fractions). Geometry begins with scale drawing for surveying, maps, and architecture. Perhaps scale drawings or shadow ratios and plumb lines were used even before there was a way to name in mathematical words the length of a line; certainly they were used before there was a way to name areas or volumes ("square miles," "cubic feet").

The natural world, both materially and socially, is about both *kinds* and *degrees*. Animal and plant species come in discrete kinds. Humans artificially divide themselves into discrete kinds (e.g., tribes, races, and nations).

Natural language abets the creation of artifacts that are of discrete kinds. It also abets the creation of concepts that are discrete and often contrasting (e.g., beauty and ugliness, good and evil, horizontal and vertical, and mass and weight). However, between horizontal and vertical, for example, there is only one concept (i.e., oblique or angled) but an arbitrarily large number of realities and meanings that need to be distinguished for practical purposes. What matters to humans about material phenomena very often is a matter of degree rather than kind—size, shape, speed, rate, height, weight, density, composition, tensile strength, salinity, acidity, and so on. And the great discovery on which science is based is that there are mathematical regularities in the relations among these quantities of degree. Indeed, mathematics largely was developed to describe just these empirical relationships—constant ratios, linear proportionalities, geometrical means, quadratic and cubic ratios, and additivities.

Early mathematics grew out of practical activity. It was not a formal and systematic field but an artisanal craft, built of rubrics and algorithms and very often made sense of through diagrams that were abstracted from drawings of real situations. People solved practical problems that required them to use meaning-by-degree as well as meaning-by-kind through a combination of natural-language concepts, gestures, technological artifacts and the practices of using them, measurements, drawings, abstract diagrams, and mathematical tables and procedures. In their origins and functions, these precursors of the hybrid meaning resources of modern science were already interdependent. And so they remained for most of their histories. Mathematics frequently branched off as an abstract study, but until the 20th century, most of its conceptual advances came from work on scientific and technological problems. Long before Descartes made coordinate geometry the basis for a homology between graphs and algebraic equations, equations were translated into numerical tables and diagrams of the results were presented in forms that look very much like our modern scientific data graphs. Early numerical tables were constructed linguistically as much as visually: Every row was a complete sentence of Latin, with numbers inserted before nouns. Abstract diagrams owed as much to schematic drawings as to geometrical forms: Bernoulli calculated the forces exerted by muscles on bones at various angles of the joints using Newtonian mechanics and geometrical diagrams of angles and forces abstracted from schematic drawings of the human skeleton. Galileo inserted a tiny drawing of Saturn, with the rings that he first saw in place of the word *Saturn* in a line of written text.

Science learned to combine meaning-by-kind and meaning-by-degree, and throughout its history these two modalities have influenced one another so that today the concepts and communications of science fuse them inseparably. Scientific text embodies this fusion. *Scientific literacy is not just the knowledge of scientific concepts and facts; it is the ability to make meaning conjointly with verbal concepts, mathematical relationships, visual representations, and manual-technical operations.*

Multimodal Literacy in Science: Texts and Classrooms

In one recent study (Lemke, 1998), I examined the semiotic forms found in the standard genres of research articles and advanced treatises of professional scientific publications. In a diverse corpus, across disciplines and publication venues, the clear finding was that there usually is at least one, and often more than one, graphical display and one mathematical expression per page of running text in typical scientific print genres. There easily can be three or four each of graphics displays and mathematical expressions *per page*, separate from verbal text.

In one prestigious journal of the physical sciences, each typical three-page article integrated four graphical displays and eight set-off mathematical expressions. Other articles had as many as three graphical displays per page of double-column text or as many as seven equations per page. In another journal, one in the biological sciences, each typical page had two nontabular visual-graphical representations integrated with the verbal text, and each short article, with an average length of 2.4 pages, typically had six graphics, including at least one table and one quantitative graph.

To appreciate the absolutely central role of these nonverbal textual elements in the genres being characterized, it may help to ponder a few extreme (but hardly unique) cases that follow:

- In one advanced textbook chapter, a diagram was included in a footnote printed at the bottom of the page.

- In one seven-page research report, 90% of a page (all but five lines of main text at the top) was taken up by a complex diagram and its extensive figure caption.

- The main experimental results of a 2.5-page report were presented in a set of graphs occupying one-half of a page and a table occupying three-fourths of another. The main verbal text did not repeat this information but only referred to it and commented on it.

- In most of the theoretical physics articles, the running verbal text would make no sense without the integrated mathematical equations. These could not, in most cases, be effectively paraphrased in natural language, even though they can be, and are normally meant to be, read as part of the verbal text (in terms of semantics, cohesion, and, frequently, grammar).

A more detailed analysis in this study showed how absolutely normal and necessary it is to interpret the verbal text in relation to these other semiotic formations, and vice versa. They are not redundant, each presenting the complete relevant information in a different medium; rather, the nature of the genre presupposes close and constant integration and cross-contextualization among semiotic modalities.

In a recent analysis of videotape data of one student, John, going through a day of advanced chemistry and physics classes (Lemke, 2000; see also Cumming & Wyatt-Smith, 1997), I observed that in his chemistry lesson, John had to interpret the following:

- A stream of rapid verbal English from his teacher
- The writing and layout information on an overhead transparency
- Writing, layout, diagrams, chemical symbols, and mathematical formulas in the open textbook in front of him
- The display on his hand-held calculator
- Writing, layout, diagrams, symbolic notations, and mathematics in his personal notebook
- The teacher's gestures, blackboard diagrams, and writing
- The actions and speech of other students, including their manipulation of demonstration apparatus
- The running commentary of his next-seat neighbor

In fact, John quite often had to integrate and coordinate most of these semiotic modalities either simultaneously or within the span of a few minutes. He could not have kept up with the content development and conceptual flow of these lessons without integrating at least a few of these different semiotic modalities almost constantly.

In one episode during the physics lesson, there was no use of the notebook and no diagram, just a pure interaction of language and gestural pantomime, including whole-body motion. The teacher, Mr. Phillips, was standing just in front of the first (empty) row of student desk tables at the opposite end of the room from where John was sitting. John saw his teacher's hands cupped together to form a sphere, then the hands moved a foot to the left and cupped together to make another sphere. Then, they moved back to the first position, and one hand and Mr. Phillips's gaze made a sweeping gesture from one position in space to the other. Next, Mr. Phillips began to walk to the left, repeating these gestures and walking down toward John's end of the room. Fortunately, Mr. Phillips also was talking, so by integrating the teacher's precise and conventionalized mime with his accompanying technical speech, John could interpret that the cupped hands were atoms and the sweeping hand was a photon emitted by the first atom that traveled to the second, was absorbed there, and was reemitted after a while to pass down, atom by atom, through a ruby crystal, producing a "snowball effect" of more and more photons of exactly the same energy. In other words, the crystal was a laser.

Then, Mr. Phillips said he was going to add more complexity to the picture. An atom "might shoot out a photon in this direction," he said as he gestured away from the axis of the room-sized imaginary ruby crystal and toward the students, "Or in this one," he said as he gestured back toward the blackboard, "Or...," he said as he made an oblique gesture. "How do we get a laser beam, then?" He walked back and forth between the ends of his now-lasing, imaginary ruby crystal, describing the mirrors that he gestured into imaginary being at each end, saying that the mirrors differed in reflectivity and transmissivity to build up and maintain the avalanche of photons while letting some photons out in the form of the laser beam.

John had seen pantomimes such as this before; he also had seen diagrams of atoms and crystals and of photons being absorbed and emitted by atoms. He was able to use the visual literacy of these past diagrams, together with his literacy in pantomime and his verbal discourse literacy in atomic physics, to synthesize a model of how a laser works.

John was lucky. He appeared to have the required literacies and ability to combine and synthesize them across media, events, and semiotic modalities. There was a great deal that John already had to know in order to make sense of what he was learning in these lessons from minute to minute—not just language and verbally expressed discourse formations (such as the intertextual thematic formations I have described in Lemke [1990, 1995] and elsewhere), but conventional diagrams of atomic arrangements in a crystal, standard graphs of atomic energy levels, typical ways of gesturing to show directionality in space, and common notations for the algebraic and symbolic representation of chemical reactions and stoichiometric calculations of concentrations and the pH of solutions. His literacy extended to motor routines in operating a calculator, social discourse routines of question and answer in a classroom, and technical practices in manipulating a spectroscope and diluting a solution. He constantly had to translate information from one modality to another—numerical to algebraic, algebraic to graphical, graphical to verbal, verbal to motor, pantomime to diagrammatic, and diagrammatic to discursive. But simple translation is not enough; John had to be able to integrate multiple media simultaneously to reinterpret and recontextualize information in one "channel" in relation to that in the other channels, all to infer the correct or canonical meaning on which he would be tested. In most such cases with students, the complete meaning in a science lesson or text is not expressed by using only one channel, but only when using two or more or even all of them taken together (see detailed examples in Lemke, 2000; Roth, 2002; Roth & Bowen, 1999; Wells, 2000).

Implications for Science and Literacy Education

The implications of these semiotic facts about scientific literacy for science education seem fairly obvious: We need to devote more explicit attention to teaching students how to read hybrid text. We need to help them understand the conventions that connect verbal text with mathematical expressions and graphs and diagrams of all kinds. We need to help them reproduce the fusion of conceptual kinds and quantitative degrees that is central to scientific meaning-making by giving them practice in translating back and forth among verbal accounts, mathematical expressions and calculations, schematic diagrams, abstract graphs, and hands-on actions. In many cases, teachers can expand their own teaching repertories by making more use of gestural and visual representations and numerical tables and simple graphs, even before students are ready for more formal mathematical expressions. Students need not only to do hands-on science and talk and write science in words; they also need to draw, tabulate, graph, geometrize, and algebrize science in all possible combinations.

But what does this view from science education have to say to the wider field of literacy education? Is this multimodal, hybrid language of science special and unique and of no relevance to literacy education in general? Or does it point to a broader, more ethnographic approach to all of literacy—

one that situates word meanings in the larger context of students' visual and cultural experience? One that fuses verbal and visual literacy back together again across the widest range of genres and insists that students learn to write as well as read multimodally in every subject area?

Cultural historians have written much in recent decades about the logocentrism of modern academic traditions. Contemporary cultural theorists have been impressed by the "visual turn" in the meaning-making habits of first the television generation and now the Internet generation. Open any magazine or view any website, and you will see how rich are the complex hybrids and fusions of visual and verbal meaning resources. They have more in common with scientific articles and textbooks than they do with the pure verbal text of traditional literacy. Scientific and technical disciplines today are leading the way in incorporating animations, dynamic simulations, and video in the explication of research questions. Websites are becoming full multimedia presentations, including interactive dynamic media, audio, video, and animation for all subject areas. CD-ROMs, although only a transitional technology, display the future of the Web in these respects. Immersive environments, whether of the virtual-reality type or akin to the existing multiplayer online gaming environments, are the next stage in this evolution.

Text is becoming more and more integrated into multimedia. Purely textual literacy will survive, but it will not continue to hold the dominant place that it has in the past. Students in all subjects need to know how to critically interpret and analyze video and animations, schematic drawings and diagrams, and other visual resources in relation to verbal text, and vice versa. All of literacy education has a great deal to learn from scientific literacy, which was long ago the pioneer of this multimodal fusion.

To teach the literacies of science well, science educators need to create partnerships with verbal literacy educators and with visual media educators. I hope I have at least suggested in this chapter why such a partnership would be mutually beneficial for us all.

What Literacy Education Has to Say to Science Educators

Although I began my career as a physicist and science educator, I also have worked in the area of literacy education, particularly on its theoretical foundations in the fields of text semantics; discourse analysis; genre structure; rhetorical analysis; and the study of academic, bureaucratic, and scientific language. As coeditor of the international research journal *Linguistics and Education*, I have had a wide overview of research relevant to literacy education.

There are a number of trends and developments in literacy education research to which science educators would do well to pay attention. I want to identify just a few of these in the following list:

1. **The role of social dialect and community culture in students' writing and their interpretation of texts.** Literacy educators today are acutely aware of the divergences between home and school language for many students, and also of the differences in attitudes, values, and priorities of students' home and peer cultures relative to those of the school and its curricular areas. Science educators need to be aware of issues in science learning that are associated with speaking English as a second language, writing standard English for speakers of non-standard dialects, and coming from home communities that may not agree with the secular value system of modern science as a culture.

2. **Research on students' language and literacy experiences outside the school.** Science education seems implicitly to assume that students' only relevant exposure to science is through the school curriculum. There is very little systematic research on students' reactions to science as portrayed in various popular media or to their experience with various forms of technology in daily life (including medical and pharmaceutical technologies).

3. **"Across the curriculum" approaches to multiplying the effects of language arts instruction.** To some extent, mathematics educators have tried to follow this lead, but "science across the curriculum" is a notion that seems to exist at best in sporadic efforts in specialized schools. If science would define itself somewhat more inclusively—to include all of technology and the social, ethical, and political issues arising from the applications of science in the contemporary world and at least a partial claim on the history of science and technology and the interpretation of literature and media that address issues of science and technology—then "science across the curriculum" could be a powerful means to engage students and sustain their engagement with scientific thinking.

A Note on Gender Issues

In preparing an initial dialogue for the Crossing Borders: Connecting Science and Literacy conference (a set of remarks that served as the basis for this chapter), Donna Alvermann (see chapter 12) and I were well aware of the gender implications of giving a male voice to science and a female voice to literacy in the dialogue. Historically, both literacy and science—indeed, all public academic knowledge and standing—were reserved for males. This restriction was not accidental, nor even an inheritance from time immemorial. It was created by the repeated work of generations, against resistance, and despite briefer and longer historical periods in which women's rights to participation in the world of public knowledge were effectively maintained against perennial opposition. The story, at least for Europe and the United States, is a fascinating, enlightening, and appalling one (see David Noble's [1992] book *A World Without Women* for one male historian's version).

But literacy—in private, and later in public—was attained by women long before they succeeded to any significant degree in opening up the institution of science to their full participation. In education, women have taught literacy in significant numbers for a very long time; they have only recently come, and still in relatively small numbers, to the teaching of science. The teaching of literacy has been associated with primary education, and so with women's traditional role in the education of children. The teaching of science until very recently has been limited to adolescents and adults. Women are far more than proportionally represented among literacy researchers and far less than proportionally among science education researchers.

The legacy of history lives still. Female graduate students in the "hard" sciences still report feeling excluded from a world of masculine camaraderie. But the deeper, still largely unanswered question is this: How have centuries of male domination and female exclusion affected the intellectual structure of science itself as a discipline? It is very clear that male scientists do still try to perform a masculine gender identity (cf. Butler, 1993) through their scientific activities. Male scientists are disposed to "hard data," "tough-minded argument," and an adversarial approach to resolving conflicting scientific claims. They admire risk-taking in general and manual dexterity in the laboratory. They form hierarchical research groups led by an "alpha male." They respect abstract and quantitative argumentation for their own sake. They swagger and intimidate and are admired by other males for doing so.

Traweek (1988) describes this scientific culture and its effect on female students. Walkerdine (1990) looks at the masculinization of scientific forms of rationality. It is more difficult for female scientists to perform a feminine gender identity through the same practices, and it is likely that the practices themselves will have to change or be expanded, even as the nature of gender identities in our society changes (cf. Walkerdine, 1990).

Correspondingly, has literacy education and its study and research become at all "feminized" in recent generations, either in its practices or in its academic image?

Are the dialogues of literacy education and science education significantly gender dialogues? Do my proposals that we refocus literacy education to include multimedia and multimodal literacies, including mathematics and formal abstract representations and with a computational technological base, tend to shift the gendering of literacy and literacy education toward the masculine pole? Would such a shift tend to put off younger female researchers and attract more male researchers?

Should we take special care to open the door also to more artistic and aesthetic modes of visual and verbal representation and to greater emphasis on social relationships and collaborations? Cultural divisions by gender may be mostly arbitrary and sometimes rather foolish, especially in their stereotypes, but they also are all too often quite real and socially pervasive. No institution in our society is immune; no practice with a long history avoids shaping by dead hands. Only critical vigilance, and dialogues not only between science educators and literacy educators but also among people of the widest variety of gender identities, will make our own contributions to this history progressive ones.

Some Further Areas for Collaboration

There are three other thematic areas in which I think one could explore fruitful dialogue between science and literacy educators.

First, we ought to examine together the criteria for what counts as sophisticated and critical literacy for scientific-technical, literary, and popular media texts, chipping away at false dichotomies that make reading literary and scientific texts seem serious and reading popular media texts seem frivolous. Intelligent and critical reading has many common features, regardless of the genre or register (i.e., specialized discourses) of texts, and we need more systematically to identify and encourage these features of thoughtful reading so students can bring them to bear on all kinds of texts. How they choose to read depends on the context of the activity and their current agendas, but even this can surprise us because people can be serious and critical even in their leisure activities.

Students who excel at reading in one register or genre either may not choose to read other texts as carefully or may not know how to do it. It is also important for educators from both science and literacy fields to define what counts as sophisticated reading for scientific texts and to define the relation between critical reading of expository text and critical analysis of data, argumentation, and evidence. I think we educators will find that we all have a lot to say to one another about these issues.

A second thematic area is that of literacy and identity issues: How do students perform their various identities in the medium of popular culture, and what space is there for linkages between their identity development and school culture, including "serious" literature and science? If education means helping students make a transition from only participating in local worlds and communities to knowing how to participate in more diverse worlds and larger communities, then how do we build bridges between what they are doing with popular media and who they are and who they imagine they could become? This is a very crucial issue for science educators because the stereotypical way in which science presents itself so often is at odds with the kinds of identities students, especially adolescents, want to perform.

Finally, there is a large body of literature written by outstanding scientists, mathematicians, and engineers attesting to the key role of intuition, aesthetic sensibility, and playfulness in scientific and mathematical creativity (e.g., Tauber, 1996; Wechsler, 1981). Too often, science presents itself only in terms of the results of research and does not say much about the process itself. When it does address process, there is an overemphasis on the straight and narrow, hard-work, highly technical, controlled, and systematic processes of research—to the neglect of the more creative and intuitive aspects of scientific inquiry, which are precisely the ones for which connections to adolescent identity potentially can be made. Research on identity and adolescents' engagement with literature and with their own writing should provide helpful guidance to a science education program that is serious about the humanistic side of real scientific work.

REFERENCES

Butler, J. (1993). *Bodies that matter.* New York: Routledge.

Cumming, J., & Wyatt-Smith, C. (Eds.). (1997). *Examining the literacy-curriculum relationship in post-compulsory schooling.* Brisbane, QLD, Australia: Griffith University.

Lemke, J.L. (1990). *Talking science: Language, learning, and values.* Norwood, NJ: Ablex.

Lemke, J.L. (1995). *Textual politics: Discourse and social dynamics.* London: Taylor & Francis.

Lemke, J.L. (1998). Multiplying meaning: Visual and verbal semiotics in scientific text. In J.R. Martin, & R. Veel (Eds.), *Reading science: Critical and functional perspectives on discourses of science* (pp. 87–113). London: Routledge.

Lemke, J.L. (2000). Multimedia demands of the scientific curriculum. *Linguistics and Education, 10*(3), 1–25.

Noble, D.F. (1992). *A world without women: The Christian clerical culture of Western science.* New York: Knopf.

Roth, W.-M. (2002). Reading graphs: Contributions to an integrative concept of literacy. *Journal of Curriculum Studies, 34*(1), 1–24.

Roth, W.-M., & Bowen, G.M. (1999). Of cannibals, missionaries, and converts: Graphing competencies from grade 8 to professional science inside (classrooms) and outside (field/laboratory). *Science, Technology, & Human Values, 24*(2), 179–212.

Tauber, A.I. (Ed.). (1996). *The elusive synthesis: Aesthetics and science.* London: Kluwer Academic.

Traweek, S. (1998). *Beamtimes and lifetimes: The world of higher energy physicists.* Cambridge, MA: Harvard University Press.

Verran, H.W. (2001). *Science and an African logic.* Chicago: University of Chicago Press.

Walkerdine, V. (1990). *The mastery of reason.* London: Routledge.

Wechsler, J. (Ed.). (1981). *On aesthetics in science.* Cambridge, MA: MIT Press.

Wells, G. (2000). Modes of meaning in a science activity. *Linguistics and Education, 10*(3), 307–334.

CHAPTER 3

Gestures: The Leading Edge in Literacy Development

WOLFF-MICHAEL ROTH

Quantitative and qualitative studies of knowing and learning in science and mathematics show that physical gestures used in conjunction with spoken utterances represent the leading edge of cognitive development (Goldin-Meadow, 1999). That is, gestures express new levels of understanding before a student can put this new understanding into words; also, gestures express the student's understanding of new concepts, although his or her language still holds on to the old, incorrect concepts (Goldin-Meadow, 1997). Being attuned to gestures while recognizing both how students learn and when it makes sense for teachers to intercede is important. Alibali, Flevares, and Goldin-Meadow (1997) already have demonstrated that even untutored individuals are able to distinguish phases in a student's development by attending to the relationship between the content, especially mathematics and science content, expressed in gestures and that expressed in language. Furthermore, Roth and Welzel (2001) have shown that students are attuned to the gestures teachers use and sometimes appropriate these gestures into their own expressive repertoires, thereby accelerating the development of scientific literacy.

In this chapter, I provide several detailed examples that demonstrate the role of situation and gesture in the development of oral and written scientific discourse. Teachers who are sensitive to contextual and gestural clues can identify scientific understanding from gestures even before students are ready to articulate verbally or in writing their observations and explanations. When discrepancies between gestures and talk exist, teachers should understand that students whose gestures represent a more sophisticated understanding are likely to comprehend new concepts and, therefore, are ready for additional instruction (Goldin-Meadow, Alibali, & Church, 1993). Teachers also can employ gestures in ways that assist students in developing their scientific literacy.

From Observation to Explanation of Natural Phenomena

Since 1990, I have conducted many studies in school science laboratories, closely attending to students' talk while they have investigated phenomena and attempted to construct explanations (e.g., Roth, 1996, 1999, 2000; Roth & Lawless, 2002a, 2002b, 2002c); I also have studied what the students subsequently wrote. These observations show that students often begin with "muddled talk" and end up, given a lot of time, with viable ways of speaking and writing about science phenomena in observational and theoretical terms. Gestures are an important aspect of this development because they allow students to communicate content before they are able to do so verbally, in part because gestures support the development of verbal modes by decreasing the mental effort required for producing communication. In this way, viable language emerges from what are, to the scientific ear, almost chaotic and incomprehensible utterances. Once students develop consistent ways of verbally representing particular entities, the use of gestures decreases.

An Exemplary Episode of Gesturing

Phil and Marcel were two students in a 10th-grade physics class whose members had explored static electricity and, in the videotaped lesson I discuss in this section, the electroscope. This instrument consists of a vertical bar to which a pointer is attached by means of a pivot or hinge (see Figure 3.1). If an electrostatically charged object is brought close, the pointer deflects away from the bar; if the object is removed, the pointer returns to its normal position, parallel to and touching the bar. In this lesson, the students were asked to touch the bottom of the bar while the charged object (a transparency) was held close to it on the opposite side and then to remove the charged object after the touching hand already had been withdrawn. Much to everyone's surprise, the pointer remained deflected away from the bar. The teacher asked her students to explore the device and its functioning in order to come up with an explanation of the phenomenon.

Part of the way through their investigation, Phil suggested, "This way it deflects," and Marcel responded, "Yes." He paused and then continued, "Now, it is there on top." Phil interrupted by repeating what Marcel had said, "Now, it is there on top," and then continued,

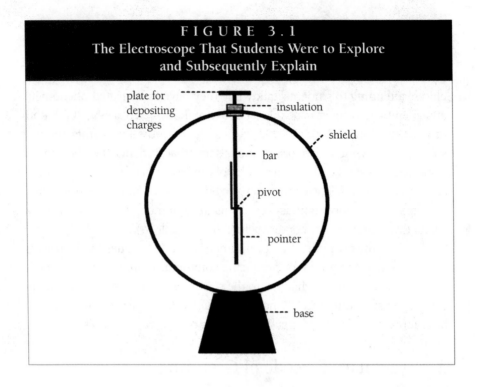

FIGURE 3.1
The Electroscope That Students Were to Explore and Subsequently Explain

Now, we have this problem again. This way—now I put the electrons down here again, which are drawn away up to here. I put them down here again with my finger. Then, I pull it away and because now there is, again, an equilibrium inside, it remains like this.

If we only take the recorded words and sentences that Phil and Marcel exchanged here and throughout the 10-week curriculum, we do not understand much about their conversations. That is, if their teacher had found this "explanation" in the students' laboratory report, she would not have understood it and probably would have been forced to give these students a low mark.

Let us now consider other aspects of the interaction that I culled from the videotape. These aspects concern the objects and events in their setting, prior conversations that a speaker could be familiar with, and the pointing and representational (iconic) gestures students made while talking.

The following transcript, which recovers some material elements from the situation as well as the students' gestures, provides us with a much greater insight into what the students said and what their talk was about. From the viewer's perspective, Marcel sat on the right and Phil on the left.

To get an impression of the students' hand gestures, you may find it beneficial to visually scan the images one after another, paying particular attention to the positions of the hands (shaded gray). The asterisks indicate which points in the transcript correspond to the images, and the square brackets indicate overlap of the two speakers' utterances.

01 Phil: This way, it deflects. *

(*He gets the transparency and moves it above the electroscope.*)

02 Marcel: Yes. (Pauses for 1.27 seconds.) * Now, it is there on [top].

(*His index finger moves up until it touches the transparency.*)

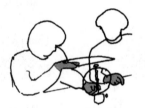

03 Phil: [Now] it is there on top. Now, we have this problem again.

04 This way (pauses 0.43 second)

(*His hand, previously poised in his lap, comes above the table and moves toward the suspension.*)

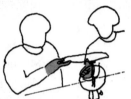

05 * now I put the electrons down here again,

(*Touches the suspension.*)

06 * which are drawn away up to here. (Pauses 0.20 second.)

(*His hand turns, and his index finger starts pointing upward; it does so for 0.36 second.*)

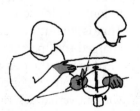

07	I now put * them down here again with my finger. *(He moves the hand back to the electroscope and touches the bottom of the suspension with his finger.)*
08	*(Pauses for 1.56 seconds.)*
09	Then I pull it away * *(Begins pulling the hand with the transparency back.)*
10	and because (pauses 0.50 second) * now there is, again, *(Hand moves way past his ear and stays in that position for 0.48 second.)*
11	* an equilibrium inside, it remains like this. *(Both hands drop below the tabletop.)*

Already in line 01, we see multiple resources provided by Phil for making meaning. He says, "This way," while bringing a charged transparency over the electroscope and adds, "it deflects." Uttering "This way" invites Marcel to attend to the concurrent action of bringing the transparency film close to and above the electroscope. The second part of the utterance invites Marcel to look out for something that is appropriately described by "it deflects." That is, the utterance invites attention to that which is brought close, a charged transparency, and something that deflects in response. Out of all the things in the classroom and, more specifically, on their laboratory table, Phil's discourse is directed toward just a few things that, nevertheless, remain without verbal description. Furthermore, neither he nor Marcel has to represent these objects verbally because the objects are there, ready to be picked from the environment whenever needed. In addition, the students do not even have to name the object; rather, using a deictic term (*this*, *it*, or *there*) or a pointing gesture, each orients the other person to the relevant things in their world. These indexical terms are commonly used in everyday language (Goodwin, 2000; Haviland, 2000). Therefore, they require much less mental energy and fewer resources than less frequently used words; pointing, because it is a sensorimotor action, takes even fewer mental resources (Agre, 1997). What is required for sense making is available perceptually, and the listener can pick up the perceptual gestalt by watching where the finger (or hand, or gaze) is pointing.

Already in the first utterance, Phil expresses so much information without actually putting everything into words. He does not say that it is the transparency that is brought close or even that it is charged—at this point in their course of study, students no longer had to describe the transparency in order for others to understand that the speaker meant a charged one. In their class, holding up a transparency in most cases meant holding up a charged transparency. In the course of this unit, the transparency had come to be used metonymically for the process of charging an object and holding a charged object. The statement is even more complex than it appears on first sight because it actually incorporates an observation that is categorical, that is, pertaining to many cases. The categorical observation is in the form of a statement of a correlation: "Whenever you bring the charged transparency close to the electroscope, it deflects." It is crucial for teachers and researchers to realize that, at this point, Phil is not yet able to make the abstract verbal statement on his own, apart from the situation and without the resources that the materials and pointing provide.

As we move through the transcript, we notice that Phil continues to communicate much more than his words alone do. His gestures and the materials present, together with his words, constitute a story line that tells his listener how he understands the phenomenon. When you touch the center bar, electrons are supplied, which are subsequently drawn upward in the bar to create a charge equilibrium. The order of events as described is not yet scientifically correct. A charge equilibrium is actually created while the transparency is close, as additional electrons are supplied through the student's hand from the electrical ground. The equilibrium is indicated by the pointer moving into its zero position. However, when the transparency is moved away, the charges reequilibrate in the bar. There is now a surplus of electrons, so the pointer is deflected again.

During the next lesson, the two students continued to work on constructing their explanation. In the course of attempting to explain the phenomenon, they needed to draw decreasingly on the materials and increasingly on language to express themselves. When they used gestures, it was done without the materials present and in a relatively abstract manner, and a gesture metonymically stood for an entire process. That is, the "story line" consisted of increasingly context-independent elements.

Over the past 13 years, I have analyzed nearly 500 videotaped hours of science classes from fourth grade to university level, and for the past four years I have studied scientists in the process of doing research. From my research it appears that, independent of their age, individuals often draw on gesture to communicate, especially when they work in the laboratory context and when they attempt to explain things with which they are not yet very familiar. A number of quantitative and qualitative research studies show how students use gestures in communicating correct science and mathematics content before they can do so verbally (e.g., Roth, 2002). In fact, conceptual discrepancies between correct gestures and incorrect language indicate that students are ready for instruction; in other words, instruction will have greater impact on these students than on those whose gestures and words are consistent but both incorrect. For example, in one study, fourth- and fifth-grade students were asked to solve equivalence problems of the type $a + b + c = \_\_ + c$ (Perry, Church, & Goldin-Meadow, 1988). Then, the children were given individual instruction on how to do equivalence problems. After instruction, students again were given equivalence problems and transfer tasks (e.g., multiplication). The study showed that children whose gestured and verbal explanations were discrepant benefited more from instruction than those children who had concordant but incorrect explanations in the two modalities.

This research also shows that teachers and other individuals, even without being tutored, can detect such inconsistencies (Goldin-Meadow & Sandhofer, 1999). As students' language develops, one can notice a temporal shift between gestures, which lead, and words, which follow. Thus, my studies show that the gap between gestures and words, which may initially range from 2.0 to 3.5 seconds, decreases to a range of 0.8 to 1.5 seconds and eventually disappears (Roth, 2003b); parallel to these temporal changes, students increasingly rely on words to communicate (Roth & Lawless, 2002b). The problem with which learners deal here may not be simply a missing or slowly forthcoming word but the integration of many words and situational details into a complete statement.

From Talking to Writing Science

In the previous section, Phil and Marcel talked in the presence of materials. (For a description of describing the use of gesture in another science class, refer to chapter 2 under the heading Multimodal Literacy in Science: Texts and Classrooms.) However, to examine what Phil and Marcel knew, their teacher used tests in the same way that teachers around the world use tests. We might ask, however, whether a student who is able to talk about a phenomenon is already in a position to write about the same phenomenon.

A fact that has not yet been appreciated sufficiently is that talking and writing are very different processes and pose significantly different cognitive demands; writing restructures consciousness (Ong, 1988). Science and literacy educators ought not to overlook the complexity of the change from spoken to written language. My work from elementary to high school science shows that this transition is facilitated when students are provided with opportunities to express themselves on paper by utilizing means of expression that bear iconic relations with the situations they experienced and the gestures that they used. In these situations, the benefits students accrued by talking in situation, surrounded by the material objects and events that they referred to and modeled with gestures, can be amplified (Roth & Lawless, 2002a). In fact, engaging students in discussions about diagrams that represent the phenomena they are to theorize provides an important step from doing science to writing science (Roth, 1996).

On the test in which the students from the 10th-grade physics class were asked to describe and explain basic concepts of static electricity, they used drawings of various levels of abstraction from their lived experience in the laboratory. They used pictorial means, particularly on the test item in which they are asked to describe (and explain) how one can prove that some material is electrically charged (see Figure 3.2 for the responses that several students provided to a test question [images are copies, the text was translated from the German originals]). The drawings and text in Figure 3.2 show various levels of abstraction of what previously had been ergotic (work-related) and epistemic (knowing-related, sensing) movements that are later represented in the form of symbolic movements (iconic and metaphoric-iconic gestures). (For this transformation of hand movements from ergotic to epistemic and symbolic see Roth, 2003a.)

Example A of Figure 3.2 depicts all objects in a naturalistic way and iconically represents the action of touching the charged body with the neon lamp in the hand. As we move through the examples in Figure 3.2, the material object, its charges, the hand, and the neon lamp are represented in an

A.   The left side of the glow lamp lights up.

B. 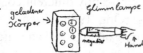 If I hold a neon lamp to a negatively charged body then that side glows which is oriented to the charged body. We know then that the body is charged negatively.

C.  You have a charged body. You touch it, at one place, with a neon lamp. There where the film and the body touch, the body will equilibrate (becomes neutral). The neon lamp always glows on the negative place!

D. 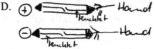 One can show that a body is charged negatively by touching it with a neon lamp. That electrode which is used to touch the body glows always when the body is charged negatively.

E. 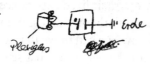 With a neon lamp. When I, e.g., charge a Plexiglas negatively and hold a neon lamp to it. If the Plexiglas is charged negatively, that electrode glows which is oriented towards the charged Plexiglas. The electrons flow from the Plexiglas through the neon lamp into my hand and return to ground. !!GROUNDING!!

F. 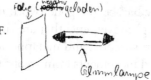 When touching that part glows which is on the side of the transparency film.

G. You can prove it by means of the neon lamp. If you hold it to a charged body, and it is charged negatively, then that part [electrode] glows which is close to the charged body. The lamp indicates the direction in which the electrons flow.

increasingly abstract way. For example, in example B, the charged bodies are indicated only by a circled plus or minus sign rather; the corresponding text is in the first person. In example C, the student used simple plus and minus signs in circles to stand for the charged bodies, but shows an iconic depiction of the hand holding the bulb. In example D, the hand is replaced by the word *hand*. In example E, the person holding the lamp is no longer present. The last two examples abstract from the experimenter (the experimenter does not appear in drawing or there is no drawing) and simply represent in words the action and results. Interestingly enough, the young females had a greater preference (11 out of 12) for using drawings than their male counterparts (4 of 7). (Boys produced examples A, F, and G; girls produced examples B, C, D, and E.)

How can these results be explained and understood? Discourse is what refers to the world, a world shared by people engaged in dialogue. The situation surrounds them and can be referred to by pointing (to the bottom of the electroscope), making a gesture (moving the hand up), or designating something by discourse ("it deflects"). That is, oral discourse is ostensive; it points out and articulates the world surrounding the speaker and listener. In written text, however, that which is referred to also has to be evoked because the two situations normally distinguished in linguistics—the speech event in which talk is produced and the scene the talk is about—are separated in space and time (Hanks, 1996). That is, the things to which students point or that they highlight by means of a gesture or designate by means of ostensive discourse need to be included in the text. This process, however, is much more complex than speaking about things, events, and the world at hand.

Think of it this way: In a lived situation, humans make use not just of one communicative medium (language) but of three mediums concurrently—language, gesture, and the semiotic resources in the perceptual environment. Writing involves more than merely fixing or freezing speech. In writing, the text is rendered autonomous with respect to the intentions of the author: Writer and reader no longer share a common situation, and the concrete act of pointing is no longer available as a means of communication. In this sense, the written text transcends the psychosocial conditions of its production and thereby opens itself to unlimited series of readings (Ricœur, 1986/1991). The writer, therefore, has to supply additional resources so that the reader can recontextualize the meaning in an appropriate way. Good scientific writing provides resources that limit the number of readings (Bastide, 1990); this requires additional work. Whether or not this work has been accomplished appropriately sometimes becomes the subject of teacher-student debates, when a student claims to have provided a sufficient answer but the teacher notes that the point of contention does not appear on paper.

As someone who continues to teach science in school, I have gained from this research on gestures and transitions into writing science many pointers about what to do to facilitate students' development of scientific literacy. I increasingly have created opportunities for students to talk in the presence of the materials; most important, I have asked them to describe and explain the relevant phenomena. When students attempt to describe what they have seen, they invariably, in the absence of words, use gestures to express themselves. These gestures bear great resemblance to the earlier sensorimotor actions that Phil and Marcel employed while doing and sensing things in the hands-on activities that they conducted. Using gestures, students already communicate even before they have the correct science words and, in the process, they construct an understanding. Understanding evolves from the attempt at expressing themselves, rather than the other way around. In the next step, when asked to explain, my students will draw on the very same gestures to articulate their first explanations, which they subsequently develop because I encourage them to do so. The more opportunities for expressing themselves a teacher provides for students, the more the students' scientific literacy skills will develop. I have found that with every attempt at describing and explaining phenomena, the time for doing so decreases and the number of science words students use increases (Roth & Welzel, 2001).

Before having students write, I find it useful to engage them in whole-class conversations in which I encourage students to use diagrams on the chalkboard. Again, the presence of communicative modes other than language facilitates interactions and contributes to the development of competent science talk, in this case aided by scientific representations (e.g., drawings and diagrams) as an integral part (Roth, 1996). In this change, students take a first step toward written scientific literacy, and a bridge is created toward developing even more formal written expressions.

Another important strategy for fostering the development of scientific literacy is to listen attentively to and observe students while they attempt to communicate. Teachers initially may find observing difficult because students' talk, especially in the beginning, is often very muddled (Roth, 1995). My 1995 study showed that the effort is worthwhile: As students construct descriptions and explanations on their own, the teacher will have ample opportunities to notice discrepancies between gestures and words. If words and gestures communicate the same but incorrect idea, the teacher would do well to provide additional time for the student to become familiar with the phenomenon because he or she is probably not ready yet for further instruction and development. On the other hand, when a teacher notices a discrepancy between the concepts being communicated gesturally and verbally, it is the right time to push the students, for example, by posing questions that challenge them to elaborate even further and, eventually, to arrive at the desired level of science literacy—the ability to read, talk, and write about science. Similarly, if a teacher sees delays between gestures and the corresponding words, the teacher can be sure that the student has not yet developed the desired concepts, and the teacher may want to provide additional opportunities for the student to communicate orally before the student can express him- or herself in scientifically correct terms. Only after students have developed competent ways of talking science would I move to the next step of communicating in written form, at first encouraging a lot of drawings and then, increasingly, using words, sentences, and paragraphs. Before seventh grade, I generally have students work on glossaries, which always include diagrams in tandem with a sentence or two.

Teacher Gestures

Teachers' gestures may serve as an important resource for students' learning (Goldin-Meadow, Kim, & Singer, 1999). In the course of their lessons, teachers find themselves in different modes of teaching, including lecturing and interacting with small groups. Because these modes constitute different forms of communication, aspects of the setting, teachers' orientation toward focal artifacts, and teachers' gestures play an important role. In lectures, gestures can both help (Roth & Lawless, 2002c) and hinder students' sense making (Roth & Bowen, 1999) and, therefore, their development of science literacy. I present two examples to highlight the role of teacher gestures and body orientation in small-group interactions and lectures, respectively.

Teacher Gestures in Small-Group Interactions

The following example is from the previously mentioned unit on static electricity in a tenth-grade physics class. The two teachers present walk around the classroom, engaging the six groups of four to five students in conversation. In this example, the teacher (Sam) wants to assist the students, who apparently are struggling to understand a phenomenon that they have produced but cannot yet explain. Two metal plates lying side by side were brought into contact. Then, a charged object was brought close to one of the plates, and the other plate was pulled away. When the plates were touched with a glow lamp, it lit up on the side closer to the hand holding it in one case but on the side opposite the hand in the other case (see example C in Figure 3.2). In his explanation, Sam not only talks, but also, and even more importantly, uses gestures. His gestures metaphorically enacted the different movements of electric charges from and to the two plates, respectively:

> Sam: Here [1] they have to leave like this [2] there they must go like this [3]. (*The teacher's hand moves from the first metal plate [1] to the tabletop [2], and from there to the second metal plate [3].*)

We notice that Sam's explanation makes use of many deictic, context-dependent terms (*here, they, like this,* and *there*). Such deictic terms are crucial aspects of the coordination of meaning in the context of scientific work (Goodwin, 1995). How *here, they, leave like this,* and *there* have to be heard must be taken from the situation. The concepts of *here* and *there* are distinguished by the different positions that the same hand takes in the course of the utterance; the two terms actively distinguish two situations without actually describing in words the differences between them. The ideas of *here* and *there* became significant in the context of the different observations made in the moments immediately before. *They* refers to something not specified in the transcript—the subject that the entire unit is about. Again, using the term *they* simplifies the verbal part of the communication, which is important at this early stage in the development of student science literacy concerning the phenomenon. Finally, readers will note that the same phrase, *like this,* is used in two parts of the utterance but actually refers to different things. In the first instance, electrons "leave like this," accompanied by the hand's movement from the metal plate ([1]) to the table ([2]), representing the ground. In the second case, "go like this" is associated with the hand movement from the table (ground) to the other metal plate ([3]). That is, the hands metaphorically enact the motion of the electrons in the model presented by the teacher from the first plate to the electrical ground, and from the electrical ground to the second plate. Metaphorical gestures constitute a core category of gestures, in addition to, or *along with,* pointing (deictic gestures) and representational (iconic) gestures (McNeill, 1992).

Two issues are worth noting here: First, the different situations are characterized by different metaphorical gestures, one involving a movement from the metal plate to the ground and the other from the ground to the metal plate. Second, a potential danger in this gesture is that students may associate the hand movement with the actual movement of electrons. That is, the gesture could create the misconception that the electrons move all the way from the ground to the plate. According to physicists, what actually happens is that electrons move onto the plate from the experimenter's body (e.g., his or her feet), and new ones move into the experimenter's body from the ground. In effect, there is a train of electrons.

Just as it is easier to produce sentences that contain a smaller number of unfamiliar low frequency words (Hadar & Butterworth, 1997), it is easier to comprehend sentences that use a smaller number of unfamiliar low frequency words. In a situation in which objects and events are present and students actually perceive them in the correct way (something that has to be ascertained beforehand), the teacher can rely on the perceptual ground and his or her gestures to provide additional information that students do not need to process verbally. Another important aspect of gestures in interactions is that they are seemingly "picked up" by others who use, often without being aware of it, the same or similar gestures to talk about the same topic. In this unit, many gestures that originated with the teachers or one student subsequently were being used by other students, even though the latter students often were not aware of having "picked up" these gestures from others (Roth & Welzel, 2001). Therefore, it is important that teachers consider and reflect on the gestures that they use while talking science.

Teacher Gestures in Lectures

Gestures can be used to point out some entity in a photograph, drawing, diagram, or graph that teachers generate or project onto a chalkboard or screen. Gestures also can be used to depict a phenomenon in an iconic way (McNeill, 1992). Both forms of gestures may assist students in appropriately verbalizing scientific representations. In the following example, the teachers of a seventh-grade science class, involved in the study of a local stream called Henderson Creek, have invited a scientist and environmental activist, Meg, to speak about her work. As Meg begins to locate Henderson Creek on the aerial photograph projected against the screen in front of the classroom, she explains that she is working not only to improve the health of the creek but also the health of the watershed, which she simultaneously highlights by waving her hand above the photograph. Then, she asks students whether they know the term *watershed*, and, when there is little response from the students, she begins to explain.

01 Meg: So this is basically a—a * drainage area
            that is collecting the water
            (*Her arms make several slight pumping
            gestures.*)

02   that falls on * on the lands,
            (*Her elbows and forearms descend.*)

03   and it is all *
            (*She steps forward, and her hands come to-
            gether.*)

04   funneling * down through the stream
            (*Her hands and arms move forward, with
            her hands making a meandering motion.
            Her hands' forward movement comes to a
            stop when her arms are fully outstretched.*)

05   and ultimately * into Saanich Inlet.
            (*She steps forward and turns toward the
            map to point to the spot where Henderson
            Creek sheds into the inlet.*)

In this excerpt, Meg provides two forms of assistance for the construction of meaning from her presentation. First, she turns her body away from the projected aerial photograph and toward the students, and second, she uses her arms to represent water as it flows from the higher to the lower points of the land, is funneled into the stream, and is ultimately shed into the inlet near which the community is located. Her turning away from the aerial photograph clearly indicates that the content of her utterances is no longer perceptually available in the photograph; she moves into a narrative mode in which her gestures no longer highlight elements perceptually available but rather elaborate the content of the narrative (Roth & Lawless, 2002c). That is, this movement is a resource for interpreting in which way the gestures have to be understood. The gestures themselves provide perceptual clues for interpreting what Meg might mean by saying *watershed* and *drainage area*. As she completes her explanation, Meg turns back toward the map and, just before describing where all the water that falls on the land is funneled into the stream, points to the place where the creek empties into the inlet. Turning her body, she highlights that now her gestures have to be understood differently, directly pertaining to entities perceptually available on the map.

Gestures and the associated body movement allow teachers to communicate more than they say with their words (Goldin-Meadow, Kim, & Singer, 1999). When gesture and talk work in concert, the movements provide resources that allow the listening students to make sense of otherwise more abstract talk. The gestures and other movements literally provide a body to go with the talk. But gestures also can interfere with comprehension. In one study, I was able to link undergraduate ecology students' difficulties in understanding a lecture topic to temporal and conceptual shifts between gestures and the associated words (Roth & Bowen, 1999). Even mathematics education professors and graduate students could not understand what the ecology professor had said because, as I suggest in the study, his gestures tuned listeners to the average height of a curve, whereas his talk was about the average width—the concepts expressed in the two different communication modes were different. Sometimes, gestures and corresponding words were shifted, with the words following the associated gestures. In this case, too, the listeners found the lecture difficult to follow and had "a hard time understanding what the professor was talking about." They missed an important part of what was communicated. Although it is not clear whether listeners privilege gesture, object, and diagram over talk, evidence exists that they find solutions to the inherent indeterminacy of meaning arising from multiple, sometimes inconsistent information in the different modalities by always understanding in terms of their familiar world (Hanks, 1996). (Some readers may be familiar with the research in which students asked questions to a "counselor" and found the responses meaningful although the responses were generated at random or, in other research, by ELIZA, a computer therapist [see Baumgartner & Payr, 1995]. That is, while listening, we always attribute to the speaker the intention to produce utterances that make sense in our world.)

This point is important to remember when reflecting on note taking. Many teachers have heard students say that when they listened, it all made sense, but when they tried to study or recall the material during a test, they could not put it together. My work on gestures and on teachers' body positioning suggests that teachers communicate more than they say—body position and gestures provide resources for making sense. Students who copy into their notebooks merely what the teacher says will miss all the gestures and shifts in body position that allows observant students to make sense of the talk in the situation.

Implications of Gesture Studies to the Classroom

Important implications for teachers come from these examples. On the one hand, our students use the same gestures that we previously have used while talking science (most often unconsciously) to make sense of our talk. Sometimes, especially from small-group interactions, students pick up such gestures and employ them in their own communication efforts. At other times, especially during lectures, the gestures allow students to become attuned to relevant visual elements on the chalkboard or in a science demonstration. On the other hand, these gestures never make it into notebooks when students copy from the chalkboard or when they summarize what they have learned in a lesson. When they subsequently study for a test or exam, these gestures are absent, and students find it difficult, or sometimes impossible, to reconstruct what was intelligible and comprehensible when the teacher talked about it. Providing students with opportunities to talk science, all the while attending to a lecture, may help bridge the gap between lecture and lecture notes. For example, together with colleagues in the University of Victoria physics department, I developed a set of manipulatives and printed materials that lecturers in introductory classes could use to get their students to talk about the lecture content. In this way, before they walked away from the lecture, students could engage and participate in talking physics, which included the use of gestures that supported the development of more mature physics talk. Often, students later enhanced their notes or became better attuned to aspects of the subsequent lecture parts.

The analysis of Meg's presentation reveals that she uses body positions to frame what she says and gestures about. My research in other contexts indicates that some lecturers naturally engage in such framing of talk and gestures associated with conceptual differences (Roth & Tobin, 1996). From experience, I know that many teachers and professors are not very expressive in their gestures and movements. Teachers may, therefore, want to think about ways in which they can use the space of their classroom and chalkboard layout so that changes in body orientation and gesture are naturally associated with different conceptual issues.

Gestures are inherently phenomenal and, therefore, they give, through a metaphoric transformation, physical content to conceptual entities (McNeill, 1992). Misunderstandings sometimes can arise because the physical image and the associated conceptual content are mismatched. Science teachers should learn to adapt their presentations (utterances and gestures) to the requirements of the conversation so that the essential aspects are represented "correctly." Thus, when Sam explains the discharging of the two plates via the glow lamp, he uses a gesture in which his hand moves from the first plate to the tabletop and from the table to the second metal plate. Simultaneously, he talks about "them" (electrons) that thereby move. The gesture apparently indicates something that moves from the plate to the ground. Yet, as mentioned previously, physicists do not model what actually happens in terms of electrons that move along this trajectory. That is, Sam enacted a model in conflict with the scientifically correct one, which he taught only a few weeks later in the same course. The particle model as enacted in our example, in which the electrons move along a path, is incompatible with the model of current electricity.

Conclusion

An increasing body of literature exists on gesture-talk relations among indigenous peoples, in industrial workplaces, and in schools. As a collective body, the studies provide evidence that gestures are a deep feature of cognition and that they play an important role in human development and learning at all levels. Until now, science and literacy teachers have not paid much attention to this information. Furthermore, the emphasis on expecting students to write before they can draw on the resources available from talking in a situation disadvantages students and curtails their learning opportunities. It is time that we teachers build on this other mode of communication that has such a tremendous role in the development of language and literacy. Many opportunities that go beyond what until now we have been using as pedagogical tools can be harnessed for teaching scientific literacy.

Acknowledgments

This work was supported in part by grant 410-99-0021 from the Social Sciences and Humanities Research Council of Canada. I also am grateful to Dr. Manuela Welzel for access to the materials from her physics lessons on electrostatics.

REFERENCES

Agre, P.E. (1997). *Computation and human experience.* Cambridge, UK: Cambridge University Press.

Alibali, M.W., Flevares, L.M., & Goldin-Meadow, S. (1997). Assessing knowledge conveyed in gesture: Do teachers have the upper hand? *Journal of Educational Psychology, 89*(1), 183–193.

Bastide, F. (1990). The iconography of scientific texts: Principles of analysis. In M. Lynch & S. Woolgar (Eds.), *Representation in scientific practice* (pp. 187–229). Cambridge, MA: MIT Press.

Baumgartner, P., & Payr, S. (Eds.). (1995). *Speaking minds: Interviews with twenty eminent cognitive scienctists.* Princeton, NJ: Princeton University Press.

Goldin-Meadow, S. (1997). When gestures and words speak differently. *Current Directions in Psychological Science, 6,* 138–143.

Goldin-Meadow, S. (1999). The role of gesture in communication and thinking. *Trends in Cognitive Sciences, 3*(11), 419–429.

Goldin-Meadow, S., Alibali, M.W., & Church, C.B. (1993). Transitions in concept acquisition: Using the hand to read the mind. *Psychological Review, 100,* 279–297.

Goldin-Meadow, S., Kim, S., & Singer, M. (1999). What the teacher's hands tell the student's mind about math. *Journal of Educational Psychology, 91*(4), 720–730.

Goldin-Meadow, S., & Sandhofer, C.M. (1999). Gesture conveys substantive information to ordinary listeners. *Developmental Science, 2*(1), 67–74.

Goodwin, C. (1995). Seeing in depth. *Social Studies of Science, 25,* 237–274.

Goodwin, C. (2000). Action and embodiment within situated human interaction. *Journal of Pragmatics, 32*(10), 1489–1522.

Hadar, U., & Butterworth, B. (1997). Iconic gestures, imagery, and word retrieval in speech. *Semiotica, 115*(1/2), 147–172.

Hanks, W.F. (1996). *Language and communicative practices.* Boulder, CO: Westview.

Haviland, J. (2000). Pointing, gesture spaces, and mental maps. In D. McNeill (Ed.), *Language and gesture* (pp. 13–46). Cambridge, UK: Cambridge University Press.

McNeill, D. (1992). *Hand and mind: What gestures reveal about thought.* Chicago: University of Chicago Press.

Ong, W.J. (1988). *Orality and literacy: The technologizing of the word.* London: Routledge.

Perry, M., Church, R.B., & Goldin-Meadow, S. (1988). Transitional knowledge in the acquisition of concepts. *Cognitive Development, 3,* 359–400.

Ricœur, P. (1991). *From text to action: Essays in hermeneutics, II* (K. Blamey & J.B. Thompson, Trans.). Evanston, IL: Northwestern University Press. (Original work published 1986)

Roth, W.-M. (1995). Affordances of computers in teacher-student interactions: The case of Interactive Physics. *Journal of Research in Science Teaching, 32,* 329–347.

Roth, W.-M. (1996). Thinking with hands, eyes, and signs: Multimodal science talk in a grade 6/7 unit on simple machines. *Interactive Learning Environments, 4,* 170–187.

Roth, W.-M. (1999). Discourse and agency in school science laboratories. *Discourse Processes, 28,* 27–60.

Roth, W.-M. (2000). From gesture to scientific language. *Journal of Pragmatics, 32*(11), 1683–1714.

Roth, W.-M. (2002). Gestures: Their role in teaching and learning. *Review of Educational Research, 71,* 365–392.

Roth, W.-M. (2003a). From epistemic (ergotic) actions to scientific discourse: Do gestures obtain a bridging function? *Pragmatics & Cognition, 11,* 139–168.

Roth, W.-M. (2003b). Gesture-speech phenomena: Learning and development. *Educational Psychologist, 38*(4), 249–263.

Roth, W.-M., & Bowen, G.M. (1999). Decalages in talk and gesture: Visual and verbal semiotics of ecology lectures. *Linguistics & Education, 10*(3), 335–358.

Roth, W.-M., & Lawless, D. (2002a). Scientific investigations, metaphorical gestures, and the emergence of abstract scientific concepts. *Learning and Instruction, 12,* 285–304.

Roth, W.-M., & Lawless, D. (2002b). Signs, deixis, and the emergence of scientific explanations. *Semiotica, 138,* 95–130.

Roth, W.-M., & Lawless, D. (2002c). When up is down and down is up: Body orientation, proximity, and gestures as resources for listeners. *Language in Society, 31,* 1–28.

Roth, W.-M., & Tobin, K. (1996). Aristotle and natural observation versus Galileo and scientific experiment: An analysis of lectures in physics for elementary teachers in terms of discourse and inscriptions. *Journal of Research in Science Teaching, 33,* 135–157.

Roth, W.-M., & Welzel, M. (2001). From activity to gestures and scientific language. *Journal of Research in Science Teaching, 38,* 103–136.

THE ROLE
OF LITERACY

INSTRUCTION IN SCIENCE

In the following chapters, Larry D. Yore and Robert E. Yager, both highly regarded science educators, question the relationship between literacy and science instruction. On the surface there appears to be a fundamental disagreement: Yore titles his contribution "Why Do Future Scientists Need to Study the Language Arts?" whereas Yager asserts that "Science Is Not Written, But It Can Be Written About." Both authors, however, are interested in helping students engage in authentic science, what practitioners of biology or chemistry or physics do. Their disagreement may be more related to when and how literacy is introduced rather than its role in the endeavor we call science.

Yore views language as central to the enterprise of science. Practicing scientists, he notes, not only use language to construct claims, but they also communicate regularly about their own questions, discuss procedures and science understandings, and use language to make informed decisions about what to do next or how to evaluate the work of others. Students of science need to hone these same skills; these skills are integrally related to the doing of science, he asserts. Yore shares Lemke's belief (chapter 2) that science communication involves multiple modalities and that science learning and literacy learning support one another. Yore examines the work of scientists to better understand the tasks and approaches as well as the habits of mind he hopes students will adopt and teachers will invite. He also asks educators to look closely at those situations in which crossing borders might be less effective; for example, where definitions of terms and basic assumptions fundamentally differ. Finally, Yore points out several teaching strategies that engage students in various modes of scientific discourse. Good science educators recognize the centrality of literacy to the scientific enterprise, he argues.

Yager is more cautious about embracing literacy instruction as central to science: "We cannot cross academic borders until the barriers between these borders are bridged or eliminated." What worries Yager most is the misuse of science by practitioners in the literacy community. Science is stripped of its power when presented as a compilation of information, he asserts. Curiosity, desire to find out through experimentation, is the heart and soul of science. Yager distinguishes here between science literacy and the literacy–science connection, noting not only the confusion in terminology but also the need to view inquiry as key to anything we offer as science education. He also argues for the importance of application—that science must be experienced in a real-world context. Knowing in science means being able to use the information at hand. Yager's worry, finally, is that by melding science and literacy instruction, the essence of science may be obscured or lost.

Together these pieces function as a dialogue in which one author enthusiastically embraces the language community and the other remains worried about the misunderstandings and debilitating practices that might arise if the conversation is not monitored carefully.

CHAPTER 4

Why Do Future Scientists Need to Study the Language Arts?

LARRY D. YORE

As a student, I often asked my secondary school teachers why we were studying English, the history of Europe, and anything else that did not fit my interests. They told me I needed to know these things for next year's course or to get into a university, but these answers did little to convince me of the subject's real importance. Also, as a science teacher and science education researcher reflecting on my elementary school experiences, I wondered why I had been in the "Johnny Thug of the Buzzard" group in reading but in a somewhat more colorful bird group in science and mathematics. You may know a boy or girl like this who spends more time in the principal's office than the principal does and who thinks the classics are a type of comic book, but at other times demonstrates interesting abilities, emotional dispositions, and insights about the world. Was I just not bright enough, or was I lacking in one or more of the multiple intelligences?

Some 40–50 years later, I finally have answers to my persistent questions about language and science. My struggles as a reader and writer produced a weak self-concept as a language user, developed unproductive coping strategies as a learner, and influenced me to pick courses in science and mathematics, preferably those with short reading lists. My struggles in school instilled in me a lifelong passion to make sense out of the problems children have with language arts and out of the ways the language arts are involved in doing, reporting, and learning science. I have realized that part of my own struggles had to do with my early image of science. My—and many other people's—vision of science was of old, white-haired men in lab coats engrossed in working with bubbling colored solutions, complex apparatus, and high-voltage electricity in front of chalkboards filled with abstract symbols, mathematical formulae, and numerical calculations.

Now that I am an old, white-haired man with metal-rimmed eyeglasses, I have come to realize that this early image was fanciful and that I was missing a critical communication and thinking tool—language, which is an integral part of science. Language is both a means of doing science and of constructing scientific claims and an end in that it is used to communicate inquiries, procedures, and science understandings so that other people can assess the validity of the knowledge claims, make critical decisions about the claims, and take informed actions on related problems.

Scientific language consists of both mathematical symbols and cultural language (English, French, Swahili, or whatever other languages the scientists speak). There traditionally has been an emphasis on mathematical formulae in school science, which appears to have convinced many people that there is nothing else to scientific language. When the vision is expanded beyond science classrooms to include authentic science practices within the scientific community, however, it becomes apparent that mathematics is not the sole means of communicating science information. Rather, spoken and written language form the symbol system that scientists use to construct, describe, defend, and present ideas. Oral discourse is vital for sharing ideas and stimulating thinking. Printed language is essential for documenting the detailed associations among evidence, warrants, and claims; making utterances permanent; allowing scientists time to reflect on their thoughts, mental images, and claims; and establishing proprietorship of intellectual properties. Chaopricha (1997) states, "Verbal or informal communication is not sufficient. The production of a written scientific research paper is needed as a record in case of dispute" (p. 12). Furthermore, scientific language is a problem-solving tool that utilizes unique patterns of argumentation and form and function (genre) to surface relations among variables, and causality among natural elements and events.

Talking, listening, reading, and writing are important abilities for scientists as they seek research funds; make sense out of their experiences; and present their research questions, experimental procedures, knowledge claims, and evidence to inform and persuade other scientists and laypeople about their work. Observations, surveys, and interviews of scientists about their language uses, habits, and strategies have found the following (Florence, 2001; Yore, Hand, & Florence, in press; Yore, Hand, & Prain, 2002):

- Debate (argument) and oral presentations are common activities in the science community.
- Research reports, grant proposals, and teaching materials are the most frequent uses of writing.
- Scientists read the same journals for which they write, and their reading is pragmatic in its purpose.

- Scientists devote little effort to crossing boundaries to promote public awareness of science by writing for laypeople and nonscientific audiences.
- Most scientists perceive talking, listening, reading, and writing as strategies for reporting their science, but they do not explicitly recognize these language arts as thinking tools and strategies for constructing science and scientific understanding.

The remainder of this chapter considers scientists' contemporary views of science, how scientists use language in their science work, and how teachers can use similar language tasks to create authentic science learning experiences to more fully promote science literacy.

Scientists as Language Users

Teacher education programs frequently are built on specific course work requirements in the social sciences, humanities, arts, and sciences, with little attention paid to giving the novices authentic experiences in doing and applying these disciplines. In science, this normally means seat time in several introductory courses and a few advanced courses, which consist of chalk-and-talk lectures, textbook readings, questions, problem set assignments, and weekly or biweekly structured laboratories that may or may not relate to the lectures and assignments. The professors in these courses are identified as scientists with specific research interests, but students seldom see these people "doing science." This dominant model of teacher education presents *science as a noun*, emphasizing encyclopedic volumes of facts, concepts, principles, laws, theories, and lengthy lists of experimental procedures and processes about science, rather than *science as a verb*, emphasizing the human endeavors, successes, failures, and emotional dispositions associated with doing science as inquiry.

This context and experience provides the foundation for most teachers' beliefs about science and scientists, a set of beliefs that frequently reinforces their childhood images. It is not surprising that many teachers have less-than-accurate comprehensive views of the nature of modern science and scientists (Bright, 2001). McComas (1998) has identified the following myths that people, teachers included, have about the nature of science:

- Hypotheses become theories, which become laws.
- Hypotheses are simply educated guesses.

- There is a single, universal scientific method.
- Carefully compiled evidence results in reliable knowledge claims.
- Science provides absolute proof about reality.
- Doing science involves mechanistic lock-step procedures more than creativity.
- Science can address all questions.
- Scientists are particularly objective people.
- Experiments are the main way of establishing science knowledge.
- All work in science is evaluated prior to becoming public information.

These myths about the nature of science and scientists also are common among elementary, middle, and high school students. Studies of children's drawings of scientists reveal that children are becoming more informed about scientists and the range of activities scientists do but that they still hold persistent stereotypical images of scientists as old, white men in lab coats who have eyeglasses, funny hairstyles, weird smiles, facial hair, wild eyes, and scars and who build robots and complex apparatus (Barman, 1997; Huber & Burton, 1995). Bodzin and Gehringer (2001), Bright (2001), and Stiles (1997) demonstrate that preservice teachers' views and children's views of science and beliefs about scientists could be improved with explicit instruction and considerations.

Recent survey and observation studies provide contemporary information about scientists' views of science (Florence, 2001; Yore et al., in press). The scientists report that a modern, evaluativist view of science most closely describes their beliefs about the nature of science, rather than a traditional, absolutist or a postmodern, relativist view of science. The modern view of science proposes that science knowledge is a temporary explanation that best fits the existing evidence and current thinking. Science is progressing toward accurate explanations of reality but may not have reached this goal yet. Science knowledge claims develop with the aid of a hypothesis about possible causes and effects that is tested or evaluated against collected data that support or refute the hypothesis. Hypothetico-deductive (hypothesis-driven deductions, i.e., a general statement of relationship to specific events) reasoning relies on the absence of refuting evidence and the presence of confirming evidence as support for a hypothesis (Yore, 1993). Hypotheses are not proved, only supported, or disconfirmed and rejected. Science knowledge claims in the evaluativist view are believed to be temporary and are open to repeated evaluation against the available evidence from nature, but some well-established claims are unlikely to change. The scientific method is not bound by a single set of steps but rather reflects the hypothesis being tested and the development of the science background related to the hypothesis. Scientists are women and men of all cultures with the human frailties of all people, including objectivity or the lack of it.

The modern, evaluativist view of science is in direct contrast with the traditional view of science that suggests science knowledge is developed through observations, measurements, and human reasoning. Scientific knowledge, according to the absolutist view, is a collection of truths about reality that are unchanging. Therefore, facts are accumulated by making observations and measurements, and these data are generalized to form a big idea, or intellect is used to produce rational speculation. This view of science proposes that the theory or concept is generated by inductive reasoning (i.e., specific events used to formulate general rules) using the evidence gained through a series of observations. In this view, deductive reasoning occurs when a general rule exists and is used to predict or explain other events and observations. The scientific method is a single, universally accepted process. The process itself provides validation to the knowledge claims, as this process controls for unknown influences and scientists are a particularly objective group of people.

Furthermore, the modern view is in contrast to the postmodern view of science that proposes that scientists construct explanations in the context of their own personal beliefs. Different interpretations and explanations of the natural world are expected because of the limitations of people and the lack of a single reality. The relativist view of science does not question, evaluate, or judge sources of information and divergent interpretations or explanations because one source, interpretation, or explanation cannot be judged as more valid than another because different interpretative frameworks were used: All data and claims are of equal merit. Science knowledge claims are viewed as individualistic and products of unique sociocultural contexts in which issues of equity, power, gender, class, and ethnicity influence the outcomes.

The studies of scientists' views of science also reveal that there is a clear difference between scientists' responses (science as inquiry) and engineers' responses (technology as design, not strictly applied science). Engineers suggest that researchers in technology do not resonate totally with images of science or with the idea that engineering is an applied science. They describe a design method that differs from scientific inquiry in that it leads to a product, innovation, or application and considers constraints—practicality, feasibility, flexibility, economics, sociopolitics, ecology, and ethics. This process potentially leads scientific understanding or follows it by applying established science ideas to relevant problems. Inventions can precede the understanding of the science ideas involved. For example, Roman arches were built before scientists understood the vector properties of forces, and crystal radios entertained people prior to the understanding of microelectronics. Engineers see themselves as problem solvers and service providers, devoted to adapting the environment to address the needs of people such that they can remediate persistent issues and enjoy an improved lifestyle. The engineers are sensitive to societal and environmental needs and to priorities and influences on public funding of technology research, and they seek reasonable compromises among the external influences.

Further consideration of science as inquiry and technology as design illustrates that there is no clear demarcation between science and technology. The interface between these fields is becoming fuzzy with the development of some of the hybrid science areas (such as atmospheric physics, environmental assessment, and ecological toxicology) that straddle the science and technology communities. These areas generate new knowledge, seek applications, solve problems, and provide services.

Oral and written communication and the processes of speaking, listening, writing, and reading are highly valued within the scientific community; scientists who communicate well are successful in gaining support from members of their own communities, funding agencies, and the wider society. In the studies, scientists with modernist views of science accept that science discourse had a rhetorical component (persuasion) as well as a communicative component, but they are uneasy about using the language of constructivism to describe their speaking and writing experiences in doing science. They fully agree that discussants', editors', and referees' feedback on their research reports improve the clarity of the science ideas and that this improved clarity not only focused on style, spelling, grammar, or other linguistic features but also included conceptual and explanatory clarity. However, they cannot break free of the strict, evidence-driven limitations of the traditional view of science (see McComas's myths discussed previously, especially the third, fourth, sixth, and ninth ones on the list) to accept that debating, writing, and linguistic techniques (metaphors, analogies, and so on) generate insights, construct new conceptions, and clarify ambiguities in their science.

Several researchers have attempted to investigate the specific language, purposes, and approaches scientists use to get funding, do science, report results, influence public policy with their work, and inform others about how it relates to current science-technology-society-environment (STSE) issues.

Florence (2001) conducted a multiple case study to examine how language was used in research teams and to cowrite research reports in microbiology and atmospheric physics. The roles of the research team leader and the research assistants; the interactions among the researchers; the activities and processes inherent in the coauthorship process; and the researchers' expertise, scientific writing, and entry into an academic discourse community were documented. Participants were given a questionnaire used in earlier studies of scientists in the United States and Canada (Yore et al., 2002, in press) to ascertain their respective backgrounds in science and their beliefs about science writing. The teams' activities were documented during the five-month drafting process of a research report manuscript. Meetings between research leaders and research assistants were observed and audiotaped, and field notes and reflective notes were taken by the observers. Edited drafts with conceptual and language comments were collected. During their writing or soon thereafter, research assistants were given a second part of the questionnaire to describe the methods they used when they wrote and to document their views about the nature of science. Finally, the participants were asked to reflect on their coauthoring experiences and to suggest any other activities that would aid them in becoming proficient science communicators.

Collectively, the studies revealed common tasks, strategies, and processes across groups of scientists and research teams, including language-use aspects, reading habits and planning, and report drafting and revising. Habits of mind (i.e., emotional dispositions), beliefs about the nature of science, and abilities to communicate the big ideas of science were evident in these activities and processes. Elements of scientific language and writing expertise, facets of enculturation into expert discourse communities, academic civility, and the dynamics of collaborative groups were apparent. Audience and journal selection were surpassed in importance only by the writers' perceptions of the rigor of their science and the resulting scientific claims. There was healthy tension and mutual respect in the research groups as they attempted to make sense of science, report their results clearly and persuasively, and share the responsibilities of expertise. These results provided a clear vision of science literacy, which is the central focus of the U.S. National Science Education Standards (National Research Council [NRC], 1996).

Scientists as Speakers and Listeners

Conversation, for scientists, involves a full range of verbal tasks—talking to another scientist face to face or at a distance; speaking to small and large groups of students and scientists; presenting and debating ideas on radio and television; and leaving voicemail messages for staff, colleagues, and family members. These one- and two-way communications require scientists to establish purpose, consider audience, and mentally compose understandable messages designed to achieve their purpose with the targeted audience. Likewise, scientists listen to other scientists, students, and laypeople in one-to-one, small-group, and large-group settings face to face or at a distance.

The language that effective scientists use varies with the setting and purpose. When speaking to laypeople, scientists may use an informal style containing minimum terminology to respect the vernacular language of the intended audience, frequent nonverbal gestures to augment spoken words, and appropriate metaphors and analogies to connect the new material to their audience's prior experiences and knowledge. Likewise, a scientist in an instructional setting uses somewhat more formal language and technical vocabulary to match the students' academic level. For example, a first-year introductory course for nonmajors approximates the style and terminology of lay audiences, but an advanced graduate course approximates the style and technical vocabulary of an academic conference presentation.

Each of these communications is intended to convey a message without distorting the science or overstating their presenters' certainty of their claims. Scientists who wish to communicate, inform, and persuade listeners use the linguistic tools necessary to bridge the gap between speaker and listener. This bridging may involve metaphors or analogies to connect the audience's prior experiences and understanding with the central science ideas of the message, or it may involve oral citations of other scientists' work to connect their messages to established ideas. The effectiveness of these communications depends on the speaker's ability, the listener's background, and the target ideas' complexity and abstractness. There are examples in which crossing borders between science and nonscience discourse communities are not effective, such as when an evolution biologist debates a religious creationist. In this situation, the terminology of the two communities is different (theory as an umbrella concept that integrates well-established science ideas vs. theory as an unproven speculation); unless the debaters agree to use a shared vocabulary, communications often will fail, and the debate will result in a shouting match in which speakers talk past their audience rather than talking with their audience (Good, Shymansky, & Yore, 1999).

Frequently, scientists are portrayed as good talkers and bad listeners, but this is not generally true. Scientists in research team meetings and conferences must listen intently to assess the significance of the presenters' claims, the credibility of their data, the supportiveness of their evidence, and the augmentation value of their citations (warrants, or cited established research findings and theoretical foundations) in an attempt to evaluate the strength of the argument presented. The acuity of their listening can be gauged by their questions for the presenter and their comments during subsequent discussions of the presentation, rebuttals, and counterclaims. In the case studies of the research teams mentioned previously, it was frequently observed that senior scientists gave junior scientists intense attention because these novice researchers possessed specific information critical to the success of the research project and to making sense of the specific ideas under consideration (Florence, 2001). This academic civility and the recognition of distributed expertise form the central pedagogy behind jigsaw cooperative learning involving home groups and expert groups (Slavin, 1990). The jigsaw approach, like doing a picture puzzle, constructs a complex view or knowledge claim in the heterogeneous composed home group of students based on the unique but narrow contributions made by each expert student returning from different learning activities or information sources.

Oral language is essential to doing science because it is a flexible medium for debate, ease of production, and instant response potential (Lemke, 1990). Oral communication and debate in science are interactive and constructive. Scientists plan their speech to construct a coherent and convincing verbal message and to revise, elaborate, and augment the original plan based on the nonverbal responses of, and verbal interactions with, the audience. Speaking and listening are interactive-constructivist processes affecting both the speakers and the listeners.

Scientists as Readers and Writers

Oral language is necessary in science but not sufficient. Scientists need permanent records of conversations to establish their priority for discoveries and to use as documented sources for reflection, analysis, and evaluation. Print-based language skills are a critical attribute for scientists to fully become members of their scientific discourse community.

Scientists read the journals they believe best represent their discourse communities. They are utilitarian and pragmatic readers, reading with specific purposes to access information, procedures, and opinions required by their teaching assignments or research agendas (Bazerman, 1988). Scientists read journals before, during, and after doing experiments that relate closely to their research interests and for which they write research reports and articles (Yore et al., 2002; in press). These readings inform their actions and influence their print language uses, style, and conventions.

Scientists read with pencil in hand, noting interesting ideas, drawing diagrams, and writing margin notes to make sense of the text. As Mallow (1991) says, "Unclear points are pondered over, references are looked up, numerical calculations are checked" (p. 331). Clearly, scientists are interacting with the print to construct understanding of the text. This illustrates science reading as an interactive, constructive, meaning-making process, not a meaning-taking process (Yore, 2000). Science reading requires scientists to engage their prior knowledge about the general domain, textual topic, scientific inquiry, and nature of science—as well as their reading strategies—from long-term memory in an effort to make sense of the printed information extracted from text in the short-term memory. To aid comprehension, additional information can be obtained from concurrent sensory experiences, such as making observations of the central ideas, conducting an activity related to the topic, or consulting with another reader or knowledgeable person. Science readers must accurately assess the validity of claims, the quality of evidence, and the coherence of claims and established science knowledge of the field. In fact, many readers of science ascribe greater authority and certainty to print and textual messages than is intended by the authors or justified by reality (Craig & Yore, 1995, 1996; Norris & Phillips, 1994; Phillips & Norris, 1999). This interactive-constructivist process requires that the prior conceptual and strategic knowledge, sensory experiences, and real-time reflections are orchestrated by the readers' metacognitive awareness and executive control. Metacognitive awareness involves the what, how, and why/when knowledge about science reading and specific strategies, while executive control involves the management of the reading task—planning your approach, evaluating your comprehension, and regulating your cognitive plan. Readers set a purpose, then monitor progress and regulating actions by activating supplementary knowledge sources and appropriate complementary strategies as needed (Yore, Craig, & Maguire, 1998).

Scientists as writers are involved in a variety of writing tasks to meet their responsibilities and purposes in teaching, research, and supervision roles. Surveys and interviews of university scientists from academic science, applied science, and technology departments in the United States and Canada indicate that the most frequent writing tasks involve their teaching, research, and administrative responsibilities (see Table 4.1). Inspection of the composite low-frequency choices (1 and 2) and the higher frequency choices (3, 4, and 5) provides a clear vision of writing for real scientists and engineers. Surprisingly, these composite data indicate that the surveyed university faculty members were not involved in writing research grants, reports,

TABLE 4.1
Frequency of Use of Types of Writing—American University and Canadian University Scientists and Engineers (N = 36)

Writing Type	1	2	3	4	5
Journal articles	37%	33%	13%	10%	7%
Lecture notes (handouts or Web)	16%	6%	14%	53%	11%
Grants proposals	19%	56%	22%	3%	0%
Reports (research summaries, etc.)	38%	42%	17%	3%	0%
Posters	17%	71%	6%	6%	0%
Abstracts	11%	49%	31%	6%	3%
Editorials/opinion pieces for science journals	72%	22%	6%	0%	0%
Seminars or talks	3%	47%	42%	8%	0%
Letters to the editors of newspapers	81%	19%	0%	0%	0%
Essays or short articles	53%	39%	8%	0%	0%
Lab or field notebooks	22%	25%	25%	11%	17%
Personal use to understand your research	22%	14%	19%	11%	34%

1 = Never used; 2 = Infrequently used (a few times each year); 3 = Occasionally used (several times per month); 4 = Frequently used (several times per week); 5 = Daily

and peer-refereed journal articles every day and that they put little priority or effort into writing for the broader public audience in the form of letters to editors and essays for nonscience audiences.

The research report is the dominant genre for academic scientists, but some scientists do write opinion pieces, editorials, committee reports, research grant applications and reports, instruction manuals, and descriptive articles (Yore et al., 2001, in press). Each genre involves a specific function and form such as narrative, description, explanation, instruction, and argument (Callaghan, Knapp, & Noble, 1993; Yore, 2000). Narrative text involves the temporal, sequenced discourse found in diaries, journals, field logs, and conversations that are ordered and that emphasize the internal beliefs, priorities, and values of the writer. Science narratives are far more personal and informal than most published scientific writing. Descriptive text involves personal, common sense, and technical descriptions, as opposed to informational books and scientific reports with embedded definitions. Science descriptions frequently are structured by chronological events, classification systems, or the five-Ws pattern—who, what, where, why, and when. Explanatory text involves sequencing elements and events into cause-effect relationships. Science explanations attempt to establish causality by linking established ideas or models with observed effects using logical connectives (*if/then, resulting in, affecting the,* etc.). Instructive text involves ordering a sequence of procedures to specify a direction, experimental process, or operation manual. Science instructions use a series of numbered steps or bulleted declarative statements reflecting established protocols, measurement techniques, technical operations, or safety concepts. Argumentative text involves logical orders of propositions to persuade the audience that the claims are supported and justified. Science arguments establish boundaries and conditions of the issue and then set out to develop a compelling message that uses data and warrants to base and augment a knowledge claim or to compare and contrast their claim against established conceptual criteria or competing claims.

Scientists describe writing any lengthy piece of text as a coordinated effort between authors and research associates, and the articulation of ideas in smaller related writing tasks spread over several months or a year. Scientists consult databases, other scientists, and related texts while writing to access expert opinions, additional data, and other established claims. On some occasions, scientists return to the laboratory to verify data and collect additional evidence.

Scientists use writing as an interactive-constructivist process to build knowledge claims, develop compelling arguments, transform data into generalizations, report research results, and persuade colleagues and other people. They move between knowledge about science and specific topics and knowledge about science discourse and writing strategies to compose comprehensible text and resolve conceptual problems (Keys, 1999; Yore, 2000). The transition between science and discourse domains and the resolution of problems is guided by scientists' metacognitive awareness and executive control of science writing and science inquiry. Clearly, scientists set purpose, monitor progress, and regulate actions based on internal and external assessments of the conceptual validity and the linguistic clarity of the written argument (Yore et al., 2002).

Making Informed Decisions About Language-Oriented Tasks in Science Instruction

Scientists use language to access ideas, interact with other people, and construct science claims. Debating, reading, and writing are interactive-constructivist processes, and teachers need to recognize these factors when forming pedagogical models of science talking, listening, reading, and writing for their classrooms. A summary of the work of Lemke (1990), Ruddell and Unrau (1994), and Bereiter and Scardamalia (1987) provides insights into general models and their application to all students in science classrooms (Yore, 2000; Yore, Bisanz, & Hand, 2003). These theoretical frames, the English language arts and science reform documents (American Association for the Advancement of Science [AAAS], 1993; National Council of Teachers of English & International Reading Association, 1996; NRC, 1996; Rutherford & Ahlgren, 1990), and the prototypical images of scientists as language users buttress the following criteria for making decisions about incorporating language-oriented tasks into inquiry science instruction:

- How do the language-oriented tasks contribute to achieving science literacy?

- Do the language-oriented tasks reflect age-appropriate teaching and authentic science inquiry?

- Do the language-oriented tasks prepare students to be lifelong learners of science?

Literacies involve a fundamental dimension of language and a derived dimension of knowing the academic domain (Norris & Phillips, 2003). Science literacy, similar to language literacy, cultural literacy, technological literacy, and numeracy, involves critical thinking, cognitive and metacognitive abilities, and habits of mind to construct understanding in the specific disciplines, the big ideas or unifying concepts of the disciplines, and the communications to share these understandings and to persuade others to take informed action (Ford, Yore & Anthony, 1997). Hurd (1998) summarizes the following central attributes of a science-literate person:

- Distinguishes experts from the uninformed, theory from dogma, data from myth and folklore, science from pseudoscience, evidence from propaganda, facts from fiction, sense from nonsense, and knowledge from opinion

- Recognizes the cumulative, tentative, and skeptical nature of science; the limitations of scientific inquiry and causal explanations; the need for sufficient evidence and established knowledge to support or reject claims; the environmental, social, political, and economic impact of science and technology; and the influence society has on science and technology

- Knows how to analyze and process data; knows that some science-related problems in a social and personal context have more than one accepted answer; and knows that social and personal problems are multidisciplinary, having political, judicial, ethical, and moral dimensions

These attributes are essential for people to cross borders between discourse communities and to take a more active part in the public debate about STSE issues and to differentiate science from other ways of knowing (NRC, 1996). (See chapter 5 of this book for additional attributes of a science-literate person.)

The current science education reform promotes inquiry science instruction, but little attention has been given to developing a concise, clear image of constructivism and associated classroom practices as described in the NSES (NRC, 1996). This list of recommended "changing emphases" in science teaching is shown in chapter 5 on page 101. When the full spectrum of changing emphases in science teaching is considered in the context of world views, definitions of science as inquiry and technology as design, the ontology of science (realist, naïve realist, or idealist), the epistemology of scientific inquiry, the judgment criteria for science, the locus of control for learning, the source of pedagogical structure, and the role of language in science instruction, it becomes apparent that several versions of constructivism could be supported. But the view of real scientists, theoretical models of communication, reading and writing, and scientists as language users promote a middle-of-the road face of constructivism—interactive-constructivist teaching models such as conceptual change, guided inquiry, and modified learning cycles (Yore, 2001).

Several popular science programs for elementary, middle, and high schools utilize an interactive-constructivist modified learning cycle (engage, explore, consolidate, and assess). This teaching approach recognizes that contemporary science learning is based on a dynamic, hybrid ecology world view and stresses an epistemology (way of knowing) in which the interactions with the physical world and the sociocultural context, and interpretations of these experiences, reflect that the lived experiences and cultural beliefs of the knowers are important (Prawat & Floden, 1994). An interactive-constructivist perspective also assumes a naïve realist ontology that recognizes the limitations of people and procedures in progressively attaining a more accurate interpretation of the reality and stresses evaluation of all knowledge claims. This evaluation requires that explanations and interpretations are judged against the available data and canonical theories, using evidence from nature and established scientific warrants to justify claims about reality (Hofer & Pintrich, 1997; Kuhn, 1993). The locus of mental activity and construction of understanding for the learner involve both a private and a public component, unlike social constructivism (see chapter 12), which assumes understanding as group consensus building, or radical constructivism, which defines understanding as a uniquely individual decision (Hennessey, 1994).

An interactive-constructivist perspective assumes that discourse reveals the variety of alternative interpretations but that consensus need not be reached. In this view, evidence from nature augmented by canonical science, not sociodemocratic consensus, supports or rejects the interpretations. The pedagogical structure for learning in an interactive-constructivist model is shared by the learner and the teacher. The basic constructivist assumptions about the role of prior knowledge, the plausibility of alternative ideas, and the resiliency of these ideas are preserved in an interactive-constructivist perspective; however, professional wisdom, the accountability of public education, and the priorities of schools mediate decisions about what and how to teach in the science classroom.

Language-oriented tasks in the interactive-constructivist approach closely parallel the theoretical interpretations of debating, reading, and writing as interactive and constructive processes. Furthermore, inquiry science provides numerous and meaningful discourse opportunities in which explicit instruction and specific language-oriented assignments can be introduced. The critical issue is to select language tasks that respect the nature of science and the nature of education. Five general criteria are based on the theoretical frames of science, scientists, and scientific inquiry; the pedagogical frames of interactive-constructivist learning and teaching; and practical frames of science classrooms. A synthesis of the collective of theory, research results, literature reviews, and teaching experience supports the following criteria (Yore, 2000; Yore et al., 2003). The criteria were crafted to guide teachers' selection and design of language tasks for science inquiry instruction.

1. Ensure that any attempt to enhance students' speaking, listening, reading, and writing is based on compatible models of language arts and science learning as interactive and constructive.

2. Make language tasks and instruction pay off now and later by using authentic communicative strategies that enhance fundamental and derived literacy, are applicable in later life, and recognize the limitations of some "cute" activities.

3. Make debating, reading, and writing instruction an integral part of any science program and science course by starting in upper primary grades and continuing into middle school, secondary school, and university science courses with developmentally appropriate cognitive and metacognitive goals.

4. Provide explicit strategy instruction for the language arts similar to any embedded instruction of requisite science processes, laboratory procedures, or safety rules.

5. Select language tasks that encompass the range of genre, information sources, and communication technologies encountered by real scientists and science-literate adults.

Using these criteria, several promising practices are documented in the professional literature, other chapters of this book, and other volumes in this series.

Oracy (oral literacy) tasks need to stress discussion and argumentation in which students delineate the alternative interpretations of inquiry experiences, data, perspectives, or controversial STSE issues and justify their claims based on the available evidence and established science ideas (Yore et al., 2003). Argumentation within contemporary science "critically examines and evaluates the numerous and at times iterative transformations of evidence into explanations" (Duschl & Ellenbogen, 1999, p. 1) to produce an argument about descriptive or causal claims. Arguments have three generally recognizable forms: analytical, dialectical, and rhetorical. Duschl and Ellenbogen (1999) state,

> Essentially in the analytical approach an argument proceeds inductively or deductively from a set of premises to a conclusion. For analytical arguments of categorisation, the form is the syllogism [a=b, b=c, therefore a=c]. For the analytical argument of causation, the form is material implication: If p, then q; p, therefore q....

Dialectical arguments are those that occur during discussion or debate and involve reasoning with premises that are not evidently true. Dialectical arguments are a part of the informal logic domain. Rhetorical arguments are oratorical in nature and are represented by the discursive techniques employed to persuade an audience. In contrast to the other two arguments where the evidence is paramount, rhetorical arguments stress knowledge of audience.

Dialectical arguments focus on the burden of support, presumption, and plausibility to determine probable claims or actions when all required evidence was not available. These arguments are not totally based on knowledge and probability, but instead based on the refutation of the counterclaims and rebuttals of the opposing sides. Rhetorical arguments focus on persuasion of the target audience by presenting a more compelling case than the alternative cases. These patterns of argumentation should be an integral part of class debates and discussions, but experience indicates that some degree of structure is necessary. The structure can be provided by the goals, the task demands, or the teacher. (p. 1)

Structured controversy (Johnson & Johnson, 1986) provides a manageable and practical approach to classroom debate in which traditional debating procedures are extended to include analysis of cases presented in the first round and a switch in sides for a second round of debate. Conflicting positions about an STSE issue can be the central focus and motivation for this cooperative learning activity. Johnson and Johnson (1986) point out that "conflicts among students' opinions and plans of action are inevitable in any learning situation involving decision making or problem solving" (p. 229). Structured controversy capitalizes on these differences and turns them into productive conflict resolution opportunities and opportunities to learn analytical argumentation and critical thinking (judgment, deliberation, and justification). Structured controversy involves the following seven steps:

1. Divide the class into an even number of groups, with about four students in each group.

2. Assign pro and con positions on controversial issues, with one issue required for every two groups.

3. Have the two groups that are assigned to an issue prepare and present their positions to the class.

4. Have each group meet independently to evaluate the strengths and weaknesses of its own case and the opposing case.

5. Assign the opposite positions to the two groups; they will now prepare and present a second case that addresses the identified

weaknesses of their opposition's first case and the strengths of their own first case.

6. Have the two groups meet jointly to evaluate the strengths and weaknesses of the cases presented on the issue and to develop a consensus on the resolution of the issue.

7. Have the two groups write a joint report for the class on the issue, including descriptions of the opposing positions, their joint decision, and justification for the final judgment.

Structured controversy provides students with the motivation and framework that are characteristic of critical thinking, productive argument, and scientific rationale involving claims, evidence, and warrants.

The reading of science material in textbook explanations, informational trade books, and electronic text can elaborate on and enrich concepts developed from inquiry science activities (Yore et al., 2003). The reading of science material can be used as a form of exploration, but it most frequently fits into the consolidation phase of the modified learning cycle—do first, read later. Science text can be obscure if readers are not properly prepared to make sense from this unique text structure and language. Explicit comprehension and strategy instruction should be an integral part of any science reading assignment. The instruction should be embedded in the actual text assigned and should reflect the interactive, constructive aspects of making sense of text and of effective explicit instruction (Pearson & Dole, 1987; Spence, Yore, & Williams, 1999). Numerous instructional activities can be modified to the specific characteristics of the textual material being used in your classroom (Paris, 1987). The selected strategy should be modeled by the teacher, practiced by the students with guidance from the teacher, used in controlled situations by students with assigned text, and transferred to other reading assignments and texts by the students. Explicit instruction can improve science reading comprehension, science achievement, and metacognition (Holden & Yore, 1996; Spence et al., 1999). Several strategies have been shown to be important to science literacy, to have the potential to improve learning from text, and to respond to explicit instruction (Dole, Duffy, Roehler, & Pearson, 1991; Norris & Phillips, 1994; Phillips & Norris, 1999; Pressley, Johnson, Symons, McGoldrick, & Kurita, 1989; Spence et al., 1999). The strategies are as follows:

- Assessing the importance, validity, and certainty of textual claims
- Generating questions about the topic to set the purpose for reading

- Detecting main ideas and summarizing them
- Inferring meaning
- Skimming, elaborating, and sequencing
- Utilizing text structure to anticipate and comprehend ideas
- Improving conceptual networks (concept mapping) and memory
- Monitoring comprehension
- Self-regulating to address comprehension failures

A more comprehensive model of the expert science reader identifies other aspects of metacognitive awareness and executive control that are related to effective science reading from an interactive-constructivist perspective (Yore et al., 1998).

Writing-to-learn science needs to move away from knowledge-telling approaches and toward knowledge-building approaches (Bereiter & Scardamalia, 1987). Similar to science debating and science reading, science writing is an interactive-constructivist process in which students address a specific conceptual problem with written discourse (Yore et al., 2003). Writing tasks are very effective means of consolidating, elaborating, and assessing science explorations. Writing tasks in science should be associated with explicit instruction on an as-needed basis and should encourage writers to write for an authentic audience; model scientific argumentation involving claims, evidence, and warrants; seek feedback, and revise their writing in light of the feedback from their audience (Hand, Prain, Lawrence, & Yore, 1999).

Prewriting is difficult to develop with young writers and only slightly easier to develop with more mature writers. But without prewriting composition actions, writing devolves into simply telling what one knows about the issue and does not fully explore alternative perspectives. Young writers need to recognize the things scientists do before starting to write: identify their audience; survey and read the established literature about the topic; collect, analyze, and interpret data; identify, consider, and evaluate alternative interpretations; and outline the pathway to address their goal. The revision process also is difficult to "sell" to young writers. Expecting elementary and middle school students to write a draft and revise it is optimistic in a time of life when people are interested in instant reinforcement. The important purpose of revision in writing-to-learn science is in the transformation of ideas and the improvement of argument more than in the improvement of the writing style, grammar, and language features. Research has found that the interactive-constructivist dimensions of writing can be achieved by sequential writing tasks that promote revision of ideas without repetition of actions—composing a data table for an inquiry, drawing a graph based on the data table, and constructing a description of the pattern illustrated by the graph (Hand, Prain, & Yore, 2001; Tucknott & Yore, 1999). The science writing heuristic (Keys, Hand, Prain, & Collins, 1999; see also chapter 19 of this book) provides an effective way to get students to transform their data and ideas without "turning students off" to science writing. Writing summaries and reactions to STSE articles, co-composing individual manuscripts with a jigsaw approach, writing concept maps, and labeling diagrams are effective writing tasks that help students make sense from inquiry science explorations (Yore, 2000).

Conclusion

In more than 30 years of working with language and science, my most difficult task has been—and continues to be—to convince science educators and other teachers of the importance of language in science and the importance of language-oriented tasks in inquiry science instruction. Many science educators and other teachers believe that yet another activity is all that is needed to rectify students' lack of understanding. Clearly, the meta-analyses of science curriculum and teaching, the conceptual change research, and the recent work in the history and philosophy of science should help teachers of science realize that scientists and science students need more than hands-on experiences and data to construct reliable claims about reality.

The habits-of-mind benchmarks for communication and critical response skills provide the single best source of age-appropriate descriptors and learning outcomes upon which to anchor the inclusion of language-oriented tasks in science instruction (AAAS, 1993). The following criteria should guide the selection of language-oriented tasks for science inquiry instruction:

- Keep science literacy central in all tasks infused into inquiry science instruction.
- Select language tasks that involve and promote interactive-constructivist learning.
- Provide explicit instruction and scaffolding for support of language arts strategies and abilities, then help students build an improved understanding of the science ideas involved.

- Use authentic tasks, information sources, issues, and audiences in the language-oriented tasks embedded into the science inquiries.

- Spend time preparing students to debate, read, and write with preliminary activities; accessing various primary print and electronic information sources; refining problem focuses; and planning strategies.

- Revisit language-oriented tasks in a sequential and developmental manner (using a language strategy or ability only once for motivational purposes and then never using it again is wasteful and ineffective).

- Demonstrate the explicit value of language in science; let students see you as a science-language user who values the products of language-oriented tasks by processing the results in class and making the products available to students.

This chapter emphasizes the value of including language-oriented tasks in science inquiry to help able science students address the fundamental components of science literacy and to motivate able language students to address the derived components of science literacy. The inclusion of language-oriented tasks in science instruction is just authentic science. With what we now understand about the nature of science and science inquiry, the role of linguistics in human thinking, learning theory, and classroom pedagogy, we clearly are ready to address the disregard shown for language in the science reform efforts of the 1960s and to accept the challenges presented by the digital age for an expanded set of language arts including presenting, viewing, and interpreting as well as speaking, listening, reading, and writing.

REFERENCES

American Association for the Advancement of Science (AAAS). (1993). *Benchmarks for science literacy.* New York: Oxford University Press.

Barman, C.R. (1997). Students' views of scientists and science: Results from a national study. *Science and Children, 35*(1), 18–23.

Bazerman, C. (1988). *Shaping written knowledge: The genre and activity of the experimental article in science.* Madison, WI: University of Wisconsin Press.

Bereiter, C., & Scardamalia, M. (Eds.). (1987). *Psychology of written composition.* Hillsdale, NJ: Erlbaum.

Bodzin, A., & Gehringer, M. (2001). Breaking science stereotypes. *Science and Children, 38*(4), 36–41.

Bright, P.G. (2001). *Elementary preservice teachers' beliefs about the nature of science and their influence on classroom practices.* Unpublished master's thesis, University of Victoria, Victoria, British Columbia, Canada.

Callaghan, M., Knapp, P., & Noble, G. (1993). Genre in practice. In B. Cope & M. Kalantzis (Eds.), *The powers of literacy: A genre approach to teaching writing* (pp. 179–202). Pittsburgh, PA: University of Pittsburgh Press.

Chaopricha, S. (1997). *Coauthoring as learning and enculturation: A study of writing in biochemistry.* Unpublished doctoral dissertation, University of Wisconsin, Madison.

Craig, M.T., & Yore, L.D. (1995). Middle school students' metacognitive knowledge about science reading and science text: An interview study. *Reading Psychology, 16,* 169–213.

Craig, M.T., & Yore, L.D. (1996). Middle school students' awareness of strategies for resolving comprehension difficulties in science reading. *Journal of Research and Development in Education, 29,* 226–238.

Dole, J.A., Duffy, G.G., Roehler, L.R., & Pearson, P.D. (1991). Moving from the old to the new: Research on reading comprehension instruction. *Review of Educational Research, 61,* 239–264.

Duschl, R.A., & Ellenbogen, E. (1999, August). *Middle school science students' dialogic argumentation.* Paper presented at the conference of the European Science Education Research Association, Kiel, Germany.

Florence, M.K. (2001). *A study of the enculturation of novice scientists into expert discourse communities by coauthoring research reports.* Unpublished master's thesis, University of Victoria, Victoria, British Columbia, Canada.

Ford, C., Yore, L.D., & Anthony, R.J. (1997, March). *Reforms, visions, and standards: A cross-curricular view from an elementary school perspective.* Paper presented at the annual meeting of the National Association for Research in Science Teaching, Oak Brook, IL. (ERIC Document Reproduction Service No. ED406168)

Good, R.G., Shymansky, J.A., & Yore, L.D. (1999). Censorship in science and science education. In E.H. Brinkley (Ed.), *Caught off guard: Teachers rethinking censorship and controversy* (pp. 101–121). Boston: Allyn & Bacon.

Hand, B.M., Prain, V., Lawrence, C., & Yore, L.D. (1999). A writing-in-science framework designed to improve science literacy. *International Journal of Science Education, 21,* 1021–1035.

Hand, B.M., Prain, V., & Yore, L.D. (2001). Writing for learning in science using a sequence of tasks. In P. Tynjälä, L. Mason, & K. Lonka (Eds.), *Writing as a learning tool: Integrating theory and practice* (pp. 105–129). London: Kluwer Academic.

Hennessey, M.G. (1994, May). *Alternative perspectives of teaching, learning, and assessment: Desired images—A conceptual change perspective.* Paper presented at the annual meeting of the National Association of Research in Science Teaching, Anaheim, CA,.

Hofer, B.K., & Pintrich, P.R. (1997). The development of epistemological theories: Beliefs about knowledge and knowing and their relation to learning. *Review of Educational Research, 67*(1), 88–140.

Holden, T.G., & Yore, L.D. (1996, March/April). *Relationships among prior conceptual knowledge, metacognitive self-management, cognitive style, perception-judge, attitude toward school science, self-regulation, and science achievement in grade 6–7 students.* Paper presented at the annual meeting of the National Association for Research in Science Teaching, St. Louis, MO. (ERIC Document Reproduction Service No. ED395823)

Huber, R.A., & Burton, G.M. (1995). What do students think scientists look like? *School Science and Mathematics, 95*(7), 371–376.

Hurd, P.D. (1998). Scientific literacy: New minds for a changing world. *Science Education, 82*(3), 407–416.

Johnson, R.T., & Johnson, D.W. (1986). Using structured controversy in science classrooms. In R.W. Bybee (Ed.), *Science technology society: 1985 yearbook of the National Science Teachers Association* (pp. 228–234). Arlington, VA: National Science Teachers Association.

Keys, C.W. (1999). Revitalizing instruction in scientific genres: Connecting knowledge production with writing to learn in science. *Science Education, 83,* 115–130.

Keys, C.W., Hand, B.M., Prain, V., & Collins, S. (1999). Using the science writing heuristic as a tool for learning from laboratory investigations in secondary science. *Journal of Research in Science Teaching, 36*, 1055–1084.

Kuhn, D. (1993). Science as argument: Implications for teaching and learning scientific thinking. *Science Education, 77*(3), 319–337.

Lemke, J.L. (1990). *Talking science: Language, learning, and values.* Westport, CT: Ablex.

Mallow, J.V. (1991). Reading science. *Journal of Reading, 34*(5), 324–338.

McComas, W.F. (1998). The principal elements of the nature of science: Dispelling the myths. In W.F. McComas (Ed.), *The nature of science in science education: Rationales and strategies* (pp. 53–70). London: Kluwer.

National Council of Teachers of English & the International Reading Association. (1996). *Standards for the English language arts.* Urbana, IL: Author; Newark, DE: Author.

National Research Council (NRC). (1996). *National science education standards.* Washington, DC: National Academy Press.

Norris, S.P., & Phillips, L.M. (1994). Interpreting pragmatic meaning when reading popular reports of science. *Journal of Research in Science Teaching, 31*, 947–967.

Norris, S.P., & Phillips, L.M. (2003). *How literacy in its fundamental sense is central to scientific literacy. Science Education, 87*, 224–240.

Paris, S. (1987). *Reading and thinking strategies.* Boston: Houghton Mifflin.

Pearson, P.D., & Dole, J.A. (1987). Explicit comprehension instruction: A review of research and a new conceptualization of instruction. *The Elementary School Journal, 88*(2), 151–165.

Phillips, L.M., & Norris, S.P. (1999). Interpreting popular reports of science: What happens when the reader's world meets the world on paper? *International Journal of Science Education, 21*, 317–327.

Prawat, R.S., & Floden, R.E. (1994). Philosophical perspectives on constructivist views of learning. *Educational Psychology, 29*, 37–48.

Pressley, M., Johnson, C.J., Symons, S., McGoldrick, J.A., & Kurita, J.A. (1989). Strategies that improve children's memory and comprehension of text. *The Elementary School Journal, 90*, 3–32.

Ruddell, R.B., & Unrau, N.J. (1994). Reading as a meaning-constructive process: The reader, the text, and the teacher. In R.B. Ruddell, M.R. Ruddell, & H. Singer (Eds.), *Theoretical models and processes of reading* (4th ed., pp. 996–1056). Newark, DE: International Reading Association.

Rutherford, F.J., & Ahlgren, A. (1990). *Science for all Americans* (American Association for the Advancement of Science Project 2061). New York: Oxford University Press.

Slavin, R.E. (1990). *Cooperative learning.* Englewood Cliffs, NJ: Prentice Hall.

Spence, D.J., Yore, L.D., & Williams, R.L. (1999). The effects of explicit science reading instruction on selected grade 7 students' metacognition and comprehension of specific science text. *Journal of Elementary Science Education, 11*(2), 15–30.

Stiles, K.R. (1997). *Influencing children's perceptions of scientists with a major focus on gender equity.* Unpublished master's project, University of Victoria, Victoria, British Columbia, Canada.

Tucknott, J.M., & Yore, L.D. (1999, March). *The effects of writing activities on grade 4 children's understanding of simple machines, inventions, and inventors.* Paper presented at the annual meeting of the National Association for Research in Science Teaching, Boston, MA. (ERIC Document Reproduction Service No. ED428973)

Yore, L.D. (1993). Comment on "Hypothetico-deductive reasoning skills and concept acquisition: Testing a constructivist hypothesis." *Journal of Research in Science Teaching, 30*, 607–611.

Yore, L.D. (2000). Enhancing science literacy for all students with embedded reading instruction and writing-to-learn activities. *Journal of Deaf Studies and Deaf Education, 5,* 105–122.

Yore, L.D. (2001). What is meant by constructivist science teaching, and will the science education community stay the course for meaningful reform? *Electronic Journal of Science Education, 5*(4). Retrieved from http://unr.edu/homepage/crowther/ejse/yore.html

Yore, L.D., Bisanz, G.L., & Hand, B.M. (2003). Examining the literacy component of science literacy: 25 years of language arts and science research. *International Journal of Science Education, 25,* 689–725.

Yore, L.D., Craig, M.T., & Maguire, T.O. (1998). Index of science reading awareness: An interactive-constructive model, test verification, and grades 4–8 results. *Journal of Research in Science Teaching, 35,* 27–51.

Yore, L.D., Hand, B.M., & Florence, M.K. (in press). Scientists' views of science, models of writing, and science writing practices. *Journal of Research in Science Teaching.*

Yore, L.D., Hand, B.M., & Prain, V. (2002). Scientists as writers. *Science Education, 86,* 672–692.

CHAPTER 5

Science Is Not Written, But It Can Be Written About

Robert E. Yager

A common misconception in modern society is that the contents of science textbooks and trade books are, in fact, science. This is not necessarily true. Rather, most written materials offered to students in the course of science instruction are but descriptions of past science explorations. Great stories can be written about doing science, and interesting histories can be recorded, but such narratives rarely are included in the textbooks or supplementary materials used for the typical courses labeled *science*. What students encounter are but declarations of "fact"—the explanations of the natural world that are generally accepted by the current academy of scientists. These explanations and, therefore, the textbooks that repeat them are likely to change as new observations and investigations are added to the theoretical base. Although many textbooks and other materials may be fine records of what scientists have come to know, they do not represent the heart and soul of the scientific enterprise.

First, science starts with curiosity (questions) about the natural universe. Second, science continues with an attempt to formulate explanations to answer these questions, often in ways that correspond to the same forms of reasoning and observation used by past scientists; sometimes, however, the interpretations of past scientists prove to be inaccurate after more careful scrutiny. Third, science involves seeking evidence through observations, experiments, and other means of verifying the proposed explanation. Finally, science is communication with other scientists about whether or not the evidence is compelling and offers an accurate explanation of the observed objects and events. Simpson (1963) has advanced these views of science that are generally accepted within the science community.

What Is Scientific Literacy?

The term *scientific literacy* is related to all the basic ingredients of science (questions, possible answers, evidence to support answers, and gaining general acceptance of the answers from others). Too often, the term is taken literally to mean being able to read with understanding—that is to comprehend—what is written about science. Until there is agreement and understanding of a broader and more useful meaning of the term *scientific literacy*, there is little or no chance that it can be related to the general field of literacy as it is defined by scholars of reading, language arts, and the humanities. To support reading and language arts literacy activities that violate the very essence of scientific literacy will not serve the interests of students or teachers interested in fostering the development of scientific thinking and understanding. Academic borders cannot be crossed until the barriers between these borders are bridged or eliminated.

It seems important to remember that all language is invented and used by people to communicate. No word has meaning until the people using it agree about what it means. Unfortunately, educators often fail to establish meaning before using a term, thereby making the terms meaningless or at least open to confusion and misinterpretation. The field of science is particularly troublesome in this regard because there are so many terms and new concepts given names by scientists as shortcuts and as a way of conversing with other experts. Somehow, these technical words and the complex ideas they represent become a focus in textbooks—often introduced as lists at the beginnings of chapters, italicized or offered in bold print in the narration, and used for testing purposes to see what students "know." Some science teachers argue that one cannot know science until one understands and can use the technical terms of practicing scientists, but this approach contradicts what is known about learning and only measures temporary remembering. Too often, the study of science is reduced to recognizing definitions of technical terms that are used meaningfully by experts but represent little that is of interest or use to students. Instead, students simply are parroting what they read or have been told.

To many scientists, *literacy* as a term is taken literally and becomes useless in discussions of badly needed reform in school programs. Morris Shamos, for example, saw scientific literacy as being able to read and comprehend every article in every issue of *Scientific American*. Because few (if any) research scientists can do this, he was quick to argue that scientific literacy is unachievable and should not be a central goal for science education. Shamos was a leader in curriculum development, past president of the National Science Teachers Association (NSTA), and a physics professor. His book *The Myth of Scientific Literacy* (1995) has attracted international attention and sparks much debate in science education circles.

NSTA has grappled with defining the essence of scientific literacy in ways quite different from Shamos, and has for more than 25 years identified scientific literacy as the major goal for science education. In a position statement, NSTA (2002) offers the following features of a scientifically literate person. Such an individual

- Uses concepts of science and of technology as well as an informed reflection of ethical values in solving everyday problems and making responsible decisions in everyday life, including work and leisure
- Engages in responsible personal and civic actions after weighing the possible consequences of alternative options
- Defends decisions and actions using rational arguments based on evidence
- Engages in science and technology for the excitement and the explanations they provide
- Displays curiosity about and appreciation of both the natural and the human-made worlds
- Applies skepticism, careful methods, logical reasoning, and creativity in investigating the observable universe
- Values scientific research and technological problem solving
- Locates, collects, analyzes, and evaluates sources of scientific and technological information and uses these sources in solving problems, making decisions, and taking action
- Distinguishes between scientific and technological evidence and personal opinion and between reliable and unreliable information
- Remains open to new evidence and the tentativeness of scientific/technological knowledge
- Recognizes that science and technology are human endeavors
- Weighs the benefits and burdens of scientific and technological development
- Recognizes the strengths and limitations of science and technology for advancing human welfare
- Analyzes interactions among science, technology, and society
- Connects science and technology to other human endeavors (e.g., history, mathematics, the arts, and the humanities)
- Considers the political, economic, moral, and ethical aspects of science and technology as they relate to personal and global issues
- Offers explanations of natural phenomena that may be tested for their validity. (p. 227)

This focus on scientific literacy is markedly different from the view of science undergirding science education in the post-Sputnik period (1957–1970), when the emphasis was on the identification of the central concepts, unifying themes, and major theories that characterized the various science disciplines (if not science itself). In the 1960s, a view of science arose that assumed science could be made meaningful, exciting, and appropriate for all if it were presented in a way known to scientists. (Of course, few consistently accept this view; it is nowhere to be seen in the U.S. National Science Education Standards, discussed later in this chapter.) Science educators during the 1960s and 1970s were eager to see, learn, and transmit this new view of science to students. As a result, there was no chance for student ownership, questions, or views of the world in which they lived. Rather, the attempt was to get students into the world that was seen, known, and experienced by scientists; that was identified as the major task of the science teacher. Such practices did not help to develop scientific literacy for anyone. In fact, enrollments plummeted in most schools across the United States and the world in the grades after which students were permitted to terminate their study. Studies beginning in the late 1970s revealed that student attitudes worsened the longer students studied science in schools (Yager & Yager, 1985; Yager, Yager, & Bonnstetter, 1984).

A focus on scientific literacy means viewing school science more broadly; it is more than a mere recitation and reproduction of the science concepts accepted by practicing scientists and the process skills they use to discover new concepts, test old ones, or do both. Assuming that science should deal only with specific concepts and processes and then assessing the degree to which each has been acquired is not an adequate indicator of real learning. Such practices provide no information concerning how the concepts and processes can be used in the lives of students and as a means for future problem solving.

Many science educators support and subscribe to the goal of scientific literacy but shy away from establishing any universal definition that could clarify its meaning and provide ways of determining how it is being achieved in traditional classrooms. Moreover, few science educators have explored how the teaching in traditional classrooms compares to the situation in so-called reform classrooms in which new materials and teaching strategies are employed. Most teachers assume their best students are scientifically literate because they do well on examinations. Yet research indicates that most teacher-made and textbook examinations require little more than memory and the ability to repeat information (Zehr, 1991).

The Vision of the U.S. National Science Education Standards

The U.S. National Science Education Standards (NSES) were published by the National Research Council (NRC) in 1996 after four years of debate. The project involved more than 100 professionals who worked on several drafts and literally thousands of other concerned persons who reacted to the drafts. A total of $7 million was spent to produce the map that suggested ways to achieve the visions offered by the NSES. The NSES team cautioned that the hard work of producing the vision was completed carefully and with the emerging research in learning as a base. However, the team also indicated that it would take a decade or more to make serious progress in actualizing the visions and charting new pathways for needed reform.

Scientific literacy was central to the NSES and was the first term defined for users of the Standards. The NSES offer the following definition for use in the field—both for researchers and practitioners: "Scientific literacy is the knowledge and understanding of scientific concepts and processes required for personal decision making, participation in civic and cultural affairs, and economic productivity" (NRC, 1996, p. 22). This means that a scientifically literate person can

- Ask for, find, or determine answers to questions derived from curiosity about everyday experiences.
- Describe, explain, and predict natural phenomena.
- Read with understanding articles about science in the popular press.
- Engage in social conversation about the validity of the conclusions of these articles.
- Identify scientific issues underlying national and local decisions.
- Express positions on current issues that are scientifically and technologically informed.
- Evaluate the quality of scientific information on the basis of its source and the methods used to generate it.
- Pose and evaluate arguments based on evidence and apply conclusions from such arguments appropriately. (NRC, 1996, p. 22)

The NSES also state that scientific literacy has different degrees and forms; it expands and deepens over a lifetime, not just during one's years in school. The NSES also indicate that the attitudes and values established toward science in a person's early years will shape his or her development of scientific literacy as an adult. Such views of scientific literacy rarely are acknowledged or practiced by other literacy experts. Literacy scholars often do not view scientific literacy in the same way that science educators are prone to view it. Literacy scholars are content to suggest that teaching science means helping all children to read technical science materials—including text in tables, figures, and graphs—as if these artifacts represent science itself and as if not focusing on such details results in a lack of scientific literacy.

Least controversial in the NSES were the visions concerning teaching—teaching that would result in real learning. The Standards were proposed with a summary with each chapter indicating the status quo and the changes needed, i.e., a listing of "less emphasis" conditions with corresponding "more emphasis" conditions (see Table 5.1). These recommended changes in teaching are all moves to achieve scientific literacy.

Too often, science education has been defined as a two-dimensional enterprise. The first (and most important) dimension consists of concepts—constructs generally accepted as explanations of the objects and events found in nature. These concepts are thought to be the starting materials for enabling students to become scientifically literate. For more than 100 years, reformers have identified a second dimension to science literacy: the science skills used by scientists. These skills are viewed as equally important to the basic concepts that should be considered in the study of science. These skills, often called processes, also have been used to define school science, but less frequently and to a much lesser degree than the conceptual themes used to organize typical courses. During the 1960s, for instance, one popular elementary school science program was developed by the American Association for the Advancement of Science (AAAS) with National Science Foundation (NSF) funding. It was called *Science: A Process Approach* (AAAS, 1965), and the whole course centered around 14 skills that were taught directly to students, almost always in ways paralleling the way in which concepts were taught.

Many science educators still accept such a two-dimensional view of science education. Teacher training programs often are conceptualized in such a way that science concepts are taught (and learned?) in science courses and process skills are taught (and learned?) in education courses. To buy into the assumption that science education consists only of the current constructs accepted by today's scientists—and of the skills they have used in determining these constructs—misses the essence of the enterprise, at least from the point of personal involvement. Nonetheless, these ideas, included in typical courses of study, are what many literacy professionals see and accept as the raw materials for teaching and learning scientific literacy. Unfortunately, many teachers, also using such a model, accept responsibility only for directly delivering major scientific concepts—with some lip service paid to teaching processes.

TABLE 5.1
Attaining Scientific Literacy

Less Emphasis On	More Emphasis On
Treating all students alike and responding to the group as a whole	Understanding and responding to individual students' interests, strengths, experiences, and needs
Rigidly following the curriculum	Selecting and adapting the curriculum
Focusing on student acquisition of information	Focusing on student understanding and use of scientific knowledge, ideas, and inquiry processes
Presenting scientific knowledge through lecture, text, and demonstration	Guiding students in active and extended scientific inquiry
Asking for recitation of acquired knowledge	Providing opportunities for scientific discussion and debate among students
Testing students for factual information at the end of the unit or chapter	Continuously assessing student understanding
Maintaining responsibility and authority	Sharing responsibility for learning with students
Supporting competition	Supporting a classroom community with cooperation, shared responsibility, and respect
Working alone	Working with other teachers to enhance the science program

Source: NRC, 1996

Context Is Central to Success With Science Learning

The importance of context in science teaching finally has become apparent. In fact, the context for learning now is advanced as being more important in promoting learning than are the concepts and the process skills per se. These science concepts and process skills continue to be seen as important outcomes for science teaching, but neither helps to achieve real understanding unless there is a real-world situation (context) for seeing, learning, and using the ideas and skills that often are portrayed as central to school science. Teaching science concepts and process skills without context ignores the very essence of science. Establishing an appropriate and relevant context for learning science is necessary for the understanding of basic science concepts and process skills. Only in this way will students achieve a literacy that is true to the nature of science itself.

Learning science concepts and process skills together is the overarching emphasis in the NSES. Students must help develop the context if science content is to be considered important and useful to them. Often, the best context for learning occurs when issues (questions, problems, or concerns) are used to define and exemplify science content. Whenever possible, these issues should arise from student experiences, concerns, or both; many valuable organizers for science begin with technological advances students see as important and useful. This focus on technology often creates problems for teachers who lack experience and formal training in the field of technology.

The importance of context in science education hardly can be overstated (Bransford, Brown, & Cocking, 1999; Champagne & Klopfer, 1984; Resnick, 1987). In a study of university science and engineering majors, 85–90% of these very interested and capable students had no real understanding of basic science concepts (see Annenberg/CPB, 1987). The "best," as measured by typical assessments, merely were conscientious students who committed important concepts and skills (often mathematical equations) to memory. Feynman (1985) reported a similar finding from a two-month study in Brazil: Teaching did not necessarily result in learning.

How can teachers engage students in science learning? Perrone (1994) suggests the following ways:

- Students help define the content, often by asking questions.
- Students are given time to wonder and find interesting pursuits.
- Topics often have "strange" features that evoke questions.
- Teachers encourage and request different views and forms of expression.
- The richest activities are "invented" by teachers and students.
- Students create original and public products that enable them to be "experts."
- Students take some action as a result of their study and their learning.
- Students sense that the results of their work are not predetermined or fully predictable.

After student minds are engaged, Perrone suggests that learning can, and is likely to, occur.

Reinsmith (1993) describes some situations (contexts) that determine real learning. The major factors he suggests include the following:

- Real learning results from trial and error.
- Students only learn when they have some success and interest in the field.
- Students have to believe that they can learn.
- Real learning connotes use.
- The more learning is like play, the more absorbing it will be.
- Time must be wasted, tangents pursued, and side-shoots followed.
- Learning never occurs outside an appropriate context.

Typical tests are very poor indicators of real learning (Reinsmith, 1993). To be able to practice science with meaning on their own (i.e., to become scientifically literate), students must become a part of defining the content—the segment of learning. Science cannot be presented as the next chapter from a textbook, the next unit in the curriculum guide, or something teachers and researchers merely report as being important and useful in the future. Science content must be related to the real world—the world the students know and operate in.

Too often in typical science classrooms, students feel as though they are victims—charged with following directions, getting correct answers, and being part of a classroom or laboratory in which everything is predetermined. So-called laboratories rarely are places to go to investigate answers to student or class questions or explore possible explanations. Activities often (90% of the time) are only verification exercises (Yager, 1993). Good students get the right answers because they know what the correct answers are before they act. Some of the best students do not bother to do the activities because they already know what they need to do in order to score well on tests. As a result, they never experience science as wondering, exploring, and testing for the validity of personally constructed explanations.

Students must learn that new contexts produce doubt, and if the skill or concept cannot be used by each of them in a completely new context, it is not really learned. Such ideas not only ensure learning but also illustrate the final feature of real science—that of communicating results and providing to others evidence of the validity of explanations. In science, fellow "experts" must agree that the evidence is compelling before it is accepted as accurate. Students always should check results, both their own results and those that are accepted by the whole class, to see if their meanings and data agree with those held by practicing scientists. Real learning results from trial and error and through the use of one's own thinking, logic, and actions. Students must have ownership, experience success, and question their own ideas and personally constructed explanations. They must realize that to know means to be able to use.

Moreover, students should receive satisfaction and recognition for using their learning to improve the school or community. In this case, learning is experienced and viewed as useful rather than as a demonstration for teachers or a feat of memory to be recorded on an examination. Such acts have nothing to do with scientific literacy.

The NSES identify seven abilities students need in order to inquire. Interestingly, these abilities also illustrate what students need to do to become scientifically literate:

- Identify questions and concepts that guide scientific investigations.
- Design and conduct scientific investigations.
- Use technology and mathematics to improve investigations and communications.
- Formulate and revise scientific explanations and models using logic and evidence.
- Recognize and analyze alternative explanations and models.
- Communicate and defend a scientific argument.
- Develop understandings about scientific inquiry. (NRC, 1996, pp. 175–176)

(These content standards associated with concepts and processes are closely related to the teaching and assessment standards.)

But four facets of content as defined in the NSES are the important ones for casting science learning into a real-world context. The four goals for K–12 school science as advanced in the NSES are as follows:

- Experience the richness and excitement of knowing about and understanding the natural world.
- Use appropriate scientific processes and principles in making personal decisions.
- Engage intelligently in public discourse and debate about matters of scientific and technological concern.
- Increase students' economic productivity through the use of the knowledge, understanding, and skills of the scientifically literate person in their careers. (NRC, 1996, p. 13)

For developing scientifically literate persons, much more effort must be given to all eight facets of content as advanced in the NSES. Four of these facets have been used for more than a century in the United States to determine the content of school science: (1) life science, (2) physical science, (3) earth/space science, and (4) science as inquiry. Four new facets of content in the NSES—new since their use by Norris Harms as organization for his NSF-supported project synthesis (see Harms & Yager, 1981)—are (1) concepts and processes used in concert, (2) a focus on technology, (3) science for meeting personal and societal challenges, and (4) the history and philosophy of science. These new facets have rarely appeared in textbooks, curriculum guides, or teacher emphasis. Nor have they been endorsed or adequately considered in state frameworks, textbooks, or local courses across the K–12 continuum. This omission is of great concern; in too many instances, the study of science means reading what has been written and remembering only that which is assigned and discussed.

If science learning is to occur, changes in science teaching must occur. And these changes do not assume science to be what is written about it in a book. The NSES have captured in Table 5.1 the essence of the changes needed if real learning is to occur. In practice, science has nothing to do with reading and remembering what is recorded in a textbook. Instead, it focuses on student experiences with the natural and designed worlds and on arguments about explanations offered for questions about these worlds. The focus is on exploring science through the ways that it affects daily living, the exercise of citizenship responsibilities, and ways of increasing economic productivity—all of which are major goals in science classrooms.

Of course, learning can be encouraged with materials, but it is important to note that none of the changes in teaching proposed in the NSES relies solely on text materials. Unfortunately, teachers are comfortable with using texts to define what students should learn. Further, parents often demand the use of textbooks so they can help their children read and remember what the textbooks contain.

Conclusion

The climate has never been better for realizing current reform visions. Funds are available, national standards are in place, state leaders have endorsed the new directions, and international attention and efforts are in concert with national initiatives. But teachers must take a major responsibility for changing their teaching and transforming it into a science. They must ask questions about science, processes, and varied contexts for learning. They must help students question better, must propose ideas that respond to questions, must design tests, must help students establish the validity of their explanations, and must help students to communicate their results and the interpretations offered as evidence. Teachers must develop and use more accurate and complete assessments as evidence for success. And most importantly, they must help students to use their learning in new contexts, thereby providing real evidence that learning actually has occurred. When science has been learned, it becomes a functional part of the learner. It indicates the importance of continued learning for an entire lifetime for everyone—especially for teachers who are encouraging it as their professional calling. When teachers practice the ingredients of science in their teaching, we will have taken a vital step in helping all citizens achieve scientific literacy. Such literacy may help in crossing borders in schools, in preparing a new citizenry ready to tackle societal problems, and in eroding the "two cultures" chasm discussed by Snow (1959) several decades ago. Snow was concerned that the advances of science and technology in the post-Sputnik era were widening a social gap between academics and the general population concerning science and the humanities.

During the 1960s, every effort was made to distinguish between science and technology. Basic science was a focus, and technology was stricken from courses labeled *science*. Current reforms emphasize using technology as a connector between science and society. This represents a 180° change. The applications of science now are seen as closer to and more meaningful to students, including advances and issues concerning food, clothing, shelter, transportation, communications, and careers.

An important step could be taken if all traditional areas of the school curriculum were more in sync with one another. After all, the research on learning, teaching, and school and classroom environments applies to all areas of the curriculum. How much more exciting places schools would be if there were a common, coherent, and research-based philosophy! Too often, teachers compete with one another for approval and recognition from students. There are far too few instances when borders have been crossed and there has been real understanding of the part that all education professionals can and should have in producing the kind of graduates that they all want (including parents and administrators as well as teachers and the students themselves). These graduates would be lifelong learners and literate in multiple dimensions. The problem of too few persons being able and willing to cross borders would disappear. And everyone would see the fallacy of using information that is written about science as a means to achieving scientific literacy. Scientific literacy, and perhaps other forms of literacy, demands that students first choose to learn if they are to learn and realize school goals in addition to the four goals for science identified in the NSES.

REFERENCES

American Association for the Advancement of Science (AAAS). (1965). *The psychological basis of science: A process approach.* Washington, DC: Author.

Annenberg/CPB. (1987). *A private universe* [Video documentary]. Washington, DC: Author.

Bransford, J.D., Brown, A.L., & Cocking, R.R. (Eds.). (1999). *How people learn: Brain, mind, experience, and school.* Washington, DC: National Academy Press.

Champagne, A.B., & Klopfer, L.E. (1984). Research in science education: The cognitive psychology perspective. In D. Holdzkom & P.B. Lutz (Eds.), *Research within reach: Science education* (pp. 171–189). Arlington, VA: National Science Teachers Association.

Feynman, R.P. (with Hutchings, E., Ed.). (1985). *"Surely you're joking, Mr. Feynman!"* New York: W.W. Norton.

Harms, N.C., & Yager, R.E. (Eds.). (1981). *What research says to the science teacher* (Vol. 3). Arlington, VA: National Science Teachers Association.

National Research Council (NRC). (1996). *National science education standards.* Washington, DC: National Academy Press.

National Science Teachers Association (NSTA). (2002). Science/technology/society: Providing appropriate science for all. In *NSTA Handbook 2002–2003* (pp. 226–228). Arlington, VA: Author.

Perrone, V. (1994). How to engage students in learning. *Educational Leadership, 51*(5), 11–13.

Reinsmith, W.A. (1993). Ten fundamental truths about learning. *The National Teaching and Learning Forum, 2*(4), 7–8.

Resnick, L.B. (1987). Learning in school and out. *Educational Researcher, 16*(9), 13–20.

Rutherford, F.J., & Ahlgren, A. (1990). *Science for all Americans* (American Association for the Advancement of Science Project 2061). New York: Oxford University Press.

Shamos, M.H. (1995). *The myth of scientific literacy.* New Brunswick, NJ: Rutgers University Press.

Simpson, G.G. (1963). Biology and the nature of science. *Science, 139*(3550), 81–88.

Snow, C.P. (1959). *The two cultures and the scientific revolution.* New York: Cambridge University Press.

Yager, R.E. (1993). Major problems in science education: "Anything over 90% is almost all." *MSTA Journal, 38*(2), 21–23.

Yager, R.E., & Yager, S.O. (1985). Changes in perceptions of science for third, seventh, and eleventh grade students. *Journal of Research in Science Teaching, 22*(4), 347–358.

Yager, R.E., Yager, S.O., & Bonnstetter, R.J. (1984). Concern for the affective domain in science education: A study over nine years of school experience. *The Iowa Curriculum Bulletin, 8*(2), 38–40.

Zehr, E. (1991). *Analysis of student scores in five domains of science education for concordance across domains and growth within domains related to ability of teachers to pose application items during an STS intervention.* Unpublished doctoral dissertation, University of Iowa, Iowa City.

EXPANDING ACCESS

TO SCIENCE

The three chapters in this section ask us to consider how science and science-related literacy learning might be improved by attending to issues outside traditional information gathering and information passing.

Barbara J. Guzzetti, in her chapter, "Girls in Science: Creating Symmetrical Opportunities for Acquiring Scientific Literacy," reviews the research that addresses gender bias in science education, using observational and action research studies. These studies were conducted at various grade levels, primary through high school, and in a range of science subjects from life science to physical science to technology. Guzzetti promotes critical literacy instruction in the science classroom, instruction that focuses on the importance of teaching all students to interrogate texts as broadly defined. She also calls for teachers to engage in their own classroom research on this and related topics.

Michael L. Kamil and Elizabeth B. Bernhardt begin their chapter, "The Science of Reading and the Reading of Science: Successes, Failures, and Promises in the Search for Prerequisite Reading Skills for Science," with an overview of the ways literacy and science can and should connect. Using this analysis as a backdrop, they ask readers to consider issues related to second-language learners, for example, When science is taught in conjunction with literacy, how might instruction be organized to benefit second-language learners? Kamil and Bernhardt view informational text as a "critical mediating factor in the storage, transmission, and retrieval of scientific information" and in this way their focus is considerably different than those authors who have shifted toward a more expansive notion of literacy.

Allan Feldman, in "Knowing and Being in Science: Expanding the Possibilities," uses an existentialist framework to examine the ways in which science teachers and their students relate to one another in educational institutions. He points out that when we want someone to learn something new, we also are asking him or her to *become* someone new. This discussion sheds useful light on Gee's discussion of lifeworld languages in chapter 1, and suggests that teachers have an important ethical obligation to consider issues of identity—their students' and their own.

The authors of these three chapters view context not simply as one more factor to take into account while planning effective instruction. Rather, they ask educators to consider issues related to identity and identification as central to the design and implementation of strategies designed to promote literacy–science connections.

CHAPTER 6

Girls in Science: Creating Symmetrical Opportunities for Acquiring Scientific Literacy

BARBARA J. GUZZETTI

Although the percentage of science and engineering degrees awarded to women is rising (National Science Foundation, 2000), it remains true that most females do not chose careers in science, particularly not in mathematics and computer science (e.g., Harwell, 2000; Mervis, 2001). Wondering whether girls' experiences in science classrooms may be contributing to this problem, researchers have explored students' gender-related perceptions of and behaviors in science classes. Researchers observing in classrooms at all grade levels have documented extensively that in typical science instruction, girls have fewer opportunities than boys do for participation in science activity and talk about that activity (e.g., Gallas, 1995; Guzzetti, 2001; Lemke, 1990). This gender gap is evidenced by asymmetrical opportunities for females to engage in scientific activity in their classrooms, which may suggest to some students that girls are not suited for science. The lack of symmetrical opportunities for female students to do science may discourage girls from choosing careers in scientific fields.

To help address this problem, this chapter reviews the research that addresses gender bias in science instruction. The review is divided into three sections. Each section reports observational and action research that was conducted at various grade levels, from primary grades to high school, with findings and recommendations being robust across age levels. The studies in this review also represent students in a range of science classes, including life, physical, and computer science.

The first section of this chapter reviews recent (since 1990) studies of science and literacy instruction that attempt to explain how women may be discouraged from choosing science careers. This research makes clear that girls often are marginalized in acquiring scientific literacy by their science instruction and by their instructional environment—their teachers, texts, and peers. In particular, this research shows that girls often are kept from actively participating in science activity.

In the second section of this chapter, I describe the action research conducted by both university and teacher researchers who attempt to address gender disparity in science instruction by changing the instructional environment. This section does not, however, review the literature on single-sex classes in science or the myriad of special intervention programs aimed at girls because these programs have been well publicized elsewhere (e.g., Simpson, 1996; Thom, 2002) and are not generally accessible to classroom teachers. Instead, this section offers strategies that have been successful in typical science classrooms and can be attempted readily by classroom teachers.

The final section of this chapter describes interventions from action research in other content areas that also focus on creating more symmetrical opportunities for females' participation in classrooms. This research should be useful for two reasons. First, it is important to show the applicability of these sorts of interventions across content areas. Second, those readers who teach additional content areas besides science also may incorporate these strategies into other areas of their instruction.

How Are Girls Discouraged in Science?

A perusal of the literature reveals that there are three main ways in which girls are discouraged in science: (1) by their teachers (and the teachers' instruction), (2) by their texts, and (3) by their peers. Typically, teachers are unaware of sources of gender bias in their classrooms, even when the problem is their own behavior or the behaviors of their students (Jones & Wheatley, 1990). Students, however, are very much aware of the ways in which some of them are marginalized, and they can explain and describe those ways when asked (Guzzetti & Williams, 1996a, 1996b). Hence, these descriptions come from the voices of students in addition to the observations of researchers.

How Do Science Teachers Discourage Girls?

The most blatant way that teachers discourage girls in science is by devaluing their participation. Teachers may unconsciously denigrate girls' contributions by their discussion practices. Researchers have found, for example, that in teacher-led, whole-class discussions, boys are spoken to more frequently and are asked more of the teacher's higher-order questions (Becker, 1991; Guzzetti, 2001). Also, teachers in science classrooms elaborate more on males' responses than females' responses in large-group discussion of scientific concepts (Guzzetti, 2001; Jones & Wheatley, 1990). In computer science classes, teachers have been known to exclusively call on boys to solve technical problems (Singh, 1993). Female teachers in both lower and upper level elementary schools perceive boys as more intellectual and girls as more process-oriented in their scientific abilities, and this perception translates into a negative message to girls about their participation in science (Shepardson & Pizzini, 1992).

Whole-class discussions become particularly more favorable to males when students are asked to refute each other or debate, a style of discussion that is more typical of the aggressive conversational styles of European American, middle-class males who dominate science classrooms (Guzzetti, 2001; Guzzetti & Williams, 1996a, 1996b). In addition, Lemke (1990) reports that males, rather than females, tend to define the appropriate way to "talk science." Lemke has found that teachers take a student's arguments on a position more seriously when the comments are assumed to have come from a male. Mervis (2001) also has found that teachers have a tendency to put more credence in responses from boys.

Even when teachers make conscious efforts to be gender-fair in ways such as calling on proportional numbers of boys and girls, there are still subtle or unconscious ways that teachers can discourage females from participating in science (Guzzetti & Williams, 1996a; Jewett, 1996). For example, when students are asked by the teacher to appoint a spokesperson from their small groups to report to the whole class, students are more likely to appoint a male to speak. Often this type of discrimination goes unnoticed and unaddressed by the teacher resulting in gender bias (Guzzetti & Williams, 1996b). In addition, teachers may subconsciously use males in their class discussion examples that show applications of scientific concepts (Guzzetti & Williams, 1996b).

Another way in which teachers, perhaps unknowingly, marginalize girls is through their grouping practices by ignoring students' preferences that make them most productive. Past research on girls' preferences for grouping is mixed. Some researchers report that girls prefer to work on and discuss science collaboratively in small groups (e.g., Baker & Leary, 1995; Harwell, 2000). Other researchers have found that girls prefer to work individually (Oberman, 2000). The reason for this disparity in findings may be because of the composition of these small groups. Observations in classrooms by a university researcher (Guzzetti, 2001) and by a university researcher collaborating with a teacher researcher (Guzzetti & Williams, 1996a, 1996b) show that simply putting students into small groups does not make girls more prone to participate actively in science inquiry. These studies show that when placed in mixed-gender groups, males tend to dominate the equipment and make the observations, and girls tend to be designated as scribes who passively record the data. Even when only one male was present in a small group, that male dominated the group. When females were placed into small groups with only each other, however, they actively participated in science activity and in talk about that activity. Hence, girls can be more productive and active learners when grouped together.

How Do Texts Discourage Girls?

In addition to teachers' instructional activities, their selection of textbooks also can discourage females from science. For example, Potter and Roser (1992) examined five seventh-grade life science textbooks for sexist language, images, and curricular content. They found that sexist language and images existed in these science textbooks. The books contained few representations of the achievements of female scientists and lacked information related to women's health issues.

Guzzetti and Williams (1996b) identified photographs and illustrations as the greatest source of gender bias in science textbooks. One female student in honors physics paged through her textbook to see how many pictures of women she could find and how those females were portrayed (1996b). In a text that had color pictures on almost every page, she found only two pictures of women. In one of the photographs, a woman in a swimsuit was lying on an air mattress in a swimming pool reading a book. In the other photo, a woman was portrayed as an assistant to a male scientist. Photos of men, however, showed them actively involved in activities that illustrated scientific principles, such as weightlifting, pushing cars, and playing baseball. The female student reported that the message she received from the textbook was the expectation that men would succeed in science but women would not. She found this "just slightly disturbing" (Guzzetti & Williams, 1996b, p. 12).

The lack of equal gender representation may be due to textbook publishers who do not involve women in the creation and production of textbooks. For example, the textbook discussed above was created by male authors, a male consultant, male illustrators, and male photo editors. Most of the textbook reviewers were high school teachers, the majority of them men.

Trade books, as well as textbooks, also may be sources of gender bias that send sexist messages about women's roles and abilities. This may be problematic at the elementary level, particularly when teachers are using literature-based approaches in which students read narrative (story) texts as well as expository (informational) texts. For example, Letts (2001) found stories that presented sexist images of women and science. One such story was a myth about the waxing and waning of the moon. In this narrative, the sun (portrayed as a male) becomes jealous of the moon (portrayed as a female). The moon begs the sun to save her, reinforcing the negative images of women being victims and being less powerful than men in the ways of science. Hence, texts like these that show women as passive and dependent on men discourage girls from active participation in science activity.

How Do Their Peers in Science Discourage Girls?

Although most studies have focused on the teacher's role in perpetuating gender disparity, several studies have demonstrated that the greatest sources of gender bias in the science classroom are the students in their interactions with one another (Guzzetti, 2001; Guzzetti & Williams, 1996a, 1996b). Observations and surveys of, and interviews with, both girls and boys have shown that the students were well aware of and could articulate their gendered interactions. The behaviors that marginalized girls were most pronounced and prominent in the classes that contained the largest proportion of males to females.

These gendered interactions among sophomores, juniors, and seniors took place both in science activity and in talk about that activity. For example, in a study of gender relations in two regular physics classes and one honors physics class (Guzzetti & Williams, 1996b), girls in one of the regular physics classes expressed their reluctance to speak out in class discussions for fear of ridicule by the boys. The girls characterized the boys' remarks as pompous and oppressive. As a result, girls spoke out in class discussions only when they were very sure of their answers, and it was usually the same few girls who contributed their voices to class discussions.

Patterns such as these were similar in the honors physics class, in which 80% of the females reported that males dominated class discussions. Although they were in an honors class, girls expressed fear of being wrong or "not smart enough to contribute anything" (Guzzetti & Williams, 1996b, p. 14) or, as one female put it, fear that the boys would "bite off my head" (p. 14). Males contributed their ideas most often, spoke over females, and interrupted to gain the conversational floor, particularly when point values were assigned to their participation. In response, girls tended to define their participation as passive listening.

The same patterns also held constant in small-group discussions, and they extended to male dominance of the equipment and experimentation in labs. Boys set up the equipment and verbalized the observations, but the girls were assigned the passive role of recording the data. Girls seemed passively to accept this situation as the norm because only one girl ever complained about the situation to an adult in the classroom during the course of the school year. The boys recognized that they held the advantage in the class, making statements such as, "The boys rule the class," and, "There are a lot of aggressive boys in this [physics] class" (Guzzetti & Williams, 1996b, p. 16).

The same patterns were found with younger students as well. For example, freshman males in a class on the physical world dominated class discussions and teacher attention with questions to and dialogues with the teacher that excluded the females in the class (Guzzetti, 2001). Fifth-grade boys were witnessed marginalizing a girl's participation in work with electrical circuits in much the same way that the high school boys in the studies previously discussed disenfranchised their female peers (Moje & Shepardson, 1998). Even primary-grade children demonstrated the same kinds of gendered interactions seen in intermediate and upper grade science classes (Gallas, 1995).

Together, these studies document that girls are indeed marginalized, and the studies show specifically how girls are disenfranchised from doing and talking science. This situation is especially problematic because students both form and express their ideas through language (Vygotsky, 1934/1978). If girls are not encouraged to discuss their ideas, how will they be able to acquire the conceptual understandings needed to become literate in the field of science?

How Can Girls Be Empowered in Learning Science?

The issue of asymmetrical opportunity for females' participation in science learning actually is an issue of differentiated power relations. Some researchers (Alvermann & Anders, 1994) have pointed out that theorists such as Gore (1993) believe that power is not a commodity that can be transferred from one student to another. Interventions that attempt to interrupt gendered power relations may have consequences. For example, in the two-year study conducted by Guzzetti and Williams (1996a, 1996b) in Williams's classroom, although the females complained about being oppressed, they were reluctant to address the issue with the whole class. Females identified risks to disturbing the status quo and damage to their reputations and their popularity. Males alluded to the costs to them in losing their power, a source of pride among them, as evidenced by their comments. Other students expressed fear of bringing up a disturbing issue for which no action might be taken. Hence, it is important to realize that the most successful interventions are ones in which the students actively are involved in identifying and addressing the problem of gender disparity.

Addressing Asymmetrical Opportunity in Class Discussion

Despite the possible risks and costs involved in attempting interventions, some teacher researchers have been successful in addressing issues of gender disparity in science learning. For example, Gallas (1995) found with her second graders that during discussions she called "Science Talks," a boy who relinquished some of his dominant social power actually gained an ability to express his own imaginative ideas. Rather than repeating what others said and making assertive statements, he learned to listen and to phrase his ideas tentatively, in an explorative way.

One of the secrets of Gallas's success was that she involved her students in identifying how to change the dynamics of their discussions. After listening to audiotapes of their discussions, her students metacommunicated (talked about their talk) to identify the problems that arose and generate ways to provide more symmetrical opportunities for girls in the class to speak. Students' suggestions included using wait time (after "big talkers" spoke, they would have to wait at least 10 seconds to say anything else, thereby giving others a chance to speak).

Another successful intervention that Gallas (1995) tried was to separate the talkers from the girls who were nontalkers. She asked the nontalkers to draw a picture about their ideas from questions she posed, while the others discussed their ideas. One question she asked was, How is blood made? Following the work in the two separate groups, she led a whole-class discussion in which she showed everyone the drawings. The reticent talkers realized that they had the same ideas as those who took a more active role in the discussions. These reticent talkers became "new talkers" whose self-confidence was increased by being enabled to express their ideas.

Other ways students can become involved in identifying and addressing inequities in class discussions is for students to trace, share, and discuss their participation records (Guzzetti & Williams, 1996b). This activity is another more structured and perhaps revealing form of metacommunication. Metacommunication may be useful in helping to make intervention an agenda of the students as well as the teacher.

Another intervention that was successful in increasing participation for girls in science was grouping by gender for small-group activity (Guzzetti & Williams, 1996a). When girls were grouped together for lab work, they collaborated together, became more active participants, and engaged more often in a wide range of verbal interactions. Girls discussed their ideas while setting up the equipment, manipulated the experiment, identified errors and resolved them, measured, made observations, recorded the data, and negotiated the data's meaning. Their talk represented equal participation and collaborative inquiry. The freedom the girls experienced from the constraints of having boys present in their labs allowed them to talk the talk of the discipline of science as scientists do. Hence, grouping by gender can be an effective way to facilitate girls' participation in science activity and talk about that activity.

Addressing Gender Bias in Science Texts

Critical literacy activities have been incorporated into both high school biology and elementary science instruction to address gender bias in science texts (Gilbert, 2001; Letts, 2001). Critical literacy activities engage students in deconstructing texts that present stereotypical images. Through teacher modeling, students learn to critically interrogate a text, asking questions during and after reading that speak to alternative representations. Both teachers and students engage in critical reflection through discussion of the features or content of text such as ones that portray females as absent from or weak in science activity.

One example of deconstructing a text comes from a sixth-grade curriculum described by Letts (2001). Letts explains how, in a unit on measuring time, materials for students interweave an investigation of the history of science with the concepts of keeping track of time. In one lesson about predicting the phases of the moon, students read the following myth from the San people of southern Africa about why the moon waxes and wanes:

> According to the San, the full moon is a joyous sight, lighting the way for weary travelers.
>
> But the sun, fiery and jealous, doesn't want the moon to shine so brightly in the sky. He tries to chase the moon away, but the moon continues to shine in the sky. Enraged, the sun carves bits and pieces off the moon. Little by little, the moon is whittled down and almost nothing is left.
>
> The moon is afraid that she is going to die. She begs the sun to spare at least her backbone.
>
> The sun relents, leaving the wounded moon her backbone.
>
> The moon goes into hiding to recover from her injuries. Slowly, she regains her strength. She begins appearing in the night sky again until she becomes full and shines brightly all night long.
>
> Seeing this, the sun becomes angry and jealous. Once again, he repeats his monthly assault to diminish the moon's light. (Letts, 2001, p. 255)

Letts (2001) notes the stereotypical and violent portrayals of hetero-sexual masculinity and the stereotypical depictions of femininity in this text, cautioning that

> the danger of such portrayals, however alluring they may be, is that they invoke these gender regimes under the guise of science, rendering invisible the way in which such tales are culturally constituted. Silence exists where critical dialogue could exist. (p. 268)

A frank and critical discussion with students could give them the resources and skills necessary to deconstruct such texts. Through critical questioning and discussion, students can be taught to interrogate these kinds of texts and not only the images of masculine and feminine that they create, but also the images of science that these texts create and sustain.

Gilbert (2001) describes a three-step process for teaching students to interrogate and deconstruct science texts. First, students read the text to understand the main ideas on the surface of the text. In this initial reading, students concentrate on the standard ways in which the topic is understood. Second, after gaining a general understanding of the text, students reread and discuss the text to analyze its general theories, assumptions, and concepts. Third, students read to find and deconstruct the underlying assumptions and metaphors within the text. In this final stage, students explore how the text could be read in other ways.

In addition to using critical literacy activities such as these to deconstruct texts, teachers can address gender disparity in science texts by finding and discussing alternative texts. For example, if the science textbook does not provide information on the accomplishments of women in science, teachers can locate trade books (children's literature) that profile female scientists. Teachers can read aloud excerpts of these texts to students, use them for inquiry into science, and make them available in a classroom library as additional curriculum materials.

What Else Can Be Done to Address Gender Disparity?

Other interventions to address gender disparity in science education have been attempted but with limited success. For example, Hsi and Hoadley (1997) explored electronic text as a medium for gender-fair communication. Students discussed science concepts through real-time, electronic communication tools instead of in face-to-face class discussions. The researchers have reported some success in increasing females' contributions to science discussions. This study, however, relies on tallies and self-reports and does not document or describe students' interactions through observations.

Another recommendation found in the literature on gender and discussion (Guzzetti, Young, Gritsavage, Fyfe, & Hardenbrook, 2002) is to teach students critical discourse analysis techniques. In other words, teachers can model for students how to recognize and change gendered patterns by analyzing discussions. Students can be taught to track power relations through recording who makes assertions, refutes, poses tentative questions, or gains and holds the conversational floor, and whose comments get elaborated on or dropped.

Perhaps the most important suggestion of all, however, is for teachers to become action researchers in their own classrooms. Researchers have found that teachers generally are unaware of gender bias in their own classrooms, perhaps because they simply are not looking for it (Guzzetti, 2001; Jones & Wheatley, 1990). Researchers also have shown that, although teachers may be unaware of any gender bias in their classrooms, their students often are well aware of these inequities and are capable of articulating and identifying the conditions that marginalize their participation. Therefore, teachers can become action researchers and involve their students as co-researchers by examining the talk and texts in their classrooms. Teachers can examine gendered talk by designing brief questionnaires that assess their students' experiences with and perceptions of gendered interactions. Teachers can interview individuals informally and observe students' working together to determine the number, length, and chances for females' turn taking in discussions. Students may become involved as co-researchers by tracing participation records and tracking their own and their peers' behaviors. In addition, teachers can examine their textbooks, tests, and curriculum materials for gender-equitable and non-stereotypical gender representations, and teachers can ask students their opinions of gender representations in the textbooks. Only by becoming aware of gender bias in the science classroom in ways such as these can teachers and students together identify and address the problem and ensure that everyone gets an equal opportunity to acquire scientific literacy.

REFERENCES

Alvermann, D.E., & Anders, P.A. (1994, July). *Content area literacy: Exploring the possibilities.* Paper presented at the International Reading Association World Congress on Reading, Buenos Aires, Argentina.

Baker, D., & Leary, R. (1995). Letting girls speak out about science. *Journal of Research in Science Teaching, 32*(1), 3–27.

Becker, J.R. (1991). Differential treatment of females and males in mathematics classes. *Journal of Research in Mathematics Education, 12,* 40–53.

Gallas, K. (1995). *Talking their way into science: Hearing children's questions and theories, responding with curricula.* New York: Teachers College Press.

Gilbert, J. (2001). Science and its "Other": Looking underneath "women" and "science" for new directions in research on gender and science education. *Gender and Education, 13*(3), 291–305.

Gore, J.M. (1993). *The struggle for pedagogies: Critical and feminist discourses as regimes of truth.* New York: Routledge.

Guzzetti, B.J. (2001). Texts and talk: The role of gender in learning physics. In E.B. Moje & D.G. O'Brien (Eds.), *Constructions of literacy: Studies of teaching and learning in and out of secondary schools* (pp. 125–145). Mahwah, NJ: Erlbaum.

Guzzetti, B.J., & Williams, W.O. (1996a). Changing the pattern of gendered discussion: Lessons from science classrooms. *Journal of Adolescent and Adult Literacy, 40,* 38–47.

Guzzetti, B.J., & Williams, W.O. (1996b). Gender, text, and discussion: Examining intellectual safety in the science classroom. *Journal of Research in Science Teaching, 33*(1), 5–20.

Guzzetti, B.J., Young, J.P., Gritsavage, M.M., Fyfe, L.M., & Hardenbrook, M. (2002). *Reading, writing, and talking gender in literacy learning.* Newark, DE: International Reading Association.

Harwell, S.H. (2000). In their own voices: Middle level girls' perceptions of teaching and learning science. *Journal of Science Teacher Education, 11*(3), 221–242.

His, S., & Hoadley, C.M. (1997). Productive discussion in science: Gender equity through electronic discourse. *Journal of Research in Science Teaching, 27,* 9, 22–36.

Jewett, T.O. (1996). *"And they is us": Gender issues in the instruction of science.* (ERIC Document Reproduction Service No. ED402202)

Jones, M.G., & Wheatley, J. (1990). Gender differences in teacher-student interactions in science classrooms. *Journal of Research in Science Teaching, 27*(9), 861–874.

Lemke, J.L. (1990). *Talking science: Language, learning, and values.* Westport, CT: Ablex.

Letts, W.J. (2001). When science is strangely alluring: Interrogating the masculine and heteronormative nature of primary school science. *Gender and Education, 13*(3), 261–274.

Mervis, J. (2001, July 18). What keeps girls out of science. *Science Now,* p. 3.

Moje, E.B., & Shepardson, D.P. (1998). Social interactions and children's changing understanding of electric circuits: Exploring unequal power relations in "peer"-learning groups. In B.J. Guzzetti & C. Hynd (Eds.), *Perspectives on conceptual change: Multiple ways to understand knowing and learning in a complex world* (pp. 225–234). Mahwah, NJ: Erlbaum.

National Science Foundation. (2000). *Women, minorities, and persons with disabilities in science and engineering: 2000.* Washington, DC: Author.

Oberman, P. (2000, April). *Academic help seeking and peer interactions of high school girls in computer science classes.* Paper presented at the annual meeting of the American Educational Research Association, New Orleans, LA.

Potter, E.F., & Rosser, S.V. (1992). Factors in life science textbooks that may deter girls' interest in science. *Journal of Research in Science Teaching, 29*(7), 669–686.

Shepardson, D.P. & Pizzini, E.L. (1992). Gender bias in female elementary teachers' perceptions of the scientific ability of students. *Science Education, 76*(2), 147–153.

Simpson, M. (1996). What's the verdict? *NEA Today, 15*(3), 25–34.

Singh, P. (1993). Institutional discourse and practice: A case study of the role of the social construction of technological competence in the primary classroom. *British Journal of Sociology of Education, 14*(1), 39–58.

Thom, M. (2002). Girls in science and technology: What's new, what's next? *Education Digest, 67*(5), 17–24.

Vygotsky, L.S. (1978). *Mind in society: The development of higher psychological processes* (M. Cole, V. John-Steiner, S. Scribner, & E. Souberman, Eds. and Trans.). Cambridge, MA: Harvard University Press. (Original work published 1934)

CHAPTER 7

The Science of Reading and the Reading of Science: Successes, Failures, and Promises in the Search for Prerequisite Reading Skills for Science

Michael L. Kamil and Elizabeth B. Bernhardt

In this chapter, we address the relationship of science and literacy in three ways. First, we examine the role of reading in science. Then, we examine the role of science content in reading and reading instruction. Finally, as a way of illustrating the need to reconcile differences in the roles of reading in science and science in reading, we address the special case of nonnative English speakers learning science.

A Reading of Science

Science is the systematic accumulation of knowledge about how the world works. In order to accumulate knowledge, it is important to understand how knowledge is created, which means distinguishing it from the data on which it is based. *Data* are obtained from empirical observations of the world. *Knowledge* involves abstraction from those data. In other words, knowledge is different from the data that scientists collect. It is the end result of an interactive, multidimensional process of abstraction, interpretation, and construction that transforms data into something that is useful and usable. Yet the process of abstraction, interpretation, and construction is insufficient to make knowledge useful and usable. Useful and usable knowledge must be disseminated (i.e., published) so others may make use of it. Publication, of necessity, is essentially a text-based activity because it is through text that we know what knowledge already has been accumulated.

In this line of reasoning, there are at least two parts to science: (1) discovery of new data and (2) development of knowledge. Although these endeavors are interrelated, they depend on very different skills. Discovery is important because it relates to the collection of new data. It is basically a hands-on activity, although it almost always is guided by our prior knowledge of what we do and do not know about the world and by our interest in verifying whether what we claim to know about the world is consistent with the world or is merely a casual, accidental observation. In other words, verification is the process of determining the value of the data collected. That is, scientists need to be certain that they are working with the same facts that other scientists use. This is accomplished in a process that can be termed *verification*. Verification is not a simple process, because the conditions under which scientists collect data may differ, even when they are working on the same problem. Verification entails knowing what other scientists have done, how it was done, and whether the work can be replicated. Once data or findings are verified, they can be used by all other scientists. Ultimately, verifying the data leads to an economy of effort. Once scientists know that data are verified, they do not have to expend the effort to collect the same data each time they want to extend their research.

The development of knowledge is the result of abstracting conclusions about the world from data. In the modern world, this abstraction and construction process takes place interactively between and among members of the scientific community. Surely, within the context of each scientist's laboratory, there is significant discussion and oral-aural interaction affording each scientist the opportunity to develop and converse about his or her own generalizations. This oral discursive process is, however, merely a prelude or a trial run at argument and interpretation. Only when the abstraction of data has been put into written form (a form that includes written expository text as well as graphics), reviewed and argued through (again with a written text), and then published does it become a part of accumulated knowledge. In this sense, publication serves the function of organizing and making both data and the knowledge abstracted and constructed from those data available to any literate person.

Clearly, a tension exists between these elements in the scientific process. The development and integration of new knowledge is largely dependent on written literacy because most of the knowledge about science is stored in text. This material is too complex and far too extensive to be stored in oral language, and it is often too abstract to be stored solely in pictorial formats. Books and articles, as well as electronic versions of documents, provide excellent random access to the information stored in them. They, unlike oral discourse, can be reviewed and verified for content, permitting a convenient focus on parts over time.

Data collection, or the performance dimension of the scientific continuum, is publicly conveyed as more dramatic and, therefore, perhaps more interesting or more important than knowledge construction. At some level, the discovery dimension of science usually is represented in schools by the popular image of a scientist in a laboratory and wearing a white coat. This romanticized image of science that values activity fails to emphasize the verification and knowledge construction dimensions of the scientific process in which literacy skills are critical. We contend that this image is one of the reasons that there has been little emphasis on literacy in science education. (Romance, of course, may not be the only reason.) Advocates for science education often appear to assume that others will deal with literacy issues.

Despite a lack of general attention to literacy issues and language within the science education community, some significant work in science education has focused on discourse. Yet even this important work seems to ignore the written literacy dimensions to the learning and using of science. Key researchers, such as Lemke (1990, 1998) and Roth (2001), insist on focusing on nonverbal elements in that discourse when they write of scientific discourse. In a 1998 study, for example, Lemke provides survey findings on scientific articles and focuses on "the relative frequency and common type of non-verbal-textual semiotic expression" (p. 88). In the article, he casts literacy as a visual process rather than focusing on the ways in which the overwhelming portion of scientific discourse as written expository prose is comprehended.

The trend within science education with a focus on language is to investigate oral interaction and its role in the construction of knowledge. Christie (1998) examines the ways in which classrooms of science learners interact with each other and depend on oral forms of language presented by the teacher. Although presented in well-executed ethnographic form, the study never mentions whether the subjects in the study ever read anything in order to acquire scientific knowledge and new forms of language. In summary, our interpretation of the science education literature is that it fails by and large to acknowledge a key component of all schooling (the acquisition of literacy knowledge) and thereby ignores a key component in the acquisition of scientific knowledge—access to previous data collections and interpretation. We find this state of affairs bitterly ironic when, in fact, a substantial knowledge base exists within literacy research in regard to verification and knowledge construction.

What Does the Science of Reading Tell Us?

In 1944, reading education expert A. Sterl Artley issued the following injunction to content area teachers:

Every classroom teacher has the direct responsibility for developing those reading skills and abilities essential for adequate comprehension with his particular area of instruction, as well as for applying to his content field and making functional those skills and abilities being developed by teachers in other areas of instruction. (p. 464)

The need for reading skill in the content areas is crucial, regardless of the area. However, it can be argued, as noted above, that the need for literacy skills is particularly acute in science. That is, because the accumulation and publication of knowledge is largely in text, anyone lacking literacy skills will be unable to access that body of knowledge and data. Without the skills necessary to read about what came before, a scientist would be largely unable to pursue his or her profession in a principled manner.

In what follows, we deal with issues of general instruction in reading and with issues of reading and science instruction in the special case of second-language learners. The second-language environment provides us with a principled, concrete, and relatively unambiguous perspective on language and its relation to literacy, the impact that the language-literacy relation can have on meaning construction, and a perspective on the demonstration of comprehension (i.e., the "doing of science"). We will look at these issues both theoretically and empirically. We want to ask whether reading education prepares students for reading in science. If so, are there still problems that should be addressed? Finally, if reading education does not prepare students for reading in science, what are the needs that must be addressed?

Comprehending Text and Learning in Science

Reading comprehension is the criterion by which success in reading is and should be measured. The RAND Reading Study Group (2002) synthesized the existing research literature on reading comprehension and has suggested that comprehension consists of the conflation of several distinct bodies of knowledge: fluency (e.g., Dowhower, 1987), comprehension strategies (Pressley, 2000), vocabulary knowledge (Nagy & Scott, 2000), and text genre (e.g., Goldman & Rakestraw, 2000). Comprehension occurs as the reader apprehends and constructs meaning from text. We know that vocabulary is possibly the key variable in determining how well readers will comprehend (National Institute of Child Health and Human Development, 2000). We also know that specific cognitive strategies (e.g., generating questions and summarizing) can facilitate comprehension. Two additional elements complete the picture. First, the knowledge we have in these areas of fluency, comprehension strategies, and vocabulary must be delivered in instruction by teachers who understand the interactions between and among these factors. Second, another key factor in facilitating comprehension is that presenting instruction in content materials facilitates the learning of comprehension strategies (Wade & Moje, 2000).

These components are parallel to those needed in science inquiry. For example, Lemke (1990) argues that becoming a scientist is related significantly to acquiring the discourse of science. The adoption of strategies is akin to becoming familiar with the discourse and procedures of scientific inquiry. Similarly, the learning of vocabulary parallels the learning of discourse, even if there is far more to discourse than word meanings.

Echoing Lemke (1990), Alexander and Jetton (2000) show the importance of domain knowledge in learning from text under a variety of conditions. They argue for the importance of knowledge of domain structures as a key to comprehension in particular subject matter areas. An implication is that reading comprehension in science is different from reading comprehension in, for example, history. In a similar manner, text genre plays an important role in reading comprehension (Duke, 2000; Goldman & Rakestraw, 2000; Richgels, McGee, Lomax, & Sheard, 1987). Combined with the notion of understanding the structure of domain knowledge, genre knowledge is a key to comprehension. Becoming familiar with the way in which texts are structured is one more parallel to understanding the discourse of science inquiry.

Of course, reading instruction does not always prepare students to do all that is needed in reading. Consequently, the parallels might not hold when readers move from reading instruction into science inquiry. For example, not all students are taught to use effective comprehension strategies. Nor are all students taught to use text structure. Although researchers have many suggestive findings about the connections between science learning and reading, educators need a far more detailed description of the connections.

What Can Reading Instruction Contribute to Science Learning?

The first set of responses to this question centers on whether reading instruction provides the full range of skills necessary for reading science. We approach this problem on three fronts. First, we examine the assumptions behind practices in reading instruction. Second, we look at aspects of what is being taught. Finally, we look at how reading practices are applicable to science.

Much of reading instruction is accomplished with narrative or story text. Reading instruction has been focused on the use of narrative text based on the assumption that stories are easier than other text to comprehend because of their predictable structure. This assumption is ingrained so deeply that almost all of the available programs for beginning reading instruction are based on story text. Although estimates vary, Hoffman and colleagues (1994) suggest that only 12% of the text in basal readers is nonnarrative. Moss and Newton (1998) provide corroborating evidence over a wider sample of instructional materials. Their estimate is that no basal reader, from first to sixth grade, contains more than 25% text that could be classified as informational text. Because basal readers are the most common sort of teaching text, this estimate encompasses a great deal of reading instruction. This trend is long term. Basal readers have come to have more stories and less informational text over at least the past 30 years. During that time, there were brief reversals, but the overall trend has been strong and persistent. This trend is counterproductive for two reasons. First, most of the literacy tasks required of children, at least above the primary grades, involve reading and writing expository materials. Second, although there has been some argument that narrative materials are easier to read and comprehend, current evidence suggests otherwise (Pappas, 1991, 1993).

Duke (2000) has shown that students do not have access to much material beyond stories in either the classroom or the library. In effect, Duke found that the amount of informational text that students could expect to encounter would be approximately 3.6 minutes' worth of reading per day. This time period would not offer sufficient exposure to the information genre for instructional purposes. Nor would it encourage readers to explore the genre on their own.

Moreover, the learning derived from instruction in a story genre may not be appropriate for reading and comprehending text of an expository genre. Several clusters of skills set informational text apart from story text. Kamil and Lane (1997) elaborate on three of these skills: the amount of text that must be read, the truth value of the text, and the structure of the text itself. For example, stories must be read in a relatively complete fashion, but informational text can be read in pieces. It is difficult to do this kind of piecemeal instruction in the context of story material. Because most of the material used for reading instruction is story text, it cannot be used to teach the skills necessary to determine how much of the text must be read to comprehend it. That is, in typical reading instruction, students are asked to read the entire story. Almost any detail in the story can become important for later developments. By contrast, informational text often is composed of self-sustaining chunks that can be read and understood independently of what came before or after.

Informational text often has built-in typographic and content cues to aid the reader in knowing what sections are relevant to particular topics. A table of contents or an index allows the reader to access specific topics without reading the entire text. Headings also provide major typographic cues to the content and importance of text portions.

Of course, there are exceptions to this principle for expository material—for example, when the concepts explicated cannot be understood without having read the preceding material. There *are* some stories that have the cues, just as there are some examples of exposition that do not. However, the more important point is that the skills unique to comprehending exposition *cannot* be taught by using stories alone.

The second cluster of skills relates to the truth value of the text. When reading stories, readers do not have to make any assumptions about the truth value of the story. That is, whether the story is true or false is irrelevant to the quality of the story. The situation is dramatically different when reading informational text. A reader has to assume that the information has a high truth value until evidence suggests otherwise. Imagine reading a timetable for flights. Unless one assumes that the information is true, there is a high probability that one would miss a flight. Note that this assumption does not require that the information *be* true. It only requires that the reader assume it is true until evidence to the contrary is available. Again, this set of skills simply cannot be taught in the sole context of story material.

The third skill cluster relates to text structure: Story text has a relatively simple and fixed text structure compared to expository text. Work on story grammar has shown that little variation exists in the structures found in written text (see Stein & Glenn, 1975, for an example). This is not the case for expository text. Researchers and theorists distinguish among a number of expository structures. For example, Meyer (1975) identifies five expository text structures. Although the specifics of each of the five types (description, collection, causation, problem and solution, and comparison) are not immediately relevant to this discussion, the fact that there are five (rather than one) is. Niles (1965) also points out the relevance to comprehension of identifying text structure.

How, then, do students learn to read across texts if they are not provided with instruction in the skills unique to each genre? Nicolls and Kamil (2001) argue that reading instruction can be divided into (at least) two sets of skills: those that are generalizable across all genres and those that are specific to at least one, but not all, genres of text. For example, decoding words can be thought of as generalizable across genres. Using an index would be a skill that can be applied only in expository genres, not to story text. Current reading instruction deals primarily with the generalizable reading skills, not with those specific to genres. However, those generalizable skills can be used with all sorts of text. Although it is possible to read any text without having the full range of skills to do a complete job, the task of reading becomes increasingly more difficult without those skills. What might otherwise be an automatic process has to be accomplished by brute force with the most basic skills. Therefore, it is not surprising that students report that they find informational texts boring and difficult to read.

Nicolls and Kamil (2001) observed reading being taught in four classrooms over a period of three months. They made observations of reading instruction and categorized the observations by two different dimensions. The first dimension was whether or not the text being used was narrative or expository; the second dimension was the nature of the instruction delivered during the use of those texts. Almost no instruction that they observed was specific to a genre of text, except for stories. This finding provides empirical support for the conclusion that unique genre skills are not being taught as a routine part of reading instruction. Instead, reading instruction seems to be delivered independently of the text type, with the instruction being geared to only those elements that are usable in the widest possible context.

Integrating Science and Reading

A second set of issues comes from a different sort of reform in science education (Santa & Alvermann, 1991). The proposal that has been put forward from this reform movement is that scientific understanding would be improved through the integration of language arts with science. One attempt to implement and assess this notion has been reported by Morrow, Pressley, Smith, and Smith (1997). In their study, Morrow and colleagues integrated a literature-based program into both science and literacy instruction. The intervention consisted of the creation of rich literacy environments in classrooms, teacher-guided literacy activities in literacy and science, teacher-guided activities for writing narratives in literacy and science, and student-directed periods of reading and writing in social settings. Morrow and colleagues report on a wide range of measures, including free recall of story retelling and rewriting, probed recall comprehension of stories, results of the language and reading subtests of the California Test of Basic Skills, the writing of original stories, results of the science textbook test, the naming of favorite generic or science literature titles, and a measure of attitudes toward literacy and science. These measures were supplemented by observational data. However, the study included no direct measures of the ability to do science. Nor were there measures of any type of reading instruction relating to genres other than stories. (However, one comparison did include the number of expository and narrative writings that children completed.)

Morrow and colleagues (1997) did find very large effect sizes on most of their measures, often greater than two standard deviations. In the comparison of narrative and expository writing, they found that the intervention groups completed more narrative writing than the control group and that the number of narrative pieces exceeded the number of expository pieces. They list as one of the limitations of the study the fact that there were no hands-on science opportunities.

This study clearly counts as a success in demonstrating the importance of integrating reading instruction with science. Why did teaching literature work, in light of the argument advanced above, dealing with the need for instruction in expository text genres? One possibility is that the improvement in students' general level of reading ability—the generalizable skills—made all text more accessible to them. What is unclear is whether or not reading instruction targeted to the needs and demands of science would bring about different outcomes. On this point, researchers have no evidence.

Despite the fact that researchers have a great deal of information about literacy acquisition, many gaps exist in the knowledge for specific circumstances and populations. In the next section, we address the issue of whether reading skills related to narrative are the same as reading skills related to exposition. We combine this discussion with issues of second-language reading. We are concerned about the issue of language because the emphasis on doing science could lead one to assume implicitly that language is unimportant or a nuisance factor and that evidence of science learning can be generated effectively by nonlanguage methods or performance assessment.

A Critical Case: Second-Language Learners, Science, and Literacy

It is interesting to note that in the study by Morrow and colleagues (1997), the population of students is described in terms of its ethnic composition but not in terms of the native languages of the students or their parents. In what follows, we discuss in some depth the results of a study that investigates some of these issues (Bernhardt, Destino, Rodriguez, & Kamil, 1995).

The second-language backdrop is in conflict with the current belief system among many science educators that deemphasizes reading and writing in order to emphasize performance-based activities that favor doing science rather than reading about science. In fact, the early iteration of a visible reform document in science education, *Science for All Americans* (Rutherford & Ahlgren, 1990), has some focus on reading and writing; by 1993, in the American Association for the Advancement of Science's *Benchmarks for Scientific Literacy*, reading and writing had disappeared.

Millions of children across the globe study and learn their school subjects in a language they neither speak nor read as a native. Although there are political, curricular, and economic reasons for instruction in nonnative languages, the processes behind such instruction are relatively unclear. Some research has indicated that children are able to learn both school subjects and nonnative languages simultaneously without any measurable detriment to either (Harley, Allen, Cummins, & Swain, 1990). At the same time, however, anecdotal evidence from teachers who teach in bilingual or second-language settings indicates that teachers feel they frequently have to compromise both the language they use and the content the children must learn in order to meet instructional objectives. In other words, in the act of simplifying both the linguistic and the content elements, material potentially gets lost.

The potential loss of content in any subject matter is troubling. It is particularly troubling within the context of science learning, in which concepts lost or misconstrued even at the most rudimentary levels may well compound themselves into scientific misconceptions. Twelve percent of the U.S. school population receives content instruction in a language it does not speak natively. This is a large portion of science learners to remain at risk for compounding misconceptions. Second-language science research is needed in order to understand fully the implications of such instruction in student outcomes and for student success.

Second-language research has indicated that reading and writing activities are critical to the learning of content. Rather than perpetuating the myth that children must learn to speak before they can read and write, research with children learning a second language indicates that writing affords children the opportunity to demonstrate their knowledge without being inhibited by the time constraints of immediate oral performance and the social constraints of needing to look and sound like "the other kids" (Bernhardt, Dickerson, Destino, & McNichols, 1994; Destino, Bernhardt, & Rodriguez, 1994). Further, reading offers children a communication channel with which they can work on their own and at their own pace rather than being constrained by the real-time flow of rapid oral speech (Bernhardt, 1994). Reading also allows them to draw on their native-language literacy skills to enhance their achievement (Bernhardt & Kamil, 1995). Research also indicates that more socially based strategies (or actively doing science) sometimes afford children learning a second language the opportunity to act out their science knowledge nonverbally. This opportunity, too, allows children to "reveal" their science knowledge unimpeded by their lack of oral language proficiency; a negative outcome is, however, that it also allows them to "perform" by simply going through the motions.

As part of a team at the National Center for Science Teaching and Learning from 1993 to 1995, we both embarked upon a research program that examined issues related to language, literacy, and culture and their influence on science learning. We worked with 47 native English-speaking children attending an inner-city, magnet elementary school with a Spanish language immersion program. The school's program was bilingual, moving children from a homogeneous language background (English) into another homogeneous language (Spanish). Although on the surface the "magnet" was the special instructional program in Spanish for English speakers and Spanish heritage-language children, for many of the parents the "magnet" was the location of the school in their neighborhood. Of the children in the school, 501 were African American, and more than 50% of the children participated in the reduced-price lunch program. All science instruction in the school was presented in Spanish, the second language of the school's children.

We took a longitudinal perspective and observed and videotaped 40 lessons in two fourth- and fifth-grade science classrooms from September 1993 to May 1994. These observations and videotapes were accompanied by field notes and interviews with the children and their teachers. Team members transcribed all the videotaped lessons and then analyzed them for recurrent discourse and procedural patterns (Green & Wallat, 1981). From the analysis procedure, three "typical" lessons and one "outlier" (i.e., a lesson that did not fit typical patterns) were selected for additional analysis in order to respond to research questions posed in our research group about how science was being accomplished in a language-minority setting.

Beyond examining questions of a broader instructional nature, we also were curious about the relationship between literacy achievement and science achievement, given that the learner population was triply challenged by language learning, literacy learning, and science learning. Against the backdrop of a language-minority context and current wisdom in science education and language arts, we posed the following questions:

1. Given that first-language abilities contribute powerfully to second-language comprehension scores, what effect does that language ability have on measures of science content knowledge?

2. What is the relationship between student performance in hands-on, experiential instruction and reading ability?

3. Is there any relationship between the ability to read different genres of text and science ability?

Twenty children in the fourth- and fifth-grade classes were selected by their teachers and one researcher on the project as representative of children in the classes. All the chosen students were native speakers of English. These children differed in Spanish language proficiency, motivation, and science knowledge, thereby representing the spectrum existing in the classrooms under scrutiny.

The 20 children were asked to read four different texts in Spanish (their second language): one narrative (*El Campesino*) and three expository texts (*El Metódo*, *La Clasificación*, and *Las Planetas*). The children were asked to read the texts and then to recall them in the language in which they felt most comfortable. In addition, the children's English-language California Achievement Test (CAT) scores in reading, vocabulary, and mathematics were collated.

During the last month of the longitudinal study, an elaborate performance assessment in Spanish, an adaptation of Shavelson, Baxter, and Pine's (1991) suggestions, was administered to the 20 children who had read the four science texts. All reading scores in Spanish, the students' second language, were significantly intercorrelated, ranging from a high score of .83 to a low score of .78. The means and standard deviations are listed in Table 7.1, and the correlation matrix is given in Table 7.2. The correlation matrix also

TABLE 7.1
Means and Standard Deviations for Passages in Spanish and Standardized Achievement Test Scores in English (N=19)

Variable	Cases	Mean	Standard Deviation
Las Planetas	19	38.4	19.2
El Metódo	19	26.8	18.5
La Clasificación	19	18.9	16.3
El Campesino	19	27.5	19.4
Expository Score	19	28.1	16.7
Recall Score	19	27.9	16.8
Performance Assessment	19	11.2	4.6
Vocabulary	19	714.8	46.4
Reading	19	714.9	43.4
Mathematics Computation	19	728.0	41.2
Mathematics Calculation	19	731.1	39.1

Note: Missing data resulted in dropping a single case from the study.

reveals the significant relationships between the CAT vocabulary measures (in English) and two of the reading passages (*Planetas* and *Metódo*) and between the CAT reading scores in English and three of the Spanish reading passages (the exception is *El Campesino*). The four Spanish reading passages correlate significantly with the two CAT mathematics scores. The reading and vocabulary scores on the CAT do not correlate with the mathematics computation section, but they do correlate with the mathematics calculation section. Finally, the performance assessment column indicates that none of the measures—neither the Spanish reading passages or the standardized achievement test measures taken in English—correlate significantly with the performance assessment.

The lack of a relation between reading and performance assessment is of concern. The children's reading of science did not relate significantly to their performance assessment in science. Their ability to "demonstrate" knowledge did not relate to or overlap with their ability to glean knowledge from text. In other words, the children we observed reflect in their performance precisely the unproductive dichotomy we discussed in the beginning of this chapter. Collecting data (doing) and developing and verifying knowledge (literacy) remain separate, and virtually unrelated, tasks.

TABLE 7.2
Correlation Matrix for Variables in the Study (N=19)

	Las Planetas	El Metódo	La Clasificación	El Campesino	Expository Score	Recall Score	Performance Assessment	Vocabulary	Reading	Mathematics Computation	Mathematics Calculation
Las Planetas	1.00										
El Metódo	.80**	1.00									
La Clasificación	.80**	.78**	1.00								
El Campesino	.84**	.78**	.68**	1.00							
Expository Score	.94**	.93**	.92**	.83**	1.00						
Recall Score	.94**	.92**	.88**	.91**	.99**	1.00					
Performance Assessment	.30	.40	.25	.41	.34	.38	1.00				
Vocabulary	.61*	.66*	.54	.33	.65*	.58*	.33	1.00			
Reading	.67*	.79**	.64*	.45	.76**	.69**	.32	.94**	1.00		
Mathematics Computation	.58*	.71**	.59*	.71**	.68*	.71**	.21	.20	.36	1.00	
Mathematics Calculation	.80**	.78**	.70**	.71**	.82**	.82**	.51	.73**	.79**	.61*	1.00

Note: Missing data resulted in dropping a single case from the study.
Significance for a two-tailed test, *p <.01; ** p<.001

This particularly important finding relates to the issues of integration of reading instruction with science instruction. We see that there is evidence in these data for generalizable reading skills as well as for genre-specific skills. Many reading educators have assumed that reading was reading and that any skill transferred to any other context. This simply was not the case for the 20 student subjects, who were being asked to do learning in a language that was not their native one. We recently have collected other evidence that this distinction between collecting data and developing and verifying knowledge exists even when the language of instruction matches the language of the students (Nicolls & Kamil, 2001).

Conclusion

What, then, are the successes we believe we have seen? One success is that the relation between science and reading—and language arts in general—is being examined with renewed vigor. The allocation of resources toward solving this problem will go a long way toward resolving many of the complexities and questions involved. A second success is that reading researchers and educators are beginning to break from their traditional instructional patterns. We have reported on a few of these research efforts, which are only in their initial phases. Attention seems to have been directed to the issues surrounding science and reading and, again, that is a first step in making progress. Finally, we believe that the results we have presented in this chapter and elsewhere about differential reading skills are a good beginning, both for first- and second-language readers. The results point out the need for incorporating both science and reading in the same contexts. Students must learn that they need both science and reading skills to be successful.

What are the failures? The most obvious failure is that we have not been able to convince science educators and reading and language arts educators that they have at least one common interest. As previously noted, this is a long-standing issue and, unfortunately, we have seen little progress. We also have failed to make much headway in accommodating second-language learners in science education. We want to work to guarantee reading instruction that will allow *all* students to maximize their potential and abilities to read and do science. The simple expedient of turning to performance assessment is insufficient to demonstrate the development of either science knowledge or reading ability. Rather, this special case of performance assessment in multilingual contexts highlights the need for the combination.

Finally, what are the promises? The promises are many, but among the most important ones is that people are beginning to attend to these important issues. Many more researchers are focusing on the issues of second language, genre, and content. As they do, society should see the results in the form of improved instruction for students in both reading and science. We are beginning to uncover the relevant dimensions with which we can make progress in integrating reading instruction with science and vice versa. As long as text remains a critical mediating factor in the storage, transmission, and retrieval of scientific information, reading will remain a critical science skill.

REFERENCES

Alexander, P., & Jetton, T. (2000). Learning from text: A multidimensional and developmental perspective. In M.L. Kamil, P.B. Mosenthal, P.D. Pearson, & R. Barr (Eds.), *Handbook of reading research* (Vol. 3, pp. 285–310). Mahwah, NJ: Erlbaum.

American Association for the Advancement of Science. (1993). *Benchmarks for scientific literacy* (American Association for the Advancement of Science Project 2061). New York: Oxford University Press.

Artley, A.S. (1944). A study of certain relationships existing between general reading comprehension and reading comprehension in a specific subject-matter area. *Journal of Educational Research, 37,* 464–473.

Bernhardt, E.B. (1994). A content analysis of reading methods texts: What are we told about the nonnative speaker of English? *Journal of Reading Behavior, 26,* 159–189.

Bernhardt, E.B., Destino, T., Rodriguez, M., & Kamil, M. (1995). Assessing science knowledge in an English/Spanish bilingual elementary school. *Cognosos, 4*(1), 4–6.

Bernhardt, E.B., Dickerson, T., Destino, T., & McNichols, M. (1994). Writing science and writing in science: Perspectives from minority children. *Cognosos, 3*(3), 7–10.

Bernhardt, E.B., & Kamil, M.L. (1995). Interpreting relationships between L1 and L2 reading: Consolidating the linguistic threshold and the linguistic interdependence hypotheses. *Applied Linguistics, 16*(2), 16–34.

Christie, F. (1998). Science and apprenticeship: The pedagogic discourse. In J.R. Martin & Robert Veel (Eds.), *Reading science: Critical and functional perspectives on discourses of science* (pp. 152–180). London: Routledge.

Destino, T., Bernhardt, E., & Rodriguez, M. (1994). Meeting science objectives in a bilingual setting. *Cognosos, 3,* 1–5.

Dowhower, S.L. (1987). Effects of repeated reading on second-grade transitional readers' fluency and comprehension. *Reading Research Quarterly, 22,* 389–406.

Duke, N.K. (2000). 3.6 minutes per day: The scarcity of informational texts in first grade. *Reading Research Quarterly, 35,* 202–224.

Goldman, S.R., & Rakestraw, J.A., Jr. (2000). Structural aspects of constructing meaning from text. In M.L. Kamil, P.B. Mosenthal, P.D. Pearson, & R. Barr (Eds.), *Handbook of reading research* (Vol. 3, pp. 311–335). Mahwah, NJ: Erlbaum.

Green, J.L., & Wallat, C. (1981). *Ethnography and language in educational settings.* Westport, CT: Ablex.

Harley, B., Allen, P., Cummins, J., & Swain, M. (1990). *The development of second language proficiency.* Cambridge, UK: Cambridge University Press.

Hoffman, J.V., McCarthy, S.J., Abbott, J., Christian, C., Corman, L., Curry, C., et al. (1994). *So what's new in the new basals? A focus on first grade* (Reading Research Report No. 6). Washington, DC: U.S. Department of Education.

Kamil, M.L., & Lane, D. (1997, March). *A classroom study of the efficacy of using information text for first grade reading instruction.* Paper presented to the American Educational Research Association, Chicago, IL.

Lemke, J.L. (1990). *Talking science: Language, learning, and values.* Westport, CT: Ablex.

Lemke, J.L. (1998). Multiplying meaning: Visual and verbal semiotics in scientific text. In J.R. Martin & R. Veel (Eds.), *Reading science: Critical and functional perspectives on discourses of science* (pp. 87–113). London: Routledge.

Meyer, B.J. (1975). *The organization of prose and its effects on memory.* Amsterdam: Elsevier.

Morrow, L.M., Pressley, M., Smith, J.K., & Smith, M. (1997). The effect of a literature-based program integrated into literacy and science instruction with children from diverse backgrounds. *Reading Research Quarterly, 32,* 54–76.

Moss, B., & Newton, E. (1998, December). *An examination of the informational text genre in recent basal readers.* Paper presented at the National Reading Conference, Austin, TX.

Nagy, W.E., & Scott, J.A. (2000). Vocabulary processes. In M.L. Kamil, P.B. Mosenthal, P.D. Pearson, & R. Barr (Eds.), *Handbook of reading research* (Vol. 3, pp. 269–284). Mahwah, NJ: Erlbaum.

National Institute of Child Health and Human Development. (2000). *Report of the National Reading Panel: Teaching children to read: An evidence-based assessment of the scientific research literature on reading and its implications for reading instruction* (NIH Publication No. 00-4769). Washington, DC: U.S. Government Printing Office.

Nicolls, E., & Kamil, M.L. (2001, December). *Instruction implementation of information text.* Paper presented at the National Reading Conference, San Antonio, TX.

Niles, O.S. (1965). Organization perceived. In H.L. Herber (Ed.), *Developing study skills in secondary schools* (Perspectives in Reading No. 4; pp. 57–76). Newark, DE: International Reading Association.

Pappas, C.C. (1991). Fostering full access to literacy by including information books. *Language Arts, 68*(6), 449–462.

Pappas, C.C. (1993). Is narrative "primary"? Some insights from kindergartners' pretend readings of stories and information books. *Journal of Reading Behavior, 25*(1), 97–129.

Pressley, M. (2000). What should comprehension instruction be the instruction of? In M.L. Kamil, P.B. Mosenthal, P.D. Pearson, & R. Barr (Eds.), *Handbook of reading research* (Vol. 3, pp. 545–561). Mahwah, NJ: Erlbaum.

RAND Reading Study Group. (2002). *Reading for understanding: Toward an R&D program in reading comprehension.* Santa Monica, CA: RAND Corporation.

Richgels, D.J., McGee, L.M., Lomax, R.G., & Sheard, C. (1987). Awareness of four text structures: Effects on recall of expository text. *Reading Research Quarterly, 22,* 177–196.

Roth, W-M. (2001). Gestures: Their role in teaching and learning. *Review of Educational Research, 71*(3), 365–392.

Rutherford, F.J., & Ahlgren, A. (1990). *Science for all Americans* (American Association for the Advancement of Science Project 2061). New York: Oxford University Press.

Santa, C.M., & Alvermann, D.E. (Eds.). (1991). *Science learning: Processes and applications.* Newark, DE: International Reading Association.

Shavelson, R.J., Baxter, G.P., & Pine, J. (1991). Performance assessment in science. *Applied Measurement in Education, 4*(4), 347–362.

Stein, N.L., & Glenn, C.G. (1975, April). *A developmental study of children's recall of story material.* Paper presented to the annual meeting of the Society for Research in Child Development, Denver, CO.

Wade, S.E., & Moje, E.B. (2000). The role of text in classroom learning. In M. Kamil, P.B. Mosenthal, P.D. Pearson, & R. Barr (Eds.), *Handbook of reading research* (Vol. 3, pp. 609–627). Mahwah, NJ: Erlbaum.

CHAPTER 8

Knowing and Being in Science: Expanding the Possibilities

Allan Feldman

How can we improve science education? In order to answer this question, I believe that educators and researchers need to look at the ways that teachers and students relate to one another. Because of this belief, I pay special attention to the use of language, which is the primary way that human beings relate to one another. I also believe that a focus on these relationships and this language use will provide us with a better understanding of what it means to be a teacher and to teach, and what it means to be a student and to learn. In what follows, I use the term *student* rather than *learner* because I focus on people and their relationships rather than on the process of learning. I also prefer to use *student* because I believe, following on the work of Lave and Wenger (1991), that learning is inherently a part of being human and that being a learner is only one aspect of the people who are students in our classrooms. I also want to make clear that my interest is in formal, structured educational systems in which there are people called teachers and people called students, and in which there is some expectation of what will be taught and learned (Schwab, 1978).

I begin by examining what it means to learn science. Then, I provide readers with an introduction to existentialism, which I use as an alternate framework to look at what teachers and students do as they interact and relate to one another in educational situations. I end the chapter by using this existential framework to show how teachers' responsibility for their students can lead to the improvement of science learning.

The Learning of Science

What does it mean to learn science? This question can be answered by describing how students will be different as a result of having learned. That is, what is it that the students now know or can do that they were not able to do before? We can talk about knowing science in several ways. For example, we can talk about science learning in terms of standards (e.g., American Association for the Advancement of Science, 1993; National Research

Council, 1996) that are used to construct examinations to measure achievement. We can think of science learning as the development of a deep conceptual understanding of the subject matter. We also can say that students have learned science when they demonstrate that they are scientifically literate (DeBoer, 2000; Laugksch, 2000). That is, in the same way that we want people to have at least a minimum ability to read and write—and to compute with numbers—we would like people to have a minimum ability to know, use, or do science. To use science is to make use of scientific knowledge or processes (whatever they are) in everyday life. To do science is to engage in activities similar to what scientists do.

For many science education researchers, the measure of whether one does or does not know science is whether one can do science. The National Science Teachers Association's (NSTA) (2000) position statement on the nature of science describes science as being

> characterized by the systematic gathering of information through various forms of direct and indirect observations and the testing of this information by methods including, but not limited to, experimentation. The principal product of science is knowledge in the form of naturalistic concepts and the laws and theories related to those concepts. (n.p.)

From this, one could assume that to do science is to systematically gather information to construct knowledge. Because it has become apparent that the construction of knowledge is a social phenomenon (Haraway, 1989; Kuhn, 1970; Lakatos, 1978), to do science also means to participate in social events in the same way that scientists do. As a result, there has been more and more interest in helping people to learn to talk like scientists (Gallas, 1995; Lemke, 1990) in addition to other activities described in the NSTA position statement. This interest has led to more and more emphasis on science learning as a sociocultural and social constructivist process (see chapter 12).

However, most of the research in science education from the past 20 years has centered on students' conceptions of science. Unfortunately, at this time it is difficult to demonstrate that this research paradigm has had much of an effect on the teaching and learning of science in schools. One of the major deficits of this research program, and possibly a cause of its lack of effect, is that it has narrowly focused on individual cognition without examining factors such as sociocultural context and the nature of language. From a postmodern perspective, this criticism can be seen as an adherence to one metatheory to the near exclusion of all other possibilities (Lyotard, 1979).

The exclusion of other possibilities can be seen in the following examples. One summer afternoon I was sitting with a friend on a pier that reached out into the sea. We looked to the west and saw that the sun was close to the horizon and that the sky was filled with shades of red, orange, and yellow. Imagine if I had turned to her and, using my expertise in physics, including optics and planetary mechanics, had said, "Isn't it fascinating that as the Earth rotates, the light from the sun travels through more and more of the atmosphere, resulting in the refraction of light into several different frequencies?" The question would have seemed absurd in this situation, and I am not at all sure that my friend and I would have spent any more summer afternoons together. Instead, one would expect anyone, no matter what his or her areas of expertise, to say something such as, "The sunset is beautiful today," even though the latter statement conflicts with the heliocentric model of the solar system. But in much of our science instruction, especially exercises that are designed to promote conceptual change, we expect students to change their thinking so that the latter statement is seen as wrong and the former question as not sounding absurd.

I also have enough of an understanding of how modern medicines work to be highly skeptical of the alternative remedies and herbal supplements that are sold as cures for a variety of ailments. However, whenever I have a cough and cold, I drink herbal teas packaged to relieve the symptoms even though I believe that, medically, they have little or no effect on my cold. I do believe that the hot liquid and the warm vapors coming from it help loosen mucous and lubricate my throat, nasal passages, and sinuses. If that is what I believe, why not just drink hot water or any flavorful hot beverage rather than the herbal remedy? The answer is that I also believe that the herbal tea will make me *feel* better, whatever that means. Most contemporary theories of science learning do not allow for the fact that I drink the herbal tea because it makes me feel better, even though I know that there is little scientific evidence to support my claim.

The Mind as Computer

For at least two reasons, the preceding examples cannot be interpreted using an individual cognitive model of science learning. First, as I argue elsewhere (Feldman, 1997), most perspectives that we use to understand teachers and teaching rely on the metaphor of the mind as a computer or information processing device (Bruer, 1994). The most obvious examples of this perspective are the use of the language of a knowledge base for teaching (e.g., Shulman, 1986) and models of teacher reasoning that rely on logical algorithms such as syllogisms (Fenstermacher, 1986). Second, I am, as are all people, immersed in situations. Immersion in situations is different from being engaged in situated cognition. The main idea of situated cognition is that in order to understand how people learn it is important to acknowledge that "the activity in which knowledge is developed and deployed...is an integral part of what is learned" (Brown, Collins, & Duguid, 1989). This idea suggests a dialectical relation between mind and experience (Bredo, 1994). Although at first it may seem difficult to argue with this claim, the way that it is used in research on science learning is problematic because it reinforces the principle of mind-body dualism put forth by Descartes. That is, many of the researchers of science learning, because of their adherence to computational models of the mind, continue to think of the mind as being separate from our bodies and the rest of the world.

We can see the separation of mind from the body and the world in the language used by Gee (2001) to explain situated cognition. After plainly stating that "meaning in language is tied to people's experiences of situated action in the material and social world" (p. 9), Gee goes on to liken it to videotaping:

> It is almost as if we "videotape" our experiences as we are having them, create a library of such videotapes, edit them to make some "prototypical tapes" or a set of typical instances, but stand ever ready to add new tapes to our library, reedit the tapes based on new experiences, or draw out of the library less typical tapes when the need arises. As we face new situations or new texts we run our tapes, perhaps a prototypical one, or a set of typical ones, or a set of contrasting ones, or a less typical one, whatever the case may be, in order to apply our old experiences to our new experience and to aid us in making, editing, and storing the videotape that will capture this new experience, integrate it into our library, and allow us to make sense of it (both while we are having it and afterwards). (p. 10)

Although Gee acknowledges that "talking about videotapes in the mind is a metaphor that, like all metaphors, is incorrect if pushed too far" (p. 10), it is a very powerful metaphor that is difficult to dislodge once accepted because it is something that we have so much experience with and because the idea of memory as storage is so robust. But to speak of making, editing, and storing videotapes suggests that there is someone or something doing it, perhaps a homunculus in your head doing the taping, editing, and replaying. As a result, Gee's camcorder and VCR metaphor for situated cognition is not much different from the idea of our minds being information processing machines that algorithmically act on our perceptions (inputs) and memories (database).

I believe that the metaphor of the mind as a computer or VCR helps little in understanding my actions or beliefs in the sunset and herbal remedy examples presented earlier. Does thinking of my brain as a computer that acts on a set of inputs—such as the sensory data of the light in the sky, the feel of the breeze, or smell of the salt in the air—combined with data stored in my brain about my friend and about romantic settings, help to explain why I spoke of the sunset rather than the Earth's rotation? The mind-as-computer metaphor would certainly explain why a robot would speak like that, but I find it lacking when trying to explain people's intentional actions. In the same way, there is something lacking in thinking that the reason I drink herbal tea when I have a cold is because I am playing one videotape, say "Episode 54: Allan Has a Cold," rather than "Episode 72: Allan Is Skeptical of Nonmedical Remedies."

Science Learning as a Change in the Way of Being

I believe that what needs to be added to a conversation about science learning is the idea that learning not only changes what we know and do, but it also changes who we are. Returning to my two examples, we can see that my knowledge of science is somehow folded into who I am, or what I call my way of being (Feldman, 1997). My cognitive and linguistic experiences are just a portion of the way I am in the world. The way of being is also related to the idea of identity, as defined by Wenger (1998):

> An identity then is a layering of events of participation and reification by which our experience and its social interpretation inform each other. As we encounter our effects on the world and develop our relations with others, these layers build upon each other to produce our identity as a very complex interweaving of participative experience and reificative projections. Bringing the two together through the negotiation of meaning, we construct who we are. (p. 151)

What this suggests is that when we say that we want students to learn science, we must be willing to admit that we want to change who they are. By acknowledging this desire, it becomes clear why the teaching of science content is a political and moral endeavor, the awareness of which also can help us to understand the controversies surrounding the inclusion of evolution and human reproduction issues in the science curriculum. Our desire to change who students are also explains why students are reluctant to leave behind the everyday language of their lifeworld (Gee, 2001) to use the academic discourse of science.

Therefore, instead of using metaphors that treat the mind as a metaphysical entity (Searle, 1997) and make people into robots and syndicated reruns, I suggest that we begin our study of science learning from an existential perspective. To speak of learning science as a change in who we are, our identities, or our ways of being is to take an existential perspective on teaching and learning. In this perspective, learners of science are *being* students of science, and teachers are *being* teachers of science immersed in educational situations. Before I give some examples of how this perspective is useful for improving science learning, I will first provide an overview of existentialism.

Existentialism

It is not easy to come up with a definition of existentialism because it is a term loosely connected with various philosophers who worked during the first half of the 20th century. It is also difficult to define because it has been out of favor as of late, which explains why many of my references date from that time period. However, we could say that existentialism begins with a focus on the individual human being, and then raises questions about what it means to exist in the world (Morris, 1966). Existentialism asks these questions in the concrete rather than abstract by reminding us that we are each immersed in situations that are temporal, spatial, and relational; that we have no pregiven or preordained essence; that we decide our own fate and are responsible for what we make of our lives; and that we should seek the most authentic and fulfilling ways of life (Guignon, 2000; Morris, 1966; Sartre, 1956, 1995).

In the pages that follow, I give an overview of the existential concepts of situation, the construction of self, and freedom, all of which can help us to better understand what it means to teach and learn science. In doing so I switch voice to the first person plural to indicate the existentialist stance that includes myself with the readers of this chapter.

Situation

The existentialist idea that the individual is involved in a social and historical world is at first glance very similar to situated cognition. What distinguishes the existentialist concept of situation from the idea of situated cognition is that the existentialist focuses on the person *being* in the situation, but the cognitive scientist focuses on the person *thinking* in the situation. To existentialists, we are beings who exist immersed in situations that are constituted by what we have experienced—including all types of interactions with others—and are a result of choices that we have made and the intentions that we have for the future. The concept of "situation" goes beyond the human interaction with a single object or event or set of objects or events. It includes the influences on people of the "traditions, institutions, custom and the purposes and beliefs they carry and inspire" (Dewey, 1938, p. 43). It also includes human interactions. As a result, existentialists say that a person finds him- or herself thrown into a situation comprising all that has occurred in the past and from which the person projects him- or herself into the future (Heidegger, 1962).

The recognition that people exist as part of situations allows us to understand what Greene (1967) calls the "existing being"—the person being in the situation with "all of its shifting moods, feelings, impulses, [and] fantasies" (p. 7). Recognition also leads to the acknowledgement that students and teachers of science are more than rational knowers and reasoners in the classroom and that almost everything that occurs in their situations is affected by their past and present, presence, moods and gestures, expectations, intentions, the others with whom they are continually engaged, and the milieu of particular human "traditions, institutions, customs and...purposes and beliefs" (Dewey, 1938, p. 43).

Human beings are both immersed in situations and aware that they are immersed in those situations: We are beings who are aware of our own being (Heidegger, 1962). Being aware in this way allows us to attend to the situation. Attending to the situation is similar to what others have called metacognition, but it goes beyond thinking about thinking to being aware of who we are, where we are, and why we do what we do. When this awareness occurs, we can see teaching and learning as intentional activities. That is, from an existential perspective, students or teachers must not only determine to act in the sense of choosing to act, but they also must be as conscious as possible of the situation, making sure that they understand the situation and deciding upon what is useful and what can be believed (Greene, 1973). In doing this, the student and teacher acknowledge that everything around them has meaning that arises from the situation—including their own way of being, which itself arises through experience.

The Self-Construction of Self

The existential concepts of situation and intentionality are tied to a fundamental tenet of existentialism, which is that "existence precedes essence" (Sartre, 1956). In other words, as Dewey writes, "the self is not ready-made, but something in continuous formation through choice of action" (Dewey, 1916, p. 408). As with the concepts of situation and intentionality, the existential concept that we create ourselves has parallels with research in science education. Research on learning has demonstrated that we construct our conceptions of scientific ideas through our physical and cognitive experiences. The parallel is that, although in science education we say that we *construct our understandings*, the existentialist says that we *construct who we are*. In addition, although our concern in science education is the construction of learning situations for *others*, the existentialist perspective tells us that as we go about living our lives we construct *ourselves*. Therefore, as I previously claimed, to learn is to change who we are, and to teach is to attempt to change others.

Freedom

Another important aspect of existentialism is the idea of freedom. Talk of intentions, actions, and the construction of the self is meaningless if people do not have the freedom to choose and act. According to Greene (1988), human freedom "is the capacity to surpass the given and look at things as if they could be otherwise" (p. 3). Freedom also is the ability to "name alternatives, imagine a better state of things, [or] share with others a project of change" (Greene, 1988, p. 9). This idea is different from autonomy or liberty, both of which, especially in the United States, are associated with the concept of freedom. A person can be autonomous without having the capacity to be free because he or she is not aware of possibilities or the constraints that limit those possibilities. Liberty also differs significantly from existential freedom. For example, liberty in the U.S. context is conceived as being represented by a set of human rights that are protected by laws. Although those laws may ensure liberty or rights, they do not necessarily provide individuals with the capacity to act freely, and, conversely, individuals can have this capacity but be constrained from acting on it.

Freedom to choose is an essential part of being human (Sartre, 1956). However, most of us act as if we have very limited choices or none at all. To some extent, this behavior is because our actions are limited by the world in which we live. However, being limited in one's actions because of external constraints is different from acting as if one has no choices at all.

For teachers, our ability to act "to surpass the given and look at things as if they could be otherwise" (Greene, 1988, p. 3) is constrained by the real and mythical (Tobin & McRobbie, 1996). For example, as I write this chapter in Massachusetts in June 2002, teachers are constrained by decisions made by local education authorities and by the statewide policies of a conservative government that has imposed high-stakes examinations on students and teachers. At the same time, teachers feel the constraints of cultural myths such as those related to content coverage, the need to transmit knowledge, academic rigor, and the preparation of students to be successful in the next course (Tobin & McRobbie, 1996). Students also feel constraints, both real and mythic, on their freedom. This feeling was demonstrated in Gee and Crawford's (1998) profiles of two high school students—Emily, who can be labeled as successful, and Sandra, who is at risk. Emily is "oriented, in word and value, toward school.... She is connecting her everyday persona to the values and forms of life" (p. 243) in public institutions such as schools. Sandra "does not connect with school[s]...her everyday life is cut off from them, partly defined in opposition to them" (p. 243). Both girls feel that their freedom to choose and to act are constrained, and as a result, they live lives determined by others.

An existential perspective can help us to acknowledge that even if there are constraints, we do have the freedom to choose, and our choices affect the situations in which they are immersed and define who we are. As Morris (1961) explains,

> [Our] existence precedes essence. We first are; then we attempt to define ourselves. [Humanity] is the great contingency; [our] essence is not given...we have been "thrown into existence"; not knowing whence we came, we wake up to discover ourselves here. And once we discover ourselves in existence, we commence the long slow journey to find our essence. As we travel, we perform this and that activity, make this and that choice, prefer this, reject that, we are actually engaged in the process of defining ourselves, of providing the essence for which we search. (p. 74)

To change who we are as teachers so we can help students learn science better means that we have to accept the responsibility that comes with the freedom to choose, even when our choices are limited. It also means that we have to uncover which constraints are real and which are the myths that bind us.

Being an Existential Teacher

I have suggested that we can improve the learning of science by acknowledging that to learn is to change one's way of being. This suggestion led me to an exploration of existentialism, particularly the concepts of situation, the construction of self, and freedom. Although all my talk so far is fine for a piece of academic writing, it provides little in the way of guidance for teachers who seek to improve their students' science learning. Fortunately, existentialist ideas already are in line with teachers' goals for their students. For example, last year when I asked a group of preservice science teachers in my class what their goals were as teachers, they wrote of the need to respect students and create supportive relationships that foster mutual respect and a sense of community. They wrote of their desires to inspire their students and help them gain confidence and learn the knowledge and skills that empower them to think for themselves. The preservice teachers acknowledged the need to recognize students as individuals by modifying their instruction to meet different learning styles and connect subject matter to the world of the students. The preservice teachers also wrote about making school fun for their students.

What seems to be missing from these responses are the teachers' desires to help their students gain expertise in the subject area. When they did specifically mention science, it tended to be in relation to students' lives rather than to the disciplines. For example, one teacher wrote, "My goal is to help students learn how to approach problems or unfamiliar situations by using skills that they already have and will further develop in class." Another wrote, "I want to prepare students for lifelong learning." In a discussion about their goals, several other teachers agreed, "We share a desire to use our students' previous experiences and to have them apply their newly acquired skills outside of the classroom, and in fact, outside of the discipline of science." And even more telling was one teacher's sentiment to "not teach solely for [the state exam], but to incorporate our own interests and philosophies."

These teachers' goals, which I call *global objectives*, also are reminiscent of what existential philosophers of education have written about the purposes of education. For example, Morris (1966) tells us, "If education is to be truly human, it must somehow *awaken awareness* in the learner" (p. 110) so he or she can take "personal responsibility for being human" (p. 116). Morris also writes, "Existential education assumes the responsibility of awakening each individual to the full intensity of his own selfhood"

(p. 134). Kneller (1958) also addresses the goals or purposes of an existential approach to education. He sees it as being concerned

> with the unfolding of the individual as a whole in the particular situation in which he finds himself, within a definite time and space into which the individual has been born through no fault of his own, but which nonetheless defines him. (pp. 118–119)

Morris's and Kneller's existential goals for education include the recognition by both teacher and student (and I would add administrators, parents, and policymakers) that each is an individual human being who is situated, whose self emerges through experience, and who has freedom to choose. This recognition is the basis for an existential approach to education.

The fact that we are people being teachers and that our students are other people suggests the importance in education of the existential concept of the other and the relationship between the self and others. That relationship is multidimensional. We construct ourselves through our choices as we project from the situations into which we have been thrown. Other people and our relationships with them are an integral part of those situations. But our connection to others is not just the explicit interactions that occur when people are with one another. There is more than an information exchange in our relationships with others. There also is a presence of the other that affects who we are and what we do (Sartre, 1956). Sartre claims that this connection happens because we are aware of other people as being human like ourselves, which results in their perception of us affecting how we perceive ourselves.

Searle (1995), although not an existentialist per se, also has written about how being with others affects who and how we are. In *The Construction of Social Reality*, he describes *collective intentionality* as the *something* about being with others that leads to the capacity to share intentional states such as beliefs, desires, and intentions. Recall my experience of sitting on the pier looking at the sunset. My friend and I were in a romantic situation together that would not have been the same if we were each alone or with other people. Even if we had not spoken a word while sitting on that pier, we each would have felt the presence of the other. We also can see the effect of the presence of the other in a classroom. Picture this: The students have just entered the room and are beginning to sit down. The bell rings, and the teacher gains their attention. At that point, something has changed. They are now a class rather than a group of individual students, and they are each aware of being a part of that class, which results in changes in their ways of being.

The idea that it is necessary for us to recognize our students as human beings like ourselves may appear at first obvious and trite. But, too often, we relegate our students to a faceless "they" that we sometimes treat almost like things rather than the people they are. In my conversations with teachers (and in my own utterances as a teacher), I too often have heard references to the students in the class as "they," "the sixth grade," or "special education students." In the same way, adversarial relations between school boards and teachers' unions, as well as the "blame the teacher" rhetoric of policymakers, serve to turn teachers into faceless "theys." For teachers and students, the result is that we engage in an "I-It" relationship with our students rather than an "I-Thou" relationship (Buber, 1937). The problem with the I-It relationship is that in it we objectify our students, making them objects that we can manipulate through technical means. It allows for a factory model of schooling and the possibility of "teacher-proof" curricula. It also allows us to look at these "objects" and remove our responsibility for them by shifting the blame for failure from ourselves and our own efforts to defects in the raw materials. Of course, the I-It relationship also relieves us of the sense of joy that comes from acknowledging the responsibility that we would have had for their success. The I-It relationship also deprives our students of their rights as human beings: to have a voice and be heard, to search for one's own meanings, and to be a potent person in the world. And, it leads us as teachers to abandon our global objectives to focus on the subject matter rather than the person who is a student.

An I-Thou relationship between our students and ourselves begins to emerge when we acknowledge and become involved with each student as an individual. When we become involved with each one, we take on responsibility for him or her as other. The way that we interact with each student can have a profound effect on how that student sees him- or herself and on what choices the student makes about who he or she is and what he or she is becoming. Therefore, to become involved, or, as Morris (1966) calls it, to make contact with the being of the student,

> is thus to make contact with that for which there is no precedent. Each encounter between teacher and learner therefore inevitably starts from scratch. It begins anew with a fresh creation still in the act of creating itself. The teacher's task is to see to it that this subjective selfhood, *de novo*, quickens its awareness of itself, of its freedom, and eventually to its responsibility for its own way of living a single human life. (p. 152)

To accept the responsibility that we have for our students requires us to be aware of the dialectic between who we are as teachers and who our students are as human beings in our educational situations.

A Case From Middle School Science

Clearly, important parts of an existential approach to science teaching and learning are the methods that teachers can use to create situations that make explicit the I-Thou relationships between them and their students. To Pine (1974), existential teaching

> is more an attitude than a technique.... Teaching is viewed primarily as an encounter which implies a special kind of relationship requiring the teacher to be totally present to the student, to participate in the student's existence, to be fully with him.... *Knowing* the student as a person becomes more important than *knowing* about him. (p. 19)

Teachers who take an existential approach are aware that the I-Thou relationship is dialectic and that students also have concerns about the nature of the teacher-student relationship.

Ellen Coss was a student in the Action Research in Schools course that I teach each year at the University of Massachusetts (Feldman, 1998). Ms. Coss teaches middle school science in a small, western Massachusetts city. Although she is new to teaching, Ms. Coss has had a wide range of jobs, including farming, dog training, and being an emergency medical technician. While student teaching in 2000, she began to use what she calls student-driven discussions. They are "a kind of discussion in which the teacher exists merely to facilitate and organize. The students provide the ideas and questions" (Coss, 2002, p. 5). These discussions are similar to what Gallas (1995) calls "science talks." Several weeks into the semester I have students write and deliver what I call a "starting point speech." The purpose of this speech is to encourage the students to think deeply about their educational situation to identify any problems, dilemmas, or dissonances in their practice (Feldman, 1998). In Ms. Coss's starting point speech she described her goals for the use of student-driven discussions:

> The state of affairs I wish to change/improve is the difficulty in the inclusion of discussion time within our limited class time. I think this can be done by a more careful approach to my lesson plans. Many of our discussions are impromptu, but they could be scheduled, with an eye towards future assessment. I also wish to change/improve the numbers of students that feel comfortable participating, and address the needs of the students who simply will not participate in a class-wide discussion. I will address this by speaking privately to the students who do not enjoy participation, giving them a "heads up" to improve their comfort level. I will also try and include other formats of cooperative learning that make participation less threatening. I wish to change/improve my ability to facilitate these discussions, keeping them round the table rather than the

"Miss Coss Show." This too should be addressed by my lesson plans; I should have a more clear focus when the discussion begins.

In her starting point speech, Ms. Coss lays out technical goals—such as better discussion structures and greater numbers of students participating—but she also alludes to her global objectives—such as the students' comfort levels, sense of being less threatened, and roles in the classroom. Ms. Coss feels a responsibility to make sure that the student-driven discussions are democratic—that everyone has an opportunity to speak, and that all are respected by being listened to. But not only does she accept this responsibility, she also believes that she must be an advocate for her students:

> Allan [Feldman] asked me what I meant by advocacy, and do the students want me to act in this capacity. I decided that in this instance it did not matter whether they wanted me to or not, it is a primary role of a teacher. To act as interface between the student and the oncoming world. (Coss, 2002, pp. 7–8)

Part of her advocacy is an awareness that it is easy to lose students among the "they," either by her oversight or by their reticence: "Even the teacher can misplace the students, their individual grace, their highs and lows, in the rush of the curriculum" (Coss, 2002, p. 2). Therefore, she has attended to the situation:

> In my classroom I try to be aware of this situation and to make sure that I do not allow any of my students to "disappear" by virtue of their ethnicity, gender, or English language fluency. It can be difficult to remember, as a teacher, not to "forget" certain students. The students that try to be invisible usually had a lot of practice. (Coss, 2002, p. 4)

Ms. Coss also is aware that the closeness that she wants to maintain with her students is not the norm in her school:

> Most of the other teachers seem less interested in the students, many of them tell me that I will "get over it," referring to my relationship with my students. I have been told that I am letting them "in too close" by talking about my life with them. (Coss, 2002, p. 10)

Even so, she continues to connect her life with her students. On one occasion, Ms. Coss asked a friend who was studying to be a doctor to talk with her students about medical school and medicine. The students in all of her classes engaged in lively discussions with the guest, even staying after the bell rang to end the class. But what seems to stand out for Coss is her students' interest in the humanness of the guest, which can be seen in the students' questions about existential concerns such as identity, angst, and death:

> Each class seemed to focus on a different topic. First period was the most fasci-
> nated by her story of not being accepted [to medical school]. Questions arose
> like, "Did you ever get, you know, so down that you wanted to just give up?"
> "What did you do to keep going?" Third period wanted to talk about cadavers,
> dissection, and death, more good questions: "What do adults mean when they
> say someone died of old age?" "Can you ever get over being grossed out by
> blood? I want to work in medicine but it is so gross." "How did it make you
> feel to dissect a dead body?" What was so remarkable is that all my shy partici-
> pants spoke right up...each period I heard kids speak that usually do not, and
> I thought here is a way to get to them. (Coss, 2002, p. 13)

Ms. Coss also has learned the power of one-on-one conversations with her students. Most telling is her relationship with Peter, which she described in a journal excerpt that she included in her report:

> [Peter] had trouble participating in discussions without trying to be the focus.
> He cannot resist making faces, trying to outsmart everyone, talking over oth-
> ers, and ridiculing any speakers that he perceives as "stupid." He and I had a
> little conversation. I asked him what he wanted from acting this way. I pointed
> out that he could lose my respect very quickly, that it was his responsibility, as
> an exceptionally bright student to help, not hinder, other students that might be
> having difficulty. I asked him if he thought he would always be at the top of
> the class, and could he envision a moment where he might need the patience
> of his classmates. He replied that no, he had not considered that, or even what
> it might be like to struggle in school. This stopped him briefly, and I hope it will
> in the long run. (Coss, 2002, p. 11)

As it turned out, the conversation with Peter has seemed to lead toward his acceptance of responsibility for himself:

> Peter is desperate now to "help" during discussions. He wants to explain how he
> does things, how he figures things out...The problem is, he had been such a
> pain...all year that the other students just roll their eyes and boo him down....
> The other students were reluctant to let him speak, so I invoked my rule of
> everyone must listen...After class Peter approached me and expressed his
> thanks. He was very pleased that I would stand up for him in the class. (Coss,
> 2002, p. 11)

In the excerpts above, Ms. Coss wrote about how she developed the I-Thou relationship by separating Peter from the "they." She acknowledged what was special about him and urged Peter to take responsibility for his choices about how to act.

Conclusion

Ms. Coss's objectives and ways of acting in her classroom with her students are familiar to anyone who has spent time in schools. The result, when teachers are aware of the constraints on their freedom and choose to act in ways to create I-Thou relationships with students, is learning as a change in way of being. As Ms. Coss writes,

> Without journaling about it every day I would have missed important moments. The moment when Maya, who barely speaks any English, stood in front of the class and explained how to use a Punnett square. The way in which seventh period "lost" their ability to discuss by actually losing their ability to listen. How they have regained their discussion ability and the comfortable feeling that has brought. How my attention to listening to a student like Peter gives me a means of managing him in class. (Coss, 2002, p. 18)

Ms. Coss also has learned that

> Teaching is not simply the disgorging of information; it is not just chalk boards, paper clips, and grade books. In fact, teaching is a meditative art that is both about being the teacher and about being the students. In the most balanced classroom everyone may play both roles. In a classroom such as this information is shared by all participants and growth occurs both in front of and behind the desk. The reality is that each classroom occupies but a tiny space in each student's head, backpack, and locker. The teacher, the concepts, and the ideology can get folded up and squirreled away in the time it takes for a bell to ring.... In order to remain mindful, to draw the students out of the herd, to reach individuals instead of classes, we must reflect and remain aware. (Coss, 2002, p. 2)

But has science learning improved in Ms. Coss's classes? We have looked primarily at her journal entries as reported in her paper, but she collected other data, including her students' test and quiz scores and the results of an opinion survey that she administered. During the semester in which she did her action research, she saw a consistent rise in students' quiz scores. Although this improvement may support the claim that the students have learned more, the methods that Ms. Coss used might not satisfy policymakers interested in quantifiable accountability measures.

Ms. Coss's (2002) opinion survey asked students their beliefs about what helps them to learn. Ms. Coss found that the vast majority of her students valued the class discussions. Again, these types of data would not satisfy those who measure the learning of science "objectively." It also is not clear whether Ms. Coss can claim that her students are better at doing science or are even any better at talking science. But what she has seen are disaffected students who have become excited about science and science learning. This change in their ways of being students is an important beginning step in the improvement of science learning. For this change to occur, teachers need to accept the responsibility for creating their own ways of being teachers, in addition to the responsibility to help their students acknowledge that they construct their own ways of being. In addition, the others involved in teaching and learning in schools—policymakers, science education researchers and educators, administrators, and parents—must acknowledge that to learn science is to change who we are and that society must allow teachers to choose to act in ways that change children's ways of being students, so students can embrace the life-change of learning.

REFERENCES

American Association for the Advancement of Science. (1993). *Benchmarks for science literacy* (American Association for the Advancement of Science Project 2061). New York: Oxford University Press.

Bredo, E. (1994, March). *Cognitivism, situated cognition, and Deweyian pragmatism.* Paper presented at the 50th Annual Meeting of the Philosophy of Education Society, Charlotte, NC.

Brown, J.S., Collins, A., & Duguid, P. (1989). Situated cognition and the culture of learning. *Educational Researcher, 18,* 32–42.

Bruer, J.T. (1994). *Schools for thought: A science of learning in the classroom.* Cambridge, MA: MIT Press.

Buber, M. (1937). *I and thou* (R.G. Smith, Trans.). Edinburgh, UK: T. & T. Clark.

Coss, E. (2002). *Discussion in learning.* Unpublished manuscript, University of Massachusetts Amherst.

DeBoer, G.E. (2000). Scientific literacy: Another look at its historical and contemporary meanings and its relationship to science education reform. *Journal of Research in Science Teaching, 37*(6), 582–601.

Dewey, J. (1916). *Democracy and education.* New York: Macmillan.

Dewey, J. (1938). *Logic: The theory of inquiry.* New York: Henry Holt.

Feldman, A. (1997). Varieties of wisdom in the practice of teachers. *Teaching and Teacher Education, 13*(7), 757–773.

Feldman, A. (1998). Implementing and assessing the power of conversation in the teaching of action research. *Teacher Education Quarterly, 25*(2), 27–42.

Fenstermacher, G. (1986). Philosophy of research on teaching: Three aspects. In M.C. Wittrock (Ed.), *Handbook of research on teaching* (3rd ed., pp. 37–49). New York: Macmillan.

Gallas, K. (1995). *Talking their way into science: Hearing children's questions and theories, responding with curricula.* New York: Teachers College Press.

Gee, J.P. (2001, August). *Language in the science classroom: Academic social languages as the heart of school-based literacy.* Paper presented at the National Science Foundation's Crossing Borders: Connecting Science and Literacy conference, Baltimore, MD.

Gee, J.P., & Crawford, V. (1998). Two kinds of teenagers: Language, identity, and social class. In D.E. Alverman, K.A. Hinchman, D.W. Moore, S.F. Phelps, & D.R. Warr (Eds.), *Reconceptualizing the literacies in adolescents' lives* (pp. 225–245). Mahwah, NJ: Erlbaum.

Greene, M. (Ed.). (1967). *Existential encounters for teachers.* New York: Random House.

Greene, M. (1973). *Teacher as stranger: Educational philosophy in the modern age.* Belmont, CA: Wadsworth.

Greene, M. (1988). *The dialectic of freedom*. New York: Teachers College Press.

Guignon, C.B. (2000). Existentialism. In E. Craig (Ed.), *Concise Routledge encyclopedia of philosophy* (p. 265). New York: Routledge.

Haraway, D. (1989). *Primate visions: Gender, race, and nature in the world of modern science*. New York: Routledge.

Heidegger, M. (1962). *Being and time* (J. Macquarrie & E. Robinson, Trans.). San Francisco: Harper.

Kneller, G.F. (1958). *Existentialism and education*. New York: Wiley.

Kuhn, T.S. (1970). *The structure of scientific revolutions*. Chicago: University of Chicago Press.

Lakatos, I. (1978). *The methodology of scientific research programmes: Volume 1, philosophical papers*. Cambridge, UK: Cambridge University Press.

Laugksch, R.C. (2000). Scientific literacy: A conceptual overview. *Science Education, 84*(1), 71–94.

Lave, J., & Wenger, E. (1991). *Situated learning: Legitimate peripheral participation*. Cambridge, UK: Cambridge University Press.

Lemke, J.L. (1990). *Talking science: Language, learning, and values*. Westport, CT: Ablex.

Lyotard, J. (1979). *The postmodern condition: A report on knowledge*. Minneapolis, MN: University of Minnesota Press.

Morris, V.C. (1961). *Philosophy and the American school: An introduction to the philosophy of education*. Boston: Houghton Mifflin.

Morris, V.C. (1966). *Existentialism in education: What it means*. Prospect Heights, IL: Waveland.

National Research Council. (1996). *National science education standards*. Washington, DC: National Academy Press.

National Science Teachers Association (NSTA). (2000). *The nature of science*. A position statement of the National Science Teachers Association. Arlington, VA: Author. Available at http://www.nsta.org/159&psid=22

Pine, G.J. (1974). Existential teaching and learning. *Education, 95*(1), 18–24.

Sartre, J.-P. (1956). *Being and nothingness* (H. Barnes, Trans.). New York: Philosophical Library.

Sartre, J.-P. (1995). *Existentialism and human emotions*. New York: Carol Publishing Group.

Schwab, J.J. (1978). Education and the structure of the disciplines. In I. Westbury & N. Wilkof (Eds.), *Science, curriculum, and liberal education: Selected essays* [of Joseph J. Schwab] (pp. 229–272). Chicago: University of Chicago Press.

Searle, J.R. (1984). *Minds, brains, and science*. Cambridge, MA: Harvard University Press.

Searle, J.R. (1995). *The construction of social reality*. New York: Free Press.

Searle, J.R. (1997). *The mystery of consciousness*. New York: New York Review of Books.

Shulman, L.S. (1986). Those who understand: Knowledge growth in teaching. *Educational Researcher, 15*(2), 4–14.

Tobin, K., & McRobbie, C.J. (1996). Cultural myths as constraints to the enacted science curriculum. *Science Education, 80*(2), 223–241.

Wenger, E. (1988). *Communities of practice: Learning, meaning, and identity*. Cambridge, UK: Cambridge University Press.

TEACHING SCIENCE

AS A DIALOGIC PROCESS

The three chapters in this section examine the decision-making processes that various stakeholders use as they negotiate science text.

In chapter 9, "Promoting Dialogic Inquiry in Information Book Read-Alouds: Young Urban Children's Ways of Making Sense in Science," Christine C. Pappas and Maria Varelas, with Anne Barry and Amy Rife, focus on the importance of reading information books as part of science instruction, looking specifically at the intertextual connections generated by young students. The authors argue that effective instruction builds on dialogue: Students offer their own ideas and comments about text so that teachers and peers can respond contingently. Classroom examples are examined and offered as evidence of the kind of rich connections that might be made among science experience, science explanation, and literacy learning.

Laura B. Smolkin and Carol A. Donovan, in "Improving Science Instruction With Information Books: Understanding Multimodal Presentations," consider the moves made by science authors as they construct text; through this analysis educators are provided with models for thinking about how science text works. Using both narrative and non-narrative information books, Smolkin and Donovan consider different purposes and structures used in text, closely examining both verbal and visual features. They conclude that enhanced comprehension results from attention to both picture and text.

Jeanne Reardon, a classroom teacher, thinks aloud in chapter 11 about the decisions that she makes as she responds to student comments and questions. Her chapter, "Readers Are Scientists: A Reflective Exploration of the Reasoning of Young Scientists, Readers, Writers, and Discussants," reveals the complexity of the interplay between teacher, students, and science content. Reardon builds from a primary student's interpretation of what it is that goes on in science class and how that work is similar to what goes on in her reading class. What students, teacher, and reader come to realize is that an inquiry approach to literacy learning does, in fact, share much in common with an inquiry approach to science.

The approach to understanding what meaningful literacy–science connections might look like promulgated by these authors grows directly from a close analysis of classroom activity. All three chapters demonstrate how theory grows from practice and at the same time how theory informs practice.

CHAPTER 9

Promoting Dialogic Inquiry in Information Book Read-Alouds: Young Urban Children's Ways of Making Sense in Science

CHRISTINE C. PAPPAS AND MARIA VARELAS,
WITH ANNE BARRY AND AMY RIFE

> A long time ago when I was little, me and my friends Erin and Charles, we were playing in the snow and we...made angels and then had a tunnel...all the way to the (***). And then a couple weeks later when I went back um snow it looked like...the sun was on it and it like melted the whole thing down, but it was still standing.

Kristina offered this brief story about her and her friends playing in the snow and the snow's subsequent melting during the read-aloud session of *What's the Weather Today?* (Fowler, 1991). The second graders had been talking about the recent snowstorm. Amy, their teacher, talked about the warmer days that had occurred recently, and Adam noted that the snow had melted. Amy accepted Adam's comment and then asked, "What do you think caused the snow to melt?" Adam thought that the warm weather was the cause of the melting. Kristina's contribution continued that reasoning, as she told her story that the "sun was on it," causing the melting to occur, but not completely—"it melted the whole thing down but it was still standing." Later, with Amy's encouragement, Kristina explained that the partially melted snow tunnel "looked like play dough hanging down." Other children provided a few more ideas, and then Amy returned to reading the book.

This chapter focuses on the importance of reading information books as part of the science curriculum. Moreover, we argue that such books need to be read in a collaborative, dialogic manner, so children such as Kristina have opportunities to offer their own ideas, comments, and questions, to which teachers and peers can respond contingently. We use specific classroom discourse examples from read-aloud sessions of information books to explore the opportunities that dialogically oriented instruction offers teachers and students (Lindfors, 1999; Nystrand, 1997; Wells, 1999). Together, we—Christine, a literacy educator; Maria, a science educator; and Anne and Amy, teacher researchers who teach first and second grade, respectively—have developed units that have five components:

1. Hands-on explorations, plus whole-class discussions around them
2. Read-aloud sessions using a range of children's information books on the topic being investigated
3. Many writing (and drawing) experiences related to the inquiries
4. Small-group literature circle inquiries using information books
5. At-home, parent-child explorations (science activities and a related children's literature information book shared together) on the topic that are reported in the classroom later

Each unit, usually 4–6 weeks long, has common features in both Anne's and Amy's classrooms (e.g., using the same books and hands-on explorations), but each teacher researcher has flexibility in the ways in which she implements it.

This chapter is organized as follows: The first part presents reasons for using information books in elementary classrooms in collaborative ways. The second part explains *intertextual connections*, a certain type of contribution that especially highlights the ways participants made sense of new ideas by linking them with other experiences in and out of the classroom. The third and fourth parts provide two sets of examples of intertextual links that we have identified for a States of Matter unit. Finally, we discuss how these intertextual links in read-alouds offer critical ways to develop scientific understandings and language.

Using Information Books to Promote Dialogic Inquiry

Unfortunately, the use of information books in elementary classrooms is limited. For example, Duke (2000) notes that in her study of first-grade classrooms, the reading of information books was an average of only 3.6 seconds per day. One reason for this lack of information books is that many teachers believe that the story genre is primary in literacy development—that young children read and write first through story, that they do not have the linguistic or conceptual capabilities to tackle the language of information books, that they prefer stories more than information books, and so forth (Pappas, 1993). Some recent studies have challenged this view (e.g.,

Donovan, 2001; Duke & Kays, 1998; Kamberelis, 1999; Newkirk, 1989; Oyler, 1996; Pappas, 1993; Wollman-Bonilla, 2000), but the story genre still reigns.

Other reasons for the limited use of information books involve their role in science instruction specifically. Teachers may not realize that reading (and writing) science is different from reading (and writing) narrative texts (Shymansky, Yore, & Good, 1991). Even when teachers believe that certain texts might be supportive in fostering scientific understandings, they may worry that texts might constrain children's hands-on science explorations and otherwise limit their generation of explanations or "answers" in the course of investigating phenomena (Palincsar & Magnusson, 1997). In addition, because of the predominance of the story genre, especially in the elementary grades, teachers frequently are unaware that information books on various science topics are available for children (Duke, 2000).

Information books—including the photographs or illustrations in them—have a useful role in supporting children's hands-on explorations. In many ways, information books are similar to those used in the scientific inquiry conducted by scientists. As scientists engage in the ongoing process of inquiry, written texts often serve as mediators in their grappling with the ideas, thoughts, and reasoning of others (Goldman & Bisanz, 2002). In addition to informing and extending the hands-on explorations in a unit, information books also provide the kind of language that scientists read, write, and talk. Thus, these books provide ongoing sources for scientific concepts *and* ways for expressing these concepts (Ogborn, Kress, Martins, & McGillicuddy, 1996). As Sutton (1992) explains, learning science is based on the linkage between a *new way of seeing* any science topic and a *new way of talking* about it. When children are engaged in hands-on science inquiries, they have "here-and-now" experiences. Often, writing down their observations of these explorations in their science journals may have this in-the-moment orientation. However, science is necessarily concerned with typical classes of concepts and processes (Halliday & Martin, 1993; Lemke, 1990). Thus, the sharing of information books enables children to go back and forth in their explorations between instances of the here-and-now and abstractions of general concepts and processes.

Furthermore, how information books are shared in read-aloud sessions is critical. Anne and Amy work hard to make these sessions sites of dialogic inquiry (Lindfors, 1999; Wells, 1999). As previously noted, children have to feel free to offer their ideas, comments, and questions. Then, teachers can build on student offerings by asking for clarification, adding new information, helping on partial or incorrect responses, and so forth. Such an arrangement is different from cases in which the teacher controls all of the discussion—via what have been called IRE discourse structures (that is, the teacher Initiates, the student Responds, and the teacher Evaluates) (Cazden, 2001)—to check children's comprehension of the concepts covered in the books. In contrast, the dialogically oriented approach that Anne and Amy have adopted allows for the voices of both students and teacher to be heard: Both students and teacher have important roles in the ongoing discussion (Pappas & Zecker, 2001). Rather than being used to "cover the facts," the books act as "thinking devices" (Lotman, 1988) so students and teacher together propose, negotiate, debate, and develop scientific understandings.

Intertextual Connections in Dialogically Oriented Read-Alouds

As we noted, in this chapter we focus on a certain type of participant contribution that occurs in dialogically oriented read-alouds, namely, intertextual connections. Intertextual connections are those occasions when speakers refer to another text as they engage with a text in the current read-aloud session. We use the word *text* in an expansive way so intertextuality is more than just a reference to another book. It does include references to written texts—for example, other books, text in the classroom such as charts or writing on the board, or children's own writing. However, it also encompass texts that are shared orally, such as rhymes, poems, songs, and sayings, and other media such as television and radio programs and movies. The concept of text also incorporates the texts of prior classroom discourse in general, and hands-on explorations in particular, to which speakers might refer. Finally, according to Wells (1990), texts can be recounts of events that speakers have experienced and that they relate during read-alouds, such as Kristina's story of playing in the snow.

However, just mentioning a text—in any of these ways—does not necessarily "count" as an intertextual connection. We use three criteria suggested by Bloome and Egan-Robertson (1993)—recognition, acknowledgment, and social significance for the participants—to determine instances of intertextuality. Table 9.1 lists the categories of intertextuality that we have identified from first- and second-grade information book read-aloud sessions for the States of Matter unit (Pappas, Varelas, Barry, & Rife, 2003). In the next two sections of this chapter, we provide relatively detailed examples (although not for all categories because of space constraints). In the first section, we cover intertextual connections with other explorations and activities in the unit. In the second section, we focus on event intertextual links. The chapter's appendix on page 189 provides the transcription conventions. In the transcripts, Anne is the first-grade teacher and Amy is the second-grade teacher.

TABLE 9.1		
Categories of Intertextuality Identified in Read-Alouds During the States of Matter Unit		
Type of Intertextual Connection	**Definition of Connection**	**Examples**
CATEGORY I **1. Written texts** a. Information books in the unit	Refers to a particular information book by title or by noting other information books in the unit	"Ooh, lightning. We're going to read a book called *Flash, Crash, Rumble, and Roll*—and that one has some stuff about lightning...." [G2, WTWT, TI]
b. Text around the classroom (on charts, the chalkboard, etc.)	Refers to a written text found on charts, the board, etc.	"Remember how I did that on the board to show. That's kind of just to show you something that's invisible, okay?" [G2, DCTR, TI]
c. Other books available inside or outside the classroom	Refers to other books inside or outside the classroom	"Now, I'm going to go over to get a book. In fact, Alejandro, no, Manuel, you go over and get the Emperor penguin book." [G1, WSCU, TI]

(continued)

KEY Grade Levels: G1 = First grade; G2 = Second grade
Read-Aloud Books: AIAAY = *Air Is All Around You* (Branley, 1986); DCTR = *Down Comes the Rain* (Branley, 1997); WDYSC = *What Do You See in a Cloud?* (Fowler, 1996); WIWMO = *What Is the World Made Of? All About Solids, Liquids, and Gases* (Zoehfeld, 1998); WSCU = *When a Storm Comes Up* (Fowler, 1995); WTWT = *What's the Weather Today?* (Fowler, 1991)
Source: CI = Child-initiated; TI = Teacher-initiated

TABLE 9.1 (continued)
Categories of Intertextuality Identified in Read-Alouds During the States of Matter Unit

Type of Intertextual Connection	Definition of Connection	Examples
d. Children's own writing, drawings, or both	Refers to children's own writing, drawings, or both	"Just like we've done for the last couple of days.... I'm going to give you your data sheet.... You're going to draw...and you're going to write about what's the weather like today." [G1, WDYSC, TI]
2. Other texts (orally shared) such as poems, rhymes, sayings, and songs	Refers to a poem, rhyme, saying, or song by orally sharing some part or all of it	"It's raining, it's pouring, the old man is snoring." [G1, WTWT, CI]
3. Other media such as television or radio programs or movies	Refers to a television or radio program or a movie	"I was watching Ms. Frizzle it was like...it was raining and the...wind was blowing in the water and it was like the wind...flew up and made the clouds." [G2, WTWT, CI]
4. Prior classroom discourse		
a. In the current read-aloud session	Refers to prior discourse in the current read-aloud session	"You know, probably in the month of March...just like Alexandra said." [G1, WSCU, TI]
b. In the unit but outside the present read-aloud session	Refers to prior discourse in the unit but not in the present read-aloud session	"The other day Julio was kind of describing them (tornados) as having hands that can pick things up, right? 'Cause they're so strong." [G2, WSCU, TI]

(continued)

TABLE 9.1 (continued)
Categories of Intertextuality Identified in Read-Alouds
During the States of Matter Unit

Type of Intertextual Connection	Definition of Connection	Examples
c. Outside the unit	Refers to prior discourse related to previous units or other curriculum material outside the unit	"Remember we talked about the equator...and people who live around the middle part of the earth are always warm." [G1, WTWT, TI]
CATEGORY II **Hands-on explorations** 1. Within the unit and in the classroom	Refers to classroom explorations within the unit	"Now...one half of the class yesterday was up here in front with me and we were heating up the teapot and we were seeing the exact thing, right?" [G2, WIWMO, TI]
2. Other explorations	Refers to other explorations (at-home explorations developed for other units or other explorations conducted at home or in other settings)	(Students had done evaporation experiments using water.) "If you left like juice on the table would it evaporate?" [G2, DCTR, CI]
CATEGORY III **Recounting events** 1. Specific events a. Personal, specific events	Refers to a personal, specific event	"Last time I poured cold water in...my plate... 'cause...I was gonna use my mom's water, and I seen (***) and I seen air coming up." [G1, AIAAY, CI]

(continued)

T A B L E   9 . 1   (c o n t i n u e d)
Categories of Intertextuality Identified in Read-Alouds
During the States of Matter Unit

Type of Intertextual Connection	Definition of Connection	Examples
b. Personally related others-involved specific events	Refers to specific events in which speakers are not personally involved but others who they know are involved	"One time everybody was asleep, and my little cousin...she woke up early, and then she...was looking out the window, and then she's like 'Mommy, Mommy!' and they...all looked out the window. It was a tornado...." [G2, WSCU, CI]
c. Impersonal, specific events	Refers to specific events in which speakers do not indicate any personal involvement but which are known to them and are reported on	"It's 65. We're breaking records. It's not supposed to be 65. It's supposed to be the thirties. It's still winter." [G1, WDYSC, TI]
2. Generalized events a. Personal generalized events	Refers to personal, generalized events that are habitual actions	"This is what I do in the bathtub." (Student takes cup, pushes it into the water upside down, and then lets go of it.) [G2, AIAAY, CI]
b. Personally related others-involved generalized events	Refers to generalized, habitual events in which speakers are not personally involved but others they know are involved	"Like my brother, he goes downstairs, that's his room, got to go downstairs." [G1, WSCU, CI]
CATEGORY IV **"Implicit" generalized events**	Refers to generalized events in which speakers do not indicate any explicit personal involvement but which they could or should have habitually experienced	"Like when you leave your milk...for a long time in the refrigerator it will become thick." [G2, WIWMO, CI]

Connections Within the Unit

A major reason for focusing on intertextual links is that they help us see how participants connect ideas between the text used in a read-aloud session and other activities of the unit. Intertextuality helps us explore the form and function of an integrated curriculum, which provides coherence in teaching and learning, an organizing center or theme—a powerful idea—that helps children learn the parts of it (Pappas, 1997). As a result, rather than experiencing isolated lessons, students engage in connected read-aloud sessions and other explorations and activities that provide them with opportunities to study science topics in depth (Pappas, Kiefer, & Levstik, 1999). See Table 9.2 for the sequence of the read-aloud sessions and other explorations and activities of the States of Matter unit. (Note that there were seven major whole-class read-aloud sessions involving six information books—one book was read in two parts, with activities intervening.)

The first example below illustrates an intertextual connection to another information book that was available in the classroom. Anne had finished a read-aloud book that covers hurricanes and tornadoes, and the discussion in the class had centered on the damage that these storms cause and how to protect humans during such storms (especially tornadoes, which are a common concern in the school's community). At the end, Manuel asked about what penguins should do in such storms. Anne followed up on this theme by referring to another book on penguins. Note that intertextual links are underlined and in bold.

Example 1: *When a Storm Comes Up* (Fowler, 1995)

1	Manuel:	Uh, if tornados go to the Antarctica, what the penguin gonna do?
2	Anne:	<u>Oh</u>, you know what*...
3	Cm:	They could go under water.
4	Anne:	Could they go under water? What kind of protection could a penguin have?
5	Bernardo:	If there's enemies // if there's enemies, how could a penguin go underneath the water if there's enemies?
6	Anne:	Oh, he wouldn't want to go underneath the water, would he? Well, who's his enemy?
7	Cs:	<u>The seal</u>.
8	Anne:	The seals, yeah. Good thinking, questioner, yeah.

**Sequence of Seven Read-Alouds
and Other Unit Explorations and Activities**

The explorations and activities listed here occurred on the day of the read-aloud or later. Students wrote (and drew) in science journals during the whole unit. They also engaged in whole-class discussions around hands-on explorations during the whole unit.

Information Book Read-Aloud	Other Explorations and Activities
Read-Aloud 1 (RA1) *What's the Weather Today?* (Fowler, 1991)	Beginning of weather charts and logs that students would work on over several days
Read-Aloud 2 (RA2) *When a Storm Comes Up* (Fowler, 1995)	
Read-Aloud 3 (RA3) *What Do You See in a Cloud?* (Fowler, 1996)	Setup of an evaporation activity that occurred over the course of the unit. Four similar jars with tape going up and down on part of each jar were filled with colored tap water and placed around the classroom: two on a window sill (one with and one without a lid); one in cold, dark closet; and one by a heater. As students periodically observed the jars, they marked the water level on the tape with date of observation.
Read-Aloud 4 (RA4) *What Is the World Made Of?* *All About Solids, Liquids, and Gases* (Zoehfeld, 1998, part I, pp. 1–16)	Small-group exploration on categorizing items (e.g., box of juice, eraser, paper clip, balloons with air and with helium, hand lotion, empty cup, container of honey, etc.).
Read-Aloud 5 (RA5) *Air Is All Around You* (Branley, 1986)	Teacher demonstration of a cup-with-napkin activity. The napkin was stuffed in a cup that was first submerged straight down in a bowl of colored water, and then submerged in a slanted position. Then, there was a small-group exploration of the same activity.
	Explorations on melting. Half the class worked in small groups with ice melting in cups of water at different temperatures (hot and cold). The other half of the class worked in small groups with ice melting in different ways such as in a bowl or in a plastic bag held in their hands.
	Whole-class evaporation activity on paper-towel drying. Three wet paper towels were placed in three conditions: in crumbled ball, laying on a flat surface, and hanging up.

(continued)

T A B L E   9 . 2   (c o n t i n u e d)
Sequence of Seven Read-Alouds
and Other Unit Explorations and Activities

Information Book Read-Aloud	Other Explorations and Activities
	Explorations on condensation. Half the class worked in small groups with a soda can taken from the freezer. The other half of the class saw a teacher demonstration of steam on a cold cookie sheet.
Read-Aloud 6 (RA6) *What Is the World Made Of? All About Solids, Liquids, and Gases* (Zoehfeld, 1998, part II, pp. 17–31)	Whole-class activity with children pretending to be molecules of a substance in different states of matter. Children wriggled or moved around and held hands or not to symbolize molecule bonding in solids, liquids, and gases.
Read-Aloud 7 (RA7) *Down Comes the Rain* (Branley, 1997)	Parent-child home exploration project: ■ Book: *Down Comes the Rain* ■ Exploration: Paper-towel drying/evaporation— exploring ways to fold them and places to pat them ■ Writing: Child Booklet and Parent Page ■ Class reporting on home project
	Activity with food coloring dropped in a cup of room-temperature water. Small groups at separate tables observed and depicted (via drawings on handouts) how food coloring disperses in water over time.
	Teacher demonstration of the above activity with two cups—one with hot water and one with cold water. Children observed and depicted (via drawings on handouts) the dispersion of food coloring in water over time.
	Small-group literature circles with the following information books for children, which were shared with the whole class later: *Feel the Wind* (Dorros, 1989) *Snow Is Falling* (Branley, 1986) *Water* (Canizares & Chanko, 1998) *What Will the Weather Be?* (DeWitt, 1991)
	Writing of students' own individual illustrated, information book

9	Cs:	(*** ***) [several students speaking at once]
10	Anne:	Alright, Manuel had his hand up first. He asked a <u>really</u> important question. He said, "Well, what can a penguin do if he knows that a tornado is coming?" Wasn't that your question?
11	Bernardo:	No, that was mine.
12	Anne:	Well, together you were kind of talking about it. Now listen. That's a <u>really</u> good question. Now let's try and <u>solve</u> the question.

....

13	Anne:	**Now. I'm going to go over and get a book. In fact... Alejandro, no, Manuel, you go over and get the Emperor penguin book. The one from _National Geographic_ on the table over there**.

....

		[Manuel goes to find the book.]
14	Cm:	The one with the little baby.
15	Anne:	Yeah. Bring it here. Uh, I want to show you a picture of one of the things that penguins do in Antarctica to help protect them from a bad storm. One of the things is // they do not have// there are no tornados in Antarctica.
16	Manuel:	But what a happen?
17	Anne:	What would happen? They just get // I'll show you. They get really bad storms though. Very vicious storms or wind. Look what happens [shows illustrations].

....

		[Another child asks what happens if there's a hurricane. Anne answers that there are no hurricanes there. Anne further explores the book with the children.]
18	Anne:	....Uh, but look, this is the middle of a very bad weather storm...Look what the penguin // you tell me what the penguins are doing. You tell me. Manuel, what do you think they're doing?
19	Manuel:	They're getting together.
20	Anne:	They're getting together. In a what? What does it #look like#?
21	Manuel:	#In a circle.#
22	Anne:	It looks like a circle, doesn't it? Pedro knows about it.

23	Pedro:	They're getting together to get warm.
24	Anne:	To get warm.
25	Pedro:	With their feathers.
26	Anne:	With their...?
27	Pedro:	Feathers.
28	Anne:	Feathers, yeah.
29	Cm:	So the baby won't die.
....		[There is more exploration of the pictures, and the children continue to be concerned about what penguins do during a tornado. Anne reiterates that there are no tornados in Antarctica, but she agrees that the storms are windy like tornados. She further explains what penguins do, using the book's pictures to illustrate penguin behavior.]
30	Anne:	Alright, when a bad storm comes, a windy storm, they get together // they keep warm so that they don't fall away and maybe not survive. They huddle. Huddle is a good word. #Here's the other thing.#
31	Cm:	#I could see them right there.#
32	Anne:	Yeah. When the outer penguins, they get colder, the inner ones come through and come back out and around.
33	Bernardo:	It looks like a wall.

This intertextual connection was initiated by the teacher, but it is a response to Manuel's question about what penguins do during a tornado. Anne uses the book on penguins, especially the illustrations, to show how penguins protect themselves during terrible storms—but not during tornados or hurricanes, which the children continue to bring up. Pedro, a class expert on penguins, also is brought into this discussion. (It is Anne's practice to have children take books home each night to read and share with family members; she keeps track of these books and which individual readers take them home, so she is aware of students' specific interests.) In units 23, 25, and 27, Pedro explains that penguins get together (in a circle) to keep warm and that their feathers help in this effort. Anne expands on these ideas by discussing how the penguins take turns being in the inner and outer sections of the huddle, as illustrated in the book.

This intertextual link was an effort to use another book (i.e., not the one currently being discussed) to answer a specific question that Manuel posed about penguin protection. Throughout the discussion, in showing children how they might find solutions to such questions, Anne also tries to be accurate about the type of storms against which penguins have to protect themselves: Penguins endure very bad storms, but those storms are not the tornados or hurricanes that the current read-aloud book covered. In addition to the informational role that this intertextual link plays, it offers children opportunities to engage with important scientific ideas. They reason about the improbability of penguins jumping into the water to protect themselves. They consider behaviors and characteristics relative to a creature's self-protection. The use of *huddle*, a very familiar term to the children, is introduced to describe the penguins' behavior. And, the children also construct a simile for the penguins' huddle ("looks like a wall"). Thus, although the penguin book was not one of the planned read-aloud books of the unit, it ends up being topically related in this first-grade classroom.

Other intertextual links that mostly are initiated by teachers are references to prior classroom discourse. The references usually serve as a means to bring in and validate children's prior ideas. Example 2 shows how the teacher makes two links to reiterate the earlier contributions of two children.

Example 2: *When a Storm Comes Up* (Fowler, 1995)

1   Anne: .... I've got two or three more pages, and I'd really like to finish the book. I think you'd like to hear the rest of it. Now the next picture is going to be showing you a scientist. He's looking at his data. That's what he is doing right here. He works for a <u>big</u> government agency that looks at weather. A WEATHER SERVICE THAT WORKS TO LEARN WHEN A HURRICANE OR TORNADO IS FORMING AND WHICH WAY {IT'S} GOING. So they can tell us. THE WEATHER SERVICE TRIES TO WARN THE PEOPLE WHO LIVE ALONG THE STORM'S PATH IN TIME FOR THEM TO LEAVE. **Or to go, like you said, your brother // to go downstairs into shelter, lower levels**.

2   Manuel: Go underground.

3   Anne: Uh huh. If we have// in school, we go out in the hall. We have a very special place to stand if there's a tornado that will come. Even, even a practice // we might have one. **You know, probably in the month of March when it does // just like Alexandra said**. If it gets to // it changes when it changes to spring and it gets more sunny and all of those things. IN THIS WAY, MANY LIVES CAN BE SAVED BUT NOTHING CAN

STOP // {YOU CAN'T} STOP A TORNADO OR A HURRI-
CANE.

Anne finishes up the last pages of the book, but in doing so she refers back
to something that Manuel and Alexandra had said previously. Manuel had re-
counted an event about his brother going downstairs during tornado warn-
ings, and Anne connects this event with the present content of the book
being read. She also gives credit to Alexandra's prior comment about when
tornadoes commonly occur—the month of March. Both intertextual links
have a validating function—acknowledging and valuing children's contributions, giving these contributions explicit social significance.

In addition to making available connections to other information books
in the classroom and to prior classroom discourse, teachers often refer to
hands-on explorations. Example 3 illustrates two such connections made
by Anne and one made by Pedro.

Example 3: *Down Comes the Rain* (Branley, 1997)

1   Anne: WATER VAPOR IS MADE WHEN WATER EVAPORATES.
             THAT MEANS THE WATER CHANGES FROM A LIQUID TO
             A GAS. The speech bubbles say, IN THE MORNING, PUT A
             TEASPOON OF WATER {RIGHT HERE} IN {THIS} SAUCER
             {AND} BY THAT NIGHT, IT MAY HAVE EVAPORATED INTO
             THE AIR! **#I wonder if we did something in our classroom
             that maybe was just like that.#**

2   Emilio: #Last time um last time#*...

3   Anne: #Did we do something in our classroom that's just like that?#

4   Cl: #Mrs. Barry? Mrs. Barry?#

5   Anne: Any ideas?

6   Pedro: Yes. **Those little jars**.

7   Anne: What? The little jars. What about*...

8   Pedro: We left them for <days.>

9   Anne: We left them for how many?

10 Cl: Days.

11 Anne: Well, for days, didn't we? What's happening?

12 Pedro: The // the water's all getting lower.

13 Anne: The water's getting lower which means the water is what?

14 Abygail: #It's gonna disappear. It's disappearing.#

15 C2:   # Ms. Barry uh.#

16 C3:   #It's <going> into a gas.#

17 Anne: It's getting into a gas. Yes.

18 Emilio: It's turning air // it's turning into air.

....

19 Manuel: When the sun comes then uh the water dries.

20 Anne: Okay. So the sun had a little bit to do with it, doesn't it? #With the water getting into being a vapor.#

21 Cm1:   #(***) it dries off. # <If it's> hot it dries it off.

22 Anne: So if it's hotter, it dries it.

23 Cs: Off.

24 Anne: Off. Might it // might it dry it off quicker?

25 C2:   #Then what does that (*** ***)#.

26 Anne: **#What about our towels?# That were out? Maybe you could think about that one?** [Anne addresses behavior.]

27 Cm1:   The // the air was in 'cause there was enough space.

28 Anne: There was enough space for it to dry.

In unit 1, after reading about the experiment being described in the book, Anne provided the first link by hinting at an evaporation exploration that had been ongoing in the unit. Early in the unit, "those little jars"—which Pedro (unit 6) referred to as the second intertextual link—had been placed at different locations in the classroom, such as near the window, in the closet, and so forth. Children periodically checked them and wrote about their observations in their journals. In unit 12, Pedro further notes, "the water's all getting lower." When Anne asks for more elaboration about the water, Abygail remarks that "it's disappearing," and another child says that it is turning into a gas. Emilio follows up by stating that the water is "turning into air." Then, Manuel (unit 19) relates the sun to the water drying, and Anne, using Manuel's language, confirms the sun as a factor in the evaporation process. Then, she takes the drying theme further by referring to another evaporation activity in the classroom (the third link). This was the experiment that had children examining what happens when wet paper towels are put in three different conditions—crumpled up, lying on a flat surface, and hanging up. The children begin to examine it in more detail, but the rest of the discussion is not included here. Thus, Anne's and Pedro's intertextual links allow the children to reexamine their understandings from the experiments and relate them to similar ones on evaporation that are presented and explained via more technical language in the book. Thus, the links offer the children opportunities to bring up their observations (water getting lower) and interpretations of these observations (disappearing, going into gas, turning into air, or drying off from the sun), leaving the meanings and language tentative to be explored further.

Intertextuality usually involves references to prior texts or past experiences. However, we have expanded the notion of intertextuality to consider links in the future as well. For example, Anne and Amy often refer to the writing their students would be doing in relation to explorations or activities of the unit. Future-related intertextual connections also occur with respect to hands-on explorations. Example 4 illustrates such a link, plus a link to prior explorations offered by Amy.

Example 4: *Down Comes the Rain* (Branley, 1997)

1	Amy:	.... MOST OF THE WATER VAPOR IN THE AIR COMES FROM LAKES, RIVERS, AND OCEANS. IT COMES FROM THE LEAVES OF PLANTS, AND FROM THE WET GROUND. Yes, Roberto.
2	Roberto:	Um (*** ***) a cup of juice on the table*...
3	Amy:	Can you say it a little bit louder?
4	Roberto:	**If you left like juice on the table, would it evaporate?**
5	Amy:	If you left juice on the table would it evaporate? What do you think?
6	Cs:	No.
7	Brittany:	Only if you set it in the light it will.
8	Amy:	Only if you set it in the light it will. Who else has an idea? If we put juice—juice is a liquid—if we put it on the table, do you think it will evaporate?
9	Cs:	No. (*** ***)
10	Amy:	Pamela.
11	Pamela:	I think only water can evaporate.
12	Amy:	You think only water can evaporate. Is there any water in juice?
13	Pamela:	No.
14	Cs:	(*** ***)

15 Cl: Uh huh, uh huh.

16 Amy: Ahh, now wait a minute. So, so water // juice can be a mixture of things.

17 Pamela: Yeah.

18 Amy: Okay. So do you think that some of it might evaporate?

19 Pamela: [Nods]

20 Amy: Maybe some. But // and you think it would help if we put it in the light. Any other ideas about that?

21 Brittany: If it was // if it was by the light in the um // in by the light, in sun maybe evaporate, maybe if it was on the um // on the ledge or on the window sill or if it was on the table.

22 Amy: Maybe one of you can try that at home. Put a little bit of a juice, some kind of a juice into a cup and **put a piece of tape on the cup the way we did, and mark "Don't Drink" on your cups. And mark the cup**. Maybe try it over the weekend and see if // see if you notice any changes. One of you can try it and report back to us.

23 Cl: Is that homework?

24 Amy: No, it's not homework. But if one of you wants to try that, take a little bit of juice, or Kool-Aid, or something, put it in a cup, see what happens. Let us know. I'm not sure. I've never // I've never tried evaporation with juice. Shh... Craig.

25 Craig: Um, that's gonna be wasting my Kool-Aid.

26 Amy: No, that's why I said a little bit. Didn't I, right? A little tiny bit. You don't need to put a lot.

Roberto initiates an intertextual link to a future exploration—"if you left like juice on the table, would it evaporate?" He poses a hypothetical situation that leads to negotiation and further construction of the meaning of evaporation. His link is taken up by Amy and several children, thereby giving his contribution social significance and recognition. As the discourse unfolds, the children's conception about the necessity of light in order for evaporation to take place surfaces. The teacher leaves this as a tentative meaning open to examination—"And you think it would help if we put it in the light. Any other ideas about that?" Furthermore, Roberto's link allows Amy to encourage the children to perform an exploration at home that would answer Roberto's question. His intertextual link is expanded by Amy's intertextual link in unit 22. She reviews some experimental procedures, such as marking the cup and keeping track of where the juice level started, that had been used in the classroom experiments. As the children try to figure out whether they were required to perform this exploration, Craig brings up another concern—reminding the class that Kool-Aid is not to be wasted like water.

In sum, there are several ways in which intertextual links serve as connections within the thematic unit. Most of these links are initiated by teachers (except for intertextual links to future, potential hands-on explorations, which are initiated exclusively by second graders in our examples). However, event-related intertextual connections—which we illustrate and discuss in the following section—are contributed mostly by children.

Event Links: Using Funds of Knowledge to Develop Scientific Talk and Understandings

Another major reason to focus on intertextual links is that they enable us to capture the cultural resources—the funds of knowledge—that participants bring to read-aloud discussions. Too frequently, it is assumed that urban, low-socioeconomic-status children from diverse ethnic and linguistic backgrounds have little or no prior knowledge to bring to discussions about the topics in books, especially typical information books such as the ones used in this thematic unit (Bartolome, 1994; Moll & Gonzalez, 1994). However, children's intertextual links to other books—as well as rhymes, songs, poems, and sayings and media such as television and radio shows and movies—exemplify their cultural resources and counter such negative perceptions. Even more indicative of children's funds of knowledge are instances when they relate events from their lives. These instances were especially prevalent links in our classrooms, and they had an impact on the understandings coconstructed in the read-aloud sessions. The fact that children offer such responses to concepts in the read-aloud books also challenges the misconception about urban, low-socioeconomic-status children's comprehension capabilities.

Event links are significant in another way because they fall within a narrative-scientific language continuum. The continuum ranges from fully narrative tales, to expressions having both narrative and scientific linguistic features, to fully scientific accounts. Thus, event links not only provide important information about how children express and use their past experiences to make sense of scientific ideas in the read-aloud books, but they also offer a window into the paths that children take to develop scientific talk. That is, teachers get to see the ways in which students move from life-world understandings and language to new scientific ideas and linguistic genres (Gee, 2001; Lemke, 1990).

Example 5 presents intertextual links as recounts of specific events—a set of various children's contributions as Amy invites her class to talk more about actual storms during the read-aloud session of *When a Storm Comes Up*.

Example 5: *When a Storm Comes Up* (Fowler, 1995)

1   Amy: Let's talk more about the actual storms and things that we're discussing right now. Antonio.

2   Antonio: **Last // one day I went to a tunnel, um, there was like a lot of water <coming up> but escaped from there**.

3   Amy: Oh, you were in a tunnel that had a lot of water. Okay ....

4   Amy: Okay. Anything else about hurricanes or tornados <from what we were just reading>? Brittany. Shh, alright then, keep your hand up.

5   Brittany: **Um [one day] when we // when I was in my uncle's car and he was getting ready for me // and he was picking me up from school because it was // it was time to go 'cause we had half a day and then when he // when he started the car he started to go back 'cause he wanted to go front but it went back 'cause all the snow all the snow was on the ground (*** ***). And there was ice on the ground and then he started to go // go back**.

6   Amy: Yeah, it's slippery sometimes on the ground, isn't it? You're right. Khalif, one at a time, please.

....

7   Elena: **When me and my mom went to Ohio, um...um, last year, 1999 // 1988, um, there was an earthquake and I was sleeping downstairs. And then there was a vase in the bathroom and then it broke, so my mom when she got up, she went to go use the bathroom and everything was broken in the // in the bathroom, and then she wiped it // she was cleaning it up. And then when I // when I // when I went to the bath // when I went to go use // went to go take a shower, there was like one piece left on the floor of glass, so I stepped on it and it got stuck all the way in**

my foot, so I went to my mom's // my mom's doctor in Ohio. And the // the doctor, he had these glasses that he took one piece, and he took something // he had glasses or something like that // and he took it off so I had to hold on to somebody real tight.

8 Amy: Yeah, I'll bet. #(*** ***)#

9 Elena: #Their whole arm got so red.#

10 Amy: Storms can cause all kinds of different things like that to happen and earthquakes and things like that and hurricanes. Okay.

11 Roberto: Last year when we had the <snow blizzard, um, we build up all the snow and (***) in the snow> and then I stepped in it, and I could climb over the fence. I only needed to jump over the fence.

12 Amy: Yeah, sometimes the snow gets so tall and when we pile it up, sure, it can be quite a bit of snow. We got almost two feet of snow I think last year during that snowstorm that we had. That was definitely a blizzard. It's definitely what we would call a blizzard. Kristina.

13 Kristina: Well, one time a long time ago when I went to play outside...and I came back in, I was so cold um..., me and my aunt we <warmed> up hot chocolate and I told everybody to come upstairs or if they were upstairs to come (*** ***). And then I put up a sign on the window and <everywhere around the house> and it said // and the sign said "Snow Day" and then um I gave everybody hot chocolate and we watched um (***).

14 Amy: That sounds nice. A lot of times when // a lot of times when the weather is bad outside, right, we need to stay inside, inside our shelter so we can be warm and safe from // from the weather.

In this excerpt, five children initiate intertextual links to specific events they were involved in. As the children recount these experiences, they, Amy, or both use the specific events to highlight important ideas related to storms and their impact. Antonio's link captures the dramatic aspect of flooding. Brittany's link brings up the slippery property of snow and its impact on a car's movement. Elena's link focuses on the (indirect) damage caused by earthquakes. Roberto's link associates snow blizzards with a big amount of snow. And Kristina's link gives Amy the opportunity to emphasize the need for seeking shelter away from storms. All these links to personal specific events also allow the children to bring up affective elements of their experiences (e.g., fear, surprise, excitement, anxiety, and joy), thus making more explicit the interplay of affective and cognitive dimensions of experiences and linking them with science.

These intertextual links are expressed as ministories or mininarratives. As such, they include personal pronouns (*I*, *my*, and *we*), past-tense verbs (*went*, *escaped*, *was sleeping*, *stepped*, and *came back*), and temporal adverbs and conjunctions (*one day*, *last year*, and *and then*). Sometimes, these event links may include dialogue (see "Mommy, Mommy!" example in Table 9.1, Category III, 1b).

However, recounts of generalized events differ from recounts of specific events in that speakers refer to events and actions that have been habitually experienced rather than relating particular events. Example 6 shows the former kind of event link. Before reading *Air Is All Around You* (Branley, 1986), which talks about what happens when a cup with a piece of napkin stuck at its bottom is submerged upside down in water, Amy's class had made some predictions and Amy had demonstrated the experiment. Then, as Amy reads the book, Roberto recounts a generalized event. The classroom demonstration materials are available for him to illustrate his habitual action.

Example 6: *Air Is All Around You* (Branley, 1986)

1	Roberto:	**This is what I do in the bathtub.** [He takes the cup, pushes it into the water upside down, and then lets go of it.]
2	Amy:	Turn it upside down, and then let it go. And what pushes it up? What do you think pushes it up?
3	Cs:	#The water!#
4	Roberto:	#It's like the air, it's \<the\> water. And then // and then when I took it out [he fills the cup up and picks it up out of the water], it was heavy because there was water.
5	Antonio:	[Antonio gets up and wants to try manipulating the cup in the water.]
6	Amy:	Okay, alright, we're all gonna get a chance in a minute.
7	Antonio:	[Takes the cup and begins dipping it.] \<And\> like this...just like this \<with\> the whole thing \<and that goes\> down.
8	Amy:	Alright, let's read some more.

9	Cs:	(*** ***)
10	Elena:	It stayed down.
11	Amy:	That's okay, because // why? Why did it stay down now? Why isn't it floating now? Diego.
12	Diego:	Because the water's inside.
13	Amy:	Oh, because the water's inside the cup. Alright, let's read.

Roberto's intertextual connection to a habitual action in which he himself has been involved offers the class the opportunity to explore floating and sinking, despite the fact that this topic is not the focus at the moment. Roberto's contribution gains social significance as Amy encourages him to share more of his thinking with the class and as other children (including Antonio, Elena, and Diego) contribute their sense making of the phenomenon. We also notice in this excerpt Amy's pull between continuing the read-aloud and not missing out on opportunities to get the children to reveal and verbalize their thinking.

The following are other examples of generalized events taken from both Anne's and Amy's classes during different read-aloud sessions:

- **My brother gets scared of the thunder**.
- **When I'm taking a bath when // when I let the water out // when it gets to the last // when it goes down the drain, it looks like a tornado**.
- **Sometimes my brother cooks for my mom**.
- **<During a tornado warning> you got to go downstairs // like my brother, he goes downstairs, that's his room // got to go downstairs**.

These examples include the personal pronouns that are found in specific event recountings, but now some scientific linguistic features are included. For example, instead of past-tense verbs, present-tense verbs (*is*, *gets*, *goes*, *looks*, and *cooks*) are used, and temporal wordings emerge such as *sometimes* and *when I'm...*, which indicate habitual, ongoing times (as opposed to the specific times that are expressed in recountings of specific events). Thus, these intertextual links are midway on the narrative-scientific language continuum.

The implicit generalized events, then, move to the other end of the narrative-scientific language continuum as speakers tell of events that they must have somehow experienced, but there is no explicit mention of personal involvement in these events. In Example 7, the class has been discussing the part of *What Is the World Made Of? All About Solids, Liquids, and Gases* (Zoehfeld, 1998) that covers liquids, and they have been considering different liquids (e.g., water, milkshakes, and vegetable oil) and their relative thicknesses in terms of their relative speeds of flowing from a container.

Example 7: *What Is the World Made Of?* (Zoehfeld, 1998)

1 Mitch: I know something!

2 Amy: What do you know, Mitch? Tell us.

3 Mitch: **Like um...when you leave your milk // when you leave your milk for a long time in the refrigerator, it will become thick**.

4 Amy: Oh, it will become thick, you're right, when it gets spoiled. We call that curdling. If it comes... // yeah, like cream. Uh huh.

5 Mitch: <It'll become> like cream. And sometimes*...

6 Amy: And what else, Mitch?

7 Mitch: When you have syrup...and uh a milkshake // the milkshake's gonna go faster because it's like // 'cause when you pour the uh*...

8 C1: The syrup.

9 Mitch: The syrup*...

10 Amy: Uh huh.

11 Mitch: It goes slow 'cause it's more thick and like...sticky.

12 Amy: Sticky and thick. Syrup yeah, it goes real slow, doesn't it? Kind of drips down.

Mitch brings up an intertextual link to an implicit generalized event—milk spoiling, or curdling, as Amy explains. Mitch's link is related to the discussion that was generated from an earlier implicit generalized link (not included here) and offers a new example that is not in the read-aloud text. Amy and Mitch propose and discuss ideas and coconstruct language for describing properties of liquids, thereby providing social significance for these links.

Other examples of implicit generalized events that children have initiated in Anne's and Amy's classes in various read-aloud sessions are as follows:

- **When you put your flag in the car, and you have (***), it goes <back and forth like a car>.**

- **You know how water um and snow comes like a ice cube togeth-er...and when you feel it, it feels like water like snow and water like... // like if you feel water**.
- **Sometimes when it's [soup's] way // not hot enough, you put it in your microwave and zap it**.

In these implicit, generalized event links, typical scientific language is used—present-tense verbs, generic nouns, third-person (rather than personal) or the general "you" pronouns, *if-then* or *when-then* and *because* constructions, and so forth.

Information Books as Important Cultural Tools for Developing Scientific Understandings and Language

Intertextuality in Dialogic Inquiry

The aim of this chapter is to show how intertextual links—the referencing of texts, broadly defined—operate in dialogically oriented read-aloud sessions of information books in a States of Matter unit. We have shared examples of links among various components within the unit and event links that highlight primary grade, urban children's funds of knowledge. These examples illustrate the various ways in which the links operate in the classroom discourse to foster dialogic inquiry—ways through which both students and their teachers coconstruct and express scientific ideas stemming from the read-aloud books (Vygotsky, 1934/1987).

In all the examples, Anne and Amy have important roles to play in recognizing, acknowledging, and underscoring the social significance of intertextual links. Teacher-initiated intertextual links are frequent in connecting ideas in the read-alouds and other explorations and activities in the unit. Even these teacher-initiated links, however, often are sparked by a student question or remark—as in Example 1 when Anne refers to a book on penguins to answer Manuel's question about how penguins protect themselves during a tornado. Many of the prior classroom links that the teachers have made serve as means to validate the prior ideas that children had provided (see Example 2). Finally, the teachers' intertextual links also help to connect the scientific concepts and processes covered in the books with the embodied meanings in the hands-on explorations (see Examples 3 and 4). Even the teacher-initiated links offer children opportunities for their voices to be heard and their ideas to shape the talk and the meanings developed.

The event intertextual links reveal the ways in which these urban children bring facets of their lives into the read-aloud sessions. For example, they show how affect and cognition are intertwined in recounting specific events, such as when children tell of the storms they have experienced (see Example 5). Generalized event links indicate how children make sense of book concepts via participation in repeated, habitual events, such as when Roberto explains the floating and sinking ideas related to the hands-on activities covered in a read-aloud book and in class (see Example 6). The implicit generalized event links do not mention explicit involvement but offer insights into events children must/could have observed or experienced such as Mitch's account of milk becoming thick when it spoils or curdles (see Example 7).

Information Books as Critical Cultural Tools

Scientific activity consists of two major, interrelated elements—developing theories (the theoretical element) and collecting and analyzing data (the empirical element). A theory is a network of concepts and ideas linked logically together that have explanatory power. It is not just the formulation of isolated hypotheses or predictions. In contrast, data include information collected through observations and experiments. Both elements interact with and influence each other and are integral to the practice of science (Varelas, 1996). In the States of Matter unit, children have many opportunities to be involved in both of these components of scientific activity. Of course, the hands-on explorations that the children and their teachers work on are also important tools. As they talk and write about what they are observing, the children and teachers offer various ways of explaining their data, thus engaging in theorizing. But information books play a critical role, too. These books provide ways of understanding and relating concepts and ideas, as well as formal examinations of students' everyday experiences and scientific phenomena. Moreover, the read-aloud sessions of information books become occasions during which event intertextuality links occur. When discussing such links, the children and teachers refer explicitly or implicitly to "data" they have. These data sometimes are experiences in the world, but many times students also wrap these data around their ways of making sense of and theorizing about them (e.g., Kristina's chapter-opening example). Thus, event intertextuality is many times the catalyst for the "theory-data dance" (Varelas, Luster, & Wenzel, 1999).

Furthermore, another analysis (Varelas & Pappas, 2002) that we have completed reveals an interesting and important trend over time regarding the three types of event links. Across the seven read-aloud sessions, the fully narrative recounting of specific events decrease and the more scientific-type recountings—those about generalized events and implicit generalized events—increase. Thus, information book read-aloud sessions foster scientific understandings and teach students how to express these ideas in scientific language. This finding is significant because it shows that the colloquial lifeworld language (Gee, 2001) of urban children from various ethnic and linguistic backgrounds can be generative and transformative in promoting scientific understandings and talk in the dialogically oriented read-alouds (Kress, 1999; Lemke, 1990). If they are viewed as "knowers" and given opportunities to offer their ideas for teachers to take up and extend, urban children have the cultural resources to develop new ways of talking to go with their learning new ways of scientific thinking (Sutton, 1992). Thus, information books, used in the ways we have illustrated in this chapter, can serve as critical cultural tools (Wells, 1999; Wertsch, 1991) in this process.

Authors' Note

This project was funded by the University of Illinois at Chicago's (UIC) Center for Urban Educational Research and Development, the Research Foundation of the National Council of Teachers of English, and the UIC Campus Research Board. The data presented, the statements made, and the views expressed in this chapter are solely the responsibility of the authors. Joint authorship of this chapter belongs to Pappas and Varelas, who are listed alphabetically here; Barry and Rife were collaborating teacher researchers and also are listed alphabetically.

REFERENCES

Bartolome, L.I. (1994). Beyond the methods fetish: Toward a humanizing pedagogy. *Harvard Educational Review, 64,* 173–194.

Bloome, D., & Egan-Robertson, A. (1993). The social construction of intertextuality in classroom reading and writing lessons. *Reading Research Quarterly, 28,* 305–333.

Cazden, C.B. (2001). *Classroom discourse: The language of teaching and learning.* Portsmouth, NH: Heinemann.

Donovan, C.A. (2001). Children's development and control of written story and informational genres: Insights from one elementary school. *Research in the Teaching of English, 35,* 394–447.

Duke, N.K. (2000). 3.6 minutes per day: The scarcity of informational texts in first grade. *Reading Research Quarterly, 35,* 202–224.

Duke, N.K., & Kays, J. (1998). "Can I say 'Once upon a time'?" Kindergarten children developing knowledge of information book language. *Early Childhood Quarterly, 13,* 295–318.

Gee, J.P. (2001, August). *Languages in the science classroom: Academic social languages as the heart of school-based literacy.* Paper presented at the National Science Foundation's Crossing Borders: Connecting Science and Literacy conference, Baltimore, MD.

Goldman, S.R., & Bisanz, G.L. (2002). Toward a functional analysis of scientific genres: Implications for understanding and learning processes. In J. Otero, J.A. Leon, & A.C. Graesser (Eds.), *The psychology of science text comprehension* (pp. 19–50). Mahwah, NJ: Erlbaum.

Halliday, M.A.K., & Martin, J.R. (1993). *Writing science: Literacy and discursive power*. Pittsburgh, PA: University of Pittsburgh Press.

Kamberelis, G. (1999). Genre development and learning: Children writing stories, science reports, and poems. *Research in the Teaching of English, 33*, 403–460.

Kress, G. (1999). Genre and the changing contexts for English language arts. *Language Arts, 76*(6), 461–469.

Lemke, J.L. (1990). *Talking science: Language, learning, and values*. Westport, CT: Ablex.

Lindfors, J.W. (1999). *Children's inquiry: Using language to make sense of the world*. New York: Teachers College Press.

Lotman, Y.M. (1988). Text within a text. *Soviet Psychology, 26*(3), 32–51.

Moll, L.C., & Gonzalez, N. (1994). Lessons from research with language-minority children. *Journal of Reading Behavior, 26*(4), 439–456.

Newkirk, T. (1989). *More than stories: The range of children's writings*. Portsmouth, NH: Heinemann.

Nystrand, M. (1997). *Opening dialogue: Understanding the dynamics of language and learning in the English classroom*. New York: Teachers College Press.

Ogborn, J., Kress, G., Martins, I., & McGillicuddy, K. (1996). *Explaining science in the classroom*. Buckingham, UK: Open University Press.

Oyler, C. (1996). Sharing authority: Student initiations during teacher-led read-alouds of information books. *Teaching and Teacher Education, 12*(2), 149–160.

Palincsar, A.S., & Magnusson, S.J. (1997, December). *The role of text in supporting and extending first-hand investigations in guided inquiry science instruction*. Paper presented at the National Reading Conference, Scottsdale, AZ.

Pappas, C.C. (1993). Is narrative "primary"? Some insights from kindergarteners' pretend readings of stories and information books. *Journal of Reading Behavior, 25*, 97–129.

Pappas, C.C. (1997). Reading instruction in an integrated language perspective: Collaborative interaction in classroom curriculum genres. In S.A. Stahl & D.A. Hayes (Eds.), *Instructional models in reading* (pp. 283–310). Hillsdale, NJ: Erlbaum.

Pappas, C.C., Kiefer, B.Z., & Levstik, L.S. (1999). *An integrated language perspective in the elementary school: An action approach* (3rd ed.). New York: Longman.

Pappas, C.C., Varelas, M., Barry, A., & Rife, A. (2003). Dialogic inquiry around information books: The role of intertextuality in constructing scientific understandings in urban primary classrooms. *Linguistics and Education, 13*, 435–482.

Pappas, C.C., & Zecker, L.B. (Eds.). (2001). *Working with teacher researchers in urban classrooms: Transforming literacy curriculum genres*. Mahwah, NJ: Erlbaum.

Shymansky, J.A., Yore, L.D., & Good, R. (1991). Elementary school teachers' beliefs about perceptions of elementary school science, science reading, science textbooks, and supportive instructional factors. *Journal of Research in Science Teaching, 28*, 437–454.

Sutton, C. (1992). *Words, science, and learning*. Buckingham, UK: Open University Press.

Varelas, M. (1996). Between theory and data in a seventh-grade science class. *Journal of Research in Science Teaching, 33*(3), 229–263.

Varelas, M., Luster, B., & Wenzel, S. (1999). Meaning making in a community of learners: Struggles and possibilities in an urban science class. *Research in Science Education, 29*(2), 227–245.

Varelas, M., & Pappas, C.C. (2002, June). *Exploring meaning-making in integrated primary science-literacy units: The nature of intertextuality*. Paper presented at the joint conference of the Society for Text and Discourse and the Society for the Scientific Study of Reading, Chicago, IL.

Vygotsky, L.S. (1987). Thinking and speech. In R.W. Rieber & A.S. Carton (Eds.), *The collected works of L.S. Vygotsky: Problems of general psychology* (N. Minick, Trans., pp. 39–285). New York: Plenum. (Original work published 1934)

Wells, G. (1990). Talk about text: Where literacy is learned and taught. *Curriculum Inquiry, 20*, 369–405.

Wells, G. (1999). *Dialogic inquiry: Towards a sociocultural practice and theory of education.* New York: Cambridge University Press.

Wertsch, J.V. (1991). *Voices of the mind: A sociocultural approach to mediated action.* Cambridge, MA: Harvard University Press.

Wollman-Bonilla, J.E. (2000). Teaching science writing to first graders: Genre learning and recontextualization. *Research in the Teaching of English, 35*, 35–65.

CHILDREN'S LITERATURE CITED

Branley, F.M. (1986). *Air is all around you.* Ill. H. Keller. New York: HarperTrophy.

Branley, F.M. (1986). *Snow is falling.* Ill. H. Keller. New York: HarperCollins.

Branley, F.M. (1997). *Down comes the rain.* Ill. J.G. Hale. New York: HarperTrophy.

Branley, F.M. (1999). *Flash, crash, rumble, and roll.* New York: HarperCollins.

Canizares, S., & Chanko, P. (1998). *Water.* New York: Scholastic.

DeWitt, L. (1991). *What will the weather be?* Ill. C. Croll. New York: HarperCollins.

Dorros, A. (Ill.). (1989). *Feel the wind.* New York: Crowell.

Fowler, A. (1991). *What's the weather today?* San Francisco: Children's Book Press.

Fowler, A. (1995). *When a storm comes up.* San Francisco: Children's Book Press.

Fowler, A. (1996). *What do you see in a cloud?* San Francisco: Children's Book Press.

Zoehfeld, K.W. (1998). *What is the world made of? All about solids, liquids, and gases.* Ill. P. Meisel. New York: HarperTrophy.

Appendix: Conventions of Transcription for Classroom Discourse Examples

Key for Speakers:	First name is listed for teacher researcher. Pseudonym first name is noted for an identified child. *C, C1, C2*, and so forth are noted for individual children (with *m* or *f* to refer to the gender of a child): *C* is used if a child's voice cannot be identified; *C* followed with a number is used to identify a particular child in a particular section of the transcript (so that *C1* or *C2*, etc., is not necessary the same child throughout the whole transcript). *Cs* represents many children speaking simultaneously.
//	False starts or abandoned language replaced by new language structures
...	Small or short pause within sentence
... ...	Longer pause within sentence
*...	Breaking off of a speaker's turn because of the next speaker's turn
< >	Uncertain words
(***)	One word that is inaudible or impossible to transcribe
(*** ***)	Longer stretches of language that are inaudible and impossible to transcribe
Underscore	Emphasis
# #	Overlapping language spoken by two or more speakers at a time
CAPS	Actual reading of a book
{ }	Teacher's miscue or modification of text being read aloud
[ ]	Identifies gestures and other nonverbal contextual information
....	Omitted part of a transcript

CHAPTER 10

Improving Science Instruction With Information Books: Understanding Multimodal Presentations

LAURA B. SMOLKIN AND CAROL A. DONOVAN

A s our previous writings have indicated (Donovan & Smolkin, 2001, 2002; Smolkin & Donovan, 2001; see also chapter 16 in this volume), we are committed to the use of trade books in science instruction. We believe that teachers who choose to use trade books are doing so because they want their science instruction tailored to their students' interests and needs. Often, however, teachers may read the books aloud without making the best possible use of the books' features to deepen students' understandings of the content or to support students' future encounters with texts on their own (Smolkin & Donovan, 2001). Given Peacock and Gates's (2000) findings on new teachers' views of science texts and our own (Donovan & Smolkin, 2001) findings on experienced teachers' views of science texts, what seems to be needed is further assistance with how to look at text materials for teaching science. In this chapter, we take the stance that encounters with science texts are multimodal, or multiliteracy, experiences. We apply this stance to two subgenres of science trade books—the narrative information book and the nonnarrative information book. Two of noted information book writer Gail Gibbons's science books serve to demonstrate how teachers might examine information books to enhance not only their science teaching but also children's comprehension of science texts. Because some of our analysis is visual, we recommend reading this chapter with copies of Gibbons's *Weather Words and What They Mean* (1990) and *From Seed to Plant* (1991) close at hand.

Science Texts as Multimedia, Multimodal Experiences

Perhaps more than any other discipline, science involves multiple modes of making meaning. Teachers use gestures and animations of objects accompanied by verbal commentary as they seek to explain how things work in the world. They also communicate through other visual channels such as drawing diagrams or displaying pictures. Science ideas are communicated through written texts as well, either as teachers read aloud or as children read to themselves. In his discussion of multimedia genres in science, Lemke (1998) makes clear that scientific communication is far more than a verbal system:

> When scientists think, talk, write, work and teach...they do not just use words;...they combine, interconnect, and integrate verbal text with mathematical expressions, quantitative graphs, information tables, abstract diagrams, maps, drawings, photographs and a host of unique specialised visual genres seen nowhere else. (p. 88)

When Lemke surveyed professional science materials, he found that they contained very high numbers of graphic displays, usually at least one such visual display per page of running text. His discussion of multiple meanings notes that visual figures in scientific text are usually "*not* redundant with the verbal main text" (Lemke, 1998, p. 105). Instead of simply illustrating the text concepts, visual representations add information and complement (or compete with) the text.

Kress, Jewitt, Ogborn, and Tsatsarelis (2001) take this idea one step further, suggesting that certain modes may work better than other modes for particular purposes. For those attempting to convey scientific information, the question becomes, "If there are these various modes, and they have different affordances [possibilities], which mode shall I use for what purpose?" (p. 2). Gibbons, who both illustrates and writes her own texts, has commented on the different roles of text and pictures in her books:

> I know that the pictures will show stuff that I won't have to say. They carry information that I won't have to write about. And I don't want to put that down on paper if the picture will be explaining it. (Personal communication, March 21, 2002)

Science-related trade books such as Gibbons's communicate through an array of visual structures—graphs, tables, pyramids, diagrams, cutaways, food chains, and so on. Authors and illustrators make decisions regarding pictures and various other types of graphic representations to contextualize, reinforce, clarify, extend, and expand verbal explanations that appear in the written text. To make the best use of science information books, teachers need to view these texts in terms of at least two modes of communication—the verbal and the visual.

Verbal Communication

To assist us in our discussion of the verbal aspects of science trade books, we rely upon the works of systemic functional linguists (e.g., Halliday, 1985; Hasan, 1984; Martin, 1992; Unsworth, 2001). Systemic functional linguists seek to understand how the structure of language has been affected by the ways we use language for different purposes and in different situations. Basically, these linguists suggest that in order to understand what is meant through language, we need to consider how different lexical items function within a particular structure. Halliday (1985) saw lexical/grammatical choices as falling into three broad metafunctions—ideational, interpersonal, and textual. Each metafunction addresses a different component of the world in which we are communicating; each metafunction concerns a different type of meaning conveyed in a clause.

When an author sits down to write a trade book on a particular science topic, he or she makes decisions about the type of text he or she is going to compose. In this case, let us suppose the author wishes to inform children about the weather. This is the function, or social purpose, of his or her text. Different aspects of the author's particular situation will determine the shape of his or her effort. For instance, the author will need to determine the audience for this text. A book on weather for upper elementary school children will be different from one for primary students. For older audiences, authors frequently create information books with chapters, but for younger audiences, authors generally use a particular type of picture book format. Each of these formats may be seen as subgenres of children's information books (whose function is to inform). And, as a representative of a particular genre, the book will have certain ordered elements in common with all other books in that genre (Hasan, 1984), constituting its generic structure.

In systemic functional linguistics, the world of meaning-making is seen as consisting of three major variables that will influence choices made in actual language—tenor, field, and mode. When ideas move beyond concept into a language communication system, linguists refer to this area of meaning as the interpersonal metafunction. The relationship between author and audience is termed *tenor* (Martin, 1992). As the tenor is expressed in actual words, through what linguists refer to as lexicogrammatical choices, the author will make decisions about the complexity of sentences and words his or her audience is likely to know. He or she will also make language choices that indicate the veracity of the information. For example, if scientists are not yet sure about a topic, the author may use the phrase "Some scientists think..." or "Scientists believe..." (Gibbons, 1995).

The author also will need to decide upon the content or the subject matter to include for his or her readers. Systemic functional linguists refer to this variable as the *field*, which they say is present in language as the ideational metafunction. Thus, ideas from the field appear in the lexicogrammatical system by showing what happens to what (or to whom) in what circumstances.

Finally, the author will need to make decisions regarding what linguists term *mode*, which begins in language as the textual metafunction. What channels will he or she use to communicate the information? Because the text is a book, instead of a classroom discussion, we know that the channel will be graphic rather than aural. And if the author has decided to create a picture book, we know that a certain amount of the graphic representation will be in a visual form (e.g., pictures, diagrams, and photos) rather than in a completely verbal form (running text). Here, too, are decisions to be made regarding the actual shaping of the text. What ideas belong together in paragraph form? What kinds of cohesive choices must appear in the lexicogrammatical structure to help the reader best link ideas within and between sentences?

Visual Communication

For a long time, the analysis of graphic representations in text proved challenging for those interested in looking at the relationships between the verbal and visual aspects of text. Without a system to examine those relationships, people often turned to principles from art (e.g., Arnheim, 1956), but those ways of looking at pictures did not serve particularly well in linking the meanings of text and graphics. Confronted with this difficulty, Kress and van Leeuwen decided to create "a visual grammar that would be compatible with Halliday's systemic functional grammar...and Martin's theory of cohesion...in other words, a kind of 'visual English'" (van Leeuwen, 2000, p. 276).

Kress and van Leeuwen's (1996) visual grammar operates within the same three-part, metafunctional organization for meaning making that we previously described (but with different terminology): (1) interpersonal (now termed *interactional*), (2) textual (now termed *compositional*), and (3) ideational (now termed *representational*). As with verbal text, the interpersonal resources of graphic representations convey the nature of relationships, and the compositional meanings inform viewers about topics such as relative emphasis among the various elements of the picture. The representational structures serve to inform the viewer about the people, objects, and events involved, set within the circumstances particular to their encounters.

Unsworth (2001) supplies a concise, clear presentation of Kress and van Leeuwen's visual grammar, specifically applied to children's texts and schooling experiences. Within the representational meanings of pictures are efforts to model the material world. There are images that seek to show what is going on between different participants (e.g., beings, objects, and diagram components). There are images that classify, and images that show part or whole relationships (whether labeled or not). There are timelines, and occasionally there are symbolic images that serve to add a further, often affective, meaning. Within the interactional meanings are those aspects that construct the relationships between the viewer and the image. Here are located aspects of visual representations that convey social distance, attitude, and power. Photographs, for example, mirror social relationships between people. People tend to stand closer to those with whom they have more intimate relationships; this intimacy would be portrayed through a close-up shot. People tend to keep their distance from those with whom they have little acquaintance; long shots capture this emotional distance. Also within the interactional meanings are images that reveal more than can be seen from a surface view: cross sections, cutaways, and explosions (an image in which component pieces appear to be "separated or 'exploded' as if ready for assembly" [Unsworth, 2001, p. 101]). Addressed within the interactional metafunction is the question of what counts as real (just as our hypothetical author previously had to determine veracity). Unsworth makes the point that as children move through the grades, the images they encounter move from being mostly naturalistic to "highly schematized images of a scientific coding orientation" (p. 103). Within the third metafunction, compositional meaning, are located aspects that address given and new information, the relative importance of ideas achieved through centering or framing, and aspects of pictures made in some way salient by drawing the eye first to that element.

It is important to note that even the verbal aspect of text, the print, carries visual information (e.g., Lemke, 1998). For instance, in terms of interpersonal meanings, text carries visual information through aspects that indicate importance—italic and bold typefaces or the relative size of the font telling readers, "Pay attention here." And textually or compositionally, it does so through the use of paragraphs and sections, letting readers know which ideas belong together.

Applying Multimodal Analyses to Science Information Books

As we have looked at trade books for science instruction (Donovan & Smolkin, 2001, 2002), we have considered four different genres: stories, dual-purpose texts, narrative information books, and nonnarrative information books. These genres differ in terms of purposes and structures. Stories, based around an event-oriented structure in which characters encounter challenges in certain settings, have as their major function the aesthetic engagement of readers. Similar to stories, dual-purpose texts also present characters involved in various events. These books also seek to aesthetically engage readers, usually by presenting characters in humorous predicaments, but they also intend to convey accurate scientific information. We have termed this type of text dual-purpose books because in some senses they offer readers several choices of reading paths. Those readers who wish to focus on the story alone may do so, and those readers who wish to focus on the pure science content will find paths that allow them to accomplish this end. Some of the best-known books in the dual-purpose category are Cole's and Degen's Magic School Bus books, published by Scholastic.

Then there are the books whose major purpose is to inform. Sometimes these information books, similar to stories and dual-purpose books, are narrative in nature; however, narrative information texts stress the processes, sequences, or time-related patterns in which particular factual phenomena usually occur. They also contain many features in common with our final category—the nonnarrative information book. Nonnarrative information books "describe the way things are" (Kress, 1994, p. 9). These books tend to present a topic and its various subtopics, or attributes. Although nonnarrative information books often contain descriptions of characteristic events (just as narrative information books frequently contain descriptions of attributes), these descriptions usually are found within a given subtopic rather than as part of the overarching generic structure of the text. It is upon these two latter subgenres of information books that we focus our discussion because their primary function is to inform.

In the following sections, we will look first at the verbal features of these two subgenres, and then we will see how they are realized in two of Gibbons's books. Finally, we will look at the visual features of those books.

Verbal Features

Systemic functional linguists adopt a view of language operating on different levels, or planes, with each level contributing to the final realization, or form, of a message. Martin (1992) presents a three-plane model with genre at the top, register (language determined by relationship between participants, subject matter, and channel—written or oral) in the middle, and language at the bottom. Within this model, a text's structure—its elements and their relationships—is determined at the top level, genre. These elements will be visible to us in the generic structures of the text. To some degree, once the genre has been selected, choices at the level of register are predetermined. These generic structures and register choices are discernable through the actual language we can see in a text. In the next two sections, we will examine the generic structure and the actual language of information books.

Generic Structures in Information Books: Elements and Their Order

In 1986, Pappas applied the thinking of systemic functional linguists (particularly Hasan, 1984) to books that children's literature experts usually describe as information books. Pappas's goal was to determine which elements constituted what Hasan (1984) describes as the Generic Structure Potential (GSP). This abstract category would indicate which elements a text of a particular genre must contain (obligatory), which elements it might contain (optional), and the order in which those elements were to occur. Through her analyses, Pappas determined that information books typically contain four obligatory elements and two optional elements. The first obligatory element, the topic presentation, always precedes the others. Descriptions of attributes associated with the topic or class and characteristic events, descriptions of events typically associated with the topic, precede the final element; their orders may be changed. The last obligatory element identified by Pappas is the final summary, a closing statement that sometimes recaps the book's content. Pappas also determined that information books can contain two types of optional elements. The first, category comparisons, serves to contrast members of the class or aspects of the book's topic. This element always appears before the final summary. The second optional element is an afterword, in which authors can include additional information about the topic in a variety of formats.

In terms of the ordering of the elements, topic presentation generally comes first, and the ordering of descriptions of attributes, characteristic events, and category comparisons is variable. The final summary appears after these elements, and the afterword, if there is one, is the last element.

Particular elements also can be interspersed, meaning they might be contained within other elements. As Pappas, Kiefer, and Levstik (1999) explain, "The Topic Presentation can be interspersed in any one of the three elements—Description of Attributes, Characteristic Events, or Category Comparison—and any of these three can be interspersed in each other" (p. 232).

Generic Structure in a Nonnarrative Science Trade Book. Figure 10.1 displays the generic scheme, or global structure, for Gibbons's (1990) nonnarrative text *Weather Words and What They Mean*. The top level in this generic structure shows the title, and the second level shows the major elements of the text. The topic presentation occurs first and is followed by a series of subtopics, which may be seen as attributes of the topic. Within each of the subtopics there are descriptions of attributes. Though not depicted in Figure 10.1, characteristic events are located within these descriptions, as when Gibbons explains that temperatures rise with the rising of the sun and fall with its setting, or that they change with the seasons. Gibbons's final summary in this text consists of two sentences, which simply express that weather changes daily and that that's what makes it interesting. This book contains only one afterword, a piece of the structure that Gibbons herself refers to as "my page 32" (personal communication, March 21, 2002). On this final page, Gibbons includes information that somehow did not fit within the running text or visual displays in the book, either because it would have made the section of text too long or because it was in some way deserving of additional emphasis. Variations on this generic structure are found in many of Gibbons's books as well as other nonnarrative science trade books.

Generic Structure in a Narrative Science Trade Book. Figure 10.2 displays the generic scheme, or global structure, for Gibbons's (1991) narrative information book, *From Seed to Plant*. This book, similar to the nonnarrative text described in Figure 10.1, begins with a topic presentation. However, because this is a narrative information book, its next major element is a sequence of characteristic events. Within this sequence are interspersed descriptions of attributes of the event. For example, under the event Seeds Travel, Gibbons's running text includes several pages devoted to the ways in which seeds travel, such as by floating on water or blowing away. Following the presentation of a full-grown plant, Gibbons concludes her final double-page spread of running text by explaining that people "eat seeds, fruits, and pods" from plants, which are "full of nutrition, vitamins and minerals and...they are tasty too" (n.p.). These sentences certainly do not

FIGURE 10.1
Generic Structure of *Weather Words and What They Mean*

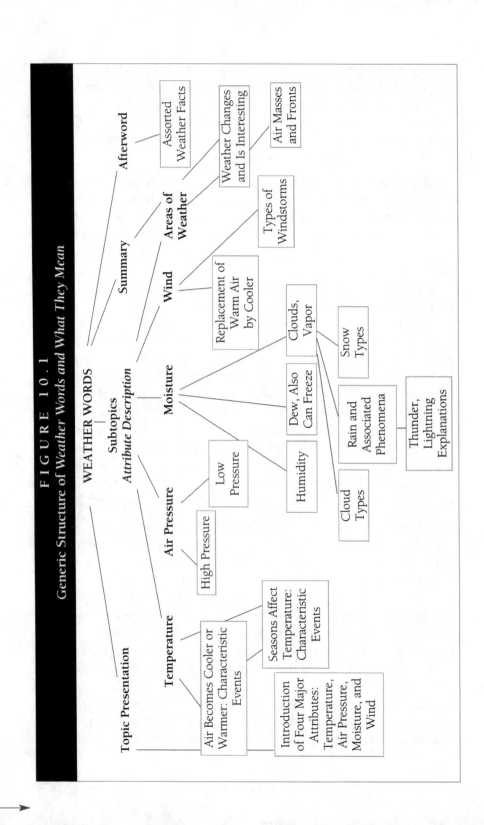

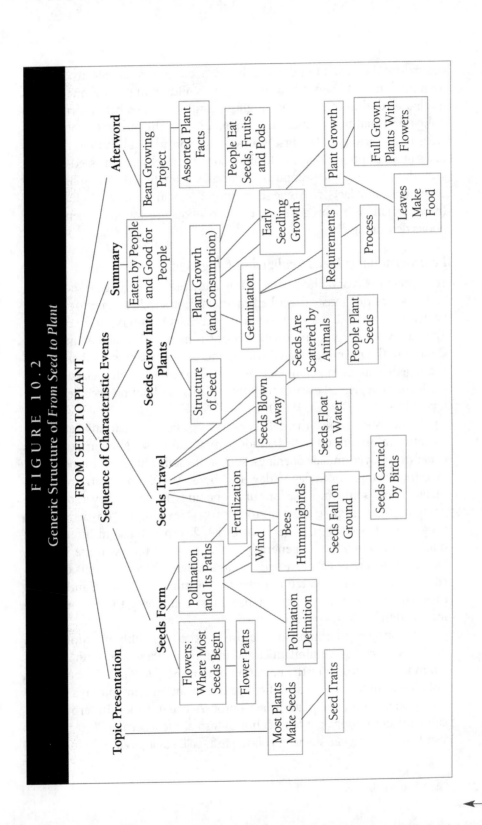

F I G U R E 1 0 . 2
Generic Structure of *From Seed to Plant*

summarize the content of the text, but they do serve as an effective closing for a book meant to engage primary grade children in plant growth. (This has led us to think that *closing* might in some ways be a better term for an obligatory final text element than *summary*.) In this book, Gibbons provides two afterwords. The first is a two-page spread that describes the steps in a suggested project that would allow students to observe the seed-to-plant growth of beans. The second is Gibbons's characteristic "page 32," with such interesting facts as "Some seeds sprout only in the heat of a forest fire" (n.p.). Variations on this genre structure are frequently found in science trade books describing changes over time.

Lexicogrammar: Ideas Realized in Language

To express ideas and choices regarding audience in language (tenor, field, and mode as previously described), writers (and speakers) employ linguistic features such as tense, lexicon (vocabulary), syntax, and cohesion. Typically, vocabulary in information books is more technical than in stories. Cohesion, the meaning created within and between sentences that holds a text together, in information books is created in part through coclassification, the focus on a general class of the topic (plants) and not on specific characters as in stories (Pappas, 1986).

Linguistic features that reflect differences between narrative and non-narrative information books include syntax and tense. Nonnarrative texts usually employ formulaic openings, such as the following topic introduction: "Weather changes from day to day" (Gibbons, 1990, n.p.). Narrative information books sometimes use formulaic openings; however, they also can use openings that resemble those of story texts—for example, "Cassie has been pregnant for two months" (Schilling, 1972, n.p.). Tense in information books, unlike stories, is generally present, or a timeless tense is used. However, in certain narrative information books, when the events of a specific case are being explored in order to generalize to all cases, authors occasionally may employ the past tense. Most commonly, though, narrative information books use present tense.

Looking at the linguistic features of the two Gibbons information books, we can observe similarities and important differences. Both are written in present tense. For the narration of *From Seed to Plant*, Gibbons does not choose to focus on a specific case (the bean seed in Tommy's garden) but speaks of how the plant growth process usually goes. In terms of vocabulary, both books contain technical terms. *From Seed to Plant* includes words such as *stigma, stamens, pollen, pistil, pollination, seed coat,* and *germi-*

nation in its running text, with additional technical terms appearing in the pictures (flower names, *ovules*, and *sepal*) and in the afterword (*annuals, perennials, minerals*, and flower and plant names). *Weather Words and What They Mean* focuses on the technical vocabulary involved in discussions of weather factors, and consequently, it contains many more technical terms—*air pressure, moisture, air particles, vapor, ice crystals, cumulous clouds, cirrus clouds, stratus clouds, evaporates, air mass*, and *boundary*. Also included are more commonplace terms that children are more likely to have heard such as *rain, fog, sleet, breezy*, and *windy*. Gibbons creates cohesion in both books partly through coclassification. Chains of related or repeated terms continue a thread of meaning across several pages (for a pictorial representation of coclassification, see Pappas, 1991). In narrative information books such as *From Seed to Plant*, the word *seed*, for example, is found on 18 different pages of the running text, as the development from seed to plant is explained across the characteristic events. In the nonnarrative *Weather Words and What They Mean*, this type of lexical cohesion through chaining, linking threads of meaning as described above, is visible within the subtopics.

Visual Features: Metafunctions and Subgenres

Our verbal analyses have proceeded from the top-level plane of genre—which indicates obligatory and optional elements of information books—to a look within the third plane at how language reveals various choices from the second plane of register in the writer's meaning-making efforts. Following others working in this area (Kress et al., 2001; Kress & van Leeuwen, 1996; Unsworth, 2001), our visual analyses of these books are based strictly in the third plane—in this case image rather than language. This decision allows us to concentrate on the three essential functions that any communicative, meaning-making system has—representation, interaction, and composition—and how these functions play out in the pictures of science trade books. Our goal in this section is not to be comprehensive in our analysis, nor to claim that every narrative or nonnarrative book will work in the same way as our examples, but to give readers a sense of how more attention to pictures may deepen children's encounters with and understandings of science information books. As before, we use Gibbons's narrative and nonnarrative texts for our examples. Our first section, focusing on the covers, shows the three meaning-making systems in action. Our second section moves inside the books to explore how visual and verbal features work separately and together to present science concepts.

Covers: Setting the Stage Through Three Metafunctions

If we adopt a multimodal view, the distinctions between Gibbons's narrative and nonnarrative texts begin before readers enter the verbal environment between the covers. In this section, we look closely at the cover of each book, noting how Gibbons has worked with representation and composition (and interactional meaning, where appropriate) to set the stage for how each text will convey its science content.

A Visual Environment for a Narrative Presentation. The cover of *From Seed to Plant*, the narrative information book, displays in the upper left-hand corner a sun in the distance. Below the sun and closer to the reader are a seed on the left-hand side and a vigorously growing bean plant (complete with flowers and pea pods) on the right-hand side. Superimposed on a cross-sectional diagram of the soil that reveals the seed and the plant's root system is a framed white box containing the book's title. Its words appear to narrate the progression of images above it and to inform us of what the book will address—how a seed (similar to the one shown) develops into a plant (similar the one shown). To achieve her representational meaning (the ideas), Gibbons employs what Kress and van Leeuwen (1996) term a *vector*. The reader's eyes skim along the white text box beneath the pictures, moving from left to right, from the seed to the plant, and connecting the two in a partial timeline of two stages in which a seed becomes a plant. The cross-sectional diagram plays a role in interactional meaning; the removed soil surface lets readers know that the artist is revealing to them what is normally hidden. In terms of compositional meaning, the left-to-right placement of the seed and the plant follows Kress and van Leeuwen's (1996) "given" and "new" principle: The seed on the left is given, or more known to the viewer, and the effusively growing plant on the right is new "information not yet known to the reader, and hence deserving of his or her special attention" (p. 55). Gibbons draws our eyes to the plant: Its roots break the lower blue, white, and black frame at the bottom of the picture, and its leaves cross the frame at the top of the page and continue beyond the cover itself. This breaking of the frame, this catching of the reader's eye, gives the plant what Kress and van Leeuwen (1996) term *salience*, heightening our sense that this book is about growth, even if that concept is not included in the verbal information of the title.

A Visual Environment for a Nonnarrative Presentation. The cover of Gibbons's nonnarrative information book, *Weather Words and What They Mean*, operates very differently. Three equally sized, separately framed boxes, each of which represents a weather condition or phenomenon, are used instead of a narrative feel similar to the cover of *From Seed to Plant*. These three boxes suggest that readers are looking at an analysis, something that shows parts (in this case, potential subtopics) of a whole (the varied phenomena of weather). This representation reveals the topic-oriented organization of this book: Readers will learn about temperature, thunder and lightning, precipitation, and so forth. Because each separate image is labeled (in this case with a speech balloon), Kress and van Leeuwen (1996) would term them *structured analytical images*. The speech balloons connect human activity with each weather representation, introducing the idea that there are words, technical vocabulary, that allow people to talk about the weather forces that affect them.

As part of the compositional meaning, the three boxes form what Kress and van Leeuwen term a *triptych*, a three-paneled structure that creates symmetry among the different weather depictions. Although triptychs often serve to indicate the progression of the "given" to "new" information as described earlier, in this instance the reader's eyes are drawn to the center box. Spilling from its frame, the speech balloon for "thunder & lightning" encroaches on the space of the temperature depiction; this encroachment and the balloon's larger size make it salient. Readers attend to it more carefully and realize that, unlike the speech balloons in the other two boxes, this balloon emerges from the cumulonimbus cloud rather than from unseen speakers who serve interactionally to bond readers to the other two images. In this way, the sounds of weather (e.g., the rumble of thunder and the crack of lightning) also are introduced into readers' auditory awareness.

Gibbons also has made compositional use of the vertical axis. Unlike the horizontal layout of the cover of *From Seed to Plant*, this vertical presentation speaks less to connection and movement and more to a sense of contrast. Kress and van Leeuwen (1996) explain that "the upper section [of a vertical display] tends to make 'emotive' appeal and show us 'what might be'; the lower section tends to be more informative and practical" (p. 193), and that is exactly how the vertical layout functions here. One can feel the heat radiating from the diagonal orange, yellow, and gold rays surrounding the sun in the left-hand image; the darkness of the cumulonimbus cloud and the sharpness of the lightning in the middle image remind readers of the fear many people feel during a thunderstorm; and the powdered-sugar dots of snow in the right-hand image engender a sense of calm and wonder. Below these emotionally charged images, readers find the practical labels that society has supplied so people can communicate easily about these weather phenomena. The two sections of the book's title work in a similar fashion. Serving as a verbal frame for the weather images, the top section of the title, *Weather Words*, presents more generalized information, and the bottom section of the title, *And What They Mean*, indicates the specific approach the book will take.

Inside the Covers: Continuing Presentations of Genre

In many ways, the visual contents of the books continue in the visual forms established on the covers. *From Seed to Plant* has 19 pages that resemble the cover—single pictures surrounded by frames—and even three pictures that cover two-page spreads (one that includes the copyright page), all contributing to the sense of narration. Even the seven pages subdivided into separate boxes add to the narration, as seen in a two-page spread on which a bee and hummingbird fly right from one flower to another or on the pages that represent seed travel of various types, again showing movement to the right. *Weather Words and What They Mean* has 15 pages that resemble its cover, subdivided into boxes (although the boxes often appear in greater numbers and different sizes than those seen in the cover triptych). Two pages use the boxes to narrate a weather process (e.g., how raindrops are formed); all others use the subdivisions just as the cover does, to present the weather terms. The book also contains 16 pages that present single pictures, but none of these pages conveys movement to the right or a sense that its ideas will be continued on a following page. And, there are no pictures that cover a two-page spread. These repetitions of form reinforce the generic compositions of each text type.

Verbal and Visual Features Together: What Each Contributes

We now return to the relationships between visual and verbal information in science texts to understand better what each contributes to scientific comprehension. Lemke (1998) has suggested that different modes "are essentially incommensurable" (p. 110); each presents some aspect of the idea communicated that the other does not or cannot. To examine how the visual and verbal aspects each contribute to science understanding, we have selected a particular page from Gibbons's *From Seed to Plant* because it is an example of a structured analytical image, a part-whole labeled figure that Unsworth (2001) has identified as very commonly occurring "in texts associated with schooling" (p. 83).

Verbal Contributions to Meaning

In terms of the book's generic scheme (see Figure 10.2 on page 199), our selected page is located within the characteristic event Pollination and Its Paths. Because the page gives the Pollination Definition, it serves as an interspersed description of attributes within an event. A very similar-looking page (Flower Parts in Figure 10.2), also a description of attributes diagram, precedes our selected page, setting the stage for the text's pollination discussion. Two bright red poppies associated with Pollination and Its Paths in Figure 10.2 appear on the page to the right of our selected page, providing an opportunity to move beyond the static image to pollination in action. The running text for the Pollination Definition reads as follows: "Before a seed can begin to grow, a grain of pollen from the stamen must land on the stigma at the top of the pistil of a flower like itself. This is called pollination" (n.p.).

A functional analysis of the first sentence of this running text indicates that it is serving to set out a series of circumstances under which pollination occurs. The first clause of the sentence, including the words *seed* and *begin*, provides cohesive links to ideas on preceding pages. (This is the first time the concept of growth has been verbally introduced; visually, though, readers already have had their thoughts directed to it through the salient growing plant on the cover.) The sentence also informs readers of an if-then condition: If pollination does not occur, then no seed will grow. Other words address important locations. The grain of pollen comes *from* the stamen; the stigma is located *at the top* of the pistil. The pollen must land *on* the stigma, and the stigma must be located *in* a flower similar to the one from which the pollen has come in order for a seed to grow. The second sentence uses the pronoun "this" to refer to the entire process just described and supplies a term for the process. This running text does what verbal descriptions do particularly well—provide a linear sense of the order of events and clearly indicate all the circumstances under which something must occur (a concept often difficult for visual representations to capture).

Visual Contributions to Meaning

Had Gibbons been using her pictures merely to mirror her running text, we might imagine her using a picture that shows the landing of the pollen grain on top of a pistil. (The two-poppy picture on the right-hand side of the spread actually performs this function). However, utilizing the interconnectedness of images in pictures books, Gibbons opts instead for a central diagrammatic image on this page that deepens the reader's understanding of the flower's reproductive structure. She also reminds readers of the physical setting in which the process takes place. In the upper left-hand corner of the picture is a whole flower, representing "a flower like itself," and possibly reminding children how the cross-sectional diagram in the center of the page has removed parts to reveal what is not normally seen. This whole flower suggests what the text does not, that similar flowers frequently are found close to one another when growing in gardens or fields (the physical setting). In the upper right-hand corner of the page, against the blue sky background, is the word *pollination*, indicating that this picture (similar to the text below) supplies information about the process. The positioning of the word places it close to the right-hand page of the spread in which the pollen of one poppy lands on the pistil of another.

In the salient center of the page, the cross-sectional diagram is repeated from the previous page. The labeling on this diagram, however, has been shortened from sentences (e.g., "The sticky part at the top of the pistil is called the stigma") to single words ("stigma"), and only terms associated with reproduction now appear. Short lines draw readers' eyes to the representations of the parts pertinent to reproduction: the stigma, the pollen, the pistil, and the stamen. Two different label lines and the diagram's central location on the page make the stigma salient. Unlike the linear, verbal description in the text, the diagram enables readers to see the pistil's central location among the pollen-laden stamens. Again, there is information the text does not supply: Although there is only one pistil, there are several stamens, increasing the amount of pollen available for causing pollination. Attending to the salient image, readers see on its surface not only the grains of pollen but also a scattering of white. Visually, this white coating reminds us of the verbal information from the preceding page—that the stigma is sticky—and suggests that the sticky surface enables the stigma to hold on to the pollen grains. Just as the speech balloon emanating from the cumulonimbus cloud on the cover of *Weather Words and What They Mean* brings in additional auditory information, this depiction of stickiness introduces a tactile aspect to readers' understanding, an aspect absent in the running text below the image but important to descriptions of scientific phenomena.

The Combined Impact of the Verbal and Visual Modes

The child whose attention has been directed to the visual information on this page of *From Seed to Plant*, as opposed to the verbal information alone, will know much more about the reproductive process of plants than the child whose teacher has read the text without commenting on the pictures. Repetition of certain terms in both the text and the picture (e.g., *pollen*, *sta-*

men, stigma, and *pistil*) deepens children's conceptions of plants' reproductive parts. Additionally, the text defines conditions and event ordering, while the picture supplies locational information far more succinctly than the text could and introduces a tactile component and its consequences without a lengthy verbal section.

Kress and colleagues (2001) point to the real importance of attending to the visual and verbal modes in science trade books: "What is taken in in one mode interacts with what is taken in in other modes via other senses" (p. 7). This interaction leads to improved understanding. Research has demonstrated that students who have had content presented in both visual and verbal forms have better comprehension of ideas than students who have had content presented in verbal forms alone (e.g., Mayer, Bove, Bryman, Mars, & Tapangco, 1996; Purnell & Solman, 1991).

Closing Thoughts

This chapter has shown why enhanced comprehension results from attention to both picture and text. This discussion has supplied examples for teachers of how they might use both visual and verbal modes of meaning making and has pointed out the additional information available for students if this approach has been taken. Seeing science information books as multimodal presentations is an important step for both new and experienced teachers in making these texts serve students in the best possible ways.

REFERENCES

Arnheim, R. (1956). *Art and visual perception: A psychology of the creative eye.* London: Faber.

Donovan, C.A., & Smolkin, L.B. (2001). Genre and other factors influencing teachers' book selections for science instruction. *Reading Research Quarterly, 36,* 412–440.

Donovan, C.A., & Smolkin, L.B. (2002). Considering genre, content, and visual features in the selection of trade books for science instruction. *The Reading Teacher, 55,* 502–520.

Halliday, M.A. (1985). *An introduction to functional grammar.* London: Edward Arnold.

Hasan, R. (1984). The nursery tale as a genre. *Nottingham Linguistic Circular, 13,* 71–102.

Kress, G.R. (1994). *Learning to write* (2nd ed.). New York: Routledge.

Kress, G.R., Jewitt, C., Ogborn, J., & Tsatsarelis, C. (2001). *Multimodal teaching and learning: The rhetorics of the science classroom.* New York: Continuum.

Kress, G.R., & van Leeuwen, T. (1996). *Reading images: The grammar of visual design.* London: Routledge.

Lemke, J.L. (1998). Multiplying meaning: Visual and verbal semiotics in scientific text. In J.R. Martin & R. Veel (Eds.), *Reading science: Critical and functional perspectives on discourses of science* (pp. 87–113). London: Routledge.

Martin, J.R. (1992). *English text: System and structure.* Amsterdam: Benjamins.

Mayer, R., Bove, W., Bryman, A., Mars, R., & Tapangco, L. (1996). When less is more: Meaningful learning from visual and verbal summaries of science textbook lessons. *Journal of Educational Psychology, 88,* 64–73.

Pappas, C.C. (1986, December). *Exploring the global structure of "information books"* (Report No. CS-008-683). Paper presented at the annual meeting of the National Reading Conference, Austin, TX. (ERIC Document Reproduction Service No. ED278952)

Pappas, C.C. (1991). Fostering full access to literacy by including information books. *Language Arts, 68,* 449–462.

Pappas, C.C., Kiefer, B.Z., & Levstik, L. (1999). *An integrated language perspective in the elementary school: An action approach* (3rd ed.). New York: Longman.

Peacock, A., & Gates, S. (2000). Newly qualified primary teachers' perceptions of the role of text material in teaching science. *Research in Science and Technological Education, 18*(2), 155–177.

Purnell, K.N, & Solman, R.T. (1991). The influence of technical illustrations on students' comprehension in geography. *Reading Research Quarterly, 26,* 277–299.

Smolkin, L.B., & Donovan, C.A. (2001, December). *Science concepts and comprehension during science trade book read alouds.* Paper presented at the 51st Annual Meeting of the National Reading Conference, San Antonio, TX.

Unsworth, L. (2001). *Teaching multiliteracies across the curriculum: Changing contexts of text and image in classroom practice.* Buckingham, UK: Open University Press.

van Leeuwen, T. (2000). It was just like magic: A multimodal analysis of children's writing. *Linguistics and Education, 10*(3), 273–305.

CHILDREN'S LITERATURE CITED

Gibbons, G. (1990). *Weather words and what they mean.* New York: Holiday House.

Gibbons, G. (1991). *From seed to plant.* New York: Holiday House.

Gibbons, G. (1995). *Planet Earth/Inside out.* New York: William Morrow.

Schilling, B. (1972). *Two kittens are born: Birth to two months.* New York: Scholastic.

CHAPTER 11

Readers Are Scientists: A Reflective Exploration of the Reasoning of Young Scientists, Readers, Writers, and Discussants

JEANNE REARDON

This book seeks to understand science-literacy connections from different vantage points. My chapter brings us into an elementary school classroom to explore several science-literacy relations. I have chosen the term *reflective exploration* rather than *teacher research* to describe what I have done. I do not have a body of data, systematically collected and analyzed, to answer my questions. Instead, I have explored and reflected on my classroom observations of children, their conversations, and their work. In preparing this chapter, I have drawn heavily on my journals, observations, audiotapes, and student work from a class I taught as first graders and later as third graders, and from another first-grade class. I collected much of this material as part of two investigations: (1) an investigation of questions posed by third-grade students about a variety of texts they were reading and (2) an investigation of the evidence that first-grade children find convincing in science.

A classroom is more than people, materials, resources, and curriculum. It also is time, space, activities, expectations, rules, decisions, questions, problems, interactions, and so on. In this chapter, I focus on students' reasoning as observed during literacy and science explorations and investigations. Exploration and investigation are central to all learning in the classroom in which I teach. While engaged in these activities, my students read, write, discuss, and mingle the content and processes of science and language arts. Exploration and investigation provide a rich source for the study of students' science and literacy reasoning.

As I revisited material for this chapter, I kept organizing and reorganizing the collection in search of a useful framework. My observations are grouped into three large categories: (1) questions and problems; (2) interpretations, explanations, and evidence; and (3) discussions and community-stimulated reasoning. Before I look at the variety of reasoning patterns I observed, I will provide a glimpse of our classroom. I briefly will visit a discussion that followed a third-grade reading exploration, a first-grade science exploration and investigation, and a third-grade writer's investigation.

All names used in this chapter, except Danielle Smith, are pseudonyms. Danielle was the student who first "crossed the border" between reading and science, and so I have used her name. Throughout this chapter, I raise questions for further consideration, which appear in italics.

Classroom Setting

Classroom Explorations and Investigations

In our classroom, my students and I distinguish between exploration and investigation and make time for both. Exploration is an engaged wandering and wondering through materials and ideas. It usually begins as an individual activity. The student explorer is free to select from material to explore and to select the manner of exploration. (As a teacher, I usually limit the materials or provide a focus for the exploration in order to guide students' attention toward particular content, form, function, problems, and so forth.) Exploration brings with it responsibilities. Students must be able to discuss what they did, what they noticed, and what they are thinking about. This means having a written record to refer to during the follow-up discussion time. The record usually is an entry in a student's exploration log or perhaps notes on bookmarks or sticky notes, or drawings. Explorations enlarge the child's reservoir of information and experiences. The exploration discussions open the child to alternative ways of "seeing" and describing, other ways of interpreting and explaining. The exposure to language in the context of exploration is especially beneficial to the Title I and English as a second language (ESL) students in the classroom. Open, wide-ranging explorations and the follow-up discussions are generative. They promote flexibility and result in connections, questions, problem identification, and possibilities to pursue.

Investigations are focused pursuits in response to a question, curiosity, or problem. They have rules and standards for evidence. Student investigators expect to be asked, How do you know? The student audience expects to be shown evidence. (In an exploration discussion, a student might say, "That's how I feel," or "It's a dumb book." These responses are not accepted in an investigation discussion.) An investigation requires a different kind of record keeping: a "scientific drawing," the exact words spoken by a character, a photograph or illustration, words quoted from the text, observations, and careful descriptions of what the student did and noticed. Students often conduct surveys or interviews as part of their investigations. Investigations provide students with a process to use when gathering and analyzing data to answer questions, solve problems, and build their explanations. Investigations also provide an opportunity for discussions that question and challenge procedures, evidence, and explanations.

Examples of Explorations and Investigations

Discussion Following a Reading Exploration: "Readers Are Scientists." Most of the third-grade class had read and discussed *Shoeshine Girl* (Bulla, 1975) as part of the third-grade language arts curriculum. On one particular day, the class had spent half an hour exploring a large collection of books by Bulla in preparation for individual book selection. As usual, the children brought their exploration logs and pencils to our follow-up discussion. (These logs are not discipline-specific but rather a jumble of responses to explorations carried out across the curriculum.) We were in the midst of the follow-up discussion when Danielle Smith made her comment, "Readers are scientists." "What an interesting idea," I thought. "This book collection is primarily fiction; I wonder where this comment came from. What factors, what qualities is she considering: What connections does she see?"

"Readers are scientists. Can you tell us more about that?" I asked.

"I didn't write that in my log. I was listening [pause] was listening to Martha talk about what she paid attention to in the books and, [pause] and, [pause] and it just came out," Danielle replied.

I responded, "Well, it's an interesting idea to consider. Let's think about readers and think about scientists. Then, take some time to write. Danielle said she was listening to what Martha paid attention to in these books. You might write about what readers and scientists pay attention to. You might write about how, in what ways, readers are scientists—if you agree with that—or maybe write how you could find out if readers are scientists—what you would do to find out."

The writing began quite slowly, and it progressed, as it often does, in spurts and sputters. My notes of the discussion that followed the writing indicate that only one child addressed the problem of how to find out if readers were scientists. He said he would watch them to see what they do, talk to them, and ask them questions. Many students worked through the problem by comparing what readers and scientists *do*. One student wrote about what readers and scientists *know*. Both similarities and differences were noted. The structure and flow of this discussion followed a typical pattern:

One student made a comment, and other students built on this comment by confirmation through examples and qualifying distinctions, or by disagreement with supporting examples. The following excerpts came from the discussion:

> "Readers and scientists both notice stuff."
>
> "Scientists observe—authors, too."

Although these students frequently linked readers with writers, and reading with writing, during class discussions, they also made distinctions. The student's switch from "readers and scientists" to "authors and scientists" is not surprising, but it is difficult to know whether the second student agrees with the statement "Readers and scientists both notice stuff" and is adding authors, or whether the student is making a distinction between readers and authors.

There also was the following interesting interchange comparing readers, writers, and scientists:

> "Writers are more 'scientist' than readers. Writers have to watch everything."
>
> "They [authors] have to hear stuff, too." (This probably reflected a series of writing workshop minilessons about how authors listen to and write "conversation.")
>
> "They [writers] have to keep going back and doing it over, just like scientists." (Our class also had minilessons about editing and revising; replication is something I stress during science investigations.)
>
> "Readers go back and read again." (This response was to the comment that writers are more like scientists because they go back and do it over.)

At this point the discussion demonstrates various ways the students sought to make connections among the practices of readers, writers, and scientists. Then one of the students brought up a difference in practice:

> "Yeah, [pause] readers got words to start. Writers an' scientists jus' got stuff...got no words to start."

This statement agrees with the position that readers as well as writers "go back," but it also points out a significant difference. Whereas readers are provided with written text [words], writers and scientists work from "stuff" and must search for the words they need.

> "They [referent unclear—readers and scientists, or writers and scientists?] both got to figure out problems, [pause] like what makes something happen how it does in a story, and where to make the chapter end, and what to illustrate, how to illustrate [pause] why you can move big heavy rocks with a pry bar."

The examples of writers' and scientists' problems provided by this student indicate that she understands writers and scientists must identify and solve problems, but then the conversation turns to how they work.

> "Authors explain in words, and scientists show you."
>
> "But they can't just show you with no words."

Another student builds on what she knows about genres and purposes for writing in her comments:

> "Writers can write what they know from themself and what they imagine, and they can write information that's true. Scientists can't make up stuff. They have to show how they know."

Now the discussion moves back to problems, drawing on real problems that class members have encountered. The students continue to make connections by describing their experiences as practicing scientists, readers, and writers.

> "Scientists and writers have bigger problems [than readers.] Like how to know what is happening underground when you can't see. And how to write loud or quiet."
>
> "Readers are quieter than scientists."
>
> "That's 'cuz scientists are in a bunch and they talk and show everyone else what they're doing." (This comment was followed by disagreement about how much, when, why, and how loud readers and scientists talk.)
>
> "Sometimes readers argue. Like now."
>
> "So do scientists."
>
> "Scientists know more. They know lots of information, lots of facts. Readers don't have to know as much."
>
> "If you're a reader, you know a lot from what you read. Besides, readers know words, punctuation, and readers know how books work, like dictionaries and indexes and biographies and how to read poems. Scientists know how things work, like rockets and eyes, and they know why things happen like volcanoes and tornadoes."
>
> "Well, writers have to know how the things work to write information books. Everybody has to know [pause] just different stuff."

The discussion points toward the many opportunities these students have to explore and investigate authentic problems encountered by practicing scientists, writers, and readers.

The ways in which students write in their logs have long interested me, and although I no longer have these students' prediscussion logs, I have my notes about the forms the students used for their log writing. Some students were very specific in their responses, and others generalized. Many responses reflected personal or classroom experiences or both. As I reread my transcripts and notes, I was not surprised that these children viewed and used themselves as models of scientists, readers, and writers in their writing and discussion. I was surprised by their awareness of the range of scientists' activities and behaviors: observing, going back and replicating, talking, asking questions, solving problems, explaining, and disagreeing. *What role does awareness play in the reasoning of scientists, readers, writers?*

At the conclusion of exploration discussions I usually invite the students to add to their logs. No one added to their readers and scientists writing that morning. I took this response as an indication that students had little interest in moving to an investigation of the ideas discussed. My own journal entry for that day indicates that I was still thinking about the connections and wondering how an exploration of fiction sparked Danielle's comment. I would like to have pursued the comparison of scientists, readers, and writers with the class, but experience has taught me that if an issue is not important to the students, there is little point in pushing them to investigate it.

A Science Exploration and Investigation of Water Drops. This science exploration and investigation began with the sound of rain pounding against the windows of our first-grade classroom. After watching the drops and talking about our observations, we began a three-month exploration of water drops. We began with a problem: How can we study and find out more about those raindrops inside our classroom? What if a scientist wanted to find out more about raindrops falling on the window? Would he or she have to wait until the next rain? We started with a "quick write." Some children wrote; others drew experimental designs. Everyone had an idea as we worked on a problem common to other scientists—how to replicate natural phenomena in a laboratory setting. Indira even wondered if the drops would be the same when we brought them inside. We talked about laboratory study and field study.

We decided that we would need a substitute for window glass and noted that we had plenty of water at the sink. The children would bring in materials that water would drop onto or run off of. I would bring in several pieces of Plexiglas. We already had a large supply of Styrofoam trays, Popsicle sticks, drinking straws, plastic cups, newspaper, foil, waxed paper, and so forth.

We used a workshop format for science lessons, beginning with a mini-lesson, followed by hands-on exploration and investigation time that included writing. The workshop concluded with a "Scientists' Meeting." During this meeting, there was general sharing, in-depth reporting by one or two of the scientists in our classroom, and time for planning the next workshop. On the first day of our exploration, I asked the children to share one thing they each did, observed, or wondered about:

"I used my fingers to make drops, and the water hung on and wouldn't let go."

"I made puddles."

"I cut my drop in two with the Popsicle stick."

"You can pull water around with a stick. It just follows the stick."

"I can pick up water with a straw and let it go in big drops."

"Some drops are taller than others."

"Drops fall 'cause they're heavy."

"I had drop races."

"You can blow drops all around and make them bump into other drops until they get so big they aren't drops."

"Drops jiggle."

"Drops are hard to see. It'd be easier if we colored them."

"I put foil on my tray, and they went faster."

"When I put a stick in my cup, it looks sort of broke. I took it out, and it's not. I put it back, and it's broke again."

"Just before drops fall they change shape."

A variety of student initiated activities led to observations of drop size, shape, movement, and change. Some children manipulated variables and noted changes in the speed at which drops moved on different surfaces. A problem was identified and a solution proposed. One child provided an explanation, "Drops fall 'cause they're heavy." This explanation led to a question, "What makes drops let go?" Another child repeatedly put her stick in water, noting that it looked sort of broke, and then took it out, noting that it was not. This range of comments and detailed observations is typical of those made by 6-year-old children during science exploration.

After a few days of general exploration, messing about, and getting to know the materials and the possibilities, the children identified investigations they were interested in conducting. These investigations began with each child writing about something he or she wanted to try out or find out more about. As the children continued to work, they found more questions and problems to investigate and observations and explanations to test.

Investigation of a Writer. Keith was sharing a piece of writing in progress with his response group when he stopped and said, "Here is where I want to write loud. I don't mean loud with giant letters or loud with bold. I know how to do it with letters. I don't mean the way we make comparisons, like 'loud as fireworks on the fourth of July,' or...I can make loud illustrations. That's not what I mean. I mean the kind of loud that startles and shakes you when you read." Keith's response group was having a hard time helping him. Keith insisted that, sometimes when he was reading, he was startled and shaken, and he wanted to know how the author did it. He could not remember a specific place in a book where this happened. One person in the group suggested that the next time it happened to him, he should mark the place and show the group. Then, they would figure out how the author wrote loudly.

Keith eventually came up with two examples, but still no one could figure out how "loud" worked. Keith told me, "I'm going to quit working on 'loud.' I'm going to try 'quiet,' and if I get it, then I'll come back to 'loud.'" Keith put up a message asking class members to show him any place in a book where they felt quiet when they read. At his request, I copied these pages of text on the copy machine. The collection of pages grew over several weeks. Keith and some friends studied the text closely, trying out different explanations. First, they agreed on a text that was "really quiet" and analyzed it. It had lots of *L*s, so they began looking at letters in other samples. After working on the "quiet sound" explanation, they began looking at the words that contained *L*, and then someone asked about word length. The investigation continued. The group's final report stated the following:

1. Some sounds make you feel quiet. *L* can make you feel quiet and sometimes *M* or *F*.

2. The sounds have to be in long words with at least two syllables.

3. It helps if the words are in long sentences.

4. What's really important is the sentences that come before and after. When the sentences before and after are short and have lots of short words it makes the quiet part quieter.

Keith never did return to his "loud" problem, at least not publicly.

Reflections

I have provided these three descriptions of exploration and investigation from my classroom as background for my reflective exploration of children's literacy and science reasoning. The reflection is in three sections: (1) questions and problems; (2) interpretations, explanations, and evidence; and (3) discussions and community-stimulated reasoning.

Questions and Problems

What do questions posed and problems encountered by students while reading, writing, and engaging in science reveal about students' reasoning? The following three questions illustrate ways students use their assumptions, observations—including those of unanticipated or inconsistent events—awareness, and reasoning by exclusion.

A Reader's Question. "Why did he [Clyde Bulla, author of *Shoeshine Girl* (1975)] put Kicker in the story, anyway?" Kanesha asked. Kanesha's reasoning may go something like this: She begins with an assumption, based on her observations as a reader and her knowledge of herself as a writer, that authors make decisions about the way they construct a story. An author does not randomly drop characters into a story. In Kanesha's reading of the book, the inclusion of Kicker in the story serves no purpose; it is inconsistent with her assumption about writing. Why put him in? Still, she reasons, he is there, and so she asks, "Why did he put Kicker in the story?"

A Writer's Problem. "How can I write loud? I don't mean loud with giant letters or loud with bold. I don't mean the way we make comparisons, 'loud as fireworks on the fourth of July,'" remarks Keith. Keith knows what kind of loud he is searching for. He demonstrates awareness and reasoning through exclusion—"What I don't mean...." As a reader, he has experienced the kind of "loud" for which he is searching. He assumes there is a way that a writer does this to a reader. "How can I write loud?" is a request for information that Keith poses to his fellow writers and readers.

A Scientist's Question. "How come my Popsicle stick pulls water drops around?" asks Celeste. This question is a response to an unanticipated observation. Celeste has been dropping water from a Popsicle stick, watching small drops merge into larger drops, tipping the tray, and observing the drops. She puts her Popsicle stick down on the tray, picks it up, and a drop "follows [her] stick!" She pulls the drop around the tray and asks, "What's going on? How come my Popsicle stick pulls water drops around?" Celeste has spilled liquids on the kitchen and lunchroom floors, and she has splashed in puddles and made drops. She has cleaned up liquids with paper towels, napkins, and rags. She knows what happens when drops come in contact with different materials such as paper, cloth, and rubber shoe soles. But the behavior of the water drops is something unexpected, something to question. Questions driven by the unexpected or inconsistent in science or reading demand investigation.

Students' assumptions, observations, awareness, and reasoning by exclusion are found in many student questions I have analyzed. However, perhaps the most interesting and important component in the students' questions is the role of the inconsistent or the unexpected observation. *How do observations, results or findings (science) and information, or outcomes (literacy) that run counter to assumptions or expectations affect students' reasoning?* These student questions also prompt me to ask, *What and how much does a student, or adult, need to know in order to ask a productive question or recognize a problem?*

In each example, the student possesses enough background knowledge to make assumptions. Kanesha's observations of text and her own experience as a writer lead her to assume that characters are included for some purpose. Celeste found that her assumptions, based on previous experiences with water, were challenged by her new observations. Keith has enough reading experience and experience with personal response to text to pose his question. One implication for teachers is clear: Students need information. *What is less clear is when and how much, from whom, and in what form information is most useable—that is, most conducive to questioning, connecting, and problem solving.*

Interpretations, Explanations, and Evidence

The previous section discussed students' reasoning as evidenced in their questions and problems. There are students who look for the answer or want to know what is "true," and for some of their questions there *is* an answer. However, in our classroom my students and I have found that the questions and problems we most often pursue, the questions that we find interesting, often do not have a clear or single answer. (In our third-grade classroom, students submit questions about their current reading to their discussion groups. Next, the group discusses the questions in terms of their potential for exploration, without responding to the question, and after that discussion they select the questions to pursue.) As we read and investigate, we search for interpretations, explanations, and understandings—often speculative ones—rather than answers. Likewise, rather than looking for answers, this section looks at the explanations that students found and the evidence they presented as they pursued the questions posed in the previous section.

Explanations for the Author's Inclusion of a Character. Kanesha's question about why the character Kicker was included in the book *Shoeshine Girl* (Bulla, 1975) was selected by her discussion group as one question to explore. Everyone in the group had read the book, and each group member came to the next meeting prepared to share explanations. Each student had notes and a copy of the book marked with paper bookmarks at places with supporting evidence for their assertions. I sat in on the group's response discussion. Some of the students' explanations follow:

> "You get to know the main characters better by having Kicker around. You can compare how he acts, how he talks with how the important characters do. See, here Kicker says.... That's real different from here...."

> "Putting in other characters is a way for the author to tell you stuff. You find out stuff you'd never know 'cause it might've happened before the story began. Right now I'm reading... And I found out...."

> "I got an idea. Take Kicker out of the story, [pause] just in your head. What's missing? What don't you know? [Discussion among group] OK, now put him back in. [Discussion among the group] Maybe that's what Mr. Bulla did."

These three students provide possible explanations in response to Kanesha's question. The first explains by making comparisons, and providing evidence from *Shoeshine Girl*, the text the group was reading. The second student makes a generalization based on data she has collected from reading other texts, and provides an example, evidence, from a different text. The last student controls a variable, the presence of Kicker, then together with classmates compares results. Each student used different processes to arrive at alternative explanations. All provided evidence for their explanations.

Explanation of Ways to Write so the Reader Feels Quiet. Keith abandoned his original investigation of how to write "loud" in hopes that finding more about the opposite—writing "quiet"—would help him. Then came a cycle of observation and further questions, more focused observation and analysis, and more questions. This group of students carried out their own research as they attempted to solve Keith's problem. Although they used text as data, they did not look to books as resources or authorities to build their explanation. There were enough "quiet text" samples so that Keith and his friends were able to test the same explanation on different texts. (They did not test their explanations on "nonquiet" text. I wonder about those results and how the students would handle findings that did not confirm their explanations.)

Explanations for a Popsicle Stick Pulling Water Around. After some time spent pulling different sizes of water drops around on a Styrofoam tray, aluminum foil, a laminate tabletop, and waxed paper, Celeste wrote and drew in her science journal what she had observed. She also wrote, "Wood is a magnet for water. It's like a bar magnet and iron." Other first graders were interested and began "pulling drops." Celeste's explanation appeared to be satisfactory until one child reported that the stick had to touch the water. It was different from a magnet pulling iron. The stick would not pull the water without touching it. Celeste studied her Popsicle stick for a long time, and then got a hand lens for a closer look. The entry in her Science Journal states, "First I thought wood was a magnet for water. I looked under the hand lens. The stick has little hooks. Now I think it's like Velcro." Scientific drawings accompanied her writing. One was a tracing of the Popsicle stick. This drawing was labeled, "What I saw first." A second drawing showed the Popsicle stick with a hand lens laid over it. An arrow from this drawing pointed to another drawing of a magnified section of the stick within a circle. The "little hooks" were labeled.

Celeste used observation, and she changed the material that the drops rested on. She was looking for a causal explanation for her observations and, reasoning by analogy, she explained that wood was a magnet for water. When challenged, she continued to study the stick under a hand lens and developed an alternative explanation. It is interesting to me that she identified the material as being important and wrote about wood, not the color or shape of the stick. Many 6-year-olds identify color as an essential and causal factor in their explanations.

How do children determine which characteristics are essential in science and which are peripheral? To what kinds of things do scientists pay attention? Just as in science, some children are able to identify important information in reading, but others find every detail equally important. *What kinds of things do readers pay attention to? When reading informative text, how do children decide what is essential to their query and what information is peripheral?*

I find that children who most easily identify the essential in science write and use analogies more frequently than other children. These children also recognize metaphors and can tell how metaphors work. (That spring, Celeste wrote, "Spring is a feather, tickling the ground with flowers.")

I also find that children who abstract the critical features and information in text frequently use analogies in science.

In both reading and science, I have heard students develop their explanations in the same ways: by using additional focused observations and by asking more questions; through feelings and intuition, causal reasoning, and reasoning by analogy; by working from the opposite position; by using outside authorities; and by carrying out research. I also have heard explanations stimulated by the classroom community reasoning. I have not observed any differences in the process and reasoning used to reach explanations in science and in reading.

However, the kind of evidence that students provide for explanations is different in reading and in science. Reading explanations require textual evidence. Young readers often use experiential evidence to support the textual evidence. They sometimes use the experiences of their peers to support interpretations: "You used to live in the country. Does this make sense to you?" I find that most children begin to use textual evidence in reading before they show any concern for evidence in science.

In science, we look for evidence from testing and replication. This task is difficult for first graders, but we try to see if a particular explanation really explains what is happening. I often introduce an evidence problem in a science workshop. See the following example:

> "Yesterday, Mike reported that he could push water through wood. He said that he had two Popsicle sticks and when he pushed down on the top stick he could push water right through the bottom one. Mike told us how he knew— what evidence he had. Remind us how you knew, Mike."
>
> "I felt under the bottom stick and it was wet, and I'd been pushing down on it."
>
> "I want each of you to write down or draw pictures of a test you could use to convince yourself that Mike's explanation, pushing down, really explains the water under the stick. Then we'll share our tests and try them out."

Most first graders see explanations as evidence and find no need for tests. "There's a hole in the stick, that's how the water gets there" became a test. Indira was the first student in this class, and one of the few, to isolate and control variables when designing tests. She said, "First, you have to make sure your hands are dry and the sticks are dry. Then, you put the top stick in water and press it down hard on the other stick. You get someone else with dry hands to feel if the water went through." Acceptance of the professional scientific community's standards for evidence comes slowly to elementary students.

By the time children are in second grade, they are very concerned with fairness. The cry often goes out, "That's not fair!" The fairness issue translates into controlling variables. However, replication does not usually become important until third grade. First and second graders are strong believers in the one-time occurrence, especially if it is based on the authority of a friend.

Discussions and Community-Stimulated Reasoning—Social Construction of Individual Understanding

During explorations and investigations in science, writing, or reading, we organize and reorganize our observations, materials, data, and ideas. This time is for raising questions and pushing for alternative explanations. The literacy and science discussion periods that are a part of these explorations and investigations bring together a diverse group to assist in organizing and reorganizing our thinking. During discussion categories emerge that foster future connection making. In the discussion of explanations, I saw students use the information, questions, and comments of other students as they worked through their questions and problems and developed their explanations. I have found that children contribute to discussions in several ways.

First, some students provide information that might be closely relevant, distantly relevant, or irrelevant. These information providers may be students who are acute observers; they may be "fact collectors" who read everything they can get their hands on. These students increase the reservoir and the depth of literacy and science discussions.

Second, some students contribute connections to the discussion. These students do not become mired in the marginal information but grasp the essential information. They may not personally possess a large store of information, but they use the information provided by others to make connections, reason through analogy, and draw inferences. Many of these students make playful connections that move the group to see alternative explanations.

Third, some students challenge through their questions or alternative explanations and make waves in the reservoir so that information, ideas, and evidence bump and collide and new possibilities surface. These students often question the accuracy of information after checking a book's copyright date or wonder if the colors used by the book's illustrator have influenced the interpretation presented by another student. These students push for evidence from the text and challenge the reported scientific findings of fellow students.

Some students restate and synthesize the information and reasoning provided by others. At the beginning of the school year, I usually provide this function, but as the year goes on, students often step into this role.

The explanations and understandings that come from discussions reflect the contributions and interactions of many students. This is community-stimulated reasoning, but not community reasoning where the class members think as one, and all reach the same conclusion. The explanations and understandings constructed are individual and varied. I cannot recall a time when a literacy or science discussion in one of my classes resulted in a universally held understanding.

Role of Writing in Reasoning

Students were engaged in writing throughout the activities mentioned in this chapter. They made notes to bring to discussions, and they stopped to write during discussions to focus their thinking. They kept records and made drawings of procedures and observations; they reflected on their observations and wrote questions and explanations; and they wrote plans for what they would do next. The many types and uses of writing and the relation of writing to science and literacy could fill an additional chapter. This chapter focuses on reasoning rather than writing; however, I cannot conclude the chapter without recognizing the power of writing to form ideas.

Conclusion

Teachers often hear talk of integrating science and language arts. Visitors to my classroom comment on what they see as the integrated curriculum in action. My goal is not to integrate or merge the disciplines. I want to lose neither science, nor writing, nor reading as a discipline. Neither am I an advocate of a model where science, reading, and writing are put in compartments and taught in isolation. I am a mingler. I work to mingle familiarity and confusion; feelings and facts; writing, reading, and conversation; reading, observing, and writing; and writing and playing. I believe there are benefits in the mingling of science and the humanities. My hope is that through such mingling, children will ask provocative questions, make more productive connections, solve complex problems, and think critically in science and in the humanities.

Author Note

The title of this chapter was inspired by Danielle Smith, age 8, who coined the phrase "readers are scientists" in 1985.

CHILDREN'S LITERATURE CITED
Bulla, C.R. (1975). *Shoeshine girl*. New York: HarperTrophy.

SELF-QUESTIONING

AND METACOGNITION

This section offers a careful look at the research that specifically informs and addresses ways in which literacy instruction and science instruction might fruitfully and authentically connect.

In chapter 12, "Multiliteracies and Self-Questioning in the Service of Science Learning," Donna E. Alvermann explores the implications of conceptualizing literacy as the study of multiple communication forms (print, visual, digital), and looks specifically at what that conceptualization means in terms of science instruction. She begins with a discussion of constructivism and constructionism and moves seamlessly to a review of work on self-questioning—a strategy that holds great promise for those interested in both literacy and science instruction. She concludes with a call for research on self-questioning that permits students' multiliteracies to show themselves, particularly in relation to science learning.

Linda Baker in chapter 13, "Reading Comprehension and Science Inquiry: Metacognitive Connections," reviews research from both the reading and science communities on metacognition and self-regulated learning. After exploring the assumptions and goals both communities share, especially in their attention to social interaction as a way to foster these processes, she moves to a series of recommendations for practice. Finally, Baker looks at the question of assessment with particular attention to self-assessment, and she highlights the important role that writing plays in promoting metacognitive understanding across the curriculum.

Both of these chapters serve as a précis to and foundation for the specific recommendations set forth in Sections VI, VII, and VIII.

CHAPTER 12

Multiliteracies and Self-Questioning in the Service of Science Learning

Donna E. Alvermann

It has been said, "speech makes us human and literacy makes us civilized" (Olson, 1988, p. 175). In making this observation, Olson was referring to written language and the bias it imparts both to the way we think about knowledge—how we organize it and store it for reuse—and the cognitive consequences of schooling and literacy; in short, a bias favoring the written text over the oral tradition. Or, extending Olson's observation slightly, one might call it a bias that favors reading and writing over talking and doing. This bias would seem to have implications for the fields of reading and science education, especially when considering that, historically, there have been tensions between the two fields that have centered around ideological differences about the value of the written text versus hands-on experience (White, 2001; Yager, 2001).

These tensions have eased considerably in the last few years, however, as both reading and science educators have come to appreciate the fact that good teachers engage learners in active inquiry using multiple forms of literacy. For example, CD-ROMs, videos, the Internet, print materials, hypertexts, and hypermedia all can be used to supplement and complement students' hands-on inquiry into photosynthesis, electromagnetism, oxidation, and so on. Effective science instruction connects students' multiliteracies to science learning. It also enlists the U.S. National Science Education Standards' (NSES) concept of scientific literacy, which involves, among other things, encouraging students to ask their own questions about their everyday experiences in the world (National Research Council [NRC], 1996).

The purpose of this chapter is to explore the implications of literacy in its multiple forms (e.g., print, visual, digital) for science instruction. Specifically, I focus on the role of students' questions in constructing knowledge about science texts. Toward that end, the chapter is divided into three sections: The first section defines *multiliteracies* and situates this concept within social constructionist learning theory; the second section examines several assumptions underlying the literature on self-questioning; and the third section draws implications from this literature for using multiliteracies and self-questioning in the service of science learning.

Multiliteracies and Social Constructionist Learning Theory

The term *multiliteracies* refers to literacies that extend beyond print-based, alphabetic texts and is most closely associated with the New London Group (Cope & Kalantzis, 2000), an interdisciplinary group of scholars who argue that all meaning-making is multimodal and that new information communication technologies and media (e.g., the Internet, hypermedia, CD-ROM) make it unreasonable to speak of literacy in the singular or to view literacy as being based on written language only:

> What we might term "mere literacy" remains centred on language only, and usually on a singular national form of language at that, being conceived as a stable system based on rules such as mastering sound-letter correspondence. This is based on the assumption that we can actually discern and describe correct usage. Such a view of language must characteristically translate into a more or less authoritarian kind of pedagogy. A pedagogy of Multiliteracies, by contrast, focuses on modes of representation much broader than language alone. These differ according to culture and context, and have specific cognitive, cultural, and social effects. In some cultural contexts—in a multimedia environment, for instance—the visual mode of representation may be much more powerful and closely related to language than "mere literacy" would ever be able to allow. Multiliteracies also creates a different kind of pedagogy: one in which language and other modes of meaning are dynamic representational resources, constantly being remade by their users as they work to achieve their various cultural purposes. (as cited in Cope & Kalantzis, 2000, p. 5)

A pedagogy of multiliteracies broadens the meaning of text and relates textual reading to oral, aural, visual, tactile, and digital modes of learning as well as to the social skills necessary for communicating and collaborating while engaged in such learning. It also draws from the literature on critical literacy, and especially on "the critical literacy skills required for assessing, selecting, and rejecting information on the basis of group-negotiated criteria relevant to the problem and the situated community of practice-learners" (Luke, 2002, p. 142). Applied to school learning (a particular kind of community of practice-learners), a pedagogy of multiliteracies assumes that teachers will design and evaluate projects on a broader basis than is typically the case for print-based, alphabetic literacy. An example of how this might work is provided by the New London Group. In this example, we see that an evaluation of a school desktop publishing project calls for an expanded view of what counts as the literate features of the project:

> Desktop publishing puts a new premium on Visual Design and spreads responsibility for the visual much more broadly than was the case when writing and page layout were separate trades. So, a school project can and should properly be evaluated on the basis of Visual as well as Linguistic Design, and their multimodal relationships. (as cited in Cope & Kalantzis, 2000, p. 29)

A pedagogy of multiliteracies is compatible with a social constructionist theory of learning, which is not to be confused with a social constructivist theory of learning. Although the term *social constructionism* is frequently used as a synonym for *social constructivism*, there are numerous reasons for not conflating the two concepts (Hruby, 2001). Constructivism, generally, has become a catch-all term for a collection of theoretical approaches to learning that rely for their explanation on the cognitive developmental processes individuals use in deriving conceptual (abstract) understanding from their lived experiences. Social constructivism (Bruner, 1986) is concerned with how factors outside the head, such as the culture of a classroom and the structural aspects of schooling, form, rather than merely affect, what teachers and students do in the name of teaching and learning. Teachers whose belief systems align with social constructivism also believe that the ways in which students perceive themselves in a particular context (e.g., a science class) will mediate their motivation to learn (or not learn) the content of that class.

In contrast, social constructionism, which is of interest in this chapter, views language as the central mediating factor in what learners come to understand about their lived experiences and texts of various kinds. To subscribe to a social constructionist perspective on learning is to believe that meaning is built through particular conventions of language on which members of a particular community agree and act. Thus, in Gavelek and Raphael's (1996) explanation of how one comprehends text from a social constructionist perspective, it is the language of the classroom and how it is used to build particular meanings that is important:

> [A social constructionist perspective] has the potential to shift our focus on talk about text away from seeking "facts" or "truths" toward constructing "interpretations" and offering "warranted justifications" for interpretations. From this perspective, the teacher's role would shift from asking questions to ensure that students arrive at the "right" meaning to creating prompts that encourage students' exploratory talk.... Teachers would encourage talk that elicits a range of possible interpretations among individuals reading and responding at any

given time. Teachers would also encourage talking about previously read texts because individuals construct different readings at different periods in life or within different contexts.... Textual meaning is not "out there" to be acquired: it is something that is constructed by individuals through their interactions with each other and the world. (p. 183)

The centrality of exploratory talk in mediating what students are thought to comprehend from textual readings—whether print, oral, aural, visual, digital, or some combination of these multimodal forms of literacy—supports the use of self-questioning, a strategy that has a long and rich history in the fields of both reading and science education. The research on this strategy and some of its underlying assumptions are explored next.

Self-Questioning

Students who generate questions for the purpose of finding "answers to questions derived from curiosity about everyday experiences" are participating in scientific inquiry as defined by the NSES (NRC, 1996, p. 22). They are also comprehending more of what they read from traditional textbook assignments, though arguably their self-questioning in this capacity is guided more from textual content than from their own curiosity. Regardless, experimentally based research on self-questioning as a strategy shows that it is one of seven types of instructional strategies deemed effective in improving students' comprehension of traditional print texts (National Institute of Child Health and Human Development [NICHD], 2000).

Of the 450 text comprehension studies that members of the National Reading Panel (NICHD, 2000) identified as meeting their stringent criteria for scientific analysis, 27 involved studies of self-questioning in grades 3 through 9 (with grade 6 studies reported most frequently). According to the Panel's report, "there was stronger evidence for near transfer than for generalized effects...[with only] mixed evidence that general reading comprehension is improved on standardized, comprehension tests" (p. 4-45). Moreover, the Panel concluded, "question generation may...be best used as a part of a multiple strategy instruction program" (p. 4-45).

As with all reports, that of the National Reading Panel must be read with a clear understanding as to the limitations of its findings. For example, the Panel did not address issues specific to English-language learners or to scientific literacy. Nor did it include studies using qualitative research designs, the absence of which severely limits what can be known about the contexts in which instruction occurred. A general assumption underlying the 27 studies the Panel analyzed was that the reading process typically consists of students working individually to extract information from printed texts. This rather narrow view of comprehension risks disenfranchising students who may learn better in more socially interactive settings or whose multiliteracies (e.g., oral, aural, visual, and digital) span a broader range than those typically emphasized in school-based print literacy.

Although agreeing with the National Reading Panel's (NICHD, 2000) conclusion that explicit instruction in self-questioning can improve students' comprehension, members of the RAND Reading Study Group (2002) pointed out the need to consider the type of reader involved:

> Sometimes this explicit instruction is helpful for low-achieving students but is superfluous for normal readers.... Sometimes improvement occurs not because of the specific strategies being taught but because students have been actively interacting with the texts. This active interaction triggers the use of strategies that inactive learners possess but do not normally use. Explicit instruction generates the immediate use of comprehension strategies, but there is less evidence that students continue to use the strategies in the classroom and outside of school after instruction ends. (p. 33)

An assumption underlying the effectiveness of direct instruction in a strategy such as self-questioning with low-achieving readers is that classroom teachers will be sufficiently prepared and have the time to respond flexibly to students' needs for scaffolding and feedback on their questioning. Unfortunately, this is often not the case. For example, it is not uncommon for elementary teachers to take little satisfaction in teaching science, a subject for which they feel underprepared (Schoenberger & Russell, 1986; Tilgner, 1990). In addition, according to the multiple case study research of Edmunds, Jones, and Michaels (2002), elementary teachers often feel pressured to teach reading and math at the expense of science.

But competing demands on teachers' time are not the only deterrent to teaching students how to self-question as means of acquiring scientific literacy. Students with a history of reading difficulties present particular challenges to science teachers. Because they read so infrequently, these students typically will not have acquired the requisite background knowledge, skills, and specialized vocabulary needed for comprehending most science materials. Some teachers understandably become frustrated when this occurs, and they sometimes resort to what Finn (1999, pp. ix–x) calls a "domesticating" education. That is, they expect less of low-achieving readers in exchange for the students' good will and reasonable effort in completing their assignments, which typically require little, if any, reading.

Even high school science teachers who rate themselves well prepared to teach their subject matter specialty often find that changing classroom structures and practices to make room for students to engage in self-questioning is difficult to do. For example, Alvermann and Hayes (1989) found in their long-term classroom intervention study that the inservice teachers with whom they worked were unsuccessful in curbing certain classroom practices that led to teacher-dominated questions, despite the fact the teachers had hoped to encourage more contributions from students. Similarly, in another intervention study aimed at changing classroom interaction patterns so as to accommodate students' voices, middle school teachers discovered that interrupting certain gendered discursive practices in talk about texts was easy to theorize but difficult to accomplish (Alvermann, Commeyras, Young, Randall, & Hinson, 1997).

In cases when science teachers have been successful in promoting students' self-questioning, the change has occurred largely as a result of working within a social constructionist framework to study the mediating effects of such questioning and/or using computers, the Internet, and multimedia software to target specific interests and create a need for student dialogue. For instance, Chin (2001) conducted a case study involving six eighth-grade target students as they worked through a nine-week chemistry unit. The hands-on laboratory activities in which these students were engaged included the following:

- Separation of salt-sand mixture—This was an open-ended, problem-solving activity in which the students had to devise a method for separating a mixture of salt and sand.

- Boiling point lab—The students had to plot and compare the temperature graphs for plain water and salt water when ice and salted ice were heated until boiling.

- Chromatography—The students used paper chromatography (a technique for separating complex mixtures) to separate the dyes in the ink from different colored marker pens and calculated the retention factor (R_f) for each dye.

- Chemical change—The teacher gave a demonstration on how to carry out the activity. In their groups, the students then performed an experiment to observe the reaction between zinc and dilute hydrochloric acid.

- Acids and bases—The students were required to determine whether some common household substances (vinegar, baking soda, water, salt water, ammonia, aspirin, antacid tablets, alcohol, bleach, Coca-Cola, coffee, mouthwash, and lemon juice) were acidic, basic, or neutral using cabbage juice and blueberry juice as indicators.

As the students worked, they were encouraged to verbalize their thoughts. Chin used the students' think-alouds in conjunction with her field notes, the transcripts of videotaped classroom discourse, the students' learning journals in which they noted things that puzzled them, and their interview data to analyze how the types of questions students asked mediated the knowledge they constructed. Similar to Scardamalia and Bereiter (1992), Chin found two types of student questions: basic information questions and wonderment questions. Examples of basic information questions included factual-level processing of textual material (e.g., recalling the dictionary definition of salt) or procedural-level processing to clarify a particular task (e.g., "Did she [the teacher] say to put the salt in a pan?").

Wonderment questions, on the other hand, consisted of higher level processing, such as hypothesis verification questions (e.g., "How about we pour some water in here?"); anomaly detection questions (e.g., "How do you know the salt's in there?"); application questions (e.g., "What is the R_f used for?"); and planning or strategy questions (e.g., "How are we going to bring the salt back?"). Chin reported that on various occasions when students were not encouraged to ask wonderment questions, they did not generate them spontaneously. This suggested to her that leaving such questioning to chance was tantamount to letting students' puzzlements go undetected—in effect, stifling further inquiry.

Using molecular modeling computer software to improve high school students' understanding of chemical bonding, Barnea and Dori (1999) demonstrated the value of virtual laboratory sessions. In fact, as Treagust and Chittleborough (2001) have pointed out, the use of virtual labs in combination with multimedia software that contains text, sound, images, animations, and interactive capabilities can increase opportunities for students to self-question and engage in creative dialogue. Although virtual labs and chemistry CD-ROMs, such as the *Interactive Periodic Table* (Attica Cybernetics, 1998), can enhance and elicit student questions about representations of chemistry at the macroscopic, microscopic, and symbolic levels, Brooks and

Brooks (1996) remind us that these new instructional aids should be viewed as supplements, not substitutes, for actual laboratory experiences.

Similarly, in referring to a review of the research on the use of technology and multimedia software to teach biology—including activities such as having students generate and e-mail questions to distant biology experts—Wandersee (2001) sounds this cautionary note:

> Within the past decade, the availability of biology teaching resources and instructional alternatives has increased dramatically. The real question now is: What shall I choose that best teaches what I have already planned to teach? It's very easy to get side-tracked.... Another danger lies in using corporate-financed, attractively packaged "free" teaching materials that may be far from neutral on issues that affect their financial viability. (pp. 213–214)

Wandersee goes on to recommend that biology teachers look to sound research and the NSES (NRC, 1996) for ideas in developing students' critical and scientific literacy. Specifically, he suggests that teachers use the standards for guidance in helping students pose problem-solving questions as they work with peers during prelaboratory and postlaboratory analytical sessions—a recommendation not unlike Chin's (2001), interestingly enough.

This call for teachers to guide students' self-questioning seems largely based on the assumption that scaffolded instruction meshes well with a social constructionist theory of how students learn. The call also seems well placed, especially given that so few students spontaneously ask higher-order questions (White & Gunstone, 1992), or for that matter, questions of any kind (Alvermann & Moore, 1991; Alvermann, O'Brien, & Dillon, 1990; Alvermann et al., 1996). More than a decade ago, Dillon (1988) noted the same paucity of student-posed questions, and judging from more recent reviews of the literature on question generation as a means of improving students' comprehension (Nist & Simpson, 2000; Pressley, 2000), the situation has not changed much. Granted, the research-backed strategies are there for teaching this essential skill (e.g., Manzo, 1969; Palincsar & Brown, 1984; Singer & Donlan, 1982), but school and classroom structures that would allow for more student-centered learning are slow to evolve (Alvermann et al., 1996; Barr, 2001).

Although student self-questioning does not show up as much as one might wish in actual classroom practice, it shows no evidence of declining in popularity as a topic of inquiry among science education researchers. According to White's (2001) quantitative and qualitative analyses of changes in topics in science education research as reported in ERIC for the past 30 years, the number of studies on questioning (though not limited to self-questioning) has remained fairly constant since 1966, ranging from a high of 98 in the five-year period from 1966 to 1970 to a low of 66 from 1976 to 1980. From 1991 to 1995 (the most recent reported five-year period), there were 77 science education studies that dealt with questioning.

Much of this research has focused on students' comprehension of text-based questions, including questions that students formulated in response to textual material (e.g., Palincsar & Brown, 1984; Wong, 1985) and as participants in conceptual-change learning (e.g., Guzzetti & Hynd, 1998; Watts, Gould, & Alsop, 1997). Questions not based on text knowledge—for example, the wonderment questions of Chin's (2001) research—were the focus of a much smaller body of research. These are the questions that reflect students' interests in finding out more about the world in which they live; in short, they are the questions that Scardamalia and Bereiter (1992) regard as having the potential to generate further scientific inquiry. Keys's (1998) study of sixth-grade students who worked in small groups to generate questions to open-ended science investigations and Chin's (2001) work with eighth-grade students to explore student-generated questions are good examples of research that seeks to study the mediating effects of such questioning on students' science learning.

In sum, the research on self-questioning points to a heavy emphasis on formulating questions in relation to print-based (mostly textbook) material. This bias is not unlike the one alluded to at the start of this chapter. Although science educators (and, to a lesser extent, reading educators) have expressed interest in the use of new interactive technologies and multimedia software to "empower the student and change the emphasis from teacher-centred to more student-centred learning" (as cited in Treagust & Chittleborough, 2001, p. 259), this interest has, in truth, failed to find its way into researchers' agendas. This fact, coupled with the scarcity of research on questions not based on text knowledge, will make tying the extant literature on self-questioning to students' multiliteracies in the last section of this chapter a bit more challenging than I might have anticipated.

Implications of Multiliteracies and Self-Questioning for Science Learning

Perhaps a good starting point in this section on implications is the following excerpt taken from an audio clip of the courtroom scene from the movie *A Few Good Men* (Reiner, 1992). As the scene opens, Lieutenant Daniel A.

Kaffee (played by Tom Cruise) is questioning Lieutenant Colonel Nathan Jessep (played by Jack Nicholson) about Jessep's knowledge of the circumstances surrounding the death of a soldier:

Nicholson: You want answers?

Cruise: I think I'm entitled.

Nicholson: You want answers?

Cruise: I want the truth!

Nicholson: You can't handle the truth!

As one of my colleagues (Rieber, 2000) at the University of Georgia observed in his response to this exchange, the question is not whether one can handle the truth, but rather, what makes something true?

This seems a pertinent observation and one that speaks to the connection I am attempting to make between students' multiliteracies and the research on self-questioning. A social constructionist theory of learning would argue that generating questions aimed at shifting away from a focus on "facts" or "truths" and toward "warranted justifications" of particular interpretations is what science learning should be about. Self-questioning that prompts a range of multiple interpretations that can be evaluated based on evidence (oral, aural, visual, tactile, digital, and print) is part and parcel of learning to become scientifically literate. It is also central to making use of a host of literacies that too often take a back seat to what Street (1995) labels the "autonomous" model of reading and writing, one whereby Literacy is perceived as being singular in form and spelled with a capital L.

The tendency to assume that such a model is also "natural" (and thus free of any ideological position) is indicative, in turn, of our tendency as educators to reify written language. I want to suggest that the understandings to be gained from designing research studies of self-questioning that permit students' multiliteracies to show themselves will move us a step closer to a knowledge base that is supportive of science learning specifically, and scientific literacy more generally. A pedagogy of multiliteracies, compatible as it is with social constructionist learning theory, offers researchers a ready instructional framework within which to study the mediating effects of students' self-questioning on their learning of science content.

However, as was pointed out in the previous section of this chapter, regardless of what research may say about the efficacy of teaching students to self-question, the assumption that elementary classroom teachers will feel prepared to accommodate an increase in this kind of questioning—and particularly, to welcome questions about nonprint texts—is a dangerous assumption to make. From all indications of the research to date, elementary teachers do not have a strong background in teaching science. This fact, coupled with the pressures being exerted on them to teach reading and math for longer blocks of time, would seem to point to potential conflicts. As work by the Strategic Literacy Initiative at WestEd (Greenleaf, Katz, & Schoenbach, 2001) has shown, it is not until teachers have the time and feel comfortable in appropriating the social practices and conceptual tools necessary for effecting change that they can hope to alter school and classroom structures that militate against student-centered learning.

Finally, the assumption that students' multiliteracies might be tapped through the use of new interactive communication technologies and multimedia software remains just that—an assumption. Although the demands and complexities of living in a highly globalized and technologized society have never been more apparent, educators are a conservative lot and generally distrustful of the "bells and whistles" so often associated with high-tech learning. In fact, the extent to which the Internet, hypermedia, and other new technologies effectively support literacy teaching and learning in science classrooms is unknown. There is little empirical research on the topic in general, and even less that applies specifically to self-questioning (NICHD, 2000). A related issue is the paucity of available research sites, given that so few schools have integrated the new information communication technologies into their curricula (Leu, 2000). Nonetheless, given that the everyday out-of-school literacy practices among the youth of this country are changing at an unprecedented pace, can it be long before we in education let loose some of the comfortable assumptions that have ceased to serve us well?

REFERENCES

Alvermann, D.E., Commeyras, M., Young, J.P., Randall, S., & Hinson, D. (1997). Interrupting gendered discursive practices in classroom talk about texts: Easy to think about, difficult to do. *Journal of Literacy Research, 29*(1), 73–104.

Alvermann, D.E., & Hayes, D.A. (1989). Classroom discussion of content area reading assignments: An intervention study. *Reading Research Quarterly, 24*, 305–335.

Alvermann, D.E., & Moore, D.W. (1991). Secondary school reading. In R. Barr, M. Kamil, P. Mosenthal, & P.D. Pearson (Eds.), *Handbook of reading research* (Vol. 2, pp. 951–983). White Plains, NY: Longman.

Alvermann, D.E., O'Brien, D.G., & Dillon, D.R. (1990). What teachers do when they say they're having discussions of content area reading assignments: A qualitative analysis. *Reading Research Quarterly, 25*, 296–322.

Alvermann, D.E., Young, J.P., Weaver, D., Hinchman, K.A., Moore, D.W., Phelps, S.F., Thrash, E.C., & Zalewski, P. (1996). Middle and high school students' perceptions of how they experience text-based discussions: A multicase study. *Reading Research Quarterly, 31*, 244–267.

Attica Cybernetics. (1998). *Interactive periodic table* [CD-ROM]. Oxford, UK: Attica Interactive.

Barnea, N., & Dori, Y.J. (1999). High-school chemistry students' performance and gender differences in a computerized molecular modeling learning environment. *Journal of Science Education and Technology, 8*(4), 257–271.

Barr, R. (2001). Research on the teaching of reading. In V. Richardson (Ed.), *Handbook of research on teaching* (4th ed., pp. 390–415). Washington, DC: American Educational Research Association.

Brooks, H.B., & Brooks, D.W. (1996). The emerging role of CD-ROMs in teaching chemistry. *Journal of Science Education and Technology, 5*, 203–215.

Bruner, J. (1986). *Actual minds, possible worlds*. Cambridge, MA: Harvard University Press.

Chin, C. (2001, April). *Student-generated questions: What they tell us about students' thinking*. Paper presented at the annual meeting of the American Educational Research Association, Seattle, WA.

Cope, B., & Kalantzis, M. (Eds.). (2000). *Multiliteracies: Literacy learning and the design of social futures*. London: Routledge.

Dillon, J.T. (1988). The remedial status of student questioning. *Journal of Curriculum Studies, 20*(3), 197–210.

Edmunds, J., Jones, M.G., & Michaels, S. (2002, April). *A stronger presence for science: Three models of elementary science instruction*. Paper presented at the annual meeting of the American Educational Research Association, New Orleans, LA.

Finn, P.J. (1999). *Literacy with an attitude: Educating working-class children in their own self-interest*. Albany, NY: State University of New York Press.

Gavelek, J.R., & Raphael, T.E. (1996). Changing talk about text: New roles for teachers and students. *Language Arts, 73*(3), 182–192.

Greenleaf, C., Katz, M., & Schoenbach, R. (2001, April). *Close readings: The impact of case inquiry on secondary teachers' literacy knowledge and practice and student achievement*. Paper presented at the annual meeting of the American Educational Research Association, Seattle, WA.

Guzzetti, B., & Hynd, C. (1998). *Perspectives on conceptual change: Multiple ways to understand knowing and learning in a complex world*. Mahwah, NJ: Erlbaum.

Hruby, G.G. (2001). Sociological, postmodern, and new realism perspectives in social constructionism: Implications for literacy research. *Reading Research Quarterly, 36*, 48–62.

Keys, C.W. (1998). A study of grade six students generating questions and plans for open-ended science investigations. *Research in Science Education, 28*, 301–316.

Leu, D. (2000). Literacy and technology: Deictic consequences for literacy education in an information age. In M.L. Kamil, P.B. Mosenthal, P.D. Pearson, & R. Barr (Eds.), *Handbook of reading research* (Vol. 3, pp. 743–770). Mahwah, NJ: Erlbaum.

Luke, C. (2002). Re-crafting media and ICT literacies. In D.E. Alvermann (Ed.), *Adolescents and literacies in a digital world* (pp. 132–146). New York: Peter Lang.

Manzo, A. (1969). The ReQuest procedure. *Journal of Reading, 13*, 23–26.

National Institute of Child Health and Human Development (NICHD). (2000). *Report of the National Reading Panel. Teaching children to read: An evidence-based assessment of the scientific research literature on reading and its implications for reading instruction* (NIH Publication No. 00-4769). Washington, DC: U.S. Government Printing Office.

National Research Council (NRC). (1996). *National science education standards*. Washington, DC: National Academy Press.

Nist, S.L., & Simpson, M.L. (2000). College studying. In M.L. Kamil, P.B. Mosenthal, P.D. Pearson, & R. Barr (Eds.), *Handbook of reading research* (Vol. 3, pp. 645–666). Mahwah, NJ: Erlbaum.

Olson, D.R. (1988). From utterance to text: The bias of language in speech and writing. In E.R. Kintgen, B.M, Kroll, & M. Rose (Eds.), *Perspectives on literacy* (pp. 175–189). Carbondale, IL: Southern Illinois University Press.

Palincsar, A.S., & Brown, A.L. (1984). Reciprocal teaching of comprehension-fostering and comprehension-monitoring activities. *Cognition and Instruction, 1,* 117–175.

Pressley, M. (2000). What should comprehension instruction be the instruction of? In M.L. Kamil, P.B. Mosenthal, P.D. Pearson, & R. Barr (Eds.), *Handbook of reading research* (Vol. 3, pp. 545–561). Mahwah, NJ: Erlbaum.

RAND Reading Study Group. (2002). *Reading for understanding: Toward an R&D program in reading comprehension.* Santa Monica, CA: Science & Technology Policy Institute/RAND Education.

Reiner, R. (Director). (1992). *A few good men* [Motion picture]. United States: Columbia/Tristar Studios. Audio clip retrieved July 6, 2000, from http://cc636243-a.twsn1.md.home.com/sond0107.htm

Rieber, L. (2000). *What is really true? A lesson in understanding constructivism.* Retrieved July 6, 2000, from http://it.coe.uga.edu/~lrieber/constructlesson.html

Scardamalia, M., & Bereiter, C. (1992). Text-based and knowledge-based questioning by children. *Cognition and Instruction, 9,* 177–199.

Schoenberger, M., & Russell, T. (1986). Elementary science as a little added frill: A report of two studies. *Science Education, 70,* 519–538.

Singer, H., & Donlan, D. (1982). Active comprehension: Problem-solving schema with question generation for comprehension of complex short stories. *Reading Research Quarterly, 17,* 166–186.

Street, B.V. (1995). *Social literacies: Critical approaches to literacy in development, ethnography, and education.* New York: Longman.

Tan, S.T., & Tan, L.K. (1997). CHEMMAT: Adaptive multimedia courseware for chemistry. *Journal of Science Education and Technology, 6*(1), 71–79.

Tilgner, P.J. (1990). Avoiding science in the elementary school. *Science Education, 74*(4), 421–431.

Treagust, D.F., & Chittleborough, G. (2001). Chemistry: A matter of understanding representations. In J. Brophy (Ed.), *Subject-specific instructional methods and activities* (Vol. 8, pp. 239–267). Amsterdam: JAI.

Wandersee, J.H. (2001). High school biology instruction: Targeting deeper understanding for biological literacy. In J. Brophy (Ed.), *Subject-specific instructional methods and activities* (Vol. 8, pp. 187–214). Amsterdam: JAI.

Watts, M., Gould, G., & Alsop, S. (1997). Questions of understanding: Categorising pupils' questions in science. *School Science Review, 79*(286), 57–63.

White, R.T. (2001). The revolution in research on science teaching. In V. Richardson (Ed.), *Handbook of research on teaching* (4th ed., pp. 457–471). Washington, DC: American Educational Research Association.

White, R.T., & Gunstone, R.F. (1992). *Probing understanding.* London: Falmer.

Wong, B.Y.L. (1985). Self-questioning instructional research: A review. *Review of Educational Research, 55*(2), 227–268.

Yager, R. (2001, August). *Analysis of learning from text designed to model scientific thinking in inquiry-based instruction: A response.* Paper presented at the Crossing Borders: Connecting Science and Literacy symposium, Baltimore County, MD.

CHAPTER 13

Reading Comprehension and Science Inquiry: Metacognitive Connections

LINDA BAKER

More than 25 years ago, developmental psychologists became interested in how and when children develop knowledge and control of their cognitive processes (Brown, 1978; Flavell, 1976). This higher level cognition was given the label "metacognition." Metacognition is concerned with our ability to reflect on our own thinking, and in an academic context it includes knowledge about ourselves as learners, about aspects of the task, and about strategy use. Metacognition also involves self-regulation of our own cognitive efforts. This includes planning our actions, checking the outcomes of our efforts, evaluating our progress, remedying difficulties that arise, and testing and revising our strategies for learning (Baker & Brown, 1984). This chapter examines how the construct of metacognition has informed the work of researchers and educators in literacy and science, with particular attention to the role of metacognition in the comprehension of science text.

The Role of Metacognition in Current Thinking About Reading and Science Education

Once developmental psychologists began to study metacognition, it quickly attracted the attention of educational researchers seeking an explanation for why some students fared better in school than others. Research had consistently demonstrated better metacognitive knowledge and control among older and higher achieving students. Instructional interventions to promote metacognition became popular, especially in the domain of reading (see Baker, 2001, for a review).

Effective text comprehension requires an important metacognitive control component known as comprehension monitoring. Comprehension monitoring involves deciding whether or not we understand something (evaluation) and taking appropriate steps to correct whatever comprehension problems we detect (regulation). Research has shown that students of all ages are often surprisingly poor at monitoring their understanding of text (Baker, 1989). These difficulties are perhaps most apparent when students are asked to read information text, such as science textbooks (Otero, 1998). Failures to evaluate and regulate understanding reduce the likelihood of meaningful learning.

It is now well accepted that metacognition should be fostered in comprehension instruction (see Block & Pressley, 2001, for example). Two highly visible national committees recently analyzed the available empirical research and concluded that metacognition is indeed important to reading comprehension (see National Institute of Child Health and Human Development [NICHD], 2000; Snow, Burns, & Griffin, 1998). In addition, based on several well-controlled instructional studies, the National Reading Panel concluded that comprehension monitoring can and should be taught (NICHD, 2000). Instruction helps students to improve not only in their ability to monitor their understanding, but also in their comprehension. Children have been taught by teacher modeling and guided practice to use self-instruction or think-alouds to monitor their own comprehension during reading. Children have also been taught to regulate their comprehension once an obstacle arises, using "fix-up" strategies such as rereading and reading ahead in search of clarification.

Although the term *metacognition* does not enjoy such a prominent role in the reports of national science panels, they do give considerable attention to things metacognitive. The term may be absent from the following statement in the U.S. National Science Education Standards (NSES), but there can be no doubt as to the central concern: "Engaging students in inquiry helps students develop an appreciation of 'how we know' what we know in science" (National Research Council [NRC], 1996, p. 105).

The Social Origins of Metacognition: Fostering Self-Regulation

It is widely agreed that social interaction plays an important role in the development of metacognition (Baker, 1996). Many theorists believe that the origins of metacognitive skills lie in adult-child or expert-novice interactions. This view comes from Soviet psychologist Lev Vygotsky (1978), who proposed that children first learn how to engage in cognitive tasks through social interaction with more knowledgeable others, usually parents or teachers. The expert initially takes the responsibility of regulating the novice's activity by setting goals, planning, evaluating, and focusing attention on what is relevant. Gradually, the expert gives over more and more responsibility to the novice as the novice becomes capable of assuming it, until finally the novice internalizes the regulatory mechanisms and can perform without expert assistance. In other words, there is a sequence of development from other-regulation to self-regulation. The goal is to enable students to take responsibility for their own learning. Most instructional interventions with a metacognitive or self-regulation focus draw on Vygotsky's theory.

Other theorists focus on a different aspect of social interaction, influenced by Swiss psychologist Jean Piaget, who emphasized the important role of peer interaction. He argued that peers challenge one another's thoughts and thus advance cognitive development. Piaget also argued that discussion and collaboration help students to monitor their own understanding and build new strategic capabilities. Champagne and Klopfer (1991) discussed the value of peer interaction while students are engaged in a science task: "These peer interactions, moderated by the teacher, help students augment the quantity and quality of the information they apply to the task. This exposes students to new information and alternative ways of thinking about the task, and enables them to modify their ideas accordingly" (p. 66). The social nature of science learning has also been emphasized by Linn, Songer, and Eylon (1996), among others. It is common for instructional programs today to supplement an emphasis on individual cognition with an emphasis on social support for monitoring, reflection, and revision.

Science educators, as well as reading educators, are concerned with promoting self-regulation. They, too, express the goal that students should assume control of their own learning. Indeed, the NSES (NRC, 1996) called for a change in teacher practice to create less emphasis on maintaining responsibility and authority and more emphasis on sharing responsibility for learning with students. Teachers need to encourage and support students as they become responsible for making sense of information for themselves. One way to do this is for students to be engaged as investigators and critics (Linn, Songer, & Eylon, 1996). Wallace, Hand, and Yang (chapter 19 in this volume) describe how students can develop a greater sense of ownership by having a chance to ask their own questions about a lab activity. Such ownership increases their cognitive and metacognitive engagement in the process. Metacognitive skill is perhaps best developed when students feel independent of the teacher, instead of viewing the teacher as an authority (White & Gunstone, 1989).

Linn, Songer, and Eylon (1996) called for the science curriculum to be reformulated to emphasize metacognition and responsibility for one's own learning. They characterized the science instruction of the mid-1990s as including "activities that help students link ideas by encouraging metacognitive skills" (p. 473) through an intertwining of inquiry skills with discipline-specific information. "Focusing on the development of scientific concepts also draws attention to the metacognitive skills necessary for organizing this information and for applying it to new problems" (p. 473).

Metacognitively Oriented Processes in Reading Comprehension and Science Inquiry

In an edited volume published in 1991, Carol Santa and Donna Alvermann brought together a collection of papers by researchers interested in the connections between literacy and science processes. Although many literacy educators were focusing on metacognition at the time, relatively few science educators were doing so. In that same volume, Baker (1991) argued that there were many commonalities between reading and science that involved metacognitive processes, illustrating this point with reference to the core set of process skills that students taking science courses were expected to acquire. Most science textbooks of the day included observing, classifying, comparing, measuring, describing, organizing information, predicting, inferring, formulating hypotheses, interpreting data, communicating, experimenting, and drawing conclusions. Many of these process skills can be regarded as metacognitive skills. Consider, for example, the science process skill of formulating conclusions. This skill corresponds to the reading skills of evaluating information, critically analyzing, recognizing main ideas and concepts, establishing relationships, and applying information to other situations.

These commonalities also were noted in other chapters of that volume. For example, Padilla, Muth, and Padilla (1991) wrote,

> Students' metacognitive knowledge of a reading or scientific task involves being aware of whether they understand the material they are reading or the activity they are performing. Students' metacognitive regulation of the two tasks enables them to take corrective action if they do not understand the material they are reading or the science activity they are performing. (p. 19)

Today, of course, the emphasis has shifted from process skills to inquiry skills. But the metacognitive connections are perhaps even more apparent. Magnusson and Palincsar (chapter 17) explicitly identify parallels between the processes involved in learning from text and learning from scientific inquiry:

It is also the case that skilled comprehenders engage in metacognitive activity to the extent that they maintain an awareness of the success with which they are constructing meaning and have a repertoire of strategies to enlist if they encounter impediments to their understanding. Inquiry requires a similar disposition on the part of the learner: a mindfulness about the purpose of the inquiry; attentiveness to the relationship between the question that is guiding the inquiry and the investigation itself; and the ability to monitor the progress of the inquiry in terms of how well it is advancing one's understanding of the phenomenon under investigation.

Guthrie and Wigfield (2001) also noted that the processes of science inquiry described in the American Association for the Advancement of Science's *Benchmarks for Science Literacy* (1993) and the NRC's *National Science Education Standards* (1996) are similar to comprehension strategies recommended as effective by the National Reading Panel (NICHD, 2000). They suggested that perhaps the cognitive strategies shared between reading and science could be taught directly, in coordination with each other.

Metacognitively Oriented Recommendations for Promoting Reading Comprehension and Science Inquiry

Many commonalities exist in recommendations for promoting reading comprehension and science inquiry. To illustrate, consider this quotation from the NSES (NRC, 1996) that would apply equally well if reading were substituted for science. The questioning, planning, evaluating, reflecting, and revising described below have as much a place in text comprehension as in science inquiry.

> In successful science classrooms, teachers and students collaborate in the pursuit of ideas, and students quite often initiate new activities related to an inquiry. Students formulate questions and devise ways to answer them, they collect data and decide how to represent it, they organize data to generate knowledge, and they test the reliability of the knowledge they have generated. As they proceed, students explain and justify their work to themselves and to one another, learn to cope with problems such as the limitations of equipment, and react to challenges posed by the teacher and by classmates. Students assess the efficacy of their efforts—they evaluate the data they have collected, re-examining or collecting more if necessary, and making statements about the generalizability of their findings. They plan and make presentations to the rest of the class about their work and accept and react to the constructive criticism of others. (p. 33)

The following five recommendations are drawn from the research literature.

1. Instruction should focus on multiple strategies and skills in context. In the early years of instructional research on promoting metacognitive skills in reading, researchers tended to select one strategy for instruction at a time, and the instruction often took place in artificial learning contexts. Researchers now have good evidence to support teaching combinations of reading strategies in natural learning situations (NICHD, 2000). Consider a recent approach called collaborative strategic reading (CSR), which combines comprehension strategy instruction with cooperative learning (Klingner & Vaughn, 1999). CSR teaches four strategies, shown, through early work by Palincsar and Brown (1984) on reciprocal teaching, to be quite effective. The first strategy is previewing. Here, students need to activate knowledge and predict what the passage will be about. The second strategy is "clicking and clunking." Students monitor when comprehension is going smoothly during reading (clicking) and when they are having difficulty (clunking). They use "fix-up" strategies to correct difficulties that arise when the text does not make sense. The third strategy is getting the gist. Students restate the most important ideas in sections or paragraphs during reading. The final strategy is wrapping up, in which students summarize after reading what has been learned and generate questions that a teacher might ask.

To teach the strategies, the teacher first uses direct explanation and modeling with the full class, and then he or she divides students into small groups to practice, giving each student a defined role. An evaluation of the effectiveness of CSR revealed that students showed greater improvement on a standardized reading comprehension test relative to peers who did not use CSR (Klingner, Vaughn, & Schumm, 1998). The approach was implemented successfully in culturally and linguistically diverse classrooms that included struggling readers, English-language learners, and average and high-achieving students. Social studies text was used in the intervention study, but the approach is likely to work as effectively with science text. An article published in *The Reading Teacher* provides teachers with explicit guidance for using CSR in their own classrooms (Klingner & Vaughn, 1999).

Science educators express similar views on how cognitive and metacognitive strategies are to be taught. According to the NSES (NRC, 1996), there should be less emphasis on process skills out of context and more emphasis on process skills in context. There should be less emphasis on individual process skills such as observation or inference, and more emphasis on using multiple process skills.

2. Promoting metacognition should not be an end in itself. Recommendations for promoting metacognition in the classroom are widely disseminated to teachers. Unfortunately, sometimes these recommendations have been put forward without solid research evidence behind them (Baker & Cerro, 2000) or they reflect misapplications of research to practice. Consider the case of strategy instruction. Reciprocal teaching has been embraced by teachers and textbook publishers in such a way as to cause Brown and Campione (1998) concern: "The surface rituals of questioning, summarizing, and so forth are engaged in, divorced from the goal of reading for understanding that they were designed to serve. These 'strategies' are sometimes practiced out of the context of reading authentic texts" (p. 177). Others, too, have worried that strategy-based instruction may divert the attention of students and teachers too much from the meaning of what is being read to the features of the strategies themselves (Beck, McKeown, Hamilton, & Kucan, 1997).

Thus, facility with the metacognitive skills of reading should not serve as an end in itself; rather, construction of meaning from text should be the ultimate goal. So, too, should students be taught to combine science processes and scientific knowledge as they use scientific reasoning and critical thinking to develop their understanding of science (NRC, 1996).

3. Students need to develop and apply a critical stance toward the information they encounter. A metacognitive skill critical to reading comprehension and science inquiry is to evaluate information encountered, whether through reading, listening, or observation. Students at all levels have a tendency to accept at face value the accuracy and plausibility of information conveyed to them by perceived authorities. An approach Baker (1991) has used to help dispel this tendency in reading comprehension is to focus on the variety of ways that text can be difficult to understand. Students can be taught through teacher think-alouds to ask themselves questions such as the following: Are there any words I don't understand? Is there any information that doesn't agree with what I already know? Are there any ideas that don't fit together (because of contradictions, ambiguous referents, misleading topic shifts)? Is there any information missing or not clearly explained? Teachers can use real texts to illustrate the process, or they may choose to modify simple texts to contain inconsistencies, difficult words, conflicts with prior knowledge, ambiguous referents, and so on. Teachers then model how they would go about resolving the comprehension difficulties using fix-up strategies such as rereading, looking ahead in the text for clarification, or consulting an outside source. Transferring responsibility for thinking aloud to the students themselves helps students take ownership of the monitoring process.

Lest one object to embedding errors in text on the grounds that it creates a task that is too contrived, bear in mind that naturally occurring texts are often "inconsiderate." That is, they lack sufficient background information and explicit connections among ideas. Science textbooks are particularly notorious in this regard (Holliday, 1991). Teaching students about different standards for evaluating comprehension can help make them aware that texts are fallible. They become more willing to acknowledge comprehension difficulties and are less apt to blame themselves, as many poorer readers do. In their Questioning the Author approach, Beck, McKeown, Worthy, Sandora, and Kucan (1996) give students a subtle change in goal, from trying to understand to making text understandable, thereby "deposing" the authority of the text.

Roth (1991) discussed the need for students to be able to read science text for conceptual change, noting the difficulties this poses.

> To read for conceptual change, students must 1) recognize the similarities and the differences between their own ideas and those in the text, 2) struggle with those differences, and 3) reorganize their own conceptual framework to accommodate the scientific explanations. This process requires a sophisticated reading strategy in which students carefully monitor their own thinking and weigh the evidence to decide if a change is warranted. (p. 62)

Some researchers discuss status constructs, such as intelligibility and plausibility, as playing a role in conceptual change. These constructs are similar to standards students might apply in evaluating their comprehension. That is, students need to ask whether the ideas are clear and whether they are plausible. Beeth (1998) reported a classroom study in which students were taught to use the intelligibility and plausibility constructs when speaking about ideas related to force and motion. The students' comments provided insights into their developing conceptions of force and motion and how they were learning these concepts. Asking students to evaluate ideas for plausibility and intelligibility shifts the classroom orientation from one in which students passively receive information to one in which they actively examine their own conceptions.

Students' attention needs to be directed to the process of acquiring scientific knowledge and the mechanisms by which truth values are assigned to information. Linn et al. (1996) write, "To foster metacognition, students must abandon the belief that there are only 2 types of scientific ideas, true and false" (p. 474). Wallace et al. (chapter 19 in this volume) argue that "one essential characteristic of scientific literacy is the ability to evaluate a scientific knowledge claim" and that "an important element of scientific literacy is understanding the relationships among questions, data, claims, and evidence" (p. 355).

Whether or not students come to adopt such an evaluativist stance depends heavily on the classroom climate. Ritchie, Tobin, and Hook (1997) found that if eighth-grade science teachers emphasized content exposure in their classrooms rather than the construction of new knowledge, interactions were dominated by what the researchers referred to as an authority warrant: Rather than exploring students' alternative conceptions and mental models, teachers expected students to accept the voice of authority uncritically.

What do students do when they encounter information that is anomalous to them? Such an experience can occur either while reading or during scientific inquiry. Chinn and Brewer (1998) identified eight possible responses to science that students might make: (1) ignoring the data, (2) rejecting the data, (3) professing uncertainty about the validity of the data, (4) excluding the data from the domain of the current theory, (5) holding the data in abeyance, (6) reinterpreting the data, (7) accepting the data and making peripheral changes to the current theory, and (8) accepting the data and changing theories.

These responses have much in common with the comprehension monitoring strategies described in the reading literature. For example, in an early study of comprehension monitoring, Baker (1979) found that students dealt with anomalous text information in a variety of ways, including (a) making an inference to supplement the information explicitly presented in the text, (b) looking back at previously read information to see if some crucial bit of information had been overlooked, (c) making a mental note that a problem had occurred but continuing to read in hope of clarification, (d) deciding the problem was trivial and not worth the effort of trying to resolve, (e) assuming the author or copy editor made a mistake, and (f) assigning an alternative interpretation to the text. Recognizing that information is anomalous is an important component of critical evaluation, as is selecting appropriate strategies for resolving the anomaly.

4. A common lesson organization in both science and reading promotes metacognition. Ridgeway (2001) observed that the science learning cycle so familiar to science teachers has a counterpart in reading. A prototypical learning cycle in both science and reading involves three phases.

During the first phase, the teacher works with the students to help them activate prior knowledge, make predictions, ask questions, establish purpose, and develop motivation and interest. During the second phase, students construct conceptual understandings with the guidance of the teacher. And during the final phase, students reflect on and apply the conceptual knowledge to new situations and contexts. Clearly, metacognitive skills play a key role in each of these phases.

Blank (2000) contrasted the learning cycle approach with a revised model involving metacognition, which not only provides students with the opportunity to reveal their science ideas but also to reflect on their science ideas. In this study, two seventh-grade science classrooms studied identical ecology content over a three-month period, but one class was taught using the traditional approach and one was taught using the metacognitive approach. Students in the metacognitive classroom were asked to discuss the status of their conceptions throughout the instruction. Although these students did not gain greater content knowledge of ecology, they showed more conceptual restructuring as a result of their increased ability to reflect on their thinking.

5. Teachers need to recognize that it is hard work to foster metacognition in reading and science. Teachers are routinely encouraged to model how to monitor comprehension and use comprehension strategies when they teach reading, but many teachers find that modeling thinking processes is difficult (Dowhower, 1999). Increasing teachers' own metacognitive awareness of their reading processes is an important first step in preparing them to increase students' awareness (Edwards, 1999). The common element in all of the approaches for teaching students to monitor their comprehension is that teachers need to make explicit their own comprehension and comprehension monitoring processes. Moreover, it is well documented that it is not easy to teach students to use cognitive and metacognitive strategies for reading comprehension (Block & Pressley, 2001).

Analogously, Roth (1991) noted that teaching students to read science text for conceptual understanding is challenging for teachers. Teachers need to have "a deep understanding of both science and their students' thinking, as well as a genuine respect for the challenges students face in undergoing conceptual change" (p. 62). Providing opportunities for teachers to talk with one another about their own thinking with respect to reading and science can be helpful in fostering such understandings (Baker & Saul, 1994).

Evaluating the Metacognitive Knowledge and Skills of Students

Given the focus on metacognition in contemporary recommendations for practice, teachers may well be interested in evaluating what their students know about their cognitive processes and their ability to regulate their own learning. One approach available to teachers for evaluating what students know about reading comprehension is to administer a simple-to-score multiple-choice questionnaire. The best known one is the Index of Reading Awareness, developed originally as a research tool for use with third and fifth graders, and subsequently recommended to classroom teachers for use as an informal assessment instrument (Jacobs & Paris, 1987). The Index of Reading Awareness assesses "children's knowledge about reading and their abilities to evaluate tasks, goals, and personal skills; to plan ahead for specific purposes; to monitor progress while reading; and to recruit fix-up strategies as needed" (Jacobs & Paris, 1987, p. 268). Yore, Craig, and Maguire (1998) adapted and validated the instrument to assess metacognition specifically in science reading, creating the Index of Science Reading Awareness.

A new 30-item questionnaire for students in grades 6 through 12, the Metacognitive Awareness Reading Strategies Inventory, has been developed and validated by Mokhtari and Reichard (2002). The complete inventory, along with information on how researchers and teachers might use it with students, is included in the publication. On the inventory, students rate on a five-point scale how frequently they engage in each strategy. Students can receive a total score and an individual score for each of three different types of strategies: global reading strategies (e.g., I have a purpose in mind when I read), problem-solving strategies (e.g., I try to get back on track when I lose concentration), and support reading strategies (e.g., I write summaries to reflect on key ideas in the text). The support strategies have particular relevance for the reading of content text, including science. Other items in this category deal with taking notes, underlining information, using reference materials, paraphrasing, and question generating.

Another option for assessment is to teach students to assess their own progress and understandings. Not only is this an excellent way to integrate comprehension instruction and assessment, but also it fosters metacognitive awareness and control. Students can be taught to use journals or portfolios to set goals, check their progress, and monitor their understanding. Thinking aloud provides another means of self-assessment for students, helping them gain an awareness of whether or not comprehension is occurring. In an article in *The Reading Teacher*, Baumann, Jones, and Seifert-Kessell (1993) described how teachers can foster comprehension monitoring through a think-aloud procedure. In addition, consistent with the social interaction perspective, dialogue and discussion are valuable ways for readers to test their understanding of text, as they see that their peers have other perspectives on the meaning of the material.

Now consider the parallels in these reading-focused recommendations with those that appear in the NSES (NRC, 1996):

> Skilled teachers guide students to understand the purposes for their own learning and to formulate self-assessment strategies. Teachers provide students with opportunities to develop their abilities to assess and reflect on their own scientific accomplishments. This process provides teachers with additional perspectives on student learning, and it deepens each student's understanding of the content and its applications. The interactions of teachers and students concerning evaluation criteria helps students understand the expectations for their work, as well as giving them experience in applying standards of scientific practice to their own and others' scientific efforts. The internalization of such standards is critical to student achievement in science. (p. 42)

An Increasing Role for Reading in Science Inquiry

As important as metacognition is to the successful application of science process skills, it is even more important to the successful interpretation of science text. Standards for science education give greater prominence to learning from text than they did in the 1980s. For example, the NSES call for children "to access scientific information from books...and evaluate and interpret the information they have acquired" (NRC, 1996, p. 45). Monitoring one's understanding of what is read is an inherent aspect of such evaluation and interpretation, and students must learn to take a critical stance with respect to what they read.

Teachers need to help students acquire the skills called for in the NSES. However, science teachers may not have the training in reading comprehension instruction that will enable them to do so effectively. As noted, teaching these kinds of strategies is effortful and challenging work, even when teachers are well prepared for it (Block & Pressley, 2001). Moreover, there is widespread concern that the early reading instruction children receive does not adequately prepare them for the challenges of using science texts to support inquiry (see chapters 9, 14, and 15 in this book). Information text is seldom used for reading instruction (Dreher, 2000; Duke, 2000), but efforts to increase access and opportunity for learning from text in the primary grades are increasing.

Forging Science–Literacy Connections Through Curricular Integration

Within the past decade, we have begun to see many initiatives focused on integrating language arts and sciences. Some have argued that the integration can lead to improved reading comprehension (Guthrie et al., 1998; Morrow, Pressley, Smith, & Smith, 1997), whereas others have argued that the integration will benefit science understanding. For example, Ford (chapter 15 of this book) suggests that the role of text is to serve as a tool in support of inquiry, and Pappas, Varelas, Barry, and Rife (chapter 9 of this book) similarly identify information books as having an important role in supporting children's hands-on explorations. Still others have commented on the reciprocal benefits. For example, Ridgeway (2001) argues that using hands-on science experiences can strengthen students' reading abilities and that reading and writing can enhance science concept development. Similarly, Palincsar and Magnusson (2001) argue that using text in inquiry-based science instruction can effectively advance the goals of both text comprehension instruction and science instruction.

Many researchers advocate using trade books in elementary science instruction as a way to integrate science and literacy (Baker & Saul, 1994; Morrow et al., 1997; see also chapter 15 of this book). Indeed, in response to the new emphasis on science reading in the NSES, prepackaged science materials now include trade books along with the materials needed for hands-on exploration. Trade books are a good alternative to textbooks, with their well-documented problems, and they are more engaging and interesting for children (Dreher, 2000). Accordingly, the research efforts exploring cross-curricular connections typically incorporate trade books into their interventions. A few efforts are described here that have explicit metacognitive components; others are described elsewhere in this book (see Section VI).

Concept-Oriented Reading Instruction (CORI) (Guthrie et al., 1998) focuses on the development of reading comprehension in the context of science learning. Through direct explanation, teacher modeling, and peer interaction, students are taught to use comprehension strategies as they read science materials, both fiction and nonfiction. Through observation and inquiry, students develop an interest in a science topic, which they pursue further through reading. The original aim of CORI was to provide a more intrinsically motivating and conceptually compelling context for learning comprehension strategies. Because strategy use is effortful, the researchers argued, motivation plays a critical role, driving the use of strategies in both science and reading. Evaluations of several implementations of CORI have shown that third- and fifth-grade students made substantial gains over comparison classrooms in strategy use, reading comprehension, conceptual knowledge, and motivation.

In the Communities of Learners (COL) research of Brown and Campione (1998), reading comprehension instruction is fully integrated with science, combining coherent content and complex strategies. Students collaborate with one another in research and knowledge sharing. Metacognitive skills are emphasized throughout. In an evaluation, students in COL classrooms made greater improvement in reading comprehension than in control classrooms. More telling still is that they improved in their reading comprehension relative to those in classrooms using reciprocal teaching and its four comprehension fostering/comprehension monitoring strategies of predicting, questioning, summarizing, and clarifying (Palincsar & Brown, 1984).

Another research team has been investigating the use of researcher-developed text materials in their science-literacy integration efforts. In their work, described fully in chapter 17 of this book, Magnusson and Palincsar (see also Palincsar & Magnusson, 2001) created notebook materials ostensibly written by a scientist during the course of an investigation. The contents of the notebook reflect metacognition in the scientist's thinking and activity. For example, she identified a set of claims based on preliminary evidence. Then, upon the urging of her peers, she collected more data, leading her to revise her initial claim. The authors' research led them to conclude that the use of these texts, in combination with hands-on investigation, supported not only the development of scientific concepts and scientific reasoning, but also metacognition. Metacognitive competencies included adopting a critical stance toward text, monitoring for comprehension, and taking remedial action to restore clarity and cohesion.

Metacognition in Science Writing

Although the primary emphasis in this chapter has been on metacognitive connections between reading and science, it is important to note that metacognition plays a role in the production of science text as well as the comprehension of science text. Research on the metacognitive skills of writing, though not as extensive as that on reading, represents a significant domain of inquiry, with important applications to classroom practice (Hayes, 1996; Hiebert & Raphael, 1996; Scardamalia & Bereiter, 1985). Metacognitive knowledge and control are essential through all phases of the writing process, including planning what to write, deciding how to express it, and revising initial efforts. Earlier in this chapter it was stated that one must take a critical stance toward what is read; this comment applies not only to texts written by others but also to one's own written products. The standards people use to evaluate their comprehension of texts written by others also should be called into play to evaluate the clarity, consistency, and effectiveness of their own texts.

Writing plays an important role in science inquiry because it helps students gain insight into their scientific thought processes and the state of their content knowledge. In other words, writing promotes metacognition about science. As Santa and Havens (1991) put it, "We cannot write about something if we do not understand it" (p. 123). Virtually all curricular integration efforts linking science and literacy emphasize writing as well as reading.

One integration effort that accords a prominent role to writing was developed by Keys, Hand, Prain, and Collins (1999; see also chapter 19, this volume). These science educators developed an approach known as the Science Writing Heuristic (SWH) to promote writing as a mode of thinking in the science classroom. Their research revealed that using SWH led to improved understanding of science concepts, metacognition, and the nature of science. The questions students address when using the heuristic have strong metacognitive elements; for example, What are my questions? What can I claim? How do I know? Why am I making these claims? How do my ideas compare with other ideas? How have my ideas changed? In chapter 19 in this book, the authors provide quotations that illustrate that students acquired the metacognitive insight mentioned earlier: You have to understand something in order to write about it.

A less structured alternative widely used in science classrooms is the learning log, in which students keep written records of their thoughts and observations. This activity helps students make their thinking more explicit, contributing toward metacognitive awareness (Santa & Havens, 1991). And through their writing, students demonstrate their ability to apply science inquiry skills. Such logs need not be in the traditional paper-and-pencil format. Audet, Hickman, and Dobrynina (1996) reported a case study of physics students who kept electronic learning logs that were shared with their classmates and the teacher. This computerized journaling provided a valuable opportunity for students to reflect on their own thinking as they defended their viewpoints and reacted to those of others.

Another writing activity that promotes metacognition is creating a graphic representation of what has been learned, whether it was learned firsthand from doing science or more indirectly from reading science, or a combination of the two. Many science educators advocate concept mapping, in which concepts, supporting details, and interconnections among concepts are represented graphically on paper. Such activities help students become more reflective about their own ideas (Linn et al., 1996).

Concluding Comments

The premise of this chapter is that when students have knowledge and control of their own cognitive processes, learning is enhanced. This holds true regardless of the domain of learning, whether in reading, writing, science, or any other activity that involves thinking. To the extent that science and literacy draw on many of the same cognitive and metacognitive processes, cross-curricular connections may well have a synergistic effect in promoting development. Science educators and literacy educators have the shared goal of fostering self-regulated learners, and the means for both to accomplish this goal appear to be similar. Recommendations are as follows: (a) scaffolded instruction should focus on multiple strategies and skills in context; (b) promoting metacognition should not be seen as an end in itself; (c) students need to develop and apply a critical stance toward the information they encounter; (d) teachers should recognize that it is hard work fostering metacognition and that peer support can be beneficial; (e) students need to learn to assess their own progress and understandings; and (f) students should be provided with frequent opportunities to share their ideas with their peers. In sum, science-literacy connections can promote metacognition; at the same time, metacognition can promote development in both literacy and science.

REFERENCES

American Association for the Advancement of Science (AAAS). (1993). *Benchmarks for science literacy.* New York: Oxford University Press.

Audet, R.H., Hickman, P., & Dobrynina, G. (1996). Learning logs: A classroom practice for enhancing scientific sense making. *Journal of Research in Science Technology, 33*(2), 205–222.

Baker, L. (1979). Comprehension monitoring: Identifying and coping with text confusions. *Journal of Reading Behavior, 11,* 365–374.

Baker, L. (1989). Metacognition, comprehension monitoring, and the adult reader. *Educational Psychology Review, 1,* 3–38.

Baker, L. (1991). Metacognition, reading, and science education. In C.M. Santa & D.E. Alvermann (Eds.), *Science learning: Processes and applications* (pp. 2–13). Newark, DE: International Reading Association.

Baker, L. (1996). Social influences on metacognitive development in reading. In C. Cornoldi & J. Oakhill (Eds.), *Reading comprehension difficulties: Processes and interventions* (pp. 331–351). Hillsdale, NJ: Erlbaum.

Baker, L. (2001). Metacognition in comprehension instruction. In C.C. Block & M. Pressley (Eds.), *Comprehension instruction: Research-based best practices* (pp. 77–95). New York: Guilford.

Baker, L., & Brown, A.L. (1984). Metacognitive skills and reading. In P.D. Pearson, R. Barr, M.L. Kamil, & P. Mosenthal (Eds.), *Handbook of reading research* (pp. 353–395). New York: Longman.

Baker, L., & Cerro, L. (2000). Assessing metacognition in children and adults. In G. Schraw & J. Impara (Eds.), *Issues in the measurement of metacognition* (pp. 99–145). Lincoln, NE: Buros Institute of Mental Measurements, University of Nebraska.

Baker, L., & Saul, W. (1994). Considering science and language arts connections: A study of teacher cognition. *Journal of Research in Science Teaching, 31*(9), 1023–1037.

Baumann, J.F., Jones, L.A., & Seifert-Kessell, N. (1993). Using think alouds to enhance children's comprehension monitoring abilities. *The Reading Teacher, 47,* 184–193.

Beck, I.L., McKeown, M.G., Hamilton, R.L., & Kucan, L. (1997). *Questioning the author: An approach for enhancing student engagement with text.* Newark, DE: International Reading Association.

Beck, I.L., McKeown, M.G., Worthy, J., Sandora, C.A., & Kucan, L. (1996). Questioning the Author: A year-long implementation to engage students with text. *The Elementary School Journal, 94,* 358–414.

Beeth, M.F. (1998). Teaching for conceptual change: Using status as a metacognitive tool. *Science Education, 82*(3), 343–356.

Blank, L.M. (2000). A metacognitive learning cycle: A better warranty for student understanding. *Science Education, 84*(4), 486–506.

Block, C.C., & Pressley, M. (Eds.). (2001). *Comprehension instruction: Research-based best practices.* New York: Guilford.

Brown, A.L. (1978). Knowing when, where, and how to remember: A problem of metacognition. In R. Glaser (Ed.), *Advances in instructional psychology* (Vol. 1, pp. 77–165). Hillsdale, NJ: Erlbaum.

Brown, A.L., & Campione, J.C. (1998). Designing a community of young learners: Theoretical and practical lessons. In N.M. Lambert & B.L. McCombs (Eds.), *How students learn: Reforming schools through learner-centered education* (pp. 153–186). Washington, DC: American Psychological Association.

Champagne, A.B., & Klopfer, L.E. (1991). Understanding science text and the physical world. In C.M. Santa & D.E. Alvermann (Eds.), *Science learning: Processes and applications* (pp. 64–73). Newark, DE: International Reading Association.

Chinn, C.A., & Brewer, W.F. (1998). An empirical test of a taxonomy of responses to anomalous data in science. *Journal of Research in Science Teaching, 35*(6), 623–654.

Dowhower, S.L. (1999). Supporting a strategic stance in the classroom: A comprehension framework for helping teachers help students to be strategic. *The Reading Teacher, 52,* 672–688.

Dreher, M.J. (2000). Fostering reading for learning. In L. Baker, M.J. Dreher, & J.T. Guthrie (Eds.), *Engaging young readers: Promoting achievement and motivation* (pp. 68–93). New York: Guilford.

Duke, N.K. (2000). 3.6 minutes per day: The scarcity of informational texts in first grade. *Reading Research Quarterly, 35,* 202–224.

Edwards, M. (1999). The aim is metacognition: For teachers as well as students. In J. Hancock (Ed.), *The explicit teaching of reading* (pp. 80–96). Newark, DE: International Reading Association.

Flavell, J.H. (1976). Metacognitive aspects of problem solving. In L.B. Resnick (Ed.), *The nature of intelligence* (pp. 231–235). Hillsdale, NJ: Erlbaum.

Guthrie, J.T., Van Meter, P., Hancock, G.R., Alao, S., Anderson, E., & McCann, A. (1998). Does concept-oriented reading instruction increase strategy use and conceptual learning from text? *Journal of Educational Psychology, 90*(2), 261–278.

Guthrie, J.T., & Wigfield, A. (2001, August). *Engaging in reading through science: Motivating strategies across the disciplines.* Paper presented at the Crossing Borders: Connecting Science and Literacy conference, Baltimore, MD.

Hayes, J.R. (1996). A new framework for understanding cognition and affect in writing. In C.M. Levy & S. Ransdell (Eds.), *The science of writing: Theories, methods, individual differences, and applications* (pp. 1–27). Mahwah, NJ: Erlbaum.

Hiebert, E.H., & Raphael, T.E. (1996). Psychological perspectives on literacy and extensions to educational practice. In D.C. Berliner & R.C. Calfee (Eds.), *Handbook of educational psychology* (pp. 550–602). New York: Macmillan.

Holliday, W.G. (1991). Helping students learn effectively from science text. In C.M. Santa & D.E. Alvermann (Eds.), *Science learning: Processes and applications* (pp. 38–47). Newark, DE: International Reading Association.

Jacobs, S.E., & Paris, S.G. (1987). Children's metacognition about reading: Issues in definition, measurement, and instruction. *Educational Psychologist, 22,* 255–278.

Keys, C.W., Hand, B., Prain, V., & Collins, S. (1999). Using the Science Writing Heuristic as a tool for learning from laboratory investigations in secondary science. *Journal of Research in Science Teaching, 36,* 1065–1084.

Klingner, J.K., & Vaughn, S. (1999). Promoting reading comprehension, content learning, and English acquisition through Collaborative Strategic Reading (CSR). *The Reading Teacher, 52,* 738–747.

Klingner, J.K., Vaughn, S., & Schumm, J.S. (1998). Collaborative strategic reading during social studies in heterogeneous fourth-grade classrooms. *The Elementary School Journal, 99,* 3–22.

Linn, M.C., Songer, N.B., & Eylon, B-S. (1996). Shifts and convergences in science learning and instruction. In D.C. Berliner & R.C. Calfee (Eds.), *Handbook of educational psychology* (pp. 438–490). New York: Macmillan.

Mokhtari, K., & Reichard, C.A. (2002). Assessing students' metacognitive awareness of reading strategies. *Journal of Educational Psychology, 94*(2), 249–259.

Morrow, L.M., Pressley, M., Smith, J.K., & Smith, M. (1997). The effect of a literature-based program integrated into literacy and science instruction with children from diverse backgrounds. *Reading Research Quarterly, 32,* 54–76.

National Institute of Child Health and Human Development (NICHD). (2000). *Report of the National Reading Panel. Teaching children to read: An evidence-based assessment of the scientific research literature on reading and its implications for reading instruction* (NIH Publication No. 00-4769). Washington, DC: U.S. Government Printing Office.

National Research Council (NRC). (1996). *National science education standards.* Washington, DC: National Academy Press.

Otero, J. (1998). Influence of knowledge activation and context on comprehension monitoring of science texts. In D.J. Hacker, J. Dunlosky, & A.C. Graesser (Eds.), *Metacognition in educational theory and practice* (pp. 145–164). Mahwah, NJ: Erlbaum.

Padilla, M.J., Muth, K.D., & Padilla, R.K.L. (1991). Science and reading: Many process skills in common? In C. Santa & D.E. Alvermann (Eds.), *Science learning: Processes and applications* (pp. 14–21). Newark, DE: International Reading Association.

Palincsar, A.S., & Brown, A.L. (1984). Reciprocal teaching of comprehension-fostering and comprehension-monitoring activities. *Cognition and Instruction, 1,* 117–175.

Palincsar, A.S., & Magnusson, S.J. (2001). The interplay of first-hand and second-hand investigations to model and support the development of scientific knowledge and reasoning.

In S.M. Carver & D. Klahr (Eds.), *Cognition and instruction: Twenty-five years of progress* (pp. 151–194). Mahwah, NJ: Erlbaum.

Ridgeway, V.G. (2001, August). *Science* ◄────► *reading: Reciprocal effects of hands-on science and minds-on reading.* Paper presented at the Crossing Borders: Connecting Science and Literacy conference, Baltimore, MD.

Ritchie, S.M., Tobin, K., & Hook, K.S. (1997). Teaching referents and the warrants used to test the viability of mental models: Is there a link? *Journal of Research in Science Teaching, 34*(3), 223–238.

Roth, K.J. (1991). Reading science texts for conceptual change. In C.M. Santa & D.E. Alvermann (Eds.), *Science learning: Processes and applications* (pp. 48–63). Newark, DE: International Reading Association.

Santa, C.M., & Alvermann, D.E. (Eds.). (1991). *Science learning: Processes and applications.* Newark, DE: International Reading Association.

Santa, C.M., & Havens, L.T. (1991). Learning through writing. In C.M. Santa & D.E. Alvermann (Eds.), *Science learning: Processes and applications* (pp. 122–133). Newark, DE: International Reading Association.

Scardamalia, M., & Bereiter, C. (1985). Fostering the development of self-regulation in children's knowledge processing. In S.S. Chipman, J.W. Segal, & R. Glaser (Eds.), *Thinking and learning skills: Current research and open questions* (Vol. 2, pp. 563–577). Hillsdale, NJ: Erlbaum.

Snow, C.E., Burns, M.S., & Griffin, P. (Eds.). (1998). *Preventing reading difficulties in young children.* Washington, DC: National Academy Press.

Vygotsky, L.S. (1978). *Mind in society: The development of higher psychological processes* (M. Cole, V. John-Steiner, S. Scribner, & E. Souberman, Eds. and Trans.). Cambridge, MA: Harvard University Press. (Original work published 1934)

Yore, L.D., Craig, M.T., & Maguire, T.O. (1998). Index of Science Reading Awareness: An interactive-constructive model, test verification, and grades 4–8 results. *Journal of Research in Science Teaching, 35*(1), 27–51.

White, R.T., & Gunstone, R.F. (1989). Metalearning and conceptual change. *International Journal of Science Education, 11*, 577–586.

CHOOSING
SCIENCE

TRADE BOOKS

How to choose quality trade books is a perennial problem for educators.

In chapter 14, "Choosing Informational Books for Primary-Grade Classrooms: The Importance of Balance and Quality," Mariam Jean Dreher and Anita N. Voelker describe the imbalance between fiction and nonfiction trade books in the primary grades and provide concrete advice on what to look for in choosing appropriate titles. The authors argue for the need to carefully evaluate classroom libraries, looking particularly at the varied features represented in a collection. Using books for primary-grade children to illustrate their point, Dreher and Voelker then offer book evaluation criteria that teachers might use as the basis for selection.

In chapter 15, "Highly Recommended Trade Books: Can They Be Used in Inquiry Science?" Danielle J. Ford looks at award-winning titles, asking if and how particular texts might serve as tools to support inquiry. She then analyzes the notion of science embedded in these works: What content is represented in the books rated as outstanding by the major awards committees? What images of science are represented in these titles? How are these images delivered (i.e., what writing style and genres are used)? And finally, what do these results tell us about the suitability and practicality of these books for inquiry science instruction?

In chapter 16, "How Not to Get Lost on *The Magic School Bus*: What Makes High Science Content Read-Alouds?" Laura B. Smolkin and Carol A. Donovan describe some of the ways a teacher can negotiate fictive elements to help children attend to science content in dual-purpose texts. To this end the authors studied practitioners' read-aloud strategies to understand if and how science content is emphasized. Highlighting a particularly successful read-aloud, Smolkin and Donovan then offer suggestions for other teachers.

Together these chapters help readers ask important questions that may guide them in making trade book choices.

CHAPTER 14

Choosing Informational Books for Primary-Grade Classrooms: The Importance of Balance and Quality

Mariam Jean Dreher and Anita N. Voelker

Considerable evidence indicates that young children have much more opportunity in school to read and listen to stories than to experience informational text. In an analysis of literacy tasks in grades 2 and 6, Fisher and Hiebert (1990) noted that almost all instruction and materials read or written by students involved stories. Similarly, in a more recent survey, primary-grade teachers reported that reading in their classrooms involved informational text only 6% of the time (Pressley, Rankin, & Yokoi, 1996). Duke's (2000) research showed that informational books were scarce in first-grade classroom libraries and that instruction related to informational text averaged 3.6 minutes per day. In addition, teachers typically select stories to read to their students (Hoffman, Roser, & Battle, 1993), rather than informational books. In short, as Venezky (2000) concluded, "literacy instruction in schools concentrates almost exclusively on fictional texts and literary appreciation" (p. 22).

Yet experts have long called for change in this situation (e.g., Hiebert, 1991; Pappas, 1991; Sanacore, 1991), pointing out that not only do young children deal quite well with informational text, they are interested in it. Pappas and her colleagues have conducted several studies documenting young children's interactions with such text. For example, kindergartners were just as successful in learning new vocabulary and in pretend reading after having listened to an informational book as they were after having listened to a storybook (Pappas, 1993; see also Duke & Kays, 1998). Other studies have shown the successful use of informational book read-alouds with urban first graders (Pappas & Barry, 1997; Pappas, Varelas, Barry, & O'Neill, 2000). Similarly, Horowitz and Freeman's (1995) research demonstrated that both kindergartners and second graders enjoyed having expository science books read to them. Kletzien and Szabo (1998) found that, when given a choice, first through third graders indicated that they would choose informational books at least as often as stories for independent reading. Primary-grade teachers who have added substantial informational text to their instructional materials have reported success (Duthie, 1996; Kamil & Lane, 1997). Further, there is reason to believe that young children's achievement and motivation both would benefit from more opportunity to interact with informational books as part of reading instruction (Dreher, 2000). Indeed, some children appear to find informational books to be their preferred route to literacy (Caswell & Duke, 1998).

Although informational books are typically scarce in classrooms, we expect today's young children to do well with such materials. The Committee on the Prevention of Reading Difficulties in Young Children (Snow, Burns, & Griffin, 1998), for example, concluded that even primary-grade children must be able to read and understand both fiction and nonfiction, as well as to combine information from multiple nonfiction sources in written reports. They argued that children should enter the fourth grade "capable— independently and productively—of reading to learn" (Snow et al., 1998, p. 207). Without appropriate opportunities to interact with and learn from informational text, primary-grade children are less likely to be exposed to the academic vocabulary they need to maintain reading achievement levels as they move into the upper grades (Chall, Jacobs, & Baldwin, 1990).

Thus, teachers in primary-grade classrooms across the United States are being asked to incorporate more nonfiction into their instruction. And publishing companies have responded to this need by flooding the market with informational books. But for many teachers, adding informational text to primary-grade instruction is not without difficulties. In this chapter, we focus on two difficulties we have observed in primary classrooms. First, we discuss the lack of a full range of nonfiction books. Even when classroom libraries are large, there are often few informational books, and these books are limited to a few types. We detail the range of informational books available and why this range is important to consider. Second, we discuss the need to carefully evaluate informational books and their varied features. Using science trade books for primary-grade children to illustrate our points, we offer an evaluation guide that teachers can modify according to their needs.

Including a Full Range of Informational Books in the Classroom Library

Although children's access to both school and classroom libraries is correlated with reading achievement (Elley, 1992), we focus here on classroom collections because they provide children with immediate access to books

(Neuman, 1999). We strongly believe that all children should be in classrooms with well-stocked, well-designed classroom libraries. But evidence indicates that many classrooms have no libraries. Fractor, Woodruff, Martinez, and Teale (1993) found that less than one half of the 183 elementary classrooms they analyzed had a classroom library. Unfortunately, even when there were classroom libraries, they were overwhelmingly rated as basic, with a very small numbers of books.

We suggest that teachers with no library or a small one should start or extend their collection. Fractor et al. (1993) noted that features such as size, face-front display, and organization are important in well-designed libraries. In addition, a good classroom library should have at least four books per student, with an excellent library containing at least eight per student. Creating a well-designed library with sufficient books can be challenging. Fractor et al. (1993) and Chambliss and McKillop (2000) offer thorough discussions of how to design good classroom libraries and how to meet the challenge of assembling a substantial collection.

Our focus here is on evaluating the range of a classroom library once it is established. A good classroom library should include a balance of fiction and informational books. There is no hard rule on the proportion of each type. However, a compelling argument can be made to target approximately 50% fiction and 50% nonfiction or informational books. Doing so would reflect the need for children to become equally proficient in reading both stories and informational text (Dreher, 2000).

Within these broad categories of fiction and nonfiction, it is important to include diverse genres and structures. Just as fiction in a classroom library should include many subcategories such as realistic fiction, historical fiction, science fiction, and fantasy, so too should a collection of nonfiction be diverse. Many nonfiction books for young children are written in a story form (narrative). But children should not be limited to nonfiction in narrative forms. There are excellent informational books that give young children the opportunity to experience expository text structures. In addition, young children should also have the opportunity to experience books that do not need to be read from beginning to end but can be read out of order, as when a reader searches for particular information using features such as an index, headings, boldface type, or a table of contents.

Types of Informational books

To avoid limiting children to one type of nonfiction, we have found it useful to sort informational books into three categories: expository, narrative-informational, and mixed texts. By using these terms, we underscore the point that all nonfiction is not alike and that it is important to afford children opportunities to experience all these types.

Expository. Books in this category might be thought of as reports. These books do not have a story line with plot and characters. Instead, they have expository structures such as comparison and contrast, problem and solution, sequence, cause and effect, and description. An excerpt from *Spiders* (Cullen, 1996) illustrates this type of writing:

> Different spiders catch their food in different ways. Wolf spiders run after their victims. Jumping spiders leap onto them. Ambushing spiders wait for insects to settle near them, and spitting spiders creep up on their prey and glue them down. (p. 20)

Here spiders in general are being discussed, rather than an individual spider as in a story. In addition, the excerpt exemplifies a common feature in expository books, the use of timeless or present tense verbs rather than past tense as in stories.

Excerpts from *Zipping, Zapping, Zooming Bats* (Earle, 1995) and *The Life and Times of the Peanut* (Micucci, 1997) provide additional examples of expository writing:

> Bats have hooked claws on their toes and thumbs. When bats sleep or clean themselves, they hang upside down by their toe claws. They use their claws to move around on their roosts, to comb their fur, and to clean their ears. Bats keep themselves as clean as cats, using both their tongues and claws. (Earle, 1995, p. 19)

> Each year, Americans eat more than 800 million pounds of peanut butter. Most of it is eaten by children. But American children were not the first peanut butter eaters.
> Almost 3,000 years ago, South American Indians ground peanuts into a sticky paste....They mixed their gooey delight with cocoa, the main ingredient of chocolate. (Micucci, 1997, p. 20)

Expository books can have different patterns. Because of the way the information is presented, some are best read sequentially. Others are organized topically and can be read in any order or used to search for specific information. For example, *Zipping, Zapping, Zooming Bats* (Earle, 1995) lends itself to being read from beginning to end; it does not have a table of contents, an index, or headings that would help readers determine where they might start if they didn't want to read it in order. In contrast, many other expository books have features such as a glossary, an index, a table of contents, and headings that facilitate children's search for information. For example, although *The Life and Times of the Peanut* (Micucci, 1997) could be read sequentially, it has a table of contents that makes it easy to read topically. *Spiders* (Cullen, 1996), with both a table of contents and an index, is also easily read topically.

Narrative-Informational. Narrative-informational books present factual information in story format. In *Everybody Cooks Rice* (Dooley, 1991), a girl goes from house to house at dinnertime looking for her brother. As she visits each home, she learns about the ethnic diversity of her neighborhood via the rice dishes each family is cooking. In *Charlie Needs a Cloak* (dePaola, 1973), readers follow a shepherd through all the steps of making a cloak, but the information is presented as a story: "...in the spring, Charlie sheared his sheep. He washed the wool, and carded the wool to straighten it out. Then Charlie spun the wool into yarn" (n.p.).

Many biographies and autobiographies are narrative-informational books. For example, *The Emperor's Egg* (Jenkins, 1999) provides a wealth of information about emperor penguins as it tells the story of a male penguin who hatches an egg after his mate does her job of laying it:

> ...what's that shape over there? It can't be. Yes! It's a **penguin**! It's not just any old penguin either. It's a male Emperor penguin (the biggest penguin in the world), and he's doing a Very Important Job. He's taking care of his egg. He didn't lay it himself, of course. His mate did that weeks ago. But very soon afterward she turned around and waddled off to sea. (Jenkins, 1999, pp. 7–10)

Similarly, Caldecott Medal-winner *Snowflake Bentley* (Martin, 1998) presents rich information in story format about the life of the man who documented the uniqueness of individual snowflakes: "In the days when farmers worked with ox and sled and cut the dark with lantern light, there lived a boy who loved snow more than anything else in the world" (n.p.).

Mixed Texts. Many children's books mix narrative and expository structures in the same book. Cole's original Magic School Bus series (e.g., *The Magic School Bus in the Time of Dinosaurs* [Cole, 1994]) features a story of a fictitious teacher and her class who go on an adventure. But the story is surrounded by facts in boxes and charts, many in the guise of student reports. (Note that the newer Magic School Bus series, based on the television show, features narrative-informational books such as *The Magic School Bus Wet All Over: A Book About the Water Cycle* [Relf, 1996]). Another example of a mixed text is *The Popcorn Book* (dePaola, 1978) in which brothers become curious about popcorn as they make some for themselves. One brother reads aloud facts from an encyclopedia about popcorn; this text appears in a different typeface than the rest of *The Popcorn Book*. Similarly, *Frog's Eggs* (Ramsay & Humphrey, 1995) tells the story of a little girl and her grandmother who find frog spawn and watch it develop. As the little girl asks questions, her grandmother gives factual information that appears in a distinct typeface accompanying photographs of stages in frog development.

Inventorying Classroom Libraries

As noted previously, even in classrooms with sizable book collections, teachers may find that they have an imbalance between fiction and nonfiction. This was exactly the case in a recent inventory of the classroom libraries of nine second-grade classroom teachers (Dreher & Baker, 2003). Although two of these teachers had a large number of books in their classroom libraries, fiction greatly outnumbered the nonfiction titles.

Table 14.1 shows the results in one teacher's library. Although the teacher had more than 800 engaging books, nearly 80% of the titles were fiction. When we showed her the inventory of her classroom library by type of book, she became visibly upset. Although her classroom library was actually among the best we had seen in her school district, what upset her was that the inventory made it apparent that her library contained virtually no expository writing. As she put it, "This means my kids aren't getting an opportunity to read that kind of material!" (Dreher & Baker, 2003).

A common misconception is incorrectly equating all nonfiction with exposition. As outlined previously, nonfiction can be expository, narrative, or a combination. If children's experiences with text remain largely narrative, then they do not get exposure to and instruction about the unique sentence and paragraph structures and other features involved in nonnarrative informational books. Using multiple terms to discuss types of informational books helps capture the range of texts that are needed in classrooms.

Evaluating Informational Books for Classroom Use

If teachers inventory their classroom libraries, they will be better informed about the gaps in their collections. To fill those gaps, teachers will want to select quality books that not only appeal to their students' interests but also match their instructional needs.

Numerous checklists are available for selecting science trade books. Rice (2002) examined recent guidelines by Butzow and Butzow (2000),

Number (Percentage) of Volumes in a Sizable Second-Grade Classroom Library by Reading Level and Genre

Genre	Reading Level (A–Z)				
	A–G	H–J	K–M	N–Z	Total
Fiction	35	194	303	137	669
	(4%)	(23%)	(36%)	(16%)	(79%)
Expository	2	26	33	19	80
	(0.2%)	(3%)	(4%)	(2%)	(10%)
Narrative-Informational	4	18	28	19	69
	(0.5%)	(2%)	(3%)	(2%)	(8%)
Mixed (combines narrative and exposition)	0	2	4	0	6
		(0.2%)	(0.5%)		(0.7%)
Poetry/Song/Cartoon	0	7	7	0	14
		(0.8%)	(0.8%)		(1.7%)
Word Games/Dictionary	0	2	0	2	4
		(0.2%)		(0.2%)	(0.5%)
Textbooks	0	0	1	2	3
			(0.1%)	(0.2%)	(0.4%)
Total	41	249	376	179	845
	(5%)	(29%)	(45%)	(21%)	(100%)

Reading levels are based on Fountas and Pinnell (1999).

Mayer (1995), Pottle (1996), and Sudol and King (1996) and concluded that teachers could "use any of these sets of guidelines with confidence to quickly and efficiently select trade books for teaching science" (p. 560). These recent guidelines, along with other longstanding suggestions for evaluation (e.g., Janke & Norton, 1983; Simon, 1982) vary, but all consider the accuracy of science concepts.

However, an in-depth look indicates that not every set of guidelines is comprehensive. For example, Butzow and Butzow (2000) used elements of narrative text in their outline, including setting, characterization, plot, and theme. Although their list may be helpful for narrative-informational books or storybooks, it is relatively useless for expository writing. Simon (1982) encouraged teachers to create their own classroom library of science trade books and to use the National Science Teachers Association's list of Outstanding Science Trade Books for Children (available at www.nsta.org) as a source for making selections. Simon's other tips for selecting books were general recommendations that encouraged teachers to "select science trade books...with care and thought" (Simon, 1982, p. 6), use contemporary books, and read for accuracy and clarity. But few specifics are provided on what to look for.

Mayer (1995) provided a more structured framework by creating a list of questions for teachers to answer about the books they select. However, if this list is used as the only approach for selecting trade books, certain issues will not be considered. For example, although Mayer considered gender equity in her checklist, she did not indicate the same necessity for cultural representations. She used the passage of time as an element to consider but did not address issues such as giving children a way to compare the size of an animal to a known concept. Importantly, Mayer did consider illustrations and misrepresentations in her questions. Mayer noted that a book could be an "excellent example of children's literature but at the same time, a poor resource for learning science" (p. 18). In creating her checklist, she hoped to provide teachers with a tool to distinguish the difference. It should be noted, however, that sometimes a book that is *not* an excellent example of children's literature might be a valuable resource for science content, if children are taught how to search it for specific information. We suggest that guidelines for book selection take differential uses of books into account.

Sudol and King (1996) offered a chart that guides a teacher through the review of five categories: accuracy, organization and layout, cohesion of ideas, specialized vocabulary, and reader interest. For each of these categories, they suggest rating whether a book meets all or most criteria, some criteria, or few criteria. They also include a section for a brief open-ended comment on the book. Although these are good suggestions, teachers often have books in their libraries that would not score high on Sudol and King's evaluation form yet have potential for use. In fact, one teacher recently informed us that by being aware of a book's strengths and weaknesses, she could make any book work in her classroom (Dreher & Baker, 2003).

Our review of available checklists led us to design our own evaluation guide. Our evaluation guide seeks to provide teachers with practical steps to employ in selecting useful books for their classrooms and to create awareness about the challenges and hazards in books already housed on their shelves. Pottle (1996) championed the need for simplicity in evaluating books, and we concur. However, Moss (2001) encouraged teachers to focus both on forms of presentation and on ways of reading. Considering Moss's multimode analysis led us to create a multidimensional design for teachers to use with books they own and books they are considering purchasing. As Moss indicated, new book designs are often nonlinear and present unique passageways for the reader. Books like these include titles such as those in the Eye Wonder (e.g., *Dinosaur* [Walker & Gray, 2001]) and Eyewitness Juniors (e.g., *Amazing Flying Machines* [Kerrod, 1992]) series. These kinds of books present opportunities for both capable and struggling readers to engage on "a level playing field" (Moss, 2001, p. 110). Providing books that work for a variety of students in a classroom requires that teachers be aware of features and possibilities of the books in their libraries and of books they add to their collections. By using a comprehensive evaluation guide, teachers can become better consumers of new books as well as thoughtful proprietors of older books.

Inspiration for Our Evaluation Guide

As we pondered how to create an evaluation guide, an observation in a second-grade classroom influenced our thinking. The second graders' teacher had asked them to review informational books to decide which titles to order for the classroom library. She asked the children to take books from a stack in the middle of each table and review each one until a timer went off, at which time they each passed the title to another child:

> Twenty-five pairs of eyes and hands engage in the process. The circular seating arrangement allows access to the books piled in the middle and freedom to have eye contact with everyone in the group. Each child seems to have invented his/her own procedure but there are clear patterns to their work. Their serious expressions show that they consider this an important task. The occasional giggle behind a small hand accompanied by a pointing finger breaks the remarkable silence of the room. It is a Friday and the last day before Christmas vacation. Yet these second graders are unencumbered by the upcoming holiday excitement. Instead they are focused and thoughtful. (Dreher & Baker, 2003)

As we observed these children reviewing science trade books, we were fascinated by the manner in which they determined which books were worthy of selection. Some common patterns were evident in their exploration and critique. Much attention and time was given to the cover. If the children looked at a book with a wrap-around cover, such as *Meet the Octopus* (James, 1996), they would instinctively spread the book open on the floor to appreciate the entire view. They looked deeply into the eyes of *Watchful Wolves* (Berman, 1998), who stared unblinking back at them. Soft fingertips lightly stroked the backs of *Siberian Tigers* (St. Pierre, 2001) as the boldly colored cats raced across the snow. Ladybugs' spots (*Ladybug*, Hartley & Macro, 1998) were counted without concern for the passing of time. Surprisingly, few children moved their eyes beyond the specific book they held.

Once they opened a book, the children continued to view pictures like magnets that attracted them to a particular page. This classroom of second graders had watched their teacher explore trade books numerous times. Predictably, they modeled their teacher's style by checking the table of contents and sliding their index fingers deliberately down the list of possibilities, telling their neighbor a nugget or two about the book, even if the neighbor was too engrossed in his or her own book to hear. Staring directly into a fluffy chicken's eyes on the cover of *Life Cycle of a Chicken* (Royston, 1998), a young reader queried, "Do you think this chicken is mean? Look at his eyes. I don't know if chickens are so nice."

Some savvy readers turned directly to pages noted in the table of contents and began their soft subvocalization of the words, slowing down when respellings appeared in parentheses or bold print. Others directed their attention to the index and skimmed the topics. Notably, a handful of children were still enraptured by the cover and never cracked the spine. Their teacher was the only one in the room attentive to the time, and she produced the signal to stop reading. Chorally, the children chanted, "Book, book, pass." Hands slipped books to new readers, and the process resumed.

Many teachers would love to examine nonfiction books with no concern but enjoyment like these children did. The mental image of teachers chanting, "Book, book, pass!" as they sit together luxuriating in reading nonfiction trade books is a satisfying thought, but teachers must make their book choices with multiple issues in mind. Using this extraordinary example of free exploration along with information from previous checklists and guidelines, we have created a guide that is teacher-friendly and flexible enough for evaluating multiple types of informational books for a variety of needs.

Applying the Evaluation Guide to a Science Trade Book

The evaluation guide, shown in Table 14.2, is flexible enough that teachers can use the entire document or just sections, as they wish. To model how to use the evaluation guide, we overview our evaluation of *Meet the Octopus* (James, 1996) in the right-hand column of the table.

Type. We began by reading *Meet the Octopus* (James, 1996) to determine how to classify it. The following excerpt is typical of the writing: "Sometimes other animals try to eat the octopus. But the octopus has a special trick for

TABLE 14.2
Completed Evaluation Guide for a Primary-Grade Science Trade Book

Directions: Proceed through the tasks listed in the left-hand column. Use as many of the Points to Consider in the center columns as are helpful in reviewing the book. Record your notes in the right-hand column.

Tasks	Points to Consider		Notes for Instructional Use
Type: Determine which type of informational book this is and what patterns are used.	Category: ■ Expository ■ Narrative-informational ■ Mixed	Organizational Patterns: ■ Sequential or continuous: most often read front to back. Example: *Life Cycle of a Chicken* (Royston, 1998) ■ Topical: may be read in order but is easy to use in parts. Example: *Ladybug* (Hartley & Macro, 1998) ■ Hierarchical: builds to a theme. Example: *Body Numbers* (Looye, 1998) ■ Tiered: two texts in one; may be two stand-alones, but often read together. Example: *Come Back, Salmon* (Cone, 1992)	Title: *Meet the Octopus* Author: *Sylvia M. James (1996)* *This book is expository, with a report-like style. It discusses octopuses in general and uses timeless verbs. The table of contents indicates that this is topical in instructional design and can be read in parts. For example, you can read about getting food on pages 15–18 or read on page 14 about where octopuses live.*
Content: Read book for science concepts.	Topic: Coverage should be adequate for level and use	Facts: ■ Factual information should be noted clearly to the reader ■ Facts should add interest and engagement ■ Information should be current	Aids to Evaluating Accuracy: ■ Evidence of author expertise ■ Authorities consulted ■ Book has received awards/praise for the scientific content	<u>What evidence is there about the accuracy of the science content?</u> *Knowing the author is the director of educational programs at the National Aquarium leads me to have confidence in the science concepts. Also the photographs come from the National Audubon Society.*
Covers: Study front and back.	Front Cover: ■ Realistic image, not anthropomorphic ■ Photographs or illustrations are accurate and fit with topic	Back Cover: ■ Questions/information for reader engagement ■ Reading levels/other information for teachers	Author/Illustrator: ■ Unknown, no information given ■ Familiar author or illustrator ■ Well known, credentialed author or illustrator	<u>How does the cover information affect the way I will use this book?</u> *The wrap-around cover and interesting paragraph on the back will entice the students.*
Additional Text: Read pages that precede and follow the book's main text.	Endpapers (inside covers): ■ Adds interest to topic ■ Adds understanding to topic	Resources: ■ Additional books listed to extend topic ■ Author's notes ■ Bibliography	Features: ■ Table of contents ■ Index ■ Glossary	<u>What features are present or missing that will affect my use of this book?</u> *Since there is no glossary in the book, I will have to be certain terms are clear in the text or provide additional definitions. I will also need to locate other books for future exploration of the topic.*

Design: Skim text to assess ease of use.	Setup: ■ Font used is appropriate for this reading level ■ Text design will make sense to the students at this level ■ Reasonable chapter or segment lengths for this level ■ Page numbers	Specialized terms: ■ New terms are identified clearly (e.g., bold print, italics)	Other features: These may include additional information in sidebars, enlargements, insets, conventions to link text and illustrations, etc.	How does the book's design affect my use of this book? *Several design elements will help my students: The use of bold print for the names of different types of octopuses and the red arrows connecting new vocabulary to the illustrations. (See page 13 for an example.)* *I have a concern about the way that some of the text wraps around the illustrations. For example, on page 4, the paragraph is shaped like a backward capital L. This may confuse my students who are just learning how to write a paragraph.*
Writing: Reread one or two pages critically.	Reader Engagement: Questions or statements should connect reader to topic (e.g., caption for map, "Do wolves live near your school?")	Language Usage: ■ Words are appropriate and precise for the level of the reader ■ New words are clearly explained	Transitions/Flow: The author and the illustrator should take the reader with them in the process of explaining or informing	What are the strengths or weaknesses of the writing that will affect my use of this book? *The use of engaging questions is a plus. On page 7, the caption asks, "Can you find an octopus hiding in this picture?" The author also uses literary devices like onomatopoeia as in, "whoosh!"*
Illustrations: Look carefully at illustrations and photographs.	Pictures: ■ Fit with natural setting ■ Realistic ■ Appropriate to actual size or are shown in relationship to known items	Gender/Race: ■ Illustrations are not stereotypical ■ Gender and race are equitably illustrated	Captions/Notes: ■ Illustrations are identified and fit with the text and overall topic ■ Enlargements are noted	What are the strengths or weaknesses of the illustrations that will affect my use of this book? *The use of drawings as well as photographs from the National Audubon Society's collection provides opportunities for engagement. A wavy border around insets indicates that these illustrations differ from the rest; but these insets are not labeled as enlargements or close-ups. I will need to make note of this with the students.*
Graphics: Revisit charts, tables, figures, and maps.	Explanation: If this is a graphic for explanation, is it well placed and easy to understand?	Extension: If this graphic is for extension of thinking, is it appropriate for my students?	Emphasis: If this graphic is for emphasis, how can I be more deliberate in using it with my students?	What are the strengths or weaknesses of the graphics that will affect my use of this book? *A map of where octopuses live would be useful—I will look in other trade books or the Internet to see if this is available.*
Recommended action on this book	✔ Place in classroom library ✔ Use as a read-aloud	☐ Use only as a read-aloud ☐ Use only as a reference	☐ Use only as a read-aloud with cautions noted	☐ Reject

escaping. It shoots a cloud of black ink out of its body so the enemy cannot see and smell" (p. 10). The report-like style, with its discussion of octopuses in general and the use of timeless present tense, helps to signal that this book falls into the expository category.

As we skimmed the table of contents, we found the following headings: What Is An Octopus?; Hiding and Escaping; Where the Octopus Lives; Getting Food; Octopus Babies; and What Scientists Have Learned. These headings evidence an organization that would allow readers to go directly to the sections they are interested in.

Content. Determining the accuracy of science concepts is not a simple task for teachers who may lack extensive science knowledge. However, although not foolproof, there is sometimes evidence to help inform decision-making. In the case of *Meet the Octopus*, the author, Sylvia James, is listed as the director of the National Aquarium in Baltimore, Maryland. The photographs are part of the Audubon Society's collection. Noting these two well-known organizations lends credibility to the science concepts presented.

Covers. Together, *Meet the Octopus*'s front and back covers create a complete scene, showing an octopus in a natural setting. The cover drawing is not anthropomorphized and is a realistic representation. The wrap-around cover may entice children to open and read the book. In addition, children may be intrigued by the interesting comment on the back cover: "Some octopuses can fit in your hand, but others are as long as a school bus! Here is a book full of fascinating information about this amazing sea animal." The size comparisons are well chosen because children can easily compare octopuses to their school bus or to their hands.

Additional Text. Looking at the pages that precede and follow the text, we noted that there is no glossary in this trade book. Teachers can decide how to handle the issue in ways that fit their specific teaching needs and style. Perhaps a teacher may want to note the missing glossary and have students make their own glossary.

We also noted that no sources or suggestions for further reading are included. A bibliography is always useful, as is a listing of other resources. In *Ladybug*, for example, Hartley and Macro (1998) list other books in which children can learn more about ladybugs.

Design. When considering text design, we noted some unusual ways that print wrapped around some of the illustrations. For example, on page 4, a paragraph is shaped like a backwards capital *L*. Although this was not a ubiquitous design feature, it is worth considering how students might be affect-ed by this design. Before placing the book in the classroom library, some teachers may want to read it aloud, stopping to discuss how certain parts are formatted and modeling how to read the wrapped text.

A helpful design feature is the bold print used to highlight the names of specific types of octopuses. Also helpful are the red arrows that point to and label specific body parts (e.g., water spray, eggs, eye) in the illustrations.

Writing. The author's writing is vital to consider when selecting a trade book. In *Meet the Octopus*, James uses engaging questions in the text. For example, on page 9, she asks, "Can you find the octopuses on these pages?" This question is very appropriate because the topic is hiding and escaping, and the opportunity to look for the octopuses connects the students to the content.

James also uses onomatopoeia to engage readers in what she is de-scribing. For example, she writes, "The octopus can get away fast! It shoots jets of water out of its body, which makes the octopus move quickly in the sea. *Whoosh!*" (p. 12). *Whoosh!* appeals to children's senses and highlights the illustration that shows water gushing out of an octopus's funnel and pro-jecting it away from the danger.

Illustrations. *Meet the Octopus* is beautifully illustrated with both drawings and photographs. However, one aspect of the illustrations might cause con-fusion. There are a number of close-up views to show details. For example, there is a close-up of an octopus's suction cups. A wavy blue border indicates that these close-ups are different from the rest of the illustrations on a page, but these insets are not labeled as enlargements or close-ups. Teachers would want to be sure students understood the different scale of the details versus the rest of the illustrations.

In contrast, in *Spiders* (Cullen, 1996), the author specifies when the drawing has been magnified. For example, when the face of a spitting spi-der is shown as a close-up to note the eye pattern, the word *enlarged* is place in parenthesis after the caption. Throughout *Spiders*, most of the illustrations include size notations.

Graphics. As we judged the charts in *Meet the Octopus*, we thought a map would have enhanced the students' understanding of where these sea crea-tures could be found. This is a feature that teachers could add to their in-struction through other trade books or the Internet.

Recommended Action. By using the evaluation guide to locate strengths and weaknesses, teachers are able to think through how to best use the material and to enhance what is lacking. We would use *Meet the Octopus* in the classroom, both as a read-aloud and as a free-reading choice in the classroom library. It has excellent science information and a useful design. The concerns we identified are minimal. We can address these concerns by creating a glossary, modeling how to read wrap-around print, helping the children to understand the enlarged pictures, and searching for a map of where octopuses live.

Our evaluation guide was useful in our investigation and was user friendly. The guide is a tool that has ample flexibility and allows for a comprehensive book preview. However, teachers will want to modify it for their own interests and needs.

Conclusion

In short, although the focus in primary-grade reading has long been on stories, there is a need to provide young children with the opportunity to read and receive instruction about both fiction and nonfiction. Professional standards call for more early attention to informational text. And, as we have shown, there is much potential for promoting both achievement and motivation by balancing attention between fiction and informational text. In this chapter, we have highlighted diverse types of informational books, arguing that students need to experience the full range of such texts. Further, we have presented an evaluation guide that can be modified as needed, to help teachers select quality informational books for young children.

Authors' Note

The research by Dreher and Baker (2003) referred to in this chapter was supported by a grant from the Spencer Foundation to Mariam Jean Dreher and Linda Baker. The data presented, the statements made, and the views expressed are solely the responsibility of the authors.

REFERENCES

Butzow, C.M., & Butzow, J.W. (2000). *Science through children's literature: An integrated approach* (2nd ed.). Englewood, CO: Teacher Ideas Press.

Caswell, L.C., & Duke, N. (1998). Non-narrative as a catalyst for literacy development. *Language Arts, 75*(2), 108–117.

Chall, J.S., Jacobs, V.A., & Baldwin, E. (1990). *The reading crisis: Why poor children fall behind.* Cambridge, MA: Harvard University Press.

Chambliss, M.J., & McKillop, A.M. (2000). Creating a print- and technology-rich classroom library to entice children to read. In L. Baker, M.J. Dreher, & J.T. Guthrie (Eds.), *Engaging young readers: Promoting achievement and motivation* (pp. 94–118). New York: Guilford.

Dreher, M.J. (2000). Fostering reading for learning. In L. Baker, M.J. Dreher, & J.T. Guthrie (Eds.), *Engaging young readers: Promoting achievement and motivation* (pp. 68–93). New York: Guilford.

Dreher, M.J., & Baker, L. (2003). *Balancing learning to read and reading for learning: Achievement and engagement in young children's reading instruction.* Unpublished manuscript.

Duke, N.K. (2000). 3.6 minutes per day: The scarcity of informational texts in first grade. *Reading Research Quarterly, 35,* 202–224.

Duke, N.K., & Kays, J. (1998). "Can I say 'Once upon a time'?" Kindergarten children developing knowledge of informational book language. *Early Childhood Research Quarterly, 13*(2), 295–318.

Duthie, C. (1996). *True stories: Nonfiction literacy in the primary classroom.* York, ME: Stenhouse.

Elley, W.B. (1992). *How in the world do students read?* Hamburg, Germany: International Association for the Evaluation of Educational Achievement.

Fisher, C.W. & Hiebert, E.H. (1990). Characteristics of tasks in two approaches to literature instruction. *The Elementary School Journal, 91,* 3–18.

Fountas, I.C., & Pinnell, G.S. (1999). *Matching books to readers: Using leveled books in guided reading K–3.* Portsmouth, NH: Heinemann.

Fractor, J.S., Woodruff, M.C., Martinez, M.G., & Teale, W.H. (1993). Let's not miss an opportunity to promote voluntary reading: Classroom libraries in the elementary school. *The Reading Teacher, 46,* 469–483.

Hiebert, E.H. (1991). Research directions: Department editor's note. *Language Arts, 68,* 482.

Hoffman, J.V., Roser, N.L., & Battle, J. (1993). Reading aloud in classrooms: From modal to a "model." *The Reading Teacher, 46,* 496–505.

Horowitz, R., & Freeman, S.H. (1995). Robots versus spaceships: The role of discussion in kindergartners' and second graders' preferences for science texts. *The Reading Teacher, 49,* 30–40.

Janke, D., & Norton, D. (1983). Science trades in the classroom: Good tools for teachers. *Science and Children, 20*(6), 46–48.

Kamil, M.L., & Lane, D. (1997, December). *Using informational text for first-grade reading instruction.* Paper presented at the National Reading Conference, Scottsdale, AZ.

Kletzien, S.B., & Szabo, R.J. (1998, December). *Informational text or narrative text? Children's preferences revisited.* Paper presented at the meeting of the National Reading Conference, Austin, TX.

Mayer, D.A. (1995). How can we best use children's literature in teaching science concepts? *Science and Children, 32,* 16–19, 43.

Moss, G. (2001). To work or play? Junior age non-fiction as objects of design. *Reading: Literacy and Language, 35*(3), 106–110.

Neuman, S.B. (1999). Books make a difference: A study of access to literacy. *Reading Research Quarterly, 34,* 286–311.

Pappas, C.C. (1991). Fostering full access to literacy by including informational books. *Language Arts, 68*(6), 449–462.

Pappas, C.C. (1993). Is narrative "primary"? Some insights from kindergarteners' pretend readings of stories and informational books. *Journal of Reading Behavior, 25*(1), 97–129.

Pappas, C.C., & Barry, A. (1997). Scaffolding urban students' initiations: Transactions in reading informational books in the read-aloud curriculum genre. In N.J. Karolides (Ed.), *Reader response in elementary classrooms: Quest and discovery* (pp. 215–236). Mahwah, NJ: Erlbaum.

Pappas, C.C, Varelas, M., Barry, A., & O'Neill, A. (2000, December). *The development of science discourse genres in a primary-grade integrated science-literacy unit on states of matter: Analysis of intertextuality*. Paper presented at the National Reading Conference, Scottsdale, AZ.

Pottle, J.L. (1996). Using trade books to make connections across the curriculum. *Clearing House, 70*(1), 52–53.

Pressley, M., Rankin, J., & Yokoi, L. (1996). A survey of instructional practices of primary teachers nominated as effective in promoting literacy. *The Elementary School Journal, 96*(4), 363–384.

Rice, D.C. (2002). Using trade books in teaching elementary science: Facts and fallacies. *The Reading Teacher, 55*, 552–565.

Sanacore, J. (1991). Expository and narrative text: Balancing young children's reading experiences. *Childhood Education, 67*(4), 211–214.

Simon, S. (1982). Using science trade books in the classroom. *Science and Children, 19*, 5–6.

Snow, C.E., Burns, M.S., & Griffin, P. (Eds.). (1998). *Preventing reading difficulties in young children*. Washington, DC: National Academy Press.

Sudol, P., & King, C.M. (1996). A checklist for choosing nonfiction tradebooks. *The Reading Teacher, 49*, 422–424.

Venezky, R.L. (2000). The origins of the present-day chasm between adult literacy needs and school literacy instruction. *Scientific Studies of Reading, 4*(1), 19–39.

CHILDREN'S BOOKS CITED

Berman, R. (1998). *Watchful wolves*. Photo. W. Muñoz. Minneapolis, MN: Lerner.

Cole, J. (1994). *The magic school bus in the time of the dinosaurs*. Ill. B. Degen. New York: Scholastic.

Cone, M. (1992). *Come back, salmon: How a group of dedicated kids adopted Pigeon Creek and brought it back to life*. Photo. S. Wheelwright. Oakland, CA: Sierra Club.

Cullen, E. (1996). *Spiders*. Ill. S. Pascoe & S. Pascoe. New York: Mondo.

dePaola, T. (1973). *Charlie needs a cloak*. New York: Simon & Schuster.

dePaola, T. (1978). *The popcorn book*. New York: Holiday House.

Dooley, N. (1991). *Everybody cooks rice*. Ill. P. Thornton. Minneapolis, MN: Carolrhoda.

Earle, A. (1995). *Zipping, zapping, zooming bats*. Ill. H. Cole. New York: HarperCollins.

Hartley, K., & Macro, C. (1998). *Ladybug*. Portsmouth, NH: Heinemann.

James, S.M. (1996). *Meet the octopus*. Ill. C.A. Belcher. New York: Mondo.

Jenkins, M. (1999). *The emperor's egg*. Ill. J. Chapman. Cambridge, MA: Candlewick.

Kerrod, R. (1992). *Amazing flying machines*. Ill. M. Dunning. New York: Knopf.

Looye, J.U. (1998). *Body numbers*. Barrington, IL: Rigby.

Martin, J.B. (1998). *Snowflake Bentley*. Ill. M. Azarian. Boston: Houghton Mifflin.

Micucci, C. (1997). *The life and times of the peanut*. Boston: Houghton Mifflin.

Ramsay, A., & Humphrey, P. (1995). *Frog's eggs*. Ill. K. Mulkey. Austin, TX: Steck-Vaughn.

Relf, P. (1996). *The magic school bus wet all over: A book about the water cycle*. New York: Scholastic.

Royston, A. (1998). *Life cycle of a chicken*. Des Plaines, IL: Heinemann.

St. Pierre, S. (2001). *Siberian tigers*. Portsmouth, NH: Heinemann.

Walker, S., & Gray, S. (2001). *Dinosaur*. New York: Dorling Kindersley.

CHAPTER 15

Highly Recommended Trade Books: Can They Be Used in Inquiry Science?

DANIELLE J. FORD

The use of trade books in elementary science instruction has been strongly advocated as a means of integrating literacy and science (Madrazo, 1997; Nordstrom, 1992; Saul & Jagusch, 1991). In many cases, this is in response to a general disappointment with textbooks (Newport, 1990), which are perennially criticized for containing numerous misconceptions and errors (Abimbola & Baba, 1996), oversimplifications (Lloyd & Mitchell, 1989), poorly designed activities (Anderson, Beck, & West, 1994), significant gender bias (Bazler & Simonis, 1991), and superficial treatment of too many topics (Kesidou & Roseman, 2002). In contrast, trade books have been extolled as being more timely, relevant to children's lives, narrowly focused on content, and highly engaging and interesting for children (Barlow, 1991; Cerullo, 1997; Saul & Jagusch, 1991). Trade books are seen as informing, engaging, and supplementing elementary science instruction in ways not possible with a single science textbook. Despite the inaccuracies and errors some contain (Rice, 2002), trade books are generally viewed as an acceptable means of introducing students to science.

Those calling for the use of trade books in science education, however, must remember that texts are used differently in *inquiry* science than they are in more traditional science and literacy instruction. Inquiry science requires meaningful contexts, active engagement of learners, and opportunities for developing an understanding of the nature of science through thinking, acting, and communicating scientifically (American Association for the Advancement of Science [AAAS], 1993; National Research Council [NRC], 1996).

An authentic component of scientific inquiry is the critical use of a variety of texts. Texts are a means of communicating the major ideas and activities of science to all members of a community of practice. In scientific communities, even those for which experimentation is central, no scientific investigation is ever text-free. Scientists consult research journals to keep current in their fields, use technical manuals in laboratory experiments, and communicate in written form through electronic media (Ford, Palincsar,

& Magnusson, 1998). Though not the sole method for communicating ideas, written texts are important tools available to researchers in the construction of understandings during their investigations.

Like scientists' texts, children's texts should serve as tools in support of inquiry: they should serve the needs of investigators at a variety of stages of research and serve to communicate the ideas of other researchers. Indeed, text use is vital to elementary science, as it serves to help students learn about science as well as participate in scientific practices. However, this purpose is not served by merely reading textbooks to gain knowledge. Inquiry science requires books that can serve many purposes, and it requires that learners take a critical stance toward the information encountered (NRC, 1996).

It is trade book or textbook authors, the majority of whom are not scientists, who serve as writers and interpreters of science for children. The extent to which these authors' understandings of science is informed by practice or philosophy varies. Authors telling the stories of science may incorporate—intentionally or not—companion meanings (Roberts, 1998) about the nature of science, its practitioners, and its accessibility that are just as important to student learning as the books' factual scientific information. It is these companion meanings and the values implicit in authors' choices of subject matter and its presentation that must be brought to light in order to determine which texts are most appropriate for a given classroom context.

Finding trade books for use in inquiry science may seem as easy as a trip to the library; however, the specific contexts in which texts are used exert considerable demands on what book qualities are considered ideal. The content area, the age of the children and their familiarity with inquiry, and the importance of developing deep understandings of the nature as well as content of science are just a few of the many concerns that must be addressed when selecting science books. The variety of science trade books published each year for the commercial market, the limited resources available in school and public libraries, and the increasing emphasis on hands-on activities at the expense of other science experiences can make the choice of trade books for instruction a complicated task for educators. Researchers have suggested frameworks for evaluating science trade books (e.g., Cerullo, 1997; Sudol & King, 1996) that include attention to content accuracy, age-appropriateness, and appeal to children. (See chapter 14 in this book for more thoughts about selecting appropriate texts.)

Although helpful in organizing evaluations, in-depth examinations of books may not be feasible for busy teachers, who have little time to spend on careful analysis of trade books. As a result, teachers and library specialists are urged to consult a variety of publications dedicated to reviewing children's books. These include (but are by no means limited to) *Science Books & Films*, published by AAAS; *The Horn Book Guide to Children's and Young Adult Books*, a comprehensive critical review of published trade books; and *Science and Children*, whose publisher also issues the National Science Teachers Association's (NSTA) annual list of outstanding trade books for children. Each of these publications carefully analyzes a range of books for its recommendations and has guidelines for reviewers on the selection and evaluation of books.

What do the books recommended by these sources tell us about the suitability of trade books for use in inquiry-based science instruction? For the study detailed in this chapter, the journals listed above were consulted for their recommendations of outstanding or exceptional science trade books for the five-year period from 1996 to 2000. Also examined were preferences exhibited in the outstanding books lists and the implications of these selections for classroom teaching. The analysis here was conducted to answer the following research questions: (1) What content is represented in the books rated as outstanding? (2) What images of science are represented in the outstanding lists? (3) How are these images delivered (through writing style and genre choices)? and (4) What do the results tell us about the suitability and practicality of recommended books for inquiry science instruction?

Research Design

To analyze children's science trade books, we compiled a list of highly rated books from among the books recommended between the years 1996–2000 in *Science Books & Films*, *The Horn Book Guide*, and *Science and Children* (the annual National Science Teachers Association/Children's Book Council [NSTA/CBC] outstanding list). Our list included books that received a rating of highly recommended in *Science Books & Films* or a rating of 1 or 2 in *The Horn Book Guide to Children's and Young Adult Books*; we also included the entire list of outstanding trade books from *Science and Children*. Books across a five-year period were chosen to eliminate year-to-year variability or trends in publishing, and books from this particular period were chosen to focus on the years subsequent to the release of the U.S. National Science Education Standards (NSES) (NRC, 1996) and to represent books likely to still be in print. (Trade books in science do not often have multiple printing runs [Patent, 1998] and so may not be readily available to teachers and researchers for more than a few years.) Our sample includes 939 trade books targeted for preschool, elementary, and intermediate audiences.

We divided the books into categories according to their content; each title was coded for content based on the descriptions provided in the review sources. Initial coding followed closely the review sources' content assignments (for the most part loosely organized by Dewey decimal classifications), but a secondary analysis was also conducted in which categories were collapsed into groupings consistent with the content divisions seen in the NSES (NRC, 1996). The percentages of books found in each content category for each review source are reported in the Results section of this chapter.

Sixty-two of the books that received an outstanding rating from at least two review sources were further divided into book genres and classified according to their representations of the nature of science (implicit and explicit). These analyses also are reported in the Results section of this chapter. Genres identified were informational texts, informational picture books, biography, poetry, fiction, experiment books, and journals. Mixed genres were assigned with the code for the dominant genre. The experiment books were primarily collections of activities children could conduct in home or school settings. The journal category included personal accounts of science or nature journeys.

The books in the subset also were coded for their representations of the nature of science, initially using a set of codes covering a broad range of scientific practices and habits of mind. However, these were subsequently reduced to those consistent with the representations seen in the books themselves. As with the genre codes, if there was category overlap in the books, one code was assigned for the dominant representation of science. If there were no mentions of scientists or scientific practices in the body of the text—that is, if the text essentially only represented factual information—the book was coded "science as facts." Books that were biographies of scientists, or that used profiles of active scientists to explain a science topic, were coded "biographical/scientist's work." Books that focused on processes of science were coded as either observational (viewing natural phenomena) or experimental/measurement (manipulation of some conditions to produce results). Books that encouraged less scientifically focused interaction with nature, such as cooking vegetables, gardening, and walking outdoors, were classified as "appreciating nature." Two readers coded the titles. Discrepancies in code assignments were discussed and reconciled.

Results

Content Areas

Table 15.1 shows the distribution (in percentages) across subject areas for the three review sources consulted in this study. *Science Books & Films* rated

616 of the 1,230 books they reviewed during the five-year period as highly recommended. *The Horn Book Guide to Children's and Young Adult Books* rated 124 of the 2,183 books they reviewed as a 1 or 2 (outstanding or superior, respectively). All 199 books on the NSTA/CBC lists in *Science and Children* for the period were considered outstanding.

The content areas reported in Table 15.1 are aligned most closely with broad content categories seen in the NSES (NRC, 1996)—life, earth, and physical sciences (Standards B, C, and D); technology (Standard E); and the history and nature of science (Standard G, reported in Table 15.1 as Biography). Space science was reported separately from earth science because of its popularity in trade books, and reference/other was included to cover encyclopedia and reference books. All review sources also included mathematics books within their science reviews.

TABLE 15.1
Percentage of the Highest Rated Books by Content Area for *Science Books & Films*, *Science and Children*, and *The Horn Book Guide to Children's and Young Adult Books* Between 1996–2000

Content Area	Science Books & Films Percentage	Science and Children Percentage	The Horn Book Guide to Children's and Young Adult Books Percentage	Total Percentage
Life Sciences	60	72	63	64
Earth Sciences	10	8	3	8
Physical Sciences	9	2	4	7
Space Sciences	10	5	6	8
Technology	2	3	5	2
Biography	2	7	18	5
Mathematics	2	2	1	2
Reference/Other	5	1	0	4

Life science topics comprised 64% of all books receiving outstanding ratings. This topic includes the largest category, nonhuman animals (36%), as well as nature/ecology (13%), humans (6%), paleontology (4%), and botany (4%). Far fewer in number are highly rated books on earth and environmental sciences, space sciences, physical sciences, and technology. Biographies of scientists represent 5% of the total books reviewed but are a much higher percentage of books on *The Horn Book Guide* lists (18%).

Despite the standards' emphasis on equal consideration of life, physical, and earth sciences within the elementary curriculum, the availability of trade books to support these areas is unequal. From year to year, books published and recommended in the life sciences dominate the books available to children, with animal books representing more than one third of the recommended books. Clearly underrepresented are earth and physical science books. For example, there are only 26 chemistry books in this 939-book sample. The elementary bias toward life sciences and nature and away from physical sciences seems to be preserved in trade book publishing and reviewer choices. It is important to note, however, that this is a sample of highly recommended books—it is not possible to determine if reviewers prefer life science/nature books, if publishers produce more quality trade books in this area, or if a general preference for life science books results in publishers directing resources toward those topics.

Presenting an Image of Science and Its Practice

In order to consider more closely the presentation of science in recommended books, the 62 books that appeared on more than one outstanding list were analyzed for genre and representation of the nature of science. The interesting subset of books that appeared on multiple outstanding lists included science-themed poetry, biographies of scientists and inventors, a field guide to trees, a historical account of measurement, recipe and gardening books, and books on animals such as horses, gorillas, frogs, and kangaroos.

Genre. The genres of scientific trade books seen in this study are listed in Table 15.2. The majority of the books (62%) are informational texts that concentrate on one focused topic in science (e.g., ants). The information books present scientific content in combinations of text and illustrations, though a subset for younger readers (11%) is picture books. However, active, child-friendly writing was used throughout both information books and picture books. For example, the book on kangaroos (Markle, 1999) used the second person and a conversational tone to explain animal behavior and encourage children to think along with the author:

TABLE 15.2
Genres of Outstanding Trade Books, 1996–2000

Genre	Percentage of All Books in Sample
Informational	62
Informational—Picture Book	11
Biography	7
Poetry	5
Fiction	3
Experiment	5
Journal	7

Did you guess that these two red kangaroo males are fighting? When they fight, the males stand tall, lock their forearms, and wrestle. They throw their heads way back to protect their eyes and ears from being scratched by sharp claws. At any moment, one of the males is likely to rock back on its tail and kick the other. They will keep on punching, wrestling, pawing, and kicking until one male breaks away and retreats. (p. 23)

Approximately one quarter of the books included in this list (Table 15.2) broaden the typical notion of a science book. These include four biographies of scientists, three books of nature-themed poetry, two fiction books, and four personalized journals from scientific expeditions. Each of these books personalizes science in some manner—by telling stories about nature, using poetry to engage scientific imaginations, or describing experiences in natural settings. In particular, the journal books are helpful formats for providing examples of positive, exciting experiences with nature in far-flung locales.

Representation of the Nature of Scientific Activity. The majority of books in this subset (57%) were factual information books that did not discuss the methods or people who brought those facts into existence (see Table 15.3). Clearly, a trend toward the use of expository text to explain factual information is dominant among books that are considered outstanding.

TABLE 15.3
Representations of the Nature of Scientific Activity
in Outstanding Trade Books, 1996–2000

Representation of Science	Percentage of All Books in Sample
Science as Facts	57
Science as Observation	8
Science as Measuring/Experimenting	5
Appreciating Nature	20
Biographical/Scientist's Work	10

Although potentially helpful for learning the content of science, informational books by themselves may do little to support student understanding of the nature of scientific inquiry as emphasized in the national standards documents (AAAS, 1993; NRC, 1996). Only 13% of the books focused specifically on scientific activity, and these limited consideration of the nature of science to only two practices of science: observation and experimentation. These books primarily encourage children to independently engage in observation. In the example below from *I Took a Walk* (Cole, 1998), observation in a natural setting is modeled for elementary readers:

> I sat quietly at the edge of the pond and peered through the cattails. I saw...
> a grebe on her nest
> a heron
> whirligig beetles
> a bluegill
> water lilies
> ...Find a place to sit and watch and listen. What do you see? (n.p.)

Books that most closely fit the popular image of classroom science—hands-on experiments—comprised only 5% of the books in the subset.

Ten percent of the books in this subset focused on the lives of scientists, either through traditional biographical treatments or through books combining profiles of nonfamous scientists with scientific content. These scientist profiles are particularly intriguing, as they directly link scientific, factual information to the people who actively engaged in determining what these scientific ideas were.

Twenty percent of the books encouraged a more generalized appreciation of nature (though they were not explicit in directing children to observe it scientifically). These books provided recipes for cooking with vegetables, encouraged gardening or visits to farms, and told stories about people who enjoyed nature.

Discussion

This analysis of recommended science trade books shows trends that favor the presentation of life science and nature facts in predominantly informational formats. Accounts of science in action, rather than collections of facts, are also present in a smaller but significant percentage of the collection. These preferences align to some extent with national science standards calling for development of students' awareness of the processes of inquiry and the work of scientists (NRC, 1996). Although the quality of the recommended books and their good fit with some of the criteria for inquiry text outlined above are encouraging, there are features present in the recommended books that present challenges when considering their use in classroom settings.

Challenges and Affordances of Content Distribution

The abundance of quality life science books makes the task of integrating texts into standards-based instructional contexts much easier for life science than for other content areas. Children's familiarity with many of the topics seen in these books—trees, animal habitats, common plants—also helps to establish the relevance of science instruction. Those books that favor more interdisciplinary topics (e.g., ecology, 13% of all books recommended) can be particularly useful in the development of rich understandings about the interconnectedness of scientific fields. However, the challenges of teaching interdisciplinary topics, especially given the demands of standards-based divisions along traditional science lines, may result in the relegation of interdisciplinary-focused instruction with texts to mere extension activities for students after the "basics" are covered.

There is a serious lack of quality physical science trade books. This trend has been consistent not just in the years analyzed for this chapter, but throughout the past three decades (Ford & Tisa, 2002). There does not seem to be a compelling demand for physical science books from either education or general public markets. Although the situation may improve with increasing pressure on publishers for trade books that supplement popular kit-based curricular materials (Saul & Reardon, 1996), teachers currently need to search far and wide for appropriate physical science trade books, particularly in the "pure" science areas of chemistry and physics. There are more applied science books that can be used to help bring texts into physical science instruction, but aligning applied science topics with the concepts central to standards-based physical science can be difficult to achieve without losing focus on the big ideas. For example, many technology books focus on taxonomies of machines, vehicles, and structures without referring to underlying principles of force and motion. Teachers of science (and purchasers of books for libraries or classroom resources) should be aware that good books in physical sciences are published less frequently than in other subject areas. Therefore, any physical science books recommended and available may be worthwhile purchases for science trade book collections.

Informational Books as Tools, Not Teachers

Books that provide factual information about scientific topics dominate the review lists. These books most closely resemble textbooks in intent, if not quality, by presenting a rather narrow window into the world of science. Even when presented in the appealing format of a trade book, this emphasis on facts misses opportunities to help children understand how these ideas about nature came to be.

This does not mean there is no place for informational books in inquiry classrooms. There are a number of standards-based science topics that cannot be investigated in a hands-on manner in elementary classrooms, requiring some form of secondary resource to help children learn about them. Engaging trade books filled with interesting factual information can bring that knowledge to children. Skilled authors who make factual information sound exciting to children write many of these trade books, and many of the topics seen in children's trade books are in science areas that appeal to children. However, it is the manner in which these books are used that makes the informational books worthwhile tools for inquiry. Rather than treating a trade book as a more colorful substitute for a textbook, fact-filled trade books can serve as tools for children involved in inquiry—in developing, researching, and investigating questions of significance that are not easily tested with empirical experiments. With the use of informational books, children can engage in the scientifically authentic practices of critical evaluation of text information, comparative analysis of text resources, and building of explanations from multiple sources of evidence.

Alternative Science Trade Books

Biographies, fiction with science themes, poetry, picture books, and conversational accounts in informational books are all represented in the subset of outstanding books analyzed in this study. Consistently, these books are beautifully written and designed, filled with high-quality illustrations. However, using a narrative or artistic book effectively in science instruction can present challenges for teachers. In a practical sense, narrative books do not contain the indexes, headers, and other structures that make informational texts helpful references in the search for scientific information. Of greater concern, however, is the problem that narrative-format trade books too often can be used to sidestep deeper scientific issues in the guise of appealing to the interests of children. This is not to say that stories have no place is science; scientific storytelling provides an invitation to children to think creatively about nature. Packaged in the child-friendly words and illustrations of a trade book, these science appreciation lessons—often presenting the personal perspectives of authors—encourage children's interest in scientific areas. The excerpt from Henry Cole's *I Took a Walk* is a good example, encouraging children to pause and appreciate a typical natural setting. However, too often, appreciation of this sort remains at an entry level. Particularly critical is the content represented in these appreciation books—children are encouraged to develop an appreciation of nature, rather than science. Although this is arguably an important first step in thinking about the natural world, it does not automatically lead to scientifically authentic appreciation without mediation from knowledgeable adults. Development of authentic appreciation relies on engaging learners in deeper understandings of the nature of scientific inquiry. Teachers need to remain steadfast to goals for deep content understandings in order to effectively use narrative and artistic texts in the instruction of scientific inquiry.

Science as Observation: Only One Component of Scientific Practice

Of the books that provided images of science beyond a static body of knowledge, a limited view of science emerged. These books presented a picture of scientific practice as observation in outdoor settings—viewing the world (quite literally) in a careful and/or appreciative manner. This certainly is a form of active, hands-on science, one that is specifically seen to be important for young children. However, there is a great deal more in the practice of science missing from this representation. None of the books showed scientific practice beyond what is typically considered appropriate for children—observation, simple inference, and simple school science experiments. Observation conceptualized as simply looking at nature is a misrepresentation of the complexity of observation and of its interdependence on other science practices (e.g., questioning, theorizing, analyzing). Even the books that focus on the work of scientists or encourage children to engage in experiments fail to develop their representations of science beyond an empiricist view of observation and interaction with natural phenomena. This focus on direct observation of visible phenomena also implies a progression of scientific understandings toward a universal truth: observation leads to factual truths, and a steady improvement of scientific knowledge is based on careful observation. Science does not always work that simplistically.

Conclusion

The books recommended as outstanding children's trade books over the past five years are potentially valuable resources for integrating text experiences into inquiry science instruction. However, books must be chosen carefully and their use in classrooms planned in order to maximize authentic science learning. Books appropriate for use in classroom scientific inquiry should provide rich, accurate scientific information that is central to standards-based content. They should explicitly link that science content to the scientists who produce it, as well as explain and model the practices of science, including all components of scientific investigation and reasoning. These books also should provide opportunities for children to engage in informational text reading, including the development of fluencies in graphical representations central to scientific literacy practices. Finally, these books should invite readers to engage with, imagine, and experience science and nature beyond their own or their teachers' experiences (Ford, 2002).

Some, but not all, of these criteria are met by current trends in the content, genres, and representations of science found in science trade books. Certainly, the criterion for books that invite students to engage in science (albeit from an appreciation view, not a scientific view) is well met by the highly rated books analyzed in this study. However, most of these books are not as useful for modeling or supporting inquiry. Although the books emphasize and encourage observation and creative thinking about natural phenomena, there is minimal modeling of data analysis, theory development, and the role of the scientific community. In addition, although there are rich and varied informational books available to serve as resources for life science investigations, there are fewer resources available on physical science topics.

The particular instructional contexts in which any science trade books are used will ultimately determine their utility. It is not likely (nor is it desirable) that any single trade book can substitute directly for a classroom textbook, but a selection of trade books and other text sources is a vital part of an inquiry classroom. Using a variety of trade books in a science classroom in support of inquiry appropriately decentralizes the role of text and positions texts as one of the many tools available to students in the construction of their scientific understandings. There are exciting possibilities for the use of trade books in elementary classrooms, if appropriate matches between books and classroom contexts can be made.

REFERENCES

American Association for the Advancement of Science (AAAS). (1993). *Benchmarks for science literacy* (AAAS Project 2061). New York: Oxford University Press.

Abimbola, I.O., & Baba, S. (1996). Misconceptions and alternative conceptions in science textbooks: The role of teachers as filters. *American Biology Teacher, 58*(1), 14–19.

Anderson, T., Beck, D., & West, C. (1994). A text analysis of two pre-secondary science activities. *Journal of Curriculum Studies, 26*, 63–186.

Barlow, D.L. (1991). Children, books, and biology. *BioScience, 41*(3), 166–168.

Bazler, J.A., & Simonis, D.A. (1991). Are high school chemistry textbooks gender fair? *Journal of Research in Science Teaching, 28*(4), 353–362.

Cerullo, M. (1997). *Reading the environment: Children's literature in the science classroom.* Portsmouth, NH: Heinemann.

Ford, D.J. (2002). More than the facts: Reviewing science books. *The Horn Book Magazine, 78*(3), 265–271.

Ford, D.J., Palincsar A.S., & Magnusson, S.J. (1998, April). *Evaluating children's science literature for classroom use: Contributions from scientists and elementary teachers.* Paper presented at the annual meeting of the American Educational Research Association, San Diego, CA.

Ford, D.J., & Tisa, L. (2002, April). *Recurring cultural and scientific themes in outstanding children's science books, 1972–2000.* Paper presented at the annual meeting of the American Educational Research Association, New Orleans, LA.

Kesidou, S., & Roseman, J.E. (2002). How well do middle school science programs measure up? Findings from Project 2061's curriculum review. *Journal of Research in Science Teaching, 39*, 522–549.

Lloyd, C.V., & Mitchell, J.N. (1989). Coping with too many concepts in science texts. *Journal of Reading, 32*(6), 542–545.

Madrazo, G.M., Jr. (1997). Using trade books to teach and learn science. *Science and Children, 34*(6), 20–21.

National Research Council (NRC). (1996). *National science education standards.* Washington, DC: National Academy Press.

Newport, J.F. (1990). What's wrong with science textbooks? *Principal, 69*(3), 22–24.

Nordstrom, V. (1992). Reducing the text burden: Using children's literature and trade books in elementary school science education. *Reference Services Review, 20*(1), 57–70.

Patent, D.H. (1998). Science books for children: An endangered species? *The Horn Book Magazine, 74*, 309–314.

Rice, D.C. (2002). Using trade books in teaching elementary science: Facts and fallacies. *The Reading Teacher, 55*, 552–565.

Roberts, D.A. (1998). Analyzing school science courses: The concept of companion meaning. In D.A. Roberts & L. Ostman (Eds.), *Problems of meaning in science curriculum* (pp. 5–12). New York: Teachers College Press.

Saul, W., & Jagusch, S.A. (Eds.). (1991). *Vital connections: Children, science, and books.* Portsmouth, NH: Heinemann.

Saul, W., & Reardon, J. (Eds.). (1996). *Beyond the science kit: Inquiry in action.* Portsmouth, NH: Heinemann.

Sudol, P., & King, C.M. (1996). A checklist for choosing nonfiction tradebooks. *The Reading Teacher, 49*, 422–424.

CHILDREN'S LITERATURE CITED

Cole, H. (1998). *I took a walk.* New York: Greenwillow.

Markle, S. (1999). *Outside and inside kangaroos.* New York: Atheneum.

CHAPTER 16

How Not to Get Lost on *The Magic School Bus*: What Makes High Science Content Read-Alouds?

LAURA B. SMOLKIN AND CAROL A. DONOVAN

The Magic School Bus books series is immensely popular. To date, author Joanna Cole and illustrator Bruce Degen have seen their initial offering of *The Magic School Bus at the Waterworks* (1986) grow into a virtual industry that ranges from books to CD-ROMs to television programs to videos to a federally funded museum program. Not only are the books celebrated in the larger culture, but they also are lauded by children's literature experts. Cole's books have been recognized with numerous awards, including selection as an Honor Book for Nonfiction by the *Boston Globe*-Horn Book committee and receiving the International Reading Association and Children's Book Council Children's Choice Awards and the *Washington Post*/Children's Book Guild Nonfiction award. Leal and Kearney (1997) are particularly enthusiastic in their comments:

> These books...don't seem anything like a textbook. In fact, learning is disguised in a story with characterization, plot, and humor....At the end of the book, you have completed a mission, the mission to gain knowledge of the subject matter with the help of your peers and a wonderful, devoted teacher. (p. 65)

Leal and Kearney suggest that books with hybrid texts—part story, part information—make wonderful read-alouds.

Our own research with teachers found a similarly high regard for Cole's magical texts. In our study of factors influencing teachers' selections of science trade books, Cole's (1987) *The Magic School Bus Inside the Earth* was chosen by teachers from every grade level (first through fifth) and was second only to Gail Gibbons's (1995) *Planet Earth/Inside Out* in its frequency of selection (Donovan & Smolkin, 2001).

We were, then, very surprised when we asked a different group of 28 K–5 teachers whether they read aloud the Magic School Bus books to their students. They did not, they explained, because the pages were jam-packed with information, and it was difficult to decide how best to present the various text types during a read-aloud.

In some ways, the teachers' responses might have been predicted. Jacobs, Morrison, and Swinyard (2000) found in their survey responses from more than 1,800 elementary school teachers that information books were the least frequently read aloud genre on their questionnaire. In fact, information books were read aloud less frequently than textbooks. If teachers in that study were making their read-aloud selections from their classroom libraries, then Duke's (2000) findings on the scarcity of informational texts in classrooms suggests another reason why teachers might not have read aloud information-oriented books.

Given Leal and Kearney's (1997) statement on the effectiveness of informational storybooks as read-alouds, and given the fact that none of our 28 teachers used them, we were curious as to what would happen when a Magic School Bus book was actually read aloud. Because of the dual aspects of the text—science and story—we particularly wanted to know if and how teachers emphasized the science content in the books. This chapter presents the results of our study. In the sections that follow, we review relevant literature, look closely at one of the Magic School Bus books, and present the findings of our study. We conclude with a look at one teacher's effective presentation of a Magic School Bus book and offer suggestions for teachers.

Trade Books in Science Instruction

Since 1973, the National Science Teachers Association, in conjunction with the Children's Book Council, has been recommending children's trade books for use in science instruction. These associations, however, are not the only ones looking closely at trade books; various researchers and writers have been contemplating the role of genre in these science-related texts. In our own work, we have identified four different text types commonly recommended for science instruction: stories, nonnarrative information books, narrative information books (our category for some of the books others have termed *informational storybooks*), and dual-purpose texts (Donovan & Smolkin, 2001, 2002).

Researchers and writers have taken different stances on which of these text types should be used for science instruction. Some (Camp, 2000; Lake, 1993) have taken the stance that trade book–related science instruction must include stories because this form combats "the more sterile factual text" (Camp, 2000, p. 400) of informational trade books. Others (e.g., Moss, 1991; Vardell & Copeland, 1992) proclaim that there is nothing at all sterile about today's nonfiction texts. Instead, they contend, the books are well written and visually appealing.

Still others (e.g., Mayer, 1995; Rice, 2002) have expressed concern that the use of fictional texts that intentionally address science concepts may inculcate serious scientific misconceptions. Their concerns seem particularly related to a category of texts, which we have defined as narrative informational texts, in which authors wish to convey science content but have chosen to do so through a story. For us, these narrative informational storybooks differ from dual-purpose texts because readers cannot begin on virtually any page to read specific facts the way they can with the reports in Cole's original Magic School Bus series. And they differ from picture storybooks, in which the author's purpose has been to entertain without pretending to be factual (Kress, 1994). In the following sections, we will review research that relates to these two distinct science-related genres.

Concerns With a Refutational Narrative Informational Storybook: Dear Mr. Blueberry

Three different researchers examined children's responses to a rather unique narrative informational storybook, *Dear Mr. Blueberry* (James, 1991). James's book relates the story of a little girl who writes letters containing her misconceptions about whales to Mr. Blueberry, who corrects her misconceptions in his responses. In some ways, *Dear Mr. Blueberry* may be seen as a refutational text (see Guzzetti, Snyder, Glass, & Gamas, 1993), one in which specific misconceptions are directly contradicted.

Jetton (1994), working with two groups of second graders, informed one group that they would be listening to a story about a little girl; the other was told that they were to listen for information in a book that described the life of whales. Then the book was read aloud to both groups. Despite being given different purposes, both groups of second graders responded similarly, recalling more story idea units than informational idea units.

Mayer (1995) also used *Dear Mr. Blueberry* in a small-scale study with kindergarten through third-grade students, two boys and two girls from each grade level. Students retold the story, answered 10 questions about the book, four of which specifically dealt with the science content, and then drew a picture of a whale. Of her sixteen subjects, nine reported learning nothing new from the book, and five reported "newly acquired misconceptions about whales" (p. 17). Mayer felt that children were unable to distinguish real from fictional elements in the text. From her study, Mayer concluded, "The results of this study indicate that some fiction may impede content acquisition" (p. 19).

Rice and Snipes (1997) noted that although children frequently changed their answers between pretest and posttest for four of the books in their study, they did so infrequently following the reading of *Dear Mr. Blueberry*. Regarding this text, Rice and Snipes commented that "both sides of the coin" (p. 9) were presented. That is, the character Mr. Blueberry responds in the book to a little girl's "*incorrect* ideas about whales by giving the *correct* information" (p. 9). Children, they speculated, saw no reason to change their answers. They seemed to have found support, "whether correct or incorrect" (p. 10), for their prior knowledge.

The results of these three studies caused us concern. Could Mayer be right? Could a fictional aspect to a text impede science content acquisition?

Research With a Dual-Purpose Book: The Magic School Bus Books in Action

Researcher Dorothy Leal has been strongly supportive of using informational storybooks in science instruction. In 1992, she reported on first, third, and fifth graders' discussions of three different types of books that had been read to them—one storybook, one information book, and one that we would term a narrative informational storybook. She found that during their discussions of the narrative informational storybook, children offered significantly more comments that drew from prior knowledge, offered twice as many speculative comments, and stayed on topic longer than during discussions of the other two genres. The children's uncertainties about "what was factual and what was fantasy" (p. 329) and the book's unfamiliar structure seemed responsible for much of this response.

Later, Leal (1994) examined third graders' retention of scientific information after listening to two informational texts, one of which we would consider a dual-purpose text—Cole's (1990) *The Magic School Bus Lost in the Solar System*—versus listening to information books on the same topic. Students' knowledge was assessed with two different versions of a 10-item multiple-choice test administered before reading, immediately after reading, and after a six-week delay. With a single exception created by students from one of the eight classrooms studied, the "increases in test scores for those students who listened to the informational storybook were significantly greater" (p. 139) both at posttest and in the six-week delayed testing than for the students who had listened to the information books.

Maria and Junge (1994), also using a Magic School Bus book, sought to determine whether reading science textbooks or informational storybooks (although we would consider this book a dual-purpose text) would lead to greater comprehension and science information retention by fifth-grade children. Specifically, they wanted to know whether children would immediately recall more informational ideas from Cole's (1987) *The Magic School Bus Inside the Earth* than from a science textbook chapter on the same topic. They also wanted to know which group would be able to answer more questions on a delayed short-answer test of 14 items. Although they found that good readers recalled more informational ideas than poor readers, they found no difference by text type. They also found no differences on the delayed short-answer test. In fact, they found that children recalled very few ideas from either text. Interestingly, in examining the structure of the children's written recalls of the Magic School Bus book, Maria and Junge noted that 12 students (42.8%) used a narrative structure, 12 students (42.8%) used an expository structure, and 4 students (14.3 %) used a mixed structure. This led the researchers to suggest that in the absence of teacher directions on stance, what attitude to take toward a text, middle-grade children might adopt "either an aesthetic or efferent stance" (1994, p. 151) toward the Magic School Bus books.

The difference in Maria and Junge's findings and Leal's findings is puzzling. Maria and Junge comment that their study did not include a pretest. Possibly, the fifth graders had considerable background knowledge about layers of the Earth and different types of rocks. If that were the case, students might find little in the Magic School Bus book worth including in a written recall. Still, another distinction might have been the mode in which the students received the information from the Magic School Bus books. In Leal's study, the books were read aloud to the third graders. In Maria and Junge's study, fifth-grade children read the books themselves. Perhaps Maria and Junge's students, like our 28 teachers, were not sure how to approach the multiple text types on the pages of *The Magic School Bus Inside the Earth*. Perhaps they became lost in the book's story and jokes and did not attend to the science. These possibilities added to our curiosity about read-alouds of the Magic School Bus series. How would adults, specifically teachers, handle the information that appeared in the varied formats?

Understanding a Magic School Bus Book

Because the artistic decisions involved in dual-purpose texts determine the nature of content and visual design, we begin with a look at Cole's creative decisions in *The Magic School Bus Inside the Earth* (1987). Then, we look more closely at the structure of the book.

Creation of the Magic School Bus Books

In his description of how the Magic School Bus series began, Marcus (2001) explains that Scholastic Press editor Craig Walker approached Joanna Cole with the idea for a science picture book that could make readers laugh. Cole, who had written both science and story trade books, "hesitated. She worried that librarians and teachers might be put off by a lighter approach to dinosaurs and digestion" (Marcus, 2001, p. 50). Still, intrigued by the possibilities, Cole began planning.

> I loved it because I imagined that the teacher would be enthusiastic about the trip, while the children would think, "How boring!" I thought this combination would make the book funny, and I knew that it could be successful only if the science was rock solid and the plot was exciting and humorous. (Cole & Saul, 1996, p. 11)

As Cole considered the story aspects of the book, she knew that she would need to resort to magic to take the teacher's class on the types of trips she and Walker had discussed. She also was focused on developing the teacher's character, and she drew upon memories of one of her own science teachers to create a teacher who "just barged ahead...so involved in what she was doing that she blithely ignored our reactions" (Cole & Saul, 1996, pp. 12–13). From Cole's description of her plot creation process, it is clear that she worked hard to create the complications and "plot element[s] to make things more exciting" (Cole & Saul, 1996, p. 15). It is also clear that she intended to create an aesthetic experience to which humor and excitement would contribute significantly.

To accommodate all her fascinating science facts in the limited space of a picture book, Cole realized that she could employ not only speech balloons, but also "pages from her characters' fact-filled class reports" (Marcus, 2001, p. 52). During Cole's initial meeting with illustrator Bruce Degen, the two discussed the cluttered aspect of pages that would include text, speech balloons, reports, and illustrations. Degen noted the importance of making clear "to readers exactly what each drawing and set of words had to do with those around it" (Marcus, 2001, p. 52). Occasionally, though, Degen, too, would add to the print-heavy page, especially if he could locate a tiny space for his own humorous wording, often in the bus's destination window.

Considering Informational Structures

In their study, Maria and Junge (1994) looked closely at information-bearing structures in *The Magic School Bus Inside the Earth*. They found that the largest percentage of the informational ideas (112 or 45%) were located only in the children's reports and that 57 ideas (23%) were found only in the labeled pictures. Of the remaining reported ideas, 20 (8%) were located in the running text, 16 (6%) were found only in Ms. Frizzle's speech balloons, and 14 (6%) were found only in the children's speech balloons. Their other 31 informational ideas were found in more than one location.

When we examined informational ideas, we chose to look at the information-bearing structures a bit differently. We separated the cross-sectional diagram on pages 28 and 29 from the other labels in pictures for two reasons: first, because it provided a visual summary of the entire body of scientific information in the book, and second, because cross-sectional diagrams are frequently quite important in scientific texts. We also decided to count all the informational ideas, with the thought that a given idea in a particular structure might not be read. Our percentages and totals varied approximately 10% from those reported by Maria and Junge. Like Maria and Junge, we found the greatest number of ideas, 103 (36.8%), in the reports and the second highest number, 71 (25.4%), in the labeled items in pictures. Unlike Maria and Junge, we found the third highest number, 35 (12.5%), in Ms. Frizzle's speech balloons, and the fourth highest number, 32 (11.4%), in the running text. The remaining ideas were located in the cross-sectional diagram of the Earth (17 ideas, or 6.1%), other characters' speech balloons (12 ideas, or 4.2%), and the author's note (10 ideas, or 3.6%). In our other explorations of Magic School Bus books (Donovan & Smolkin, 2001, 2002), we have noted that the story line appears in the running text, supported by character dialogue in speech balloons. And, we have commented that readers need not read the fact-filled diagrams and reports if they simply wish to follow the plot in these dual-purpose texts.

Setting Up Our Study

In this section of our chapter, we present the decisions we made regarding our approach to our research questions. We also discuss the ways in which we made sense of the data once we had collected them.

Subjects and Setting

In a Google search of Internet references to *The Magic School Bus Inside the Earth*, we noted that its use was most frequently recommended for first-, second-, and third-grade classes. That information, and the fact that read-alouds are more common in the primary grades (Jacobs et al., 2000), led us to use these three grades for our study.

The school we used, Orchard Hill, has 50.1% of its students on free lunch, which let us know teachers might not expect highly developed background knowledge. Of its students, 71.8% are white, 26.2% are African American, and 2% are Hispanic, although the number of Hispanic migrant students increases in the fall. We decided to collect our data during the children's science fair week to make sure everyone would be excited about science topics; it was also the week before the third-grade classes would be visiting a well-known cave in the area. We invited all first-, second-, and third-grade teachers to participate in the study; four from each grade level agreed to assist us.

Procedures

We explained to the teachers that we wanted to know what happened when a Magic School Bus book was read aloud, and we told them to prepare as they usually would for any read-aloud. We said they were to share the book as they would any other text read-aloud for instructional purposes. Each teacher had time to read the book before her reading event was scheduled. Teachers were told to turn a tape recorder on when they were ready to start and turn it off when they had finished their read-aloud time. After the teachers finished their readings, we asked them to complete a short questionnaire for us. We then collected all the tapes and transcribed them.

Data Analysis

We began by assigning each teacher a code name. All first-grade teachers were given code names that began with the letter *A*; all second-grade teachers' code names began with the letter *B*; all third-grade teachers' code names began with the letter *C*.

For our first analysis, we looked for the informational idea-bearing structures that teachers actually read. To do this, we had created diagrams of each two-page spread in the book, with a different-shaped box to represent each textual structure. We then read each transcript and coded the boxes that teachers had either read or narrated (slightly different wording, possible omissions of some words or ideas) so we could consider what was and was not read as well as the order in which mature readers presented the many different text components on the page. We then counted the numbers of pages on which each teacher had read or narrated each type of informational idea-bearing structure. It was here that we noted Ms. Bowen's decision not to read any reports. She began her read-aloud by reminding children about other Magic School Bus books they had read. Then she explained, "First thing I'm going to go and read to you the story itself. Then we'll go back and look at some of the reports. And if we have a chance, and enough time, we might even talk a bit about some of those reports."

For our second analysis, we counted teachers' questions and comments that they made during their read-alouds about both the science and the story of the book. Determining when a teacher asked a question was quite easy; we could hear that they expected and waited for responses from their students. For teacher comments, we looked for statements they made when they were not directly reading or narrating text. In this category, we included directives they gave the students ("say *metamorphic*"), new ideas they introduced ("sparkly specks we see are minerals"), and reinforcements of the ideas they had just read ("So, it's hotter closer to the Earth's center"). We also inspected whether teachers emphasized the jokes on a page, and we included this in our story topics. We did so because the humor of the Magic School Bus books may be seen as part of the aesthetic response to the text (Rosenblatt, 1978). This analysis allowed us to consider both the science and the story content that teachers emphasized during their readings.

In our third analysis, we looked for correlations between the information structures read and the numbers of science questions and comments generated by each teacher. This let us consider which information structures might figure prominently in generating science-related discussions.

Results of the Study

In this section, we will share what we discovered about the read-aloud of one particular Magic School Bus book. We begin with a look at teachers' presentation of the information- and story-bearing structures, then examine teachers' questions and comments about story and science, and finish by looking at relationships between these two.

Which Information Structures Did Teachers Present to Children?

As can be seen in Table 16.1, there were certain informational structures that were presented by virtually every teacher and certain structures that were

Structure Type	Reports	Picture Labels	Frizzle Speech Balloons	Running Text	Diagram	Other Speech Balloons	Author Notes	Pronunciation Guides
# Possible Pages	16	11	13	26	2	31	2	1
Abbott	8	1	1	26	2	2	0	0
Adams	16	5	13	26	2	31	2	1
Andrews	14	4	12	26	2	25	0	0
Ashby	16	5	13	26	2	31	0	0
Baber	16	7	13	26	2	31	0	0
Bittner	15	7	13	26	2	30	0	0
Bowen	0	0	6	26	0	11	2	1
Bryant	5	7	7	26	2	4	0	0
Cabell	3	1	13	26	2	30	2	0
Chapman	12	0	1	25	0	2	0	0
Clark	16	3	12	26	2	28	0	1
Critzer	14	4	13	26	2	28	0	0

presented far less frequently. Almost every teacher in the study read the running text, which carried 11.4% of the informational ideas, on every single page of the book. Only Ms. Chapman omitted the running text, and she did so only once.

On the other hand, teachers' attention to units of the book bearing the greatest numbers of informational ideas varied considerably. Reports in the book, as previously noted, carried the highest number of informational ideas. Although four teachers read all the reports in the book, Ms. Bowen, as her comments to her students suggested, never read any. Labels in pictures were the second largest source of informational ideas in the text; not one single teacher in the study read the labels on all eleven pages on which they appeared. Two teachers, Ms. Bowen and Ms. Chapman, never read any labels, and Ms. Abbott and Ms. Cabell each read labels on only one page. In fact, the highest number of pages on which labels were read was seven, and this was by only three teachers in the study. The third largest informational idea-bearing structure, Ms. Frizzle's speech balloons, also was presented inconsistently. Still, six of the teachers read all of the balloons, and two others read almost all. Ms. Abbott and Ms. Chapman, on the other hand, each only read Ms. Frizzle's speech balloons on one page.

How Did Teachers Negotiate the Visual Environment?

Some of the teachers were very deliberate in their choices about what they would and would not read, as Ms. Bowen's comments and performance indicate. Other teachers, such as Ms. Ashby, Ms. Baber, and Ms. Bittner, appeared to have adopted a strategy of reading all the text, wherever it occurred, with the exceptions of labels on certain pages, the author notes, and the pronunciation guide.

When we worked at charting the order in which teachers moved about the two-page spreads, we were struck by the impressive variation. Ten teachers almost always read the running text on the left-hand side first. Ms. Bittner and Ms. Critzer adopted a different strategy; they began in the upper left-hand corner of the left-hand page, which meant that they often read reports before they read anything else. Teachers were very divided as to what they read second on each two-page spread. If it were a two-page spread on which running text appeared on both pages, certain teachers—Ms. Abbott, Ms. Adams, and Ms. Chapman—usually read the running text on the right-hand side next. Other teachers—Ms. Andrews, Ms. Baber, and Ms. Cabell—usually read the speech balloons on the left-hand side before moving to the running text on the right-hand side.

The three second-grade teachers who read labels on seven different pages did so differently. Ms. Baber and Ms. Bittner tended to read them after they had read running text, speech balloons, and reports. Ms. Bryant seemed not to follow a discernable pattern: Sometimes she focused on the picture (and labels) before reading anything else; on other pages, she followed Ms. Baber's and Ms. Bittner's pattern of reading them at the end.

Comments and Questions Emphasizing Science and Story Concepts

Table 16.2 displays the numbers of science and story questions asked and comments made by each teacher; it also shows the discussion content. Although we did not include them in our counts of teacher-cued questions and comments, we have also included the topics for teacher comments made in response to a child's remark (child cued, or c-c). The table shows that, except for third-grade teachers Ms. Clark and Ms. Critzer, teachers offered more questions and comments about science content than they did about story content.

Story Questions and Comments. Second-grade teacher Ms. Bryant offered the highest number of story-related questions and comments (16) and first-grade teacher Ms. Bittner offered the lowest (1). All but two teachers, Ms.

TABLE 16.2
Discussion Topics by Teacher

Name	Interactive Discussions	Teacher Discussions	Teacher's Story Comments & Questions	Teacher's Science Comments & Questions	Science Topics	Story/Other Topics
Abbott	1	1	1	5	■ Where do rocks come from? ■ These rock layers have names ■ Can rocks melt on playground? ■ There are different volcano shapes ■ There are lots of rocks here	■ Now they are deep inside Earth
Adams	1	1	4	6	■ This book is teaching us things ■ Rocks are always beneath us ■ It's neat how things become rocks ■ This is how stalagmites and stalactites differ ■ Clothing protects the characters (c-c) ■ Earth is hottest at the center ■ There are different volcano types	■ Who wrote report? (c-c) ■ Where is the Empire State building? ■ Joke: Knock on head ■ This is not real ■ The characters are scared
Andrews		2	3	5	■ Soil is dirt ■ What are fossils? ■ How do plants and animals become fossils ■ It's hotter closer to Earth's center ■ Collecting rocks can be a hobby	■ Joke: Beaver is chewing chair leg ■ Joke: His head is like a rock ■ Joke: Rock-n-roll has the word *rock*
Ashby	1	7	8	13	■ The crust is Earth's outer layer ■ Rock is under Earth's surface ■ Sea was where land is now ■ There are things inside caves ■ This is how stalagmites and stalactites differ ■ It's hotter closer to Earth's center ■ Heating and pushing makes limestone ■ This is what marble looks like ■ Which section is the mantle? ■ There are different volcano types ■ Pumice floats ■ We can place rocks in categories ■ I will bring in rocks to examine	■ You have seen *Magic School Bus* TV shows (c-c) ■ Joke: Beaver is chewing chair leg ■ Teacher provides a summary ■ The new kid is wondering ■ The Empire State building is in New York ■ Joke: His head is like a rock ■ Joke: Rock-n-roll has the word *rock* ■ Why are they nervous? ■ They were transported home (c-c) ■ This is not real

Name	Interactive Discussions	Teacher Discussions	Teacher's Story Comments & Questions	Teacher's Science Comments & Questions	Science Topics	Story/Other Topics
Baber	6	4	5	14	■ Here we see road cuts ■ They have been studying types of animal homes ■ This is the Earth's shape ■ Sparkly specks are minerals ■ This is how ground is formed (c–c) ■ There is rock under us (c–c) ■ Earth's top layer is soil ■ This fossil of seashell exists because of ancient sea ■ Limestone has many uses ■ We can look for fossils in caverns ■ This is how stalagmites and stalactites differ ■ These statues are made of marble ■ This is a formula for marble ■ There are different types of volcanoes—these we have seen on Internet, too ■ Rock can float ■ Rocks have many uses	■ Joke: Beaver is chewing chair leg ■ Who is Phil? (c–c) ■ Look at Frizzle's dress ■ Why is the bus spinning? ■ Look at Frizzle's clothes ■ Joke: His head is like a rock ■ Joke: Rock-n-roll has the word *rock* (c–c) ■ Frizzle is a neat teacher (c–c) ■ I would want to go home (c–c)
Bittner	1	3	3	16	■ We can learn real stuff about Earth and rocks ■ Rocks have weight and mass ■ Are glass, sidewalk, and Styrofoam rock? ■ Soil is ground-up rocks ■ Rock is always beneath us ■ There are different layers of rock ■ Sedimentary rock settles ■ Fossils may indicate sea ■ It took pressure and years to form fossils ■ This is how stalagmites and stalactites differ ■ Limestone changed to marble under heat and pressure ■ Shale+heat+pressure+years = slate ■ So, these are the different layers ■ The inner core is solid because of pressure ■ What type of volcano is this? ■ Pronounce rock names ■ Lava comes out with volcanic eruption (c–c)	■ Nonverbal joke: Beaver is chewing chair leg ■ Do dogs eat rocks? ■ Why do they go on a field trip? (c–c) ■ How does Frizzle get the bus to do all those things? (c–c; reality) ■ What is rumbling?

Discussion = more than single IRE pattern   c–c = child-cued   Teacher discussions develop from teacher questions/comments   (continued)

TABLE 16.2 (continued)
Discussion Topics by Teacher

Name	Interactive Discussions	Teacher Discussions	Teacher's Story Comments & Questions	Teacher's Science Comments & Questions	Science Topics	Story/Other Topics
Bowen	6	3	4	4	■ Placement of seas and land on Earth changed over time ■ You will see a cave in third grade ■ This is how stalagmites and stalactites differ ■ You saw rocks at science fair	■ Frizzle's dress has a pick ■ Define jackhammer ■ What's real? ■ Pronunciation guide can help us
Bryant	6	9	16	20	■ These are road cuts where machines have cut ground away ■ These must be long tunnels (c-c) ■ Animal homes are also animal habitats ■ How many wonder what is inside the Earth? ■ Does anyone know where rocks come from? ■ There are moon rocks (c-c) ■ Did you think about what earth would be without soil? ■ Would we find rock under our floor? ■ There are different layers (c-c) ■ Pronounce sedimentary ■ Limestone is made of shells ■ What type of rock were the fossils seen in other teacher's room? ■ Will children find more fossils in limestone cave? ■ Children will see stalagmites and stalactites in cave ■ Pronounce metamorphic ■ Teacher demonstrates pressure ■ Marble formed from heat and pressure ■ Are marbles made of marble? (c-c) ■ Did they know melted rock could push through cracks? ■ Look through the magnifying glass ■ What are islands? ■ Would rock from volcano be sedimentary rock? ■ Teacher displays pumice ■ What will happen when lava cools?	■ Remember the teacher's name ■ What might the new girl be thinking? ■ Will the new girl get to go on the trip? ■ What will the new adventure be? ■ What will Frizzle do? ■ What's on Frizzle's dress? ■ What are pick axes? ■ Do buses really do those things? ■ The bus has changed (c-c) ■ Those are names for jackhammers ■ Define layer cake ■ Joke: Layers of earth are like layers in a cake ■ Would the children be scared on falling bus? ■ Will children follow the bus? ■ They'll go through a volcano (c-c) ■ Are children afraid there will be a volcano? ■ Will the volcano erupt? (c-c) ■ What is making the rumbling sound? ■ Do you believe the bus really went inside Earth?

Name	Interactive Discussions	Teacher Discussions	Teacher's Story Comments & Questions	Teacher's Science Comments & Questions	Science Topics	Story/Other Topics
Cabell	2		5	5	■ What is the top layer? ■ Have they seen limestone? ■ We'll see stalagmites and stalactites (c-c) ■ This is how stalagmites and stalactites differ ■ How many have seen marble? ■ There are three parts inside Earth: mantle, outer core, inner core	■ Joke: Earth's crust is not pie crust ■ Are children excited about falling into Earth? ■ Joke: Character calls another character fossil ■ Joke: His head is like a rock ■ They cannot really go to Earth's center (c-c) ■ Identify octopus
Chapman	1	3	3	9	■ This book will be helpful for science fair ■ What is soil? ■ This book can help with projects ■ This book has lots of information ■ This exactly describes how caves are formed ■ They can learn more about stalagmites and stalactites in packets ■ Heat and pressure change rocks ■ Will it be hot in caves? (c-c) ■ Earth used to be hot rock all over (c-c) ■ We would die if we were inside (c-c) ■ What is name of Roman volcano? ■ Would children cook inside the Earth? (c-c) ■ Is cement a rock? (c-c)	■ Frizzle has a busy classroom ■ What is wrong with children's excuses? ■ Hope this does not happen to our field trip bus

(continued)

TABLE 16.2 (continued)

Discussion Topics by Teacher

Name	Interactive Discussions	Teacher Discussions	Teacher's Story Comments & Questions	Teacher's Science Comments & Questions	Science Topics	Story/Other Topics
Clark	5	1	9	6	■ What are those [rocks]? (c–c) ■ Here is fossil ■ How do we get fossils? (c–c) ■ What will it be like in cave? (c–c) ■ We'll need to find out if cave we visit is limestone ■ We'll see stalagmites ■ Cave we will visit will not be hot ■ Characters are further in Earth than we will be ■ This is a particular volcano type (c–c) ■ Did I pronounce the words correctly?	■ Identify beaver ■ We know about Ms. Frizzle ■ Is Frizzle happy? ■ What will happen? ■ We're going on trip too (c–c) ■ Will our bus spin? ■ Character must always think of food ■ Characters are putting labels on layers ■ Would it be scary to fall? ■ Dorothy Ann likes vocabulary ■ Characters couldn't really go inside (c–c) ■ This is what labels and speech balloons say (c–c)
Critzer	4	3	13	7	■ Is the Earth's crust like a pie crust? (c–c) ■ Can you grind up pebbles? (c–c) ■ Is rock under the water? ■ Read the labels of layers ■ Is that picture a swordfish? (c–c) ■ We'll see stalagmites and stalactites in cave ■ Stalagmites and stalactites locations ■ Can we take a rock from cave? (c–c) ■ There are different volcano shapes ■ Why does pumice float? ■ Hot lava makes steam	■ Summarizes finishing unit ■ Poor Arnold has Styrofoam ■ Our class will take a trip (c–c) ■ What is on Frizzle's dress? ■ I hope our bus does not spin around ■ Where is Florrie? (c–c) ■ Who says layers of a cake? (c–c) ■ What is the jackhammer? (c–c) ■ New kid cannot get used to Frizzle's class ■ Bus turned into steam shovel ■ Joke: His head is like a rock ■ Dorothy Ann loves vocabulary ■ What will happen? ■ Maybe child forgot his permission slip ■ Who is Rachel? (c–c) ■ Child still wants to go home ■ Things are always crazy with Frizzle ■ Children are scared

Bryant (16) and Ms. Critzer (14), produced nine or fewer remarks and questions each. Questions and comments ranged from simple interpretive remarks ("Now they're deep inside the Earth") to questions that probed inferences about characters' reactions ("Would they be scared [on a falling bus]?") to questions that dealt with the fantastic aspects of the book ("Do you believe the bus really went inside the Earth?"). With regard to the jokes in the book, four teachers never drew children's attention to them, four did so once, and four did so three times. For Ms. Andrews, jokes were the only story material on which she commented.

Science Questions and Comments. The number of science-related questions and comments teachers made while they were reading had an even greater range than those produced for story aspects, with Ms. Bowen posing only four comments but Ms. Bryant producing 20 questions and comments. Four teachers, Ms. Ashby, Ms. Baber, Ms. Bittner, and Ms. Bryant, each produced 13 or more questions and comments; just as with story questions and comments, the majority offered nine or fewer. Interestingly, three of these teachers—Ms. Ashby, Ms. Baber, and Ms. Bittner—read virtually all the text on the pages. And three of the teachers—Ms. Baber, Ms. Bittner, and Ms. Bryant—read labels on seven of the eleven pages on which they appeared. Given the higher number of science comments and questions made by these four teachers, we decided to term them "high science" teachers—individuals particularly focused on imparting the book's science concepts.

Teachers' questions and comments represented a range of purposes and functions. Some were simple restatements of text information ("Soil is dirt") while others served to check for understanding ("So, which section is the mantle?"). Some asked children to transfer text material ("Would we find rocks under our floor?"), and others called upon children to contemplate the unknown ("Did you think about what the Earth would be like without soil?").

Correlations Between Information-Bearing Structures and Science Questions and Comments

Because we had noted that most of the science ideas appeared in reports, labels, Ms. Frizzle's speech balloons, and the running text, we expected that there might be a relationship between the type of structures read and the numbers of remarks and questions teachers produced. There was only one statistically significant correlation, though; the relationship between pages with labels read and science questions and comments was significant ($r = .725$, $p = .008$). This correlation implies that teachers who took the time to read labels were also likely to spend more time discussing the science concepts with their students.

Discussions of the Book

We also looked at discussions that occurred while teachers read; we defined *discussion* as teacher-student interactions that exceeded a typical three-part question-answer-affirmation pattern (e.g., Mehan, 1979). Teacher discussions were those in which the teacher set the discussion in motion; interactive discussions were those begun by children's questions and comments, with higher numbers of student turns. Discussions ranged from a low of 1 per reading (Ms. Adams and Ms. Bittner) to a high of 15 per reading (Ms. Bryant). Some teachers had no interactive discussions (Ms. Abbott, Ms. Andrews, Ms. Bowen), and others had no teacher-launched discussions (Ms. Bittner and Ms. Cabell).

What Happens When Teachers Read Aloud Magic School Bus Books?

Our study shows that these 12 teachers approached their readings of *The Magic School Bus Inside the Earth* very differently. As mentioned previously, teachers had different styles of reading. Some read virtually everything on the page; others were more selectively attentive to parts of the book. Some had many discussions of content during the reading event; others had no more than one or two. However, what we are most concerned with here is whether, as Mayer (1995) suggests, the fictional aspects of the book overcome its science content.

What Happens to the Science Content?

It is certainly not surprising that Ms. Bowen, who decided that she would read the story first but did not return to read the reports later, raised the fewest number of science topics and issues with her students. All four science comments that did occur in her classroom were linked to experiences outside the material in the book, such as to another book the class had read (see chapter 9 on intertextual connections), to an experience they would have in third grade, and to a visit to the science fair. None particularly deepened children's appreciation of the science ideas. Although we could find no correlation between the numbers of science courses teachers indicated they had taken and the numbers of science-related questions and comments they posed, we will note here that Ms. Bowen reported that she had taken no science courses during college or after.

On the other hand, the fact that a teacher read the reports or had taken more science courses did not guarantee that the science in the book would be stressed for children. Ms. Clark, for example, read every single report in the book and had taken more science courses than any other teacher in the study (five courses), but she raised only two more science-related questions or comments than Ms. Bowen. So, we must conclude that it is possible to read these dual-purpose texts exactly as we have suggested previously—focusing almost exclusively on story content. This may, indeed, be what happened in Maria and Junge's study in which the fifth graders read the books by themselves.

Further, the failure to read reports did not necessarily lead to a low science read-aloud experience, in which a teacher spent little time discussing science concepts. Ms. Bryant, the highest science content reader with 21 questions and comments in her classroom, only read or narrated reports on 5 of the 16 pages on which they occurred. Nor did the number of discussions teachers fostered affect how much the science was stressed for children. Ms. Bittner had only one longer interchange (beyond the common, three-move Initiation-Response-Evaluation sequence [Mehan, 1979]) during her read-aloud; yet, she was second only to Ms. Bryant in terms of the number of science topics she stressed and introduced (16).

What Produced More Science Readings?

We do know that all four of the "high-science" teachers stressed science content more than they did story content, sometimes in a very pronounced fashion. Our correlations showed a link between the reading of the picture labels and higher numbers of science comments and questions. Ms. Baber, Ms. Bittner, and Ms. Bryant all read picture labels on seven pages. The other high-science teacher, Ms. Ashby, read fewer labels than the three second-grade teachers, but she adopted the same read-all-print strategy that Ms. Baber and Ms. Bittner used. For three of these teachers, then, reading reports and labels was part of the read-aloud strategy that led them to higher science content readings. They may, however, have read the text this way because they were more interested in science (Ms. Ashby, for example, had participated in a Project Wild institute, focused on environmental K–12 education) or because they were simply oriented to reading almost all science text items on the page.

Examining a High-Science, High-Story Magic School Bus Read-Aloud

Unique among the high-science teachers was Ms. Bryant. She only occasionally read reports; she approached the pages in a less systematic fashion than the other three. She was attentive to both story and science. More importantly, she was unique in the types of comments and questions she raised, and we have noted some of her distinctions with boldface words in Table 16.2. In this section, we look more closely at four of Ms. Bryant's strategies that fostered scientific responses during her read-aloud.

Encouraging Speculation. Ms. Bryant brought a sense of wonder to the scientific aspects of her read-aloud. When a child commented that it could be scary to go inside a mountain via a tunnel, Ms. Bryant also focused on the picture on the two-page title spread, directing all students to notice the size of the mountain in which the tunnels appeared. "Think," she commented to her class, "how big those tunnels must be." Instead of simply reading Ms. Frizzle's question to Arnold as to whether he wondered what was inside the Earth, Ms. Bryant turned the story question into an actual question. "How many of you wonder?" she asked her students. This same encouragement of speculation appeared as she read Florrie's report defining soil. Its concluding sentence indicated that without rock there would not be soil for plants and trees to grow in. "Wow," breathed Ms. Bryant. "Did you think about that?" Ms. Bryant, unlike other teachers in the study, encouraged a deeper processing of the way the world around us works.

Assisting Children in Transferring Knowledge. Ms. Bryant was not content with only checking children's recall of what she had read. Instead, she wanted them to transfer the science content of the book to other situations. After reading Shirley's report, which says, "There is always rock under you," Ms. Bryant asked her students, "How about if you dug through this floor?" When there was no response, she commented, "If we went deep enough, we would find rock." Then she asked another question, "What about if we were in the middle of the ocean floating on a raft?" "Rock," responded a student. "Yeah, but there's predators down there," said another. "That's true," acknowledged Ms. Bryant. "We'd have to get through the predators." Later, she asked her students if they had seen fossils in the rocks in another teacher's classroom that morning. When they indicated they had, she asked them again to transfer their new knowledge. "Fantastic. So, what kind of rock must that have been?"

Stressing Scientific Terms. Although Ms. Bryant was not the only teacher to ask her students to pronounce the names of the various types of rocks as she read the text, she encouraged, as can be seen in the child's predator comment above, the use of scientific terminology. She encouraged her students to use the term *habitats* as they looked at the first two-page spread of the book, and she was the only teacher to note the magnifying glass on the two-page spread that featured the cross-sectional diagram.

Making Science Tangible. Ms. Bryant also was unique in her preparation for her read-aloud. Though all teachers had opportunities to read the book prior to presenting it to their students, Ms. Bryant was the only teacher to bring a rock collection to the reading event. Instead of reading the author's and illustrator's notes at the end of the book, she read the names of the rocks in Ms. Frizzle's students' collection, then said, "I'm going to turn off the tape recorder now, and let's see if we can match some of our rocks to these." This was not, however, the only way in which Ms. Bryant made science tangible. Below is part of her discussion of metamorphic rock.

Ms. Bryant: [reading from the book] *Rocks that were changed are called metamorphic rocks.* Can I hear that word, please?

Children: Metamorphic rock.

Ms. Bryant: All right. So they're changed by two things. Heat and, do you remember what they said?

Child: Pressure.

Ms. Bryant: Pressure. Show me your hands together and really press hard. Ooooh! That's such pressure.

Despite the fact that Ms. Bryant read fewer reports than eight of the twelve teachers in the study, her attitude toward scientific stances and scientific understanding made her read-aloud exemplary from the standpoint of stressing the science.

Returning to the Author's and Illustrator's Intentions

In our earlier review of Cole's and Degen's statements about the creation of the Magic School Bus books, we noted that Joanna Cole sought to create a book that would be funny, exciting, and informative. The read-alouds we examined suggest that she was successful. Teachers encouraged children to be concerned with character's feelings and the little jokes they made as Ms. Frizzle forged forward with her underground science instruction. Teachers also attended to the science concepts in the books, albeit some more successfully than others.

It does appear, though, that Degen may have been less successful in his efforts to indicate "what each drawing and set of words had to do with those around it" (Marcus, 2001, p. 52). Teachers, though not random in their readings, did not seem to attend to situations in which the two pages of a spread indicated two separate events. Nor did they necessarily attend to the logical order of the book's elements, which would suggest that the reports written after the field trip be the last items read on a page.

Advice for Teachers

Given all our findings, we close with our advice for teachers who would like to share the Magic School Bus books with their students. We recommend that teachers look carefully at the books before they read them aloud. They may wish to follow Ms. Bryant's example and bring objects to the classroom that relate to the science content. Teachers should look carefully at each two-page spread and determine if each page represents a separate event. If it does, we suggest following the Ashby-Baber-Bittner approach: Read any running text first, then the speech balloons, and then any reports on the page. As to the reading of the labels, for the most part, they are part of the environment in which the characters find themselves; teachers should address them as they discuss the action of the page, whether they do so before or after the reading of connected text.

Finally, we urge all teachers to work to deepen children's understanding of science, using strategies such as those in Ms. Bryant's read-aloud. Cole and Degen's Magic School Bus books can indeed create excellent settings for considering how science operates in the world around us.

REFERENCES

Camp, D. (2000). It takes two: Teaching with twin texts of fact and fiction. *The Reading Teacher, 53,* 400–408.

Cole, J., & Saul, W. (1996). *On the bus with Joanna Cole: A creative autobiography.* Portsmouth, NH: Heinemann.

Donovan, C.A., & Smolkin, L.B. (2001). Genre and other factors influencing teachers' book selections for science. *Reading Research Quarterly, 36,* 412–440.

Donovan, C.A., & Smolkin, L.B. (2002). Considering genre, content, and visual features in the selection of trade books for science instruction. *The Reading Teacher, 55,* 502–520.

Duke, N.K. (2000). 3.6 minutes per day: The scarcity of informational texts in first grade. *Reading Research Quarterly, 35,* 202–224.

Guzzetti, B.J., Snyder, T.E., Glass, G.V., & Gamas, W.S. (1993). Promoting conceptual change in science: A comparative meta-analysis of instructional interventions from reading education and science education. *Reading Research Quarterly, 28,* 117–159.

Jacobs, J.S., Morrison, T.G., & Swinyard, W.R. (2000). Reading aloud to students: A national probability study of classroom reading practices of elementary school teachers. *Reading Psychology, 21,* 171–193.

Jetton, T.L. (1994). Information-driven versus story-driven: What children remember when they are read informational stories. *Reading Psychology, 15*(2), 109–130.

Kress, G. (1994). *Learning to write* (2nd ed.). New York: Routledge.

Lake, J. (1993). *Imagine: A literature-based approach to science.* Bothell, WA: Wright Group.

Leal, D.J. (1992). The nature of talk about three types of text during peer group discussions. *Journal of Reading Behavior, 24*(3), 313–338.

Leal, D.J. (1994). A comparison of third-grade children's listening comprehension of scientific information using an information book and an informational storybook. In C.K. Kinzer & D.J. Leu (Eds.), *Multidimensional aspects of literacy research, theory, and practice* (43rd yearbook of the National Reading Conference, pp. 137–145). Chicago: National Reading Conference.

Leal, D.J., & Kearney, M.K. (1997). What's so magical about those *Magic School Bus* books? Textual encounters of another kind. *Ohio Reading Teacher, 31*(3), 62–66.

Marcus, L.S. (2001). *Side by side: Five favorite picture-book teams go to work.* New York: Walker.

Maria, K., & Junge, K. (1994). A comparison of fifth graders' comprehension and retention of scientific information using a science textbook and an informational storybook. In C.K. Kinzer & D.J. Leu (Eds.), *Multidimensional aspects of literacy research, theory, and practice* (43rd yearbook of the National Reading Conference, pp. 146–152). Chicago: National Reading Conference.

Mayer, D. (1995). How can we best use literature in teaching? *Science and Children, 32,* 16–19.

Mehan, H. (1979). *Learning lessons: Social organization in the classroom.* Cambridge, MA: Harvard University Press.

Moss, B. (1991). Children's nonfiction trade books: A complement to content area texts. *The Reading Teacher, 45,* 26–32.

Rice, D.C. (2002). Using trade books in teaching elementary science: Facts and fallacies. *The Reading Teacher, 55,* 552–565.

Rice, D.C., & Snipes, C. (1997, March). *Children's trade books: Do they affect the development of science concepts?* Paper presented at the 70th annual meeting of the National Association for Research in Science Teaching, Oak Brook, IL. (ERIC Document Reproduction Service No. ED374467)

Rosenblatt, L.M. (1978). *The reader, the text, the poem.* Carbondale, IL: Southern Illinois University Press.

Vardell, S.M., & Copeland, K.A. (1992). Reading aloud and responding to nonfiction: Let's talk about it. In E.B. Freedman & D.G. Person (Eds.), *Using nonfiction trade books in the elementary classroom: From ants to zeppelins* (pp. 76–85). Urbana, IL: National Council of Teachers of English.

CHILDREN'S LITERATURE CITED

Cole, J. (1986). *The magic school bus at the waterworks.* Ill. B. Degen. New York: Scholastic.

Cole, J. (1987). *The magic school bus inside the Earth.* Ill. B. Degen. New York: Scholastic.

Cole, J. (1990). *The magic school bus lost in the solar system.* Ill. B. Degen. New York: Scholastic.

Gibbons, G. (1995). *Planet Earth/Inside out.* New York: Mulberry.

James, S. (1991). *Dear Mr. Blueberry.* New York: Margaret K. McElderry.

SCIENCE WRITING

HEURISTICS

In this section, Shirley J. Magnusson and Annemarie Sullivan Palincsar seek to increase the level of student engagement by peppering lessons with a series of journals by a fictional scientist who is working on the same problems as the students. This study of student reaction and action is richly detailed in chapter 17, "Learning From Text Designed to Model Scientific Thinking in Inquiry-Based Instruction." Their approach, Guided Inquiry supporting Multiple Literacies, is based on the notion that teaching science for understanding provides a powerful context for teaching literacy. Examples from a fourth-grade class support their claim that text and inquiry together can bolster children's understanding of both science and language use.

In chapter 18, "Students' Science Notebooks and the Inquiry Process," Michael P. Klentschy and Elizabeth Molina-De La Torre provide powerful data that supports the inclusion of writing in a hands-on science program. Using information gathered from the Valle Imperial Project in Science (VIPS), the authors describe a "high needs" school district in southern California, populated by the children of many unemployed workers and nonnative speakers, that showed impressive test score gains when a writing component was added to their science program. This study clearly correlates increased literacy and science achievement when a "science notebook" was added to the extant inquiry science program.

In chapter 19, "The Science Writing Heuristic: Using Writing as a Tool for Learning in the Laboratory," Carolyn S. Wallace, Brian Hand, and Eun-Mi Yang describe a procedure for helping students think through and reflect on their science experiences that they call the Science Writing Heuristic. Seventh-grade students in a life science course were given a variety of writing tasks that caused them to highlight the connections among questions, claims, data, and evidence. The authors conclude that as a result, students were better able to grapple with the concept of a knowledge claim in science and became more skilled in seeking evidence to support their claims. In addition, students' metacognitive skills improved.

In short, writing is a powerful tool for teaching both literacy and science skills.

CHAPTER 17

Learning From Text Designed to Model Scientific Thinking in Inquiry-Based Instruction

SHIRLEY J. MAGNUSSON AND ANNEMARIE SULLIVAN PALINCSAR

Rather than begin with the question, How can literacy promote an understanding of science? we begin this chapter with a claim that is a modification of this question: Teaching science for understanding provides a powerful context for promoting literacy. This claim is reflected in the perspective that we bring to the teaching of science in the elementary grades, an orientation we call *Guided Inquiry supporting Multiple Literacies* (GIsML) (Magnusson & Palincsar, 1995). The value of this claim is the leverage it provides, especially for those of us who work with elementary school teachers, many of whom have a firm commitment to the teaching of reading and writing but not necessarily to the teaching of science.

The claim that teaching science for understanding can promote literacy is an invitation to consider—at a minimum—the roles of reading, writing, and oral language in science instruction. In this chapter, we will narrow our focus to knowledge we have gleaned about the use of text in science instruction. Our interest in the use of text in inquiry-based science instruction is fueled by two observations: (1) learning from text is authentic to scientific practice, and (2) using text in inquiry-based science instruction is a powerful way to advance the goals of both text comprehension instruction and science instruction. However, there are many features of existing texts that limit their potential to support science learning; hence, the fit between text and inquiry is not always a comfortable one, leading many teachers to divorce text from inquiry-based science instruction (Shymansky, Yore, & Good, 1991).

We begin this chapter by considering the parallels between the processes integral to learning from text and learning from scientific inquiry. We then discuss some of the limitations of extant science text that prompted us to design an innovative type of text. After describing this text, we illustrate its use in one fourth-grade classroom to provide evidence of our claim that text and inquiry can be integrated in powerful ways that advance children's understanding of both scientific reasoning and reasoning from text.

Comprehending Text and Learning From Scientific Inquiry

Perhaps the most salient requisite to both text comprehension and learning from inquiry-based instruction is the construction of knowledge and understanding. In both text comprehension (Chan, Burtis, Scardamalia, & Bereiter, 1992; Coté, Goldman, & Saul, 1998; Chi, de Leeuw, Chiu, & La Vancher, 1994) and science inquiry learning (Clement, 1993; Magnusson & Palincsar, 1995; Schwab, 1962), children construct meaning by integrating new information with prior knowledge and by building representations or mental models of the referential situation.

In both text comprehension and science learning, the capacity to build these mental models is assisted by the learner's awareness and use of both general discourse structures and domain-specific knowledge structures. Comprehension is enhanced to the extent that the reader is aware of and makes use of text genre and structure (Goldman, 1997; Richgels, McGee, Lomax, & Sheard, 1987). Similarly, inquiry-based activity engages participants in learning the structure of discourse that best communicates a scientific argument (Kuhn, 1989; Lemke, 1990; van Zee, 1997).

Furthermore, becoming a skilled reader (Hartman, 1995; Perfetti, Britt, & Georgi, 1995) and engaging in scientific inquiry (Goldman, 1997; Pera, 1994) both call for the coordination of information across texts. For example, in the course of inquiry experiences, children have opportunities to compare information presented by peers with their own thinking, lab notebook entries (within and across students' notebooks), and their own experiences with those reported in science texts. Learning in these situations requires children to synthesize information across trade books and other forms of text.

One of the skills demonstrated by successful comprehenders is the capacity to flexibly interpret the multiple representations that are used to communicate ideas in text, such as graphs, charts, diagrams, and tables (Carpenter & Shah, 1998). In the course of scientific inquiry, decisions regarding how to represent one's data for the purposes of clear and compelling communication is an integral part of the inquiry process, as is the ability to interpret others' representations (Lehrer & Shauble, 2000).

There is a significant literature that speaks to the importance of vocabulary knowledge in advancing text comprehension (Stahl & Fairbanks, 1986). In fact, the relationship between vocabulary knowledge and comprehension is remarkably robust across ages and populations. Furthermore, research syntheses (National Institute of Child Health and Human Development, 2000) suggest that the context in which words are learned is critical to determining the success of vocabulary instruction. To that end, a significant portion of vocabulary instruction should occur as students learn from subject matter materials. A hallmark of engaging in science learning is the opportunity to acquire the discourse of science (Lemke, 1990). Although discourse is, of course, much more than the accretion of particular words, it is the case that in the course of "trying on" the discourse of science, students are exposed to a rich—and nuanced—vocabulary for communicating ideas. Guided inquiry science instruction, in which the teacher draws attention to the ways in which language in general, and words in particular, are being used to communicate ideas, clearly offers a prime context for this type of experience.

Finally, it is also the case that skilled comprehenders engage in metacognitive activity to the extent that they maintain an awareness of the success with which they are constructing meaning and have a repertoire of strategies to enlist if they encounter impediments to their understanding. Inquiry requires a similar disposition on the part of the learner, a mindfulness about the purpose of the inquiry, attentiveness to the relationship between the question that is guiding the inquiry and the investigation itself, and the ability to monitor the progress of the inquiry in terms of how well it is advancing one's understanding of the phenomenon under investigation.

In summary, there is exciting potential at the intersection of the teaching of text comprehension and the engagement and support of children in inquiry-based science learning. As a result, science instruction is one of the prime contexts in which teachers might effectively use informational text to advance multiple learning goals. Despite the parallels between text comprehension and inquiry, activity-based science kits prior to the U.S. National Standards Education Standards (NSES) (National Research Council [NRC], 1996) rarely included text. With the advent of the NSES calling for students to "learn how to access scientific information from books...and evaluate and interpret the information they have acquired" (NRC, 1996, p. 45), various forms of text have appeared in the major, nationally developed, kit-based materials. However, observational and survey research suggest that elementary school teachers who choose to engage in inquiry-based instruction do not typically incorporate the use of text in this instruction (Shymansky, Yore, & Good, 1991).

One explanation for this phenomenon is that learning via text is typically seen to be at odds with learning via inquiry. Rutherford's (1991) comments about the nature of textbooks intended for elementary school science provides several reasons for this view: "textbooks are more of a hindrance than a help in elementary science education..." because they "emphasize not discovery but presentation...are too ordered, too assertive by their nature, too given to explanations" (p. 27). Other criticisms of extant science texts characterize them as dense and abstruse (Lloyd & Mitchell, 1989), thin with respect to scientific explanation (Lloyd & Mitchell, 1989), and sparse with regard to the use of devices that would lend themselves to text cohesion (Farris, Kissinger, & Thompson, 1988). In their review of existing science basals, Brown and Palincsar (1989) further observed that these texts (a) concentrate on facts but not on generative understanding; (b) emphasize the products of science rather than the nature and processes of science; (c) present information in familiar but not scientifically conventional ways; and (d) are organized in such a fashion that the sequence of topics does not support cumulative reference, knowledge building, or sustained effort after meaning.

Designing an Innovative Type of Text

For the past five years, in response to the kinds of criticisms leveled at text and text use (or the lack thereof) in inquiry-based science and guided by knowledge of the authenticity of text in scientific practice, we have been engaged in the design and study of an innovative form of text to support elementary classroom teachers and their students in guided inquiry science teaching and learning.

The text is modeled after the notebook of a fictitious scientist, named Lesley, who uses her entries to (a) identify the problem she is investigating, (b) think aloud about how she can accurately model the phenomenon for the purposes of investigation, (c) make decisions about how she will most effectively represent the data that she is collecting, (d) share her data and the claims that she believes she can make from these data, (e) respond to the critical reactions of her colleagues as they weigh the evidence for her claims, and (f) revise her thinking as she gathers new data or considers alternative explanations.

Our decision to model the text on a scientist's notebook was influenced by our interest in the role that the use of text could play in advancing students' understandings related to both the topic under study (e.g., light, motion, electricity), and the nature of scientific reasoning through learning about the experiences and thinking of others. These notebook texts have been designed in conjunction with the programs of study in use in our GIsML-oriented classrooms (e.g., How does light interact with solid objects? What causes objects to float and sink? What is in soil? What explains motion down an inclined plane? What explains motion on a level plane? What makes static electricity? How do electric circuits work?).

The notebook texts include multiple ways of representing data including diagrams, tables, and figures. For example, diagrams are used to illustrate the setup of the investigation materials. Figures are used to depict data that students can interpret along with the scientist. Tables model the various ways in which data can be arrayed, and the accompanying narrative models the activity of interpreting these data.

The notebook texts also include properly cited notes from reference materials to demonstrate how a scientist would access published material, selectively read that material, and apply the newly acquired information to the problem at hand. For example, in a notebook entry regarding static electricity, Lesley consults with a historian of science who refers her to a volume containing descriptions of Benjamin Franklin's experiments with electricity. In this volume, Lesley encounters a chronology of what scientists since the sixth century B.C. have observed about static electricity. Lesley uses this reference material to help shape the claims that she wishes to investigate.

Yet another feature of these notebook texts is the extent to which they portray the ways in which scientists interact with one another, observing particular conventions. In one entry, Lesley notes that fellow scientists were not persuaded by her data because the data were imprecise. This leads her to use an instrument that will allow for more precise measurements, as well as a process that can be more readily replicated by others.

In our description of the parallels between comprehension and scientific problem solving, we noted the importance of metacognitive activity. One feature that is present in a section of the notebook texts reflects how metacognition can be captured through Lesley's thinking and activity; that is, the revisions in which Lesley engages during the course of her investigations. For example, in the notebook text that was used in the study we report in this manuscript, Lesley has identified a set of claims based upon her preliminary evidence. Subsequently, with the urging of her peers, she collects more precise data, which lead her to revise her initial claim.

Finally, because Lesley writes in the first person, there is the presence of voice in these notebook texts. Students have commented favorably on this feature (see Students' Evaluations of the Notebook Text, page 330), noting that it serves to personalize the reading. (See chapter appendix, page 334, for sample notebook text regarding how light interacts with objects.)

Investigating the Use of the Notebook Text

Through a program of research employing multiple methods, we have accrued evidence that these notebook texts, used in tandem with firsthand investigations of natural phenomena, advance children's conceptual understanding, as well as their ability to engage in scientific reasoning. In fact, these notebook texts promote learning more effectively than traditional text, even when that text is constructed to be "considerate" or friendly to the reader, meaning that it is accessible and is written to be coherent and readily understandable (Armbruster & Anderson, 1988).

For example, in one study (Palincsar & Magnusson, 2001), we compared children's learning from two types of text: a notebook text and a traditional considerate informational text. To conduct this study, we prepared texts for the topic of light: one of each type regarding reflection and one of each type regarding refraction. Designed as a within-subject study (to control for individual differences in reading and background knowledge), seven classrooms of students were taught with both types of the text, counterbalanced for order of presentation. The students first responded to a set of questions assessing their topic-specific science background knowledge, followed by a reading of either the traditional or the notebook text, and finally a post-instruction assessment of their topic-specific science knowledge. A week later, this sequence was repeated for the alternative text type on the remaining topic. For six of the seven classrooms, the children showed greater pre-instruction to post-instruction knowledge differences when learning from the notebook text rather than from the traditional informational text. An item analysis revealed that these differences were largely accounted for by the responses students made to items designed to assess students' capacity to reason within a topic-specific context (e.g., to use data to support claims about the behavior of light).

In addition to this quasi-experimental research, we have conducted a series of observational studies for specific curricular units in which inquiry-based instruction was designed to include text in interplay with firsthand investigation. Using ethnographic methods (videotaping, field notes, and teacher and student interviews), we have investigated the nature of the discourse when elementary teachers and students incorporate texts in guided-inquiry instruction (Cutter, Vincent, Magnusson, & Palincsar, 2001;

Palincsar & Magnusson, 2001). These studies demonstrate that notebook texts (used together with firsthand investigation) support not only the development of scientific concepts, but also children's engagement in scientific reasoning, adopting a critical stance toward text and metacognitive activity, such as monitoring for sense-making and taking steps to restore clarity and cohesion.

In the next section of this chapter, we examine one classroom's use of the notebook text dealing with the topic of how light interacts with solid matter. We selected this classroom for several reasons: first, the teacher, Ms. Sally Freeman, is recognized by her district as an exemplary teacher of the language arts; hence, she has a solid understanding of how to support children's learning from text. Second, prior to the development of the notebook text, we conducted a descriptive study of Ms. Freeman using traditional informational text with her class, following a week of firsthand investigation (Palincsar & Magnusson, 1997). In this research, despite Ms. Freeman's expertise, we did not see students interacting with the text in ways that we thought were key to their full understanding of science. For example, although the traditional text was useful in advancing the children's conceptual understanding, we saw little evidence in the transcripts of this instruction that children were learning about scientific reasoning. Furthermore, there was no indication that the students were assuming a critical stance toward the text. This was problematic because deferring to the authority of the text runs counter to active engagement in evaluating the relationship between the ideas in the text and the ideas the students held from their prior experiences (Guzzetti, Snyder, & Glass, 1992).

Context

This study took place during the 1999–2000 academic year, in which Ms. Freeman had 29 fourth graders. The students were engaged in a program of study on the interaction of light with matter. In the course of firsthand investigations, which occurred over six days before the investigation with the notebook text, the students used flashlights to investigate an array of objects that varied in terms of their texture, color, reflectivity, translucence, and shape. There were two sets of goals that were integral to this program of study. The substantive goals included the following:

- Light can be reflected, absorbed, or transmitted by objects.
- All objects reflect and absorb light.

- There is an inverse relationship between the amount of light reflected from and absorbed by an object.
- The behavior of light is related to the characteristics of the object with which it is interacting.

The scientific reasoning goals were for students, like scientists, to do the following:

- Observe phenomena to determine how/why they occur.
- Record observations with precision.
- Decide when and how often to observe in order to determine relationships.
- Use charts and graphs to organize and interpret data and determine patterns/relationships.
- Conduct fair and reliable tests to answer a question.
- Express findings as knowledge claims.
- Present knowledge claims to the community (classmates).
- Evaluate the adequacy of knowledge claims on the basis of the strength of the evidence (data) supporting them.

Instruction proceeded through cycles of investigation, in which pairs of students investigated ideas that had been generated by the class based on their experiential or background knowledge. The students designed their investigations, made observations, organized these data to determine what claims they could make, and then shared them with the class, prompting discussion about how the claims compared to the ideas generated by the class. Claims generated from firsthand investigations varied in terms of the amount of supporting evidence the students provided. Figure 17.1 shows the time frame for instruction.

The first notebook text used in this study of light reports what is essentially a replication of the students' investigation, using a smaller set of the materials they had used in their inquiry. There were several differences in Lesley's investigation, perhaps the most significant of which is that she used a light meter to measure the light. (See chapter appendix, page 334, for notebook text used in this investigation.)

All instruction was videotaped with the use of a sensitive microphone to capture whole-class interactions and with a microphone on the teacher to capture her interactions with small groups of students during their

FIGURE 17.1
Time Frame of Instruction

Day 1	Day 2	Day 3	Day 4	Day 5	Day 6	
Cycle 1			Cycle 2			
Question: How does light interact with objects?			Question: What happens to all of the light when it interacts with objects?			
Firsthand Investigation			Firsthand Investigation			
Engage What we think we know; how to investigate	Investigate Work with 20 different materials	Report Whole-class discussion about investigating	Engage; Investigate	Prepare to Report Groups make displays of findings	Report Focus on claims and evidence	

Day 7	Day 8	Day 9	Day 10	Day 11	Day 12	Day 13
Cycle 3		Cycle 4		Cycle 5		
Question: How does light interact with solids?		Question: How much light is reflected from and/or transmitted through an object, and how much light is absorbed?				
Secondhand Investigation		Firsthand Investigation		Firsthand Investigation		
Notebook text investigation without light meter	Notebook text investigation with light meter	Engage; Investigate	Report Discuss standards for data collection	Engage; Investigate (quantify)	Investigate; Report	Report

investigations. Transcripts were prepared for each segment of videotape during which the notebook text was in use. We then conducted a content analysis, coding specifically for practices the teacher used to mediate the students' interaction with the text for the purpose of supporting their interpretations and use of the text, and instances of students using the text to advance scientific reasoning (guided by the goals previously identified).

Finding: General Literacy Practices

The literacy teaching practices in which Ms. Freeman engaged speak to the processes we described in the introduction to this chapter. They were designed to support the students' learning from the text. For example, Ms. Freeman led the students in a quick preview of the text (less than five minutes), during which the students identified the general topic of the text (an investigation with light) and the presence of findings from the investigation. As they previewed the text, Ms. Freeman called their attention to particular features of the text (e.g., diagrams of the investigative set-up, tables that presented data), asking the students why these features were included in Lesley's notebook. A significant amount of time was devoted to examining the relationship between the information in the notebook text and the students' own experiences. This examination occurred throughout the reading of the text but was particularly active before the students even began the reading. Ms. Freeman accomplished this review of the students' experiences by revisiting the claims list arising from the students' own firsthand investigations. The students identified those claims for which there was consensus and those that were still under consideration but for which there was insufficient evidence. There were multiple examples of the class engaging in intertextual activity, with at least four "texts" being referred to in the course of the notebook reading: (1) the notebook itself, (2) the children's individual lab books, (3) the chart of class claims, and (4) the conversations that occurred as the class investigated and shared their findings. In addition, there were numerous instances when Ms. Freeman called the students' attention to the vocabulary words that were introduced in the notebook text and to how those compared with terms the students had been using in their own writing and discussion (e.g., Lesley's use of *absorbed* to describe the blocking of light).

Findings Specific to Scientific Reasoning

To support our claim that the use of the notebook text, as mediated by Ms. Freeman, engaged the students in scientific reasoning, we have identified particular transcript excerpts (taken from videotape) for which we will present the context and a brief discussion. (Note that some students could not be identified from the videotape record and therefore could not be named in the following excerpts. All names are pseudonyms.)

In the first excerpt, the students have encountered Lesley's table in which she has entered her data using candles as a unit of measure for light. Ms. Freeman is guiding the students' sense-making of the table:

Teacher:	Okay, it's the readout of how many candles. And right now it's showing the flashlight all by itself has....?
Leo:	Ten candles.
Teacher:	Ten candles.
Nabil:	Could it be, like, 10.5 or something, or 10.3?

Teacher:	I would imagine. Don't you think it could go up or down depending on how bright the light is?
Nabil:	So, if she puts zero candles, so that means it doesn't transmit at all?
Teacher:	Yes. Good observation.
Tatsuto:	Are there such thing as like, um, a millicandle?

There are several observations we can make about this excerpt. One is to call attention to the way in which Ms. Freeman mediates the students' sense-making with the table; to understand any of the other findings in this table, it is important that the students recognize that the amount of light from the light source (the flashlight) is 10 candles. This discussion, however, leads several students to wonder about this unit of measurement; transferring their knowledge of measurement about other units, they inquire about the system from which this unit is derived and how that system works (i.e., does it work like the metric system?).

In the next excerpt, the students have encountered Lesley's claim that "all objects reflect and absorb light."

Teacher:	What evidence did you see that would support that [all objects reflect and absorb light] even though that wasn't your claim?
Ian:	That almost all the objects did and maybe if we used a light meter, we might have found out that every single object did a little.
Teacher:	How about you, Megan?
Megan:	Some objects did both things—two different things, but not—we didn't, like, kind of find out that for all objects.
Teacher:	If you had done more, do you think we might have?
Megan:	Maybe.
Teacher:	If you had tested more?
Megan:	We didn't do all the objects, yet.

In this exchange, two issues are identified that are relevant to the differences in Lesley's and the class's claims: the role of measurement and the sample size. Lesley has used a light meter to collect her data, but the children had no means of measurement; they simply described their visual observations as precisely as possible. Ian suggests that with a measuring device, the class's findings might have been consistent with Lesley's. Ms. Freeman introduces the possibility that additional investigation might have yielded a different finding, to which Megan responds that the class hasn't investigated with all the materials yet. Determining how much evidence is sufficient to confidently make a broad claim, such as "all objects reflect and absorb light," is fundamental to scientific problem solving.

In the following excerpt, the students are entertaining other possible explanations for the differences between their findings and Lesley's findings. In this instance, Lesley reports the data for what happens when a flashlight shines on a piece of black felt. She reports that there was no transmitted light recorded by her light meter. The majority of students, however, report having seen transmitted light; here the class considers why there might be these different findings:

Catherine: When we stuck the lamp like—not like directly next to the black but a little bit up close to the black, it came out a maroon color on the other side.

Teacher: So we were getting some transmitted. We thought we had some transmitted light, too. She's not getting—detecting that, is she, with her light meter?

Nabil: But she would be more sure because she has a light meter and we don't.

Teacher: What might cause a difference in results from what you did and from what she did?

Student: She may have had her flashlight back farther than and we had ours up very close.

Teacher: Anything else might have made a difference? Ian?

Ian: She might have either had a weaker flashlight or a thicker piece of felt or something.

Teacher: Okay, so two things there.

Student: Yeah, or maybe it was because of the light meter.

Teacher: What about the light meter? How would the light meter make it harder to detect transmitted light?

Tatsuro: Because it's in, measuring in the tens. What if it was, like, 0.09?

Teacher: So maybe it's not measuring to the tenth or the millicandle?

Student: Or maybe she's just rounding off.

Teacher: Maybe she's rounding it off. Maybe the little machine rounds off. Good.

Louise: Or maybe it's because like, in the diagram, it shows it had the sensor pretty far back. Maybe the transmitted light didn't go that far.

In this excerpt, the students begin to identify the range of variables that might explain the differences in their outcomes when compared with Lesley's, including differences in the set-up, the materials, the strength of the light source, the device used to record the data, and the scientist's decisions regarding the reporting of the data. This exchange is significant to the extent that the students demonstrate an appreciation for the role that variables play in the design of an investigation. With this understanding, they are now situated to consider the control of variables that is necessary so that only a single contrast is featured in an experiment (Klahr, Chen, & Toth, 2001).

In the next set of excerpts, we turn to examples in which the students are observed to assume a critical stance relative to the notebook text. We begin with a brief discussion of why we think it is important that students learn to assume such a stance. Pera (1994) characterizes traditional science as the *methodological model*, in which scientific research is a game with two players: the scientist whose inquiry raises questions, and nature, which provides the answers. The impartial arbiter in this game is method, ascertaining whether the game was conducted well and determining when it is over. Pera notes, "as it is guided or forced by the rules of the arbiter, nature speaks out. And 'knowing' amounts to the scientist's recording of nature's true voice, or mirroring its real structure" (1994, p. ix). Pera contrasts this model with the *dialectical model*, in which there are three players: an individual or group of individuals, nature, and another group of individuals who debate with the first group according to the features of scientific dialectics. From this perspective, there is no impartial arbiter, nature responds to a "cross-examination," and knowing emerges from the communities agreeing upon nature's correct answer. Further, as Pera notes, agreement among the members of a community is not merely conversational because it is constrained by nature. If the dialectical process described above is going to be effective, then clearly there has to be the opportunity for community members to express disagreement and skepticism.

We indicated earlier, when describing students' interactions with the expository text that was used in Ms. Freeman's class, that we did not observe students assuming a critical stance toward the text; they simply deferred to the authority of the text. Hence, we were intrigued to determine whether there was evidence that the notebook text might elicit more critical responses from the students. We believe the following three examples speak to this issue.

The first two are examples of students questioning the generality of Lesley's claim that "all objects reflect and absorb light." In the first instance, Kit interjects, "I think that she says 'all' too much. Like she could just say 'most' or she could test more objects because 'all' is kind of a lot because she only tested like, seven." Ms. Freeman responds, "Okay, so you're saying you don't know if she's tested enough to say 'all,' to make that kind of statement."

The second example begins when one student, Katherine, expresses concern that Lesley has not provided sufficient information about the kinds of materials she has been investigating. This leads a second student, Megan, to observe that each of the objects with which Lesley has investigated is quite similar (i.e., they are all "flat") and that Lesley should have selected objects with different characteristics if she wishes to make the claim that "all objects absorb and reflect light." Ms. Freeman prompts for more specificity, to which Megan responds,

> None of them are kind of like a ball or something that's 3-D. They're all, like, flat...because something that's 3-D...it gets thicker because if you had a green ball and you shine light through, it would be...probably be a darker color because there's two sides to a ball and not just one.

In a related criticism, Kit observes that Lesley needs to consider not only the color of the object she is investigating, but also the material of which an object is made:

Kit: I don't think the claim would be as true if the white [objects] were different materials.

Teacher: Okay, so you would get a—if you had a light meter to measure like she did and you were measuring all the black objects on this list, do you think you still would get different readings? They'd absorb differently? They wouldn't all absorb the same amount?

Students: Yeah...yeah....

Teacher: How many people agree with that, that all the black objects probably wouldn't absorb the same amount of light? Okay, so they're agreeing with you.

These examples demonstrate some of the ways in which the notebook text provides the occasion for students to both engage in reasoning with the text (e.g., regarding the investigative set-up, the measurement procedures, the relationship between the claims, and the evidence that Lesley is putting forward) and assume a critical stance toward the text.

The Role of the Teacher in Mediating Students' Use of the Notebook Text

What we have not captured in these brief excerpts is the role of the teacher in facilitating these kinds of interactions with the text. Although we have explored this in other research (Cutter, Vincent, Magnusson, & Palincsar, 2001; Ford, 1999), it is too important not to mention briefly in this chapter. Studying the practices of teachers who are differentially successful with the use of the notebook texts points to several roles that teachers assume. First, teachers help to make explicit and keep present the connections between students' relevant experiences (typically acquired through their own firsthand investigations) and the information they are encountering in the text. In Ms. Freeman's case, she did this by referring the children to the class claims list, by urging the students to consult the data and claims they had recorded in their individual notebooks, and by asking the children to compare their ideas with Lesley's.

Second, teachers play a significant role in guiding and shaping the conversation in multiple ways. For example, Ms. Freeman probed to check on the depth of understanding that students were deriving from their reading of the text; she modeled her own thinking about the similarities and differences in Lesley's investigative questions, procedures, data, and claims. She also encouraged the students not to take a deferential stance toward the text.

In summary, the notebook text offers particular affordances by virtue of its content and structures. However, the extent to which these affordances are realized is a function of the students' own inquiry experiences, as well as the role that the teacher plays in supporting the students' interactions with the text.

Students' Evaluations of the Notebook Text

We conclude with some of the comments that students have shared regarding the use of Lesley's notebook text in science instruction. In particular, we share those students' comments that support the claims with which we began this chapter regarding the relationship between learning science and learning to comprehend text.

A number of students made reference to the relationship between the content of Lesley's notebook and their own experiences, signaling their awareness of the role of prior knowledge in constructing meaning. Louise comments,

> One thing that would be different if we had not, if we hadn't done this ourselves [an investigation regarding the angle of reflection], it would have been harder to agree on the claim and stuff if we didn't have any experience ourself, just taking her word for it.

Kat notes the value of a shared language between the students and Lesley: "It was perfect for fourth grade, because we learned all about the words she used in our class."

Emma comments on the graphical representations in the text: "I thought it [the notebook text] was good because everything she did, she made pictures, so it was easier to see." In a journal entry, Caitlynn also responded to this feature:

> I like it when you put tables on the sheet. It help me to understand. I thought this was very good for a scientist. I found out some real good evidence. I found out where you explained the claims and evidence. Thank you for sharing this.

Finally, Nat comments, "The diagram and the table, too, they helped us a lot because like, we didn't get exact answers and everything. So, that's what could help us trying to get exact answers."

A number of the students' comments also have metacognitive overtones. For example, Megan indicates, "I think she's much more explanatory than most scientists are about their procedure.... Is this written for kids? Because it seems like it is 'cause I really understand this and most science books I really don't understand." Anita notes, "It's pretty cool because we get to share our thinking with the class and we also get to share Lesley's thinking with the class." Ian, in reference to the revisions that Lesley makes in her thinking and her entries, suggests, "It's [the notebook text] kind of more like a first draft." These types of comments speak to the different ways in which students can compare features of the notebook text to their existing knowledge about texts, which can, in turn, help to deepen their understanding of learning from text.

Conclusion

Understanding science, like understanding any subject, requires the basic tools of reading, writing, and oral language. Thus, learning science provides an opportunity not only to build knowledge about the physical world, but also to learn about the basic tools with which that type of knowledge is built and represented for others. We provided evidence in this chapter that important aspects of literacy learning can be advanced in the process of learning science. We focused on learning to comprehend text, but results of related research we have conducted (Hapgood, Magnusson, & Palincsar, in press) have provided evidence that science learning can also support the development of informational writing and oracy. As we consider the issue of what it means to be literate in the information age, we suggest that more literacy learning should occur within subject matter areas. Learning what others have discovered about the world and sharing one's own discoveries can be powerful motivators for learning to read, write, and speak in particular ways. There is no better time than the present to bring these authentic contexts to the issue of the development of literacy.

REFERENCES

Armbruster, B.B., & Anderson, T.H. (1988). On selecting considerate content area textbooks. *Remedial and Special Education, 9*, 47–52.

Brown, A.L., & Palincsar, A.S. (1989). Guided cooperative learning and individual knowledge acquisition. In L. Resnick (Ed.), *Knowing, learning and instruction: Essays in honor of Robert Glaser.* Hillsdale, NJ: Erlbaum.

Carpenter, P.A., & Shah, P. (1998). A model of the perceptual and conceptual processes in graph comprehension. *Journal of Experimental Psychology: Applied, 4*, 75–100.

Chan, C.K.K., Burtis, P.J., Scardamalia, M., & Bereiter, C. (1992). Constructive activity in learning from text. *American Educational Research Journal, 29*, 97–118.

Chi, M.T.H., de Leeuw, N., Chiu, M.H., & LaVancher, C. (1994). Eliciting self explanations improves understanding. *Cognitive Science, 13*, 145–182.

Clement, J. (1993). Using bridging analogies and anchoring intuitions to deal with students' preconceptions in physics. *Journal of Research in Science Teaching, 30*(10), 1241–1257.

Coté, N., Goldman, S.R., & Saul, E.U. (1998). Students making sense of informational text: Relations between processing and representation. *Discourse Processes, 25*, 1–53.

Cutter, J., Vincent, M., Magnusson, S.J., & Palincsar, A.S. (2001, April). *Text-based inquiry science: How high needs students respond to instructional choices in reading and discussing scientist's notebooks.* Paper presented at the annual meeting of the American Educational Research Association, Seattle, WA.

Farris, P.J., Kissinger, R.W., & Thompson, T. (1988). Text organization and structure in science textbooks. *Reading Horizons, 28*(2), 123–130.

Ford, D.J. (1999). *The role of text in supporting and extending first-hand investigations in guided inquiry science.* Unpublished doctoral dissertation, University of Michigan, Ann Arbor.

Goldman, S.R. (1997). Learning from text: Reflections on the past and suggestions for new directions of inquiry. *Discourse Processes, 23*(3), 357–398.

Guzzetti, B.J., Snyder, T.E., & Glass, G.V. (1992). Promoting conceptual change in science: Can texts be used effectively? *Journal of Reading, 35*(8), 642–649.

Hapgood, S., Magnusson, S.J., & Palincsar, A.S. (in press). A very science-like kind of thinking: How young children make meaning from first- and second-hand investigations. *Journal of the Learning Sciences.*

Hartmann, D. (1995). Eight readers reading: The intertextual links of proficient readers reading multiple passages. *Reading Research Quarterly, 30,* 520–561.

Klahr, D., Chen, Z., & Toth, E. (2001). Cognitive development and science education: Ships that pass in the night or beacons of mutual illumination? In S. Carver & D. Klahr (Eds.), *Cognition and instruction: Twenty-five years of progress* (pp. 75–119). Mahwah, NJ: Erlbaum.

Kuhn, D. (1989). Children and adults as intuitive scientists. *Psychological Review, 96*(4), 674–689.

Lehrer, R., & Shauble, L. (2000). Modeling in mathematics and science. In R. Glazer (Ed.), *Advances in Instructional Psychology* (Vol. 5, pp. 101–159). Mahwah, NJ: Erlbaum.

Lemke, J.L. (1990). *Talking science: Language, learning, and values.* Norwood, NJ: Ablex.

Lloyd, C.V., & Mitchell, J.N. (1989). Coping with too many concepts in science texts. *Journal of Reading, 32*(6), 542–545.

Magnusson, S.J., & Palincsar, A.S. (1995). The learning environment as a site of science education reform. *Theory Into Practice, 34*(1), 43–50.

National Institute of Child Health and Human Development. (2000). *Report of the National Reading Panel. Teaching children to read: An evidence-based assessment of the scientific research literature on reading and its implications for reading instruction* (NIH Publication No. 00-4769). Washington, DC: U.S. Government Printing Office.

National Research Council (NRC). (1996). *National science education standards.* Washington, DC: National Academy Press.

Palincsar, A.S., & Magnusson, S.J. (1997, November). *The role of text in supporting and extending first-hand investigations in guided inquiry science teaching.* Paper presented at the annual meeting of the National Reading Conference, Scottsdale, AZ.

Palincsar A.S., & Magnusson, S.J. (2001). The interplay of first-hand and second-hand investigations to model and support the development of scientific knowledge and reasoning. In S. Carver & D. Klahr (Eds.), *Cognition and instruction: Twenty-five years of progress.* Mahwah, NJ: Erlbaum.

Pera, M. (1994). *The discourses of science.* Chicago: University of Chicago Press.

Perfetti, C., Britt, M.A., & Georgi, M.C. (1995). *Text-based learning and reasoning: Studies in history.* Hillsdale, NJ: Erlbaum.

Richgels, D.J., McGee, L.M., Lomax, R.G., & Sheard, C. (1987). Awareness of four text structures: Effects in recall of expository text. *Reading Research Quarterly, 22,* 177–196.

Rutherford, F.J. (1991). Vital connections: Children, books, and science. In W. Saul (Ed.), *Vital connections.* Washington, DC: Library of Congress.

Schwab, J.J. (1962). The teaching of science as enquiry. In J. Schwab & P. Brandwein (Eds.), *The teaching of science* (pp. 1–103). Cambridge, MA: Harvard University Press.

Shymansky, J.A., Yore, L.D., & Good, R. (1991). Elementary school teachers' beliefs about and perceptions of elementary school science, science reading, science textbook, and supportive instructional factors. *Journal of Research in Science Teaching, 28*(5), 437–454.

Stahl, S., & Fairbanks, M.M. (1986). The effects of vocabulary instruction: A model-based meta-analysis. *Review of Educational Research, 56*(1), 72–110.

van Zee, E.H. (1997). Reflective discourse: Developing shared understandings in a physics classroom. *International Journal of Science Education, 19*(2), 209–228.

Appendix: Sample Notebook Text

Scientist: Lesley Park   Date: 10/26/97   Page 1

Today I investigated how light interacts with different materials. I shined a flashlight on different solid objects and looked at what happened to the light. I used a light catcher to see if light reflected off the object, and I looked behind the object to see if light was transmitted by it (traveled through) or if there was a shadow. A shadow would tell me that the object was blocking the light. Figure 1 shows how I used my equipment.

Figure 1: Materials in Investigation

Positions where I described the light:
A—on the light catcher
B—area behind the object

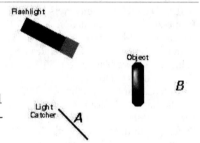

From the data I collected, I made Table 1 to list the ways light interacted with solid objects.

Table 1: How Different Places Looked When I Shined Light on Solid Objects

Object	On Light Catcher (light reflected)	On Back of Object (light transmitted)	Area Behind Object (light blocked)
Clear Glass	dim light	bright light	light shadow
Purple Glass	dim purple light	bright purple light	dark purple shadow
Silver Wrap	bright light	no light	dark shadow
White Plastic Sheet	dim light	medium light	medium shadow
White Typing Paper	bright light	dim light	medium shadow
Black Felt	no light	no light	very dark shadow
Orange Cardboard	dim orange light	dim reddish light	dark shadow

What I concluded from my data:

- Light reflects off all solid objects, except if they are black.
- Light does not go through all solid objects.
- All objects block the light some amount.
- If a lot of light is reflected off a solid object, not much light is transmitted through it. If a lot of light is transmitted through a solid object, not much light is reflected.

When I showed my claims and evidence to other scientists, they were not convinced of my conclusions because my data were not exact. The other scientists were not confident in my judgments about how the amount of light reflected from an object compared to the amount of light that was transmitted through it.

One scientist suggested that I use a **light meter** to collect more data. She told me a light meter is an instrument that measures the brightness of light. With this tool, I can actually measure the amount of light at any place. Figure 2 shows a picture of a light meter. It measures light in units of candles. I plan to repeat my experiments with the same materials but using a light meter.

Figure 2: Picture of a Light Meter

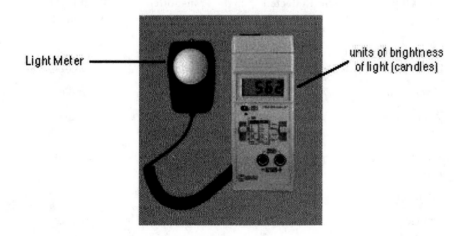

Light Meter

units of brightness of light (candles)

When I repeated the light experiments, I used the same materials in the same way. Figure 3 shows the setup when I measured the light reaching each object. The light meter told me that the light from the flashlight was 10 candles bright.

Figure 3: Using the Light Meter

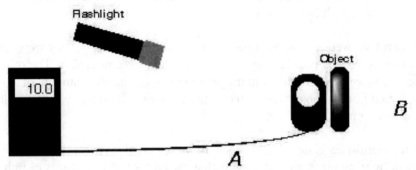

I also used the light meter to measure at two other points (shown in Figure 3). The light at point A tells me how much light reflected from each object, and the light at point B tells me how much light was transmitted through each object. I recorded these measurements in Table 2.

Table 2: Measurements of How Light Interacted With Objects

Object	Light Reflected From Object (A)	Light Transmitted Through Object (B)	Total Light Measured
Clear Glass	2 candles	7 candles	9 candles
Purple Glass	2 candles	6 candles	8 candles
Silver Wrap	7 candles	0 candles	7 candles
White Plastic Sheet	5 candles	2 candles	7 candles
White Typing Paper	4 candles	3 candles	7 candles
Black Felt	1 candle	0 candles	1 candle
Orange Cardboard	3 candles	2 candles	5 candles

What I concluded from these data is as follows:

- Light reflects off all solid materials.
- The light reflected from each solid object was always less than the amount of light on the object.
- The light transmitted through each solid object was always less than the amount of light on the object.
- The total amount of light transmitted *and* reflected from a solid object does *not* add up to the light reaching the object. A + B ≠ 10 candles.

Question for me to think about: If they don't add up, where is the other light? Can I assume it is absorbed in the material?

When I thought about whether the light was being absorbed, I thought about how all the objects made a shadow (see Table 1). I know that a shadow means light is blocked, so maybe this means that when light is blocked, some light is absorbed and stays in the object.

I wonder whether other scientists are thinking in this way? To find out, I will go to the library to read what other researchers have claimed about light.

I read several articles in the *Journal of Research on Optics* to learn about what other scientists have found out about light. Here is what one researcher said:

> Our results tell us that light is a form of energy that can interact in several ways with a material. From our measurements of the temperature of solid objects after shining light on them, we determined these relationships:
>
> - All objects reflect *and* absorb light.
> - The amount of energy that is absorbed or reflected depends on the material. White objects mostly reflect light, and black objects mostly absorb light; red and yellow objects absorb less light than green and blue objects.
> - Thin objects transmit some light through them, and the thicker an object, the more light is absorbed and the less light is transmitted.

What I learned from the writings of this scientist is as follows:

- Light is energy.
- Light can be reflected, absorbed, and transmitted by the same object.
- All solid objects reflect *and* absorb light.
- The color of an object tells us something about how light interacts with it.
- How light interacts with an object is also determined by the thickness of the object.

I need to think about how this information helps me think about my own data and conclusions.

Scientist: Lesley Park   Date: 10/30/97   Page 6

The second claim that I recorded from the work other scientists did helped me the most in my thinking. If light can reflect, transmit, *and* be absorbed by the same object, I think that helps explain why the light meter readings didn't add up to 10 candles in my investigation. I only measured the light that was reflected or transmitted. I think the "missing" light was light that was absorbed by each object.

I used my measurements from Table 2 and my thinking about absorption to describe how light interacted with each of my objects. Here's how I described the light meter readings:

1 - 3 = "a little"; 4 - 6 = "some"; 7 - 9 = "a lot."

I recorded these results in Table 3.

Table 3: Describing My Objects by How Much Light They Absorb, Transmit, and Reflect

Object	Reflects Light	Transmits Light	Absorbs Light
Clear Glass	Yes, a little	Yes, a lot	Yes, a little
Purple Glass	Yes, a little	Yes, some	Yes, a little
Silver Wrap	Yes, a lot	None	Yes, a little
White Plastic Sheet	Yes, some	Yes, a little	Yes, a little
White Typing Paper	Yes, some	Yes, a little	Yes, a little
Black Felt	Yes, a little	None	Yes, a lot
Orange Cardboard	Yes, a little	Yes, a little	Yes, some

What I concluded is that light always interacts with a solid object in at least two ways. These results tell me that light does not interact in the same way for each object. That made me wonder: why does light behave differently for different objects? I am also wondering how light can interact in *different* ways with the *same* object. What does that mean about what light is like? I will have to figure out how to investigate to answer these questions.

CHAPTER 18

Students' Science Notebooks and the Inquiry Process

MICHAEL P. KLENTSCHY AND ELIZABETH MOLINA-DE LA TORRE

Science education is currently facing an enormous challenge in the United States. This challenge may ultimately determine the direction of public education in general over the next several decades. Some observers, for example, believe that the U.S. national movement emphasizing reading, writing, and mathematics skills, as measured by high-stakes standardized tests, conflicts with efforts to make progress in science education (Jorgenson & Vanosdall, 2002). Under pressure to improve test scores in these basic skills, some school districts have reduced or eliminated science instruction. Whether science is eliminated or not, these systems of high-stakes accountability tend to reward teaching for coverage, rather than teaching for understanding, and this can have negative results on all content areas. For example, educators have argued for years that emphasis on writing as a way of learning may be impossible to implement when models of instruction emphasize the importance of coverage of content rather than mutual exploration of interpretations (Langer & Applebee, 1986).

At any rate, it is clear that many school districts, under pressure from policymakers to create and comply with standards, assessment goals, and accountability systems for language arts and mathematics, are shrinking that portion of the school day devoted to science education and are moving away from using writing as a way of learning. One way educators may be able to combat this trend is by linking science with literacy. A growing number of science educators believe that by making science a key element in strengthening literacy skills, teachers can demonstrate that a strong program of science instruction can play an important role in improving achievement in literacy (Thier, 2002).

The Science–Literacy Connection

By linking science and language literacy, science educators can demonstrate the role of science in strengthening students' language skills, thus extending and strengthening the place of science in a basic curriculum. Learning science helps children develop an understanding of the world around them. In order to learn science, children have to build up concepts that help them link their experiences together and to learn ways of collecting and organizing information and of applying and testing ideas. This learning not only contributes to children's ability to make better sense of things around them, but also prepares them to deal more effectively with wider decision making and problem solving in their lives. Learning science involves the processes both of thinking and of taking action. When literacy skills are linked to science content, students have personal, practical motivation to master language and use it as a tool to help them answer their questions about the world around them. Language becomes the primary avenue that students use to arrive at scientific understanding (Thier, 2002). Scientific literacy should emphasize scientific ways of knowing and the process of thinking critically and creatively about the natural world (Harlen, 2001).

The Learning Research and Development Center at the University of Pittsburgh and the National Center on Education and the Economy identify reciprocal skills associated with science and literacy (2000). These reciprocal skills are shown in Figure 18.1.

This analysis of the reciprocal nature of science and literacy strengthens the view that teaching for understanding is a much more powerful means to connect science and literacy than teaching them as independent disciplines. Harlen (2001) suggests that the key to effective science teaching is to enable children to develop ideas about the world around them that fit evidence they have collected from their classroom instructional experiences in science and for which they have developed personal meaning.

Children bring ideas picked up or created from their past encounters and links they have made between old and new experiences to new experiences. The learning of science is an active, continuous process whereby the learner takes information from the environment and constructs personal interpretations and meanings based on prior knowledge and experience (Driver & Bell, 1986). Learning involves both a personal and social construction of meaning. In the classroom, the child develops cognitively by becoming an agent of his or her own learning—constructing scientific concepts by drawing on their existing ideas and experience, social interactions that mediate knowledge construction, and knowledge that is personally constructed by the learner (Shepardson & Britsch, 2001). Harlen (2001) also suggests that learning science involves students who are able to communicate their thinking. This communication can be oral, written, and symbolic (i.e., in the form of drawings).

FIGURE 18.1
Reciprocal Skills

Literacy	Science
Note details	Observe and retain small details
Compare and contrast	Make notes about the way a variety of substances react (e.g., to heat)
Predict	Hypothesize about what will happen next
Work with sequences of events	Work with processes of logic and analysis
Link cause and effect	Study what causes things to react in a particular way
Distinguish fact from opinion	Use evidence to support claims
Link words with precise meanings	Develop operational definitions of a concept though experiences
Make inferences	Base hypotheses on observation and evidence
Draw conclusions	Combine data from various sources

Communication is a vital aspect of the process of science. Language is central to shaping our constructions of the world around us. Words and language are used as a way of trying out a framework for understanding; learners need to have space to reflect on ideas, and that space is created through writing. Writing in science is important for generating a personal response to experiences, for clarifying ideas, and for constructing knowledge. Howard (1988) stated that writing enables the learner to understand first and to communicate second. There is, then, a link to science and literacy through this social interaction of communication. Vygotsky (1978) concluded that personally meaningful knowledge is socially constructed through shared understandings.

Science and literacy also have another strong point of connection through the desire of many educators to develop metacognitive awareness in children. Cognition is an interactive-constructive process, and metacognition is a conscious awareness and control of this process that results in verifying, rethinking, reflecting, and reshaping information into meaningful knowledge networks.

Metacognition often takes the form of an internal dialogue. Many students may be unaware of its importance unless teachers explicitly emphasize the processes. Research has demonstrated that children can be taught these strategies, including the ability to predict outcomes, reflect to improve understanding, note failures to understand, and to plan ahead (National Research Council [NRC], 1999).

Strategies for writing are metacognitive in that they are designed to help students reflect on the process of writing. Thier (2002) suggests that metacognitive activities take students beyond basic performance to deeper levels of reflection and personal understanding. These metacognitive activities may be introduced to students through the completion of open statements such as "What really surprised me about this activity was...," or "The outcome of this activity was different from...(another activity) because...."

Teaching metacognitive strategies in context has been shown to improve understanding in physics, written composition, and problem solving, especially when language skills and science are taught in the context of each other (NRC, 1999).

The Valle Imperial Project in Science

The Valle Imperial Project in Science (VIPS), a Local Systemic Initiative funded by the National Science Foundation (NSF), serves approximately 27,500 K–8 students and 1,200 teachers in 14 school districts in Imperial County, California, USA. Imperial County, located in the southeast corner of California along the U.S. border with Mexico, is one of the largest (4,597 sq. mi.) and most sparsely populated (130,000) counties in California. The county lacks any large metropolitan areas, and residents must travel to San Diego (over 120 miles) or Los Angeles (over 200 miles) to reach the nearest urban areas.

Many Imperial County residents live in extreme poverty, with household incomes declining over the past decade. The Internal Revenue Service reported a mean per capita income of $16,353 for the year 2000, the lowest of all California counties. The county's unemployment rates increased from 17.1% in 1991 to 33.2% in 2000, while statewide unemployment rates remained lower than 5.2%. Imperial County ranks highest in poverty of all 58 counties in California.

Most Imperial County residents have strong cultural and linguistic ties to Mexico. Of the 22,500 K–6 students in the Imperial County, 81.3% are Hispanic. Caucasian (11.3%), African American (5.1%), Asian (1.3%), and Native American (1%) students make up the rest of the population.

More than 50% of the students in the county are limited English proficient, with 10% of the students in general being children of migrant workers. Nearly all of the county's schools qualify for Title I funding. Countywide, more than 67% of all students are eligible for free and reduced-cost lunches.

The science reform model implemented in the Imperial Valley is based on the National Science Resources Center Leadership and Assistance for Science Education Reform (LASER) Model for systemic reform, with five critical, interrelated elements necessary for effective reform (National Academy of Sciences, 1997). These elements include (1) a high-quality curriculum, (2) sustained professional development and support for teachers and school administrators, (3) materials support, (4) community and top-level administrative support, and (5) program assessment and evaluation.

VIPS began in the summer of 1998 as a collaborative partnership between the fourteen Imperial County school districts and San Diego State University, Imperial Valley Campus. It was preceded for three years by a pilot effort on the part of the El Centro Elementary School District, which with 6,500 elementary students is the largest district in the county. The pilot program established three pilot schools and a fully functioning materials resource center and developed a cadre of lead teachers. This pilot school effort was the result of the El Centro Elementary School District participating as a member of the NSF-funded Pasadena Center Program at the California Institute of Technology. Direct technical assistance and support was provided by the Pasadena Center to build capacity within the district for future districtwide and countywide expansion of the program.

The design of VIPS links science and literacy through the use of student science notebooks. The inquiry-based model of science instruction is based on the belief that students need to be provided with an opportunity to develop "voice" in their personal construction of meaning of the science phenomena. In VIPS, this voice comes in the form of students' science notebooks, which we view as knowledge-transforming rather than knowledge-telling. Students use their science notebooks during their science experiences, in social interactions, as a tool for reflection, and as a tool for constructing meaning. There is a pattern of significant growth in achievement in science, reading, and writing for all students participating in this program (Amaral, Garrison, & Klentschy, 2002; Jorgenson & Vanosdall, 2002). Student science notebooks have played an important part in the documented success of this program, and science in general has become an important vehicle to extend literacy for the students of Imperial County.

In order to examine the impact on student achievement, it is important to examine the role that student science notebooks play in the inquiry-based program of science instruction, the importance of student voice in a knowledge-transforming context, and the importance of feedback.

Student Science Notebooks

The use of writing as a vehicle to promote learning is consistent with the belief that the writer is engaged in active reprocessing at the level of concepts and central ideas (Scardamalia & Bereiter, 1986). Writing is, first, a process of polishing one's thinking for self-edification and, second, communicating those thoughts to others (Howard & Barton, 1986). Writing is a heuristic device with which students can achieve powerful insights and understandings about content (VanDeWeghe, 1987). Writing enables students to express their current ideas about science content in a form that they can examine and think about. Writing, then, is a symbolic activity of constructing meaning and is a tool of understanding, as well as a tool for communication. The first goal of writing is to understand. Writing is an instrument to think with. Written reasoning to discover or construct meaning must consider purpose, genre, and evidence. Written words provide cues for expressing ideas verbally to others. Achievement in science is directly proportional to a student's ability to use language (Fellows, 1994).

Children construct models of the workings of written language by interacting with people and objects in their environment. They simultaneously construct understandings of science phenomena that may be reflected in both their writing and drawing (Wells & Chang-Wells, 1992). This view establishes a foundation to an approach to teaching wherein children learn science by doing science and use writing as part of their science experiences. This suggests that in the context of science activities, student-produced science notebooks promote the use of literacy while clarifying students' emerging theories about science phenomena (Neuman & Roskos, 1993). How children interact with peers and the products they create—drawings and writings—are the means they use to create understandings of science (Doris, 1991).

VIPS holds a belief that student science notebooks are a special, essential means of communication. When used appropriately, student science notebooks provide stability and permanence to children's work, as well as purpose and form. They are a record of personally valued information and an extension of children's mental activities. This form of writing also may help students link new information with prior knowledge (Rivard, 1994). Science notebooks also can contain drawings, tables, or graphs that are essential in forming meaning for the child from the science experience. The earlier children start to learn to keep records, the better prepared they will be to make this a natural part of their science activities (Harlen, 1988). Children will recognize the importance of record keeping from experiences that require them to keep, collect, and interpret times, distances, or other measurements. The use of student science notebooks in class discussions helps students construct meaning from the science phenomena (Harlen, 2001). In fact, teachers in VIPS begin the use of student science notebooks as early as kindergarten.

The student science notebook, then, becomes more than a record of the data that students collect, facts they learn, and procedures they conduct. The science notebook also becomes a record of students' reflections, questions, speculations, decisions, and conclusions—all focused on the science phenomena (Thier, 2002). As such, a science notebook becomes a central place in which language, data, and experience operate together to form meaning for the student. Students' written ideas provide them with windows into their own thinking processes.

Thier (2002) offers two guiding questions to assist students in internalizing what they learn: (1) What new ideas do I have after today's activity? and (2) How can I use what I have learned in my everyday life? Using writing tasks that engage students in reflecting on their own alternate conceptions and in reconciling them with available evidence and current conceptions might be an effective classroom strategy for enhancing conceptual change (Fellows, 1994). It is in this context that VIPS views the role of student science notebooks as a powerful tool in the learning process of each student.

Discrete knowledge should not be learned for its own sake. Students should be challenged to use this knowledge in solving meaningful problems. Student science notebooks can serve as the medium for fleshing out responses to complex problems requiring higher-order reasoning. The way that writing is employed and evaluated in the classroom is critical in helping students perceive its potential as an aid to learning content (Rivard, 1994). By creating their own science notebook pages, students are able to describe their ways of seeing and thinking about the science phenomena, constructing and reconstructing meaning through their own lens of experience (Shepardson, 1997). This construction of meaning is done in the voice of the student, not the teacher.

VIPS has an established belief that students need time to develop the skills of self-expression and of recording their observations. In the earliest stages, children might only use their notebooks to draw what they see and what they *think* is going on. This early use of drawings is an important beginning because, if students are expected to record their observations in some way, they are likely to observe more closely, shed their preconceptions, and see what is really there (Harlen, 2001). Later, student science notebooks become useful instruments for recording what students do in their investigations and the results they achieve. The professional development program for teachers in the VIPS is designed to develop a best practice in which the teacher guides the students to record what they actually see and do, not what they think the teacher expects them to see or do.

Vygotsky (1978) referred to drawing as graphic speech and noted that young students' representations often reflect what they think they know about the object rather than what is actually perceived. These drawings can act as a guide to students' understandings. Students incorporate different selections of such details in order to draw the experience into a form that makes sense to them. Drawing and writing produced in a science investigation are valuable because they allow students to express their ideas and findings; they take the role of talk with regard to assisting students in making meaning of their ideas (Harlen, 1988). It is in this context that the VIPS views the use of student drawings as an important aspect in developing the science-literacy connection for all students.

The nature of students' contextualization of the science phenomena and the activities on the science notebook pages are dependent on students' familiarity with the phenomena and equipment and the length of exposure to the program of instruction (Amaral et al., 2002). In unfamiliar situations, students' entries reflect the immediately observed science investigation, whereas in familiar situations, entries are based on students' experiences with the phenomena, placing the science investigation into a real-world context (Shepardson, 1997). In an analysis of the initial use of student science notebooks in the VIPS, the students' first science notebooks took on the form of a narrative or procedural recount (Amaral et al., 2002). One caveat about the use of science notebooks, however, is that although they may engage students in solving problems, they less frequently engage students in finding problems (Reddy, Jacobs, McCrohon, & Herrenkohl, 1998). Also, although students may be quite interested in and excited about carrying out science activities, they may not be willing to spend time interpreting their results. Students' self-produced science notebook pages may be viewed as a story that unfolds as the observed phenomena change over time, a story molded to fit the children's way of seeing; therefore, the story may be distorted from that of a scientist or a teacher (Shepardson, 1997). The action of students interpreting their results is developmental, and teachers must guide them to be more reflective about their work. Student science notebooks have the potential to move students beyond simply completing the task to making sense of the task. In this way, these science notebooks can support the development of students' scientific thinking.

Student Voice in a Knowledge-Transforming Context

Langer and Applebee (1986) reported that students are more aware of their strategies, rhetorical structures, and background knowledge while writing than while reading, although this may vary according to the type of writing in question. Strategies and text structure usage are not as easily apparent to readers as they are to writers. By requiring the learner to organize language, the act of writing by its very nature may enhance thinking. However, much classroom writing is mechanical, leaving the student to play an unthinking, passive role. Traditional classroom science writing, for example, is directed at communicating what the writer knows to the teacher as an informed audience by filling in blanks, producing short responses to teacher-generated questions, and recording observations and information (Applebee, 1984). In this traditional approach, student science notebooks have served primarily as logs in which children simply maintain records of experiments and list their results. Simply logging the results and listing the experiments limits students in the construction of the true meaning of the phenomena and reduces the experience to knowledge and transmission of recalled information. Student writing also is limited. Studying the shortcomings of this type of writing, Shepardson and Britsch (2001) concluded that students' entries in the science notebook must function as more than a means of reporting teacher-expected results.

The use of student science notebooks is effective for most students when the teacher is more concerned with establishing a dialogue with students to monitor learning, emphasizing the thinking and learning processes involved in learning the content (Willey, 1988). Bereiter and Scardamalia (1987) described two types of writing: knowledge-telling and knowledge-transforming. The dominant use of the knowledge-telling mode may have an adverse effect on how children organize and store knowledge because it is a simplistic strategy that diminishes students' ability to reorganize their knowledge. The interactive-constructive processes involved in the knowledge-transforming model of writing parallels the constructivist model of science learning in that it involves long-term memory, working memory, and sensorimotor activity. The knowledge-transforming model may be far more inter-active and recursive than linear.

Santa and Havens (1991) suggested that meaningful writing should bridge new information and prior knowledge, provide authentic authoring tasks for an uninformed audience, encourage minds-on learning, facilitate conceptual organization and restructuring, and promote metacognition. Meaningful writing also facilitates the transformation of vague ideas into clear conceptions and stimulates the construction of meaning. In VIPS, professional development in the use of student science notebooks guides teachers to pose questions that students might ask themselves in knowledge-transforming writing in their science notebooks, such as What evidence do I have? What claims should I make? or What are some alternative explanations?

VIPS also places great emphasis on helping students develop voice in their science writing. Palincsar and Magnusson (2000) looked at the effect on students of strong voice in the notebook text of a fictitious scientist, Lesley Park (see chapter 17 in this book). The notebook was introduced as an indi-rect experience used in conjunction with the students' firsthand inquiry-based experience on the properties of light. The notebook text influenced the stu-dents' thinking when they conducted their own firsthand inquiry-based in-vestigations on the properties of light following their reading of the notebook text (an indirect, or secondhand, investigation). At first, the students were challenged in distinguishing among evidence, claims, and data. After investi-gating the fictitious scientist's notebook, the students became attentive to the organization and representation of their data, drawing heavily on the format-ting ideas presented in the scientist's notebook in their own work. The pres-ence of voice in the notebook may well have been an important factor in helping students construct meaning. Currently, VIPS is examining the impact of the combination of voice in student-generated text, along with providing students with opportunities for knowledge-transforming writing in the form of science notebooks on student achievement in science and literacy.

Holliday, Yore, and Alvermann (1994) described the need to emphasize knowledge-transformation models that demonstrate the roles of evidence, reasoning, interpretation, and thinking. Such a mode of writing emphasizes exploration, expressive inquiry, decision making, and knowledge construc-tion. It is a process of constructing understanding, enhancing personal clar-ity, and producing insightfulness. Hanrahan (1999) reported that this type of writing encouraged students to participate in their own learning. Caswell and Lamon (1998) found that when fourth-grade students were exposed to inquiry and used their own science notebooks instead of completing teacher-created products, the amount of writing the children did increased; students did more than simply observe and were more involved in the investigation. The students' science notebook writing enabled them to organize collected information in novel ways, to develop hypotheses, and to interpret and explain on the basis of collected information. Similar findings have been reported with regard to student writing accomplishment in VIPS (Jorgenson & Vanosdall, 2002). Marzano (1991) has argued that fostering higher-order thinking demands instructional activities in which the learner's existing knowledge is restructured through activities that are complex and long-term. He argues that writing is well suited to induce knowledge transformation.

Shepardson and Britsch (2001) reported that students frame their understandings of science investigations and phenomena with reference to three types of mental contexts that may be reflected graphically on the pages of their science notebooks. These contexts are their imaginary, experiential, and investigative worlds. By drawing on these three internal contexts, the children were able to place an external phenomenon in an internal context that was familiar to them. This internal context linked with the science experience to frame a way of thinking that used the students' prior knowledge and experiences to construct science understandings. The science notebooks must allow students to use various student-selected combinations of writing and drawing to construct and represent their understandings with flexibility in their use of genre. This enables the student to use science notebooks in ways that are both socially and cognitively appropriate to their developing understandings of science phenomena and are thus knowledge-transforming. It is in this same context that the Valle Imperial Project in Science utilizes student science notebooks as a knowledge-transforming device for students.

Feedback

Teacher feedback is important in the knowledge-transformational process of using student notebooks in inquiry-based science instruction. The teacher in the knowledge-transforming process has a different role than the teacher in the knowledge-telling process, however. Marzano, Pickering, and Pollock (2001) reported in a review of nine research studies that feedback that guides students, rather than telling them what is right or wrong on a test, can attain significant results in terms of student achievement. The most appropriate form of feedback in a knowledge-transforming mode of instruction is one of asking guiding questions or writing guiding questions in students' science notebooks. The feedback also can take the form of a personal written conversation between teacher and student in the student's science notebook. In VIPS, professional development activities for teachers in the use of student science notebooks stress this form of feedback, which can best be summarized as issues, evidence, and you. Some examples of good questions teachers can use include the following:

- What evidence do you have to support your claims?
- What claims can you make from your evidence?
- Is there another explanation for what happened?

For feedback to be most effective, it must be timely and specific. In general, the more delay that occurs in giving feedback, the longer it takes students to clear up misconceptions (Marzano et al., 2001). This could be especially true in clearing up the science misconceptions reported by Shepardson and Britsch (2001). Not only should feedback be timely, but it should also reference a specific developmentally appropriate level of skill or knowledge expected of students. Research has consistently indicated that this form of feedback has a more powerful effect on student learning than simply reporting to students their standing in relation to their peers (Marzano et al., 2001). These strategies and techniques are used extensively in VIPS through the use of developmental storylines for each of the units of science instruction. The developmental storylines serve as a graphic organizer that establishes a flow chart indicating the "big idea" or unifying concept of each unit of study (Amaral et al., 2002). These storylines form the basis for a rubric used by teachers in providing appropriate written feedback to students in their science notebooks.

Research on feedback also indicates that students can effectively monitor their own progress (Marzano et al., 2001). The use of student feedback in the form of self-evaluation has been strongly advocated by Wiggins (1993). Teachers in VIPS have students utilize the rubric for student science notebooks during classroom discussions of their science experiences, evidence, and claims. This self-evaluating form of feedback is also important in the construction of meaning by the students.

Conclusion

Educators across the United States are feeling the pressure of standards, assessment, and accountability. Increasingly, time is being squeezed from the instructional day in an attempt to strengthen student achievement in reading, language arts, and mathematics. As a result, science has almost become an invisible curriculum in many classrooms. Yet at the same time, there is a growing body of evidence that indicates a strong relationship between inquiry-based science instruction and improved achievement not only in science, but also in reading, language arts, and mathematics (Amaral et al., 2002; Jorgenson and Vanosdall, 2002). An extensive examination of this body of evidence indicates that there is a strong connection between science and literacy. Each discipline reinforces the other discipline in a reciprocal process. The connection between science and literacy appears to be especially strong when student science notebooks play a pivotal role in the instructional program. This connection also has the potential to assist students in developing their metacognitive abilities in science.

The student science notebook serves as an important link between science and literacy when it is utilized in the classroom as a knowledge-transforming form of writing that provides an appropriate opportunity for students to develop voice in the process of constructing meaning from their experiences with the science phenomena. This, coupled with appropriate and timely feedback from the classroom teacher, has strong potential to provide the improvement in student achievement across the curriculum that educators are seeking. As educators, we must examine the consequences of reducing or even eliminating science instruction from our classrooms for the sake of raising test scores in other curricular areas. If we allow this reduction to continue, the current generation of students may never recover either intellectually or economically.

Authors' Note

This work is supported, in part, by National Science Foundation Grant No. ESI-9731274. The opinions expressed in this work are those of the authors and not necessarily those of the National Science Foundation.

REFERENCES

Amaral, O., Garrison, L., & Klentschy, M. (2002). Helping English learners increase achievement through inquiry-based science instruction. *Bilingual Research Journal*, 26(2), 213–239.

Applebee, A.N. (1984). Writing and reasoning. *Review of Educational Research*, 54(4), 577–596.

Bereiter, C., & Scardamelia, M. (1987). *The psychology of written composition*. Hillsdale, NJ: Erlbaum.

Caswell, B., & Lamon, M. (1998). *Development of scientific literacy: The evolution of ideas in grade four knowledge-building classrooms*. Paper presented at the annual meeting of the American Educational Research Association, San Diego, CA. (ERIC Document Reproduction Service No. ED419789)

Doris, E. (1991). *Doing what scientists do: Children learn to investigate their world.* Portsmouth, NH: Heinemann.

Driver, R., & Bell, B. (1986). Students' thinking and the learning of science: A constructivist view. *School Science Review, 67*(240), 443–456.

Fellows, N. (1994). A window into thinking: Using student writing to understand conceptual change in science learning. *Journal of Research in Science Teaching, 31*(9), 985–1001.

Hanrahan, M. (1999). Rethinking science literacy: Enhancing communication and participation in school science through affirmational dialogue journal writing. *Journal of Research in Science Teaching, 36*(6), 699–718.

Harlen, W. (1988). *The teaching of science.* London: David Fulton.

Harlen, W. (2001). *Primary science: Taking the plunge* (2nd ed.). Portsmouth, NH: Heinemann.

Holliday, W., Yore, L., & Alvermann, D.E. (1994). The reading-science learning-writing connection: Breakthroughs, barriers, and promises. *Journal of Research in Science Teaching, 31*(9), 877–893.

Howard, V.A. (1988). Thinking on paper: A philosopher's look at writing. In V.A. Howard (Ed.), *Varieties of thinking: Essays from Harvard's philosophy of education research center* (pp. 86–89). New York: Routledge, Chapman, and Hall.

Howard, V.A., & Barton, J.H. (1986). *Thinking on paper.* New York: Quill.

Jorgenson, O., &Vanosdall, R. (2002). The death of science? What are we risking in our rush toward standardized testing and the three R's? *Phi Delta Kappan, 83*(8), 601–605.

Langer, J.A., & Applebee, A. (1986). Reading and writing instruction: Toward a theory of teaching and learning. In E.Z. Rothkopf (Ed.), *Review of research in education* (Vol. 13, pp. 118–123). Washington, DC: American Educational Research Association.

Learning Research and Development Center at the University of Pittsburgh & National Center on Education and the Economy. (2000). *New standards: Performance standards and assessments for schools.* Pittsburgh, PA: Learning Research and Development Center.

Marzano, R. (1991). Fostering thinking across the curriculum through knowledge restructuring. *Journal of Reading, 34*(7), 518–525.

Marzano, R., Pickering, D., & Pollock, J. (2001). *Classroom instruction that works: Research-based strategies for increasing student achievement.* Alexandria, VA: Association for Supervision and Curriculum Development.

National Academy of Sciences. (1997). *Science for all children: A guide to improving elementary science education in your school district.* Washington, DC: National Sciences Resource Center, Smithsonian Institution.

National Research Council (NRC). (1999). How people learn: Bridging research and practice. In S. Donovan, J. Bransford, & J. Pellegrino (Eds.), *Committee on learning research and education* (pp. 87–89). Washington, DC: National Academy Press.

Neuman, S.B., & Roskos, K. (1993). *Language and literacy in the early years: An integrated approach.* Fort Worth, TX: Harcourt Brace Jovanovich.

Palincsar, A., & Magnusson, S. (2000). *The interplay of firsthand and text-based investigations in science education* (Report #2-007). Ann Arbor: University of Michigan Center for the Improvement of Early Reading Achievement.

Reddy, M., Jacobs, P., McCrohon, C., & Herrenkohl, L. (1998). *Creating scientific communities in the elementary classroom.* Portsmouth, NH: Heinemann.

Rivard, L.P. (1994). A review of writing to learn in science: Implications for practice and research. *Journal of Research in Science Teaching, 31*(9), 969–983.

Santa, C.M., & Havens, L.T. (1991). Learning through writing. In C.M. Santa & D.E. Alvermann (Eds.), *Science learning: Processes and applications* (pp. 122–133). Newark, DE: International Reading Association.

Scardamalia, M., & Bereiter, C. (1986). Research on written composition. In M.C. Wittrock (Ed.), *Handbook on research on teaching* (3rd ed., pp. 779–799). New York: Macmillan.

Shepardson, D. (1997). Of butterflies and beetles: First graders' ways of seeing and talking about insect life cycles. *Journal of Research in Science Teaching, 34*(9), 873–890.

Shepardson, D., & Britsch, S. (2001). The role of children's journals in elementary school science activities. *Journal of Research in Science Teaching, 38*(1), 43–69.

Thier, M. (2002). *The new science literacy: Using language skills to help students learn science.* Portsmouth, NH: Heinemann.

VanDeWeghe, R. (1987). Making and remaking meaning: Developing literary responses through purposeful, informal writing. *English Quarterly, 20*(1), 38–51.

Vygotsky, L.S. (1978). *Thought and language.* Cambridge, MA: MIT Press.

Wells, G., & Chang-Wells, G.L. (1992). *Constructing knowledge together: Classrooms as centers of inquiry and literacy.* Portsmouth, NH: Heinemann.

Wiggins, G. (1993). *Assessing student performances: Exploring the purpose and limits of testing.* San Francisco: Jossey-Bass.

Willey, L.H. (1988). The effects of selecting writing to learn approaches on high school students' attitudes and achievement (Doctoral dissertation, Mississippi State University, 1988). *Dissertation Abstracts International, 49*, 3611A.

CHAPTER 19

The Science Writing Heuristic: Using Writing as a Tool for Learning in the Laboratory

Carolyn S. Wallace, Brian Hand, and Eun-Mi Yang

What would be the characteristics of a learner who is scientifically literate? There is currently a variety of opinions about what a scientifically literate person should know or be able to do. Some science educators propose that a knowledge of science vocabulary is important, others state that literacy is using scientific knowledge in the real world, and some believe that reading and writing scientific materials are the essential skills (Norris & Phillips, 2001). Our view is that one essential characteristic of scientific literacy is the ability to evaluate a scientific knowledge claim. A scientifically literate person is able to examine data in light of a scientific question and determine whether those data support or disconfirm a knowledge claim. Thus, the judging of evidence for a claim in the form of data is an important goal of science education. The process of perceiving sensory information, comparing it to prior knowledge, and generating meaning for data is fundamental to the process of knowledge construction in science (Osborne & Wittrock, 1983). Thus, an important element of scientific literacy is understanding the relationships among questions, data, claims, and evidence. These skills are important not only to understand the work of scientists, but also to learn how to learn science and to have the capacity to generate new scientific meanings.

A view of scientific literacy that encompasses a deep understanding of questions, knowledge claims, and evidence is similar to that expressed previously by scholars. For example, Kuhn (1993) cites the coordination of theory and evidence as the essential scientific reasoning skill without which individuals cannot use science to solve everyday problems. Yore, Hand, and Florence (2001) have identified patterns of argumentation that establish clear connections among claims, warrants, and evidence as the central feature of an understanding of the nature of science. Norris and Phillips (2001) argued that a literate individual has a deep understanding not only of constructed meanings for the content of text, but also of the creative process of the construction of the text itself. Thus, a scientifically literate person not only interprets text, but also critiques text based on his or her own knowledge of the scientific process.

Our work has focused on classroom strategies by which teachers and students may compose scientific texts that highlight the connections among questions, claims, data, and evidence in science. The view is that in creating these connections through their own work and relating their understandings to physical data as well as their own texts, students will achieve improved scientific reasoning skills, a grasp of the nature of science, and conceptual understandings.

The Science Writing Heuristic

In the interest of promoting writing as a mode of thinking in the science classroom, two researchers, Wallace (formerly Keys) and Hand, have developed the Science Writing Heuristic (SWH) (Hand & Keys, 1999; Keys, 2000; Keys, Hand, Prain, & Collins, 1999). SWH is a tool for promoting thinking, negotiating meaning, and writing about science laboratory activities. Theoretically, the SWH represents a bridge between more personal, expressive forms of writing, which have been shown to promote science understanding (Rivard, 1994), and the recognized form of the genre, the scientific laboratory report, which represents traditional patterns of thinking in science, most especially the link between claims and evidence. From a practical standpoint, SWH is a series of activities to guide teachers and their students in thinking and writing. SWH consists of two parts or templates, a teacher template (see Figure 19.1) and a student template (see Figure 19.2). Wallace and Hand designed SWH to facilitate students' understanding of science concepts and also to facilitate students' understanding of how they have come to know those scientific understandings, a process known as metacognition.

The teacher template of SWH suggests a series of activities in which students can write about and discuss their understandings of laboratory work. The student template suggests questions for students to ask themselves during each "minds-on" activity. The SWH is unique among heuristic tools in that it emphasizes the formation of a knowledge claim for the activity (for example, plant and animal cells have similarities and differences), and then requires the student to provide evidence for that claim. Implementing the heuristic in the science classroom requires teachers to adopt a more student-centered approach to teaching and encourages students to take more ownership over the procedures and outcomes of a practical activity. Our re-

---

FIGURE 19.1
The Science Writing Heuristic Teacher Template

1. Exploration of preinstruction understanding through individual or group concept mapping.
2. Prelaboratory activities, including informal writing, making observations, brainstorming, and posing questions.
3. Participation in laboratory activity.
4. Negotiation phase I—writing personal meanings for laboratory activity (e.g., writing journals).
5. Negotiation phase II—sharing and comparing data interpretations in small groups (e.g., making a group chart).
6. Negotiation phase III—comparing science ideas to textbooks or other printed resources (e.g., writing group notes in response to focus questions).
7. Negotiation phase IV—individual reflection and writing (e.g., writing a report or textbook explanation).
8. Exploration of postinstruction understanding through concept mapping.

FIGURE 19.2
The Science Writing Heuristic Student Template

1. Beginning ideas—What are my questions?
2. Tests/experiments—What did I do?
3. Observations—What did I see?
4. Claims—What can I claim?
5. Evidence—How do I know? Why am I making these claims?
6. Reading—How do my ideas compare with other ideas?
7. Reflection—How have my ideas changed?

---

search, including the study described below, indicates that SWH can improve students' conceptual and metacognitive understandings.

In addition to investigating the use of the SWH in science classrooms, we also have been examining how using different forms of writing helps generate science conceptual learning. For example, when students engage with a set of science concepts during laboratory activities and then write a textbook explanation for other students of their own age, would reformulating those ideas in new language extend learning (Hand, Prain, Lawrence, & Yore, 1999)? As with reading, writing involves the negotiation of meaning for verbal symbols and, therefore, has the potential to generate new science knowledge.

The purpose of the research described below was to examine the usefulness of SWH and a textbook writing activity for promoting conceptual understanding and metacognition with seventh-grade students in life science. Research questions that guided the study included the following:

- Do students who use SWH perform better on tests of conceptual understanding than students who use traditional laboratory reports?

- Do students who use SWH and are engaged in a second task of writing a textbook explanation perform better on tests of conceptual understanding than students who used the SWH alone?

- Within the context of the SWH classroom, to what do students attribute their own increased science understandings?

- What are students' understandings of observations, claims, and evidence in science, and how do they assess their own understandings?

- What is the value of the additional textbook writing task from the students' perspective?

Design of the Research Study

A mixed-methods design was used to evaluate learning in this study. We chose an experimental design to evaluate students' performance on tests of conceptual understanding for a control group, a treatment group who was engaged in the SWH activities, and a treatment group who was engaged in the SWH activities in addition to composing a textbook explanation. A qualitative approach was used to characterize students' understandings of questions, claims, and evidence in science and to probe their views on learning with SWH. The study took place within the context of a unit on cells that was taught for eight weeks during the fall of 2000.

The participants in the experimental portion of this study were 93 seventh-grade students enrolled in an introductory biology course at a midwestern middle school in 1999–2000. Students were enrolled in one of five class sections, with each section being taught by the same teacher. Each student participated in five 45-minute biology periods each week. The student participants were 90% European American, with the remaining 10% from a variety of ethnic origins. Special needs students were excluded from the data analyses to avoid confounding effects between the treatment and students' special needs, such as lack of fluency in English. For the qualitative portion of the study, twelve seventh-grade students—five boys and seven girls, all European American—were chosen for in-depth interviews. In selecting students for the interviews, attempts were made to ensure that there was a balanced gender mix and that there was equal representation between high-, middle-, and low-ability students within the class.

The first two class sections were chosen to be the SWH treatment group. Students used the SWH student templates to guide written work for their lab activities (see Figure 19.2). These students set up their own questions for investigation in the cell unit through all class or group discussions. During the unit, students investigated cell structure, characteristics of plant and animal cells, and movement of water across the cell membrane. The teacher helped guide the students in question formulation, but students determined the questions on the final form. These students also were allowed flexibility in laboratory procedures, again guided through teacher-class discussions. As a final project for the cell unit, students in this group were asked to turn in a research paper summarizing the results of the lab activities.

The third section served as a control group. In this group, all laboratory activities started with questions posed by the teacher and then followed step-by-step instructions written by the teacher. Students in the control group wrote a traditionally formatted laboratory report for each lab. Students in this group were asked to complete the same end-of-unit final project as the SWH group; that is, a research paper summarizing their results.

The last two sections were assigned as the SWH and textbook treatment group (SWH plus-textbook group). Students in these sections used SWH for their laboratory activities and had the same flexibility with questions and procedures as the SWH group previously described. However, their final written summary project was different. Students in this group were asked to write their summaries in the form of a textbook explanation for their peers. They were allowed to choose from a list of topics that their teacher suggested. They sent first drafts of their textbook explanations to seventh graders in a different school, who gave them feedback on clarity and understanding. Then, they composed final drafts of their textbook explanations.

Students in all groups took the same pretest and posttests, consisting of 34 multiple-choice questions and three essay questions, to measure biology conceptual understanding. The test was designed collaboratively by the teacher and the researchers. Stanford Diagnostic Reading Test scores were used to determine if there were initial differences between the groups in reading ability; no significant differences were found. Statistical tests known as analyses of covariance were used to compare posttest scores for the different groups. Twelve students total were interviewed from the SWH and the SWH plus-textbook groups to probe students' thoughts as to which class activities they found the most helpful, their understanding of claim and evidence in science, and how they valued writing in science class. The interviews were audiotaped, transcribed, and coded for major themes.

Results of the Experiment

Results of the experiment indicated that students who were engaged in the SWH group and SWH plus-textbook group performed significantly better on the multiple-choice portion of the posttest for cell concepts than those in the control group. There was no significant difference between the SWH and SWH plus-textbook groups. The mean score on the multiple-choice portion (out of 34 points) for the SWH group was 23.81, for the SWH plus-textbook group it was 23.25, and for the control group it was 19.84. These results indicate that using the SWH and the SWH plus-textbook strategies was helpful for students in learning cell concepts.

There also were three essay questions on the posttest, worth 8 points each. As with the multiple-choice portion, students in the SWH group and SWH plus-textbook group performed significantly better on one (#35) of the three essay questions. The mean scores on question 35 were 3.02 for the control group, 4.80 for the SWH group, and 5.88 for the SWH plus-textbook group. For the remaining two essay questions (#36 and #37), students in the SWH plus-textbook group performed significantly better than either the SWH group or the control group. The mean scores for question 36 were 3.39 for the control group, 3.77 for the SWH group, and 6.11 for the SWH plus-textbook group. The mean scores on question 37 were 3.25 for the control group, 3.54 for the SWH group, and 5.79 for the SWH plus-textbook group. These results indicate that the students using the SWH plus-textbook strategies were able to express the most complete and accurate cell understandings on the essay questions. Thus, we concluded that both the SWH and the textbook tasks did have a positive effect on students' science learning.

Results of the Interview

We sought to answer the following questions through our interview process: (a) Within the context of the SWH classroom, to what do students attribute their own increased science understandings? (b) What are students' understandings of questions, evidence, and claims in science, and how do they assess their own understandings? (c) How did students interpret and value the textbook explanation task?

Coding the interview data led to the following assertions for each of the research questions.

Theme One

Students cited the following SWH activities as most helpful to their science learning: framing their own questions, participating in peer group discussions, making connections between concepts, and the act of writing.

First, students enjoyed framing their own investigation questions for the laboratory activities. They believed they became more involved in the laboratory activity because they were answering questions that were relevant to their own interests. As Else said, "You don't learn about something you don't want to know about—you learn about something you do want to learn about." Only one of the twelve students we interviewed preferred having the teacher set up the question. Other students stated that framing their own questions facilitated learning through increased engagement (Else) and individualized pacing (Kether).

> Else: It makes you more interested, 'cause, like, if you have to answer something you're not interested in you already know it or something. You're bored and you don't pay attention. But, if you answer a question that you made up—helped make up—and you're wondering about, you pay attention 'cause you want to find out the answer to your question.

> Kether: I like asking my own question 'cause it allows the student to personalize the work so they understand it and 'cause, like, a student might understand it far more than the next, so it would be difficult for the other who didn't understand, so they really have to work with it at their own pace.

Second, most students stated that peer group discussions embedded in the SWH activities facilitated their learning of cell unit concepts. There were two students who stated that they learned more working alone than in the group situation. However, the majority of students attributed increased conceptual understanding to hearing their peers' explanations and having an opportunity to share their ideas in the group, as evidenced by Rob and Else, below. Students attributed increased learning to the actions of both giving and receiving information (Rob).

> Else: [Peer group discussion] does help, because if you don't have the discussion, it kind of goes in there and then you have to try

to understand it, but when you discuss it you get what other people think and you're able to understand the concept.

Rob: Usually I am probably the loudest in the group, so they usually listen to me so I usually give our information too, but sometimes they'll, like, help me too, like if I don't understand something or if I need help with something.

Third, students appreciated that the SWH promoted a deeper and more meaningful mode of science learning than they had engaged with in the past. Several of the students interviewed asserted that SWH promoted thinking. For example, Neil recognized that a higher level of learning was taking place in the classroom: "Not only did we learn, but we found out how to learn." Other students brought up features of SWH that specifically promoted deeper learning, including meaningful learning versus memorization (Jason), the promotion of firsthand knowledge (Rob), and the need for organization and synthesis of ideas (Kether). These students' comments reveal a high level of metacognition about science learning. Kether specifically draws the contrast between copying words from the textbook versus the meaningful writing activities they did, including the SWH and textbook explanation tasks.

Jason: Well, I think this [SWH] helps you out more because memorizing sometimes you don't really learn what it actually means and then but learning it and remembering it, instead of memorizing it, you learn more, I think.

Rob: I don't like lecture, but that's 'cause I like to know what's going on. I don't like when people tell me the answer and they don't show why that is right and with an SWH you know why it is right, your claim, and evidence, and everything like that.

Kether: He [the teacher] wants us to organize our thinking and he wants to make sure we've been understanding what he's been saying and Ms. Cress [student teacher] has been saying and, like, it doesn't really show you've learned a lot by answering the textbook questions because they're in bold. You don't even have to read it. You just copy down what's in bold and I know a lot of people do that, but you can't learn if you do that. And then when he assigns things like the paper [textbook explanation] and the SWH you can't fake it; you have to really know what you are talking about.

Fourth, five of the students specifically mentioned the act of writing as a useful learning tool, when asked which features of SWH helped them learn. Although not as popular a response as framing the question, group work, or promoting meaningful learning, some students appreciated the value of writing for clarifying learning, including help with remembering (Lisa and Else) and generating authentic understanding (Julie and Else).

Lisa: 'Cause you get to write it down, and when you write it down, it makes you remember it more.

Julie: Probably the research you had to do to write it was the most important part [of SWH] because you needed to know more to write about it and that helped you with your understanding and that if you didn't understand something in the research or it was confusing, writing it down sort of helped.

Else: It helps me put it down because if I didn't, 'cause I have trouble if I don't write something down, I'll forget. That's why I use my action planner so much. So, the SWH helps me put it down in the way I think of it, and then reading it over helps it get into my understanding, so it's not just a bunch of words I don't understand.

Theme Two

Students developed a sound understanding of the purpose of a knowledge claim in science, as well as an understanding that the claim must coordinate with the question and the claim must be supported by the evidence.

Students described their understanding of how to construct a knowledge claim during the interview sessions. Data revealed that students developed an understanding that the claim needed to respond to the investigation question. For example, in the excerpts that follow, Tasha indicated that the claim "deals with the question." Also, the students illustrated the notion that there may be more than one claim for an investigation. Rob acknowledged that "there were lots of claims you could have," and Julie stated, "there doesn't have to be one claim." An understanding that there could be many claims for an investigation and that scientific investigators seek a claim that matches their question is an indication that the students were developing important understandings about scientific literacy.

Tasha: I think it [the claim] deals with the question and that's, like, all because it just tells, it explains the question more and, like, this question, it says what are the parts of the cell membrane?

	And it talks and it tells the claim, it tells what are the parts of the cell membrane.
Rob:	There were lots of claims you could have, but I just didn't know what claim I needed to have so, and then, if you don't have a claim, you can't have evidence.
Julie:	And plus, a claim is sort of, it depends on what you think so there doesn't have to be one claim, so it's easier.

The students also indicated their understanding that the knowledge claim must coordinate with the evidence. Initially, this was difficult for students; for example, Julie struggled with the concept of what was considered evidence and what was not. As the unit progressed, students became aware of the need for coordination of the claim with the evidence. When asked about the relationship between claim and evidence, several of the students could articulate the appropriate relationship, such as Neil and Rob below.

Researcher:	How did you get evidence for the claim?
Neil:	Well, before I made the claim, I made sure the evidence was good.
Researcher:	Ahh!
Neil:	I can't just make the claim and have no evidence.
Rob:	Well, the claim you'd make, but the evidence, you'd have to have good evidence to support your claim.
Researcher:	Why did you think you had to have really good evidence?
Rob:	Um, 'cause, like, if you don't give good evidence, um, they won't think your claim will be right.

Third, we suggest that experience with the SWH promoted an understanding of how to construct a knowledge claim in science. This aspect is closely related to student knowledge of the possibility of multiple claims and the need for coordination of claims with questions and evidence as described above. In the excerpt below, Rob describes his knowledge of the relationships among claim construction, observations, and evidence.

Researcher:	How did you figure out how to make a good claim?
Rob:	Well, let's see. Just see what does the structure do or how does it affect it or something and then you could say, like, let's see, for example, multicell organisms have more parts

than single cell organisms because, and I said, we saw in the microscope the differences between the two cells and decided that we should look at more and we found the same thing. We found that there were more parts in the multicelled because we looked in the microscope, and we would look at a single cell bacteria and then we would look at a tick or something. And then we would see how many, the insides of it, and the single-celled organisms, there were not many parts and the multicelled organisms there were tons of parts of that's how I got that claim.

Theme Three

Students who wrote the textbook explanation for peer seventh graders valued the task for pointing out what they did not know and requiring them to explain concepts in everyday language.

Students were in agreement that the textbook writing task prompted them to organize their ideas so that they were able to determine what they did or did not know. The textbook writing task was viewed as being valuable in terms of learning, because students were able to identify gaps in their own understandings and begin to address them. Julie's excerpt below indicates that she is developing a metacognitive understanding through writing.

Else: I think I understand it, but then when I write it down, I understand that I don't understand the topic.

Julie: Yeah, because if you don't really know something very well then if you try to write about it, it will definitely show. I mean *it will tell you you need to learn more*, so then you go back and check.

All six of the students who were interviewed about the textbook writing task indicated that there was a need to change the science language in their material into "more informal language" (Julie). Two of the students indicated that they did not focus enough attention on this informal language and had put too much technical language in their first drafts. The students realized that there was a need to explain the "big words" (Rob) because the teacher was no longer the audience. The students understood that they could not "hide behind a word" and expect the teacher to interpret its meaning (Else). Further, students pointed out that the process of changing the language took some effort and was different from language used for the teacher (Lisa).

> Else: Well, it helped them saying, I don't understand this, help me. Then I read it and concentrated on the part they didn't understand. I found out that, yeah, it really is confusing, so I went back and reworded it...I just reworded it so it would make more sense, because it was more the way I was thinking of it which didn't have all the explanations in it, so I had to go back and put more detail into it, so people would understand it.

> Lisa: Well, I think I had to put a little bit more effort into it because Mr. M was studying the thing with us and he was teaching us, so he knew what we were trying to say and when you're writing to someone who doesn't understand anything you have to go into really specific details for them to understand.

Conclusion

We believe this study shows the value of the SWH for promoting student understanding of laboratory activities and improving scientific literacy. It also shows that reformulating conceptual understandings in writing, such as a textbook explanation, can improve science learning. The seventh-grade students in our study expressed quite sophisticated understandings of their own learning. They were able to grapple with the concept of a knowledge claim in science and actively seek evidence to support their claims. They also were able to understand the value of the textbook writing task for their own improved understanding. Activities such as the SWH and the textbook explanation task promote not only conceptual understanding, but also metacognition, or learning how to learn. These tools may be used throughout the students' lifetime and represent the characteristics of scientific literacy.

The U.S. National Science Education Standards (NSES) (National Research Council [NRC], 1996) emphasize the need for students to be actively engaged with science inquiry and to make logical connections between their explanations, the evidence, and the questions being asked. SWH encourages students to move past the typical cookbook approach to science inquiry to promote greater ownership and responsibility for the decisions made and the outcome of the laboratory activity. Students are able to recognize that there is a relationship between the question that they ask and the type of evidence required both to answer the question and to make a claim from the activity. Having the opportunity to personalize the question promoted a greater sense of participation in the laboratory activity and led to a greater sense of understanding of the conceptual outcome of the activity.

The NSES also emphasize the need for students to communicate and defend the results of their investigations. In undertaking this communication, "arguments must be logical and demonstrate connections between natural phenomena, investigations and the historical body of knowledge" (NRC, 1996, p. 176). As part of the process in completing SWH, strong emphasis is placed on students having to communicate their understandings to one another, both in constructing claims and in assessing their claims against current scientific understandings. We believe that this improvement in written communication skills may carry over to students' reading skills. Learning to write about questions, claims, and evidence may help students construct an understanding of how written arguments in science are structured. This, in turn, may prepare them to comprehend and interpret meaning as they read scientific texts. Our future studies will investigate the effects of SWH on students' science reading.

REFERENCES

Hand, B., & Keys, C.W. (1999). Inquiry investigation: A new approach to laboratory reports. *Science Teacher, 66*(4), 27–29.

Hand, B., Prain, V., Lawrence, C., & Yore, L.D. (1999). A writing in science framework designed to enhance science literacy. *International Journal of Science Education, 21*(10), 1021–1035.

Keys, C.W. (2000). Investigating the thinking processes of eighth grade writers during the composition of a scientific laboratory report. *Journal of Research in Science Teaching, 37*(7), 676–690.

Keys, C.W., Hand, B., Prain, V., & Collins, S. (1999). Using the science writing heuristic as a tool for learning from laboratory investigations in secondary science. *Journal of Research in Science Teaching, 36*(10), 1065–1084.

Kuhn, D. (1993). Science as argument: Implications for teaching and learning scientific thinking. *Science Education, 77*(3), 319–337.

National Research Council (NRC). (1996). *National science education standards.* Washington, DC: National Academy Press.

Norris, S.P., & Phillips, L.M. (2001, March). *How literacy in its fundamental sense is central to scientific literacy.* Paper presented at the annual meeting of the National Association of Research in Science Teaching, St. Louis, MO.

Osborne, R.J., & Wittrock, M.C. (1983). Learning science: A generative process. *Science Education, 67*(4), 489–508.

Rivard, L.P. (1994). A review of writing to learn in science: Implications for practice and research. *Journal of Research in Science Teaching, 31*(9), 969–983.

Yore, L.D., Hand, B., & Florence, M. (2001, March). *Scientists' views of science, models of writing, and science writing practices.* Paper presented at the annual meeting of the National Association of Research in Science Teaching, St. Louis, MO.

EVALUATING COMMERCIAL

TEXT MATERIALS

W hat role might science textbook materials play in science instruction?

In chapter 20, "Better Textbooks, Better Readers and Writers," Cynthia Shanahan discusses the important role textbooks play in science instruction. Although reading specialists have at their disposal a number of general teaching strategies, to be most effective these tools need to be adapted to the specific purposes of science. Students will be best served when literacy educators, science teachers, and textbook publishers work together to develop instructional plans, Shanahan argues. She then elaborates on science-relevant recommendations from the National Reading Panel and suggests that educators would do well to look carefully at the important role writing plays in helping students understand and access science content.

In chapter 21, "Choosing Science Textbooks: Connecting Research to Common Sense," William G. Holliday surveys the current state of textbook publishing, comparing the "new" science textbooks to trade books and other instructional materials. Decisions on which texts to purchase should take into account both research and practical concerns, Holliday notes. To this end, he proposes guidelines to help in the choice of textbooks.

In chapter 22, "Integrating Science and Literacy Instruction With a Common Goal of Learning Science Content," Harold Pratt and Norby Pratt warn educators about the dangers of losing sight of authentic science and literacy goals as they go about seeking to integrate instruction. Although acknowledging that literacy study embraces a multitude of goals, this chapter focuses primarily on reading comprehension. The authors delineate specific learning principles they view as key to creating sound instructional practices and then go on to present their own instructional model for learning that integrates science inquiry and literacy strategies.

Textbook purchasing committees would do well to consider the issues raised in these chapters.

CHAPTER 20

Better Textbooks, Better Readers and Writers

CYNTHIA SHANAHAN

The Problem: Students Have Trouble Reading and Writing in Science

It is no secret that students find their science texts difficult to read. The reasons for their difficulty include (a) a preponderance of text that requires students to make sophisticated inferences (Britton & Gulgoz, 1991); (b) a mismatch between students' levels of knowledge and the textbook information (Britton & Gulgoz, 1991); (c) a lack of elaboration about complex concepts; (d) a lack of liveliness in tone (Beck & McKeown, 1991; Beck, McKeown, Hamilton, & Kucan, 1998); (e) a lack of relatedness to students' real-world experiences (Guzzetti, Hynd, Williams, & Skeels, 1995); and (f) a high vocabulary load that makes thinking about the described processes difficult (Guzzetti et al., 1995; McKeown, 1985).

My colleagues and I found that the physics students we studied recognized these drawbacks to their texts and were intensely frustrated by them. In a series of studies of reading in physics classes, we asked students about their textbooks, interviewed teachers about textbook use, and observed textbook use and the lack of it in daily class periods (Guzzetti et al., 1995; Hynd, Guzzetti, Fowler, Williams, & Seward, 1997; Hynd, McNish, Qian, Keith, & Lay, 1994).The extent to which students were expected to read texts varied across levels of classes. Honors students who were expected to read the textbook on their own rarely did. Rather, they used the text as a seldom-used reference in order to solve the problems they were assigned at the end of the textbook chapters, and they remained confused about complex concepts. In one teacher's class, regular and general education students were never asked to read the textbook. In another, they were required to read it during class and to record the main ideas; the students in both classes continued to rely on the teachers' explanations to understand the concepts.

Our interviews with students about texts in these classes underscored the awareness that students had about the problems with textbooks. Here are some of the comments that students made:

Well, when I don't understand something, I get frustrated, and I don't really want to learn. It's more, I have to. I can't understand the book, so if you don't pick it up in class and you go back to try learning in the book, and it doesn't make sense.... And my parents can't help me 'cause they don't have no idea. (Hynd et al., 1997, p. 23)

The text needs to talk more to high school students, more down to earth, more interesting. (Guzzetti et al., 1995, p. 662)

They try to impress us with fancy words. (Guzzetti et al., 1995, p. 661)

Our text is like having a building with no foundation. The ideas are just floating on the air to me. I don't know how to make sense of them. (Hynd, McNish, et al., 1994, p. 661)

Yet, these same students believed that understanding their science textbooks was important. They knew that something more had to be done to help them make connections to their textbooks. Indeed, students do learn science from reading about it. The studies my colleagues and I have conducted with refutational text show that learning is improved by reading. For example, in one study (Hynd, McWhorter, Phares, & Suttles, 1994), students who read text performed better on delayed posttests (three weeks after the experiment) than students who did not but who engaged in discussion and watched demonstrations. In another study (Hynd et al., 1997), text had an effect on posttest performance despite the fact that students also engaged in experiments, listened to lectures, participated in discussions, and watched videos about the topics. And studies by Andre and Windschitl (2003) show that refutational text had an effect on long-term learning, whereas computer modeling and experimentation did not. These findings support the notion that reading is an important aspect of science learning.

Although we did not interview teachers and students about their scientific writing, we saw little evidence that students engaged in writing except to write down and solve physics problems. Research suggests writing is important in science learning (Hand, 1999; Hand, Prain, & Wallace, 2002). Writing is perhaps the most neglected part of science classes. Students have trouble with writing in science because they rarely practice writing. Yet, it is an integral part of scientific activity.

Solving the Problem

What do science teachers do about the reading and writing problem? In regard to texts, do they demand better textbooks? Do they opt for trade books? Do they continue to do what they have done in the past—fade out text use and rely on hands-on experimentation and their own explanations? Do they teach students strategies for reading the textbooks they find so frustrating?

Some researchers (e.g., Holliday, 2001; Holliday, Yore, & Alvermann, 1994) assert that the problem can be solved by aligning science and literacy educators to work with the educational publishing industry to produce better textbooks—textbooks that are easy to understand and that offer opportunities for writing. In order for this alliance to take place, however, science educators need to understand the role of literacy in the understanding of science concepts and to believe in its importance. If science teachers understand the importance of literacy in science learning, they will align with literacy teachers and work with publishers to get better science textbooks. The first step is to convince science educators that literacy is important and that the science teacher should teach literacy as well as science. Resistance to that notion is widespread.

Why Literacy Is Important to Science Learning

Reading and writing in science class is important for a number of reasons. First, science educators want to foster lifelong, independent learning and knowing how to learn science from reading about it is a prerequisite for that independence. If students continue to read about science, then science knowledge will grow even after formal schooling has been completed.

Second, reading and writing activities are important to the *doing* of science. Consider the everyday life of a scientist and the myriad ways in which literacy plays a role. The scientist reads research articles in journals and evaluates their worth based on both explicit and implicit criteria. She forms hypotheses based upon what she has read and suspects to be true then writes a grant requesting funding to test the hypotheses. She writes lab reports and reads the data that are collected. She reports those data and her interpretation of them in scientific journals after a round of reviews and much editing. She reads other scientists' reactions to the work and forms new ideas on the basis of her reading. Therefore, if one goal of science teachers is to engage students in the process of doing science, then doing science requires a high degree of literacy.

Third, even if students do not plan to become scientists, reading and writing about scientific issues will help them to participate fully in society and in the democratic process. Students who understand what it is to read a scientific paper, for example, will be much better equipped to evaluate the scientific issues that arise in our society, such as the benefits and drawbacks of stem cell research. Students who understand what it means to evaluate often-contradictory scientific data based on the scientific method will be much better equipped to look at the often-contradictory scientific reports in the media and respond to them appropriately.

Finally, students who are skilled in reading and writing in science are capable of learning concepts more deeply and thinking about them more critically. There is evidence to suggest that written text can be a powerful persuader (Chaiken & Eagly, 1976). And with written text, one can reread, cross-reference, clarify using outside sources, and take the time to consider one's thoughts—activities that are difficult with lectures and demonstrations. Reading and writing strengthen the learning of content material and raise achievement.

Students will not learn to read different kinds of science text by reading literature, just as they will not learn to engage in scientific writing by writing stories. Thus, students who participate in reading and writing activities only in language arts or English classes will not necessarily learn to be better readers and writers in science class. Scientific texts are structured quite differently (including expository descriptions of processes, data tables and illustrations, problem-solution and cause and effect structures, and specialized vocabulary) than texts in other disciplines. In addition, there are conventions in science writing that are quite different from the conventions in English, mathematics, or history classes. Structuring a laboratory report, for example, requires adherence to the scientific method, so the lab report may include hypotheses, methods, findings, and conclusions—a structure different from an argumentative paper in an English class or even a research report in a history class. Students will learn to read and write in science if they are given explicit instruction in strategies for

- reading and writing science;
- understanding and exemplifying through their own writing the structure with which scientific information is presented;
- understanding and exemplifying the ways that thinking is represented in different science texts;
- forming a full and flexible knowledge of the vocabulary of science; and
- understanding the tradition of scientific investigation, including the way scientific information is created, shared, and evaluated by the scientific community through reading and writing.

These elements of literate activity cannot be taught easily in language arts and English classes. They are part and parcel of the discipline of science.

Alexander and her colleagues (1998) note that the path to expertise in a discipline is a result of the interaction among interest, knowledge, and strategies. As a student learns more, knowledge becomes structured around principles specific to the discipline, interest becomes more intrinsic, and strategies change from global and inefficient to specific and efficient. A change in any one of the elements—knowledge, interest, or strategies—will trigger changes in the other two. Thus, arming students with more specific, efficient strategies for learning scientific information can result in increased knowledge and more intrinsic interest in science, and these outcomes are highly desired by science educators.

Science and literacy educators should work together to improve science texts. It is highly unlikely that science educators will work with literacy educators, however, unless they are convinced that reading and writing—the sort of specialized reading and writing I just discussed—are not only central to understanding science, but need to be *taught* in science class.

How Literacy and Science Experts Should Align

What would an alliance between literacy and science educators entail? Literacy experts do not have the expertise in science that science educators have. What they do have at their disposal are a number of tools or strategies for expository reading and writing that work across disciplines. But to be their most effective, these tools need to be adapted to the specific purposes and content of science, as Alexander (1998) suggests happens with growing scientific expertise. These adaptations may become so highly specific, in fact, that they look like new tools. Their development can only come about through the collaboration of literacy and science educators.

How can science educators be convinced that teaching reading and writing in science classes is an important way to help students learn science? In Illinois, it may take place as a result of the new teacher education standards put into practice in 2003. In addition to requiring science teachers to demonstrate their understanding of science content, the new standards require that "the competent science teacher understands the process of reading and demonstrates instructional abilities to teach reading in the content area of science" (Illinois State Board of Education, 2002). That statement is accompanied by 8 knowledge indicators and 10 performance indicators, listed in Figure 20.1. The knowledge indicators include knowledge of how students become motivated to read, the role of vocabulary and fluency in read-

FIGURE 20.1
Illinois Content Area Standards for Educators: Science Core

Knowledge Indicators: The competent science teacher

19A. Understands that the reading process is the construction of meaning through the interactions of the reader's background knowledge and experiences, the information in the text, and the purpose of the reading situation.

19B. Recognizes the relationships among the four language arts (reading, writing, listening, and speaking), and knows how to provide opportunities to integrate these through instruction.

19C. Understands how to design, select, modify, and evaluate materials in terms of the reading needs of the learner.

19D. Understands the importance of and encourages the use of adolescent literature in the curriculum and for independent reading.

19E. Understands the relationship between oral and silent reading.

19F. Understands the role of subject-area vocabulary in developing reading comprehension.

19G. Understands the importance of the unique study strategies required of the specific content area in developing reading comprehension.

19H. Understands the importance of the relationship between assessment and instruction in planning.

Performance Indicators: The competent science teacher

19I. Plans and teaches lessons for students that develop comprehension of content area materials through instructional practices that include analyzing critically, evaluating sources, and synthesizing and summarizing material.

19J. Plans and teaches lessons on how to monitor comprehension and correct confusions and misunderstandings that arise during reading.

19K. Plans and models use of comprehension strategies before, during, and after reading of text.

19L. Provides opportunities for students to develop content area vocabulary through instructional practices that develop connections and relationships among words, use of context clues, and understanding of connotative and denotative meaning of words.

19M. Plans and teaches lessons that encourage students to write about the content read in order to improve understanding.

19N. Plans and teaches lessons for students to develop study strategies that include previewing and preparing to read text effectively, recognizing organizational patterns unique to informational text, and using graphic organizers as an aid for recalling information.

19O. Plans and teaches units that require students to carry out research or inquiry using multiple text, including electronic resources.

19P. Provides continuous monitoring of student progress through observations, work samples, and various informal reading assessments.

19Q. Analyzes and evaluates the quality and appropriateness of instructional materials in terms of readability, content, length, format, illustrations, and other pertinent factors.

19R. Promotes the development of a literate environment that includes classroom libraries that foster reading.

Source: Illinois State Board of Education, 2002.

ing comprehension and learning, a knowledge of appropriate reading material, and a knowledge of strategies for helping students to develop key concepts from reading. Teachers will need to be able to demonstrate that they can teach students how to use comprehension strategies; recognize organizational patterns; monitor their comprehension; and synthesize, analyze, and evaluate the information they read in science class. That is a daunting task for those who have not considered teaching reading as part of their job descriptions.

How Should Science Texts Be Changed?

The quality and usability of textbooks is improving. However, some textbook publishers continue to ignore new concepts of text readability and, instead, rely on pictures and outmoded ideas about what makes books easy to read (such as decreasing the length of sentences). These measures do little to enhance the understandability of the concepts, even though they increase the books' surface-level appeal. Others, however, as Holliday (2001) suggests, are making strides in writing textbooks that are reader friendly. See, for example, *Conceptual Physics* (Hewitt, 2001) and *Modern Biology* (Towle, 2000).

Previously, textbooks included information that was inaccurate, but now error rates are lower. Previously, written explanations also sounded arcane, but in the newer books, the prose is of higher quality. The vocabulary load has possibly diminished, and now in order to explain difficult vocabulary, textbooks use elaboration, diagrams, drawings, and photographs. Now controversial topics are covered, and textbooks give explicit information rather than ambiguous and vague information on sensitive topics, such as evolution and reproduction. Textbooks are more concerned with prior knowledge than they used to be. For example, Hewitt (2001) commonly discusses students prior conceptions about physics principles and how they are different from scientific understanding. Technology is offering students tools for understanding that have heretofore been unavailable. For example, webpages that accompany textbook chapters extend lessons through simulation and video.

However, there is still a need for science educators and literacy educators to combine their efforts in order to get publishers to improve their textbooks. The direction for improvement should be twofold: (1) publishers should continue to improve the content of texts, and (2) they should provide teachers with strategies for teaching students to read their science textbooks and other materials and with strategies for writing scientific prose.

What can publishers do to continue to improve the content of science textbooks? My colleagues and I had students read a variety of physics texts about projectile motion and asked them to rate the texts. Rather than choosing current textbooks and trade books as the most useful texts and as their favorites, they chose the texts that we had written that were refutational in nature. These texts recognized that students had intuitive conceptions about projectile motion that went against current scientific thought, and they argued that the scientific explanation was better than these intuitive ones. We categorized their comments about what they liked about the refutational texts; the comments and the categorization are presented in Figure 20.2. In summary, the table shows that students believe they learn more when text information is tied to their knowledge, explained clearly and thoroughly, shown to be relevant to their lives, and reinforced by other experiences. Certainly, these principles could play a role in guiding the continued improvement of textbooks that publishers create.

What Else Needs to Be Done?

But science students must learn to make sense of a wide variety of texts, not just textbooks. They should read scientific articles, lab reports, trade books, and other materials that get them involved in the doing of science. Not all of these are going to be written for students. For example, students' first experiences with reading articles in a scientific journal may be difficult. To a novice, the articles are hardly friendly. It helps, though, to know what to look for in terms of the text organization and to have some standards for evaluation in mind when reading. My point is that all texts are not going to be reader friendly, but students should be taught strategies for reading and learning from them.

Textbook publishers can, indeed, do a better job at helping science teachers to help their students make sense of science texts and to write scientific discourse. Science educators and literacy educators should ask publishers for teachers' guides that offer help to the science teacher. These guides should be written by content literacy experts and science experts who work collaboratively to offer strategies for reading and writing that are specific to the discipline of science.

What should these guides include? The National Reading Panel published a report of their research syntheses in 2000 (National Institute of Child Health and Human Development [NICHD], 2000). This panel, commissioned by the U.S. government, analyzed experimental research in phonics and phonemic awareness, vocabulary, comprehension, and fluency. Some

FIGURE 20.2
Comments on Refutational Texts

Dissonance
There's a contrast between common people and physics.
While it was saying the wrong ideas, they fit how I believed.
It shows common ideas you can identify with but explains why they're wrong.
It makes you think twice about what you think you know.
If I thought about what it said, it would help me change my mind.

Clarity/Depth
It gets its points across...clearer than a text that beats around the bush.
Talks about how gravity really works.
It was good. It had a lot of information.
A lot of detail of vertical and horizontal motion.
Little questions. Everything I needed to know was there.

Believability
The text gave everyday life examples.
It has a lot to do with everyday life. The things you do have to do with physics.
It was half-realistic. Most people don't think of physics when an orange rolls or think of why the soda cup kept moving when he stopped.

Usefulness
It was dealing with things we could really do. It told us you can use it for the rest of your life.
Because you could explain something to somebody by reading it.
This information could be used in everyday life to better understand how objects react to forces.

Reinforcement
We did it in class. Most stuff I read says this will happen.
The information was believable because it was from other sources.
It fits what I've learned.

Credibility
It's a text, right?
I have no reason not to believe this. It's in a science book.
It doesn't seem right to me, but because it's a text, it has to be true. I believe what I read.

Identification
It was like it was talking to me.
You don't think you're stupid.
While it was saying the wrong ideas, they fit how I believed.
It explained what I believed in. It's not just me.
It's good to know that people have different theories. At least my theory was there.
It's just like me.
The story was interesting. I could identify.
It has a lot to do with everyday life, the things you do have to do with physics.

of their findings are pertinent to reading in science. For example, one finding was that structured vocabulary programs increase vocabulary and comprehension. Programs could be structured because a vocabulary text was used, but programs in which students were taught strategies for learning words in common within a discipline also were successful. What does that have to do with science? Conceptual vocabulary is one of the most central aspects of learning science. If students understand concepts in depth, they understand science in depth, too. Thus, vocabulary needs to be a focus of science instruction, and students need to be taught strategies for learning it. Teaching a strategy for learning vocabulary is different from assigning students a list of words to learn. One strategy for learning a word, for example, is to use context clues. Another strategy is to break down a word into meaningful units. Also, students could draw a picture or mnemonic of the word. For example, a student could draw a concept map that shows the relation between one scientific term and others. To learn a strategy, it must be modeled and practiced, and a teacher needs to give appropriate feedback. If a student cannot provide an appropriate example of a word, for example, a teacher would help students to think of one.

The panel also found six comprehension strategies that lead to increased reading achievement. Reading achievement is raised when teachers are engaged in (a) teaching text organization; (b) teaching students to make visual representations of ideas such as in maps, charts, and graphs; (c) teaching students question-creating and question-answering strategies; (d) teaching students to make summaries; (e) using cooperative learning strategies; and (f) teaching students to use multiple strategies (NICHD, 2000). These strategies are general in nature; they work across disciplines. However, with collaboration among literacy and science educators, these strategies could be made more specific to the content of science.

Finally, the panel found that teaching students to read fluently increased comprehension and overall reading achievement. That is, students who practiced reading text orally at an appropriate speed, with a high degree of accuracy, and with proper inflection and intonation could increase their reading achievement. This finding is significant because fluency practice has not been a feature of literacy instruction in the past.

So, what can science teachers do to help students learn to read in the discipline of science? They can work with literacy experts to modify and create vocabulary, comprehension, and fluency strategies that are specific to the discipline of science. These strategies could be the focus of the teacher's guides that would accompany the textbooks that publishers market.

The panel did not study writing, nor did it focus on studies that dealt with more than one text. Yet, these elements of literacy are important as well. Reading and writing are reciprocal processes, and, as previously stated in the explanation of a scientist's job, they are both integral parts of scientific work. Further, in order to understand, interpret, and make decisions based on the myriad sources of information about scientific topics, it is important for students not only to consider information within texts, but also to be able to analyze, synthesize, and evaluate information across texts.

Let us consider an example of a high school physics student. As part of his learning experiences about a single topic, the student may read the textbook, read supplementary materials such as trade books, read laboratory directions, listen to his teacher's explanations, watch demonstrations, perform his own demonstrations and conduct experiments, participate in discussion, write lab reports, engage in problem solving, and write explanations of scientific information. Most of these activities involve reading and writing. All of them must be integrated into a learning experience that is tied to one's prior knowledge—what a student has read in other classes and on his own, seen on TV, experienced in his out-of-school life. Yet, integrating information across these sources is not something that high school students do easily. Furthermore, it is even more difficult to integrate across sources when some of the information is contradictory or challenges a student's prior beliefs. How, indeed, does one make sense of experiments that do not support accepted scientific theory? How can students combine information that is similar across sources while not ignoring the dissimilarities? Students need to be taught strategies for integrating information and for making decisions about what to believe in the light of existing evidence. What counts as scientific rigor? How can media bias be detected? How do scientists deal with ethical questions? These questions and others reflect the higher-order thinking that is involved in thinking across scientific texts.

The field of literacy education has just begun to consider cross-textual integrations and the importance of teaching students strategies for making sense of multiple texts. The strategies that literacy educators create alone will not be as good for science students as the ones that are created in collaboration with science educators.

Conclusion

In this chapter, I have discussed the difficulties that students have with reading science texts as well as with the general lack of writing that traditionally takes place in science classes. The solution to these problems lies in a collaboration among literacy educators, science educators, and publishers to develop better textbooks and to include guides for teaching students reading and writing strategies. Textbooks should continue to improve in making ties to students' prior knowledge, explaining concepts in clear and elaborate ways, making the information relevant to students' everyday lives, and providing a number of alternate experiences that include other texts as well as activities to reinforce learning. In addition to helping teachers identify other sources of information and assign students appropriate learning activities, teacher's guides also should help science teachers teach strategies for vocabulary learning, comprehension, fluency, and writing both within and across sources—strategies that are specific to the scientific content students are learning. Publishers should no longer assume that students can read their textbooks, write scientific prose, and integrate information across sources, and they should dispel that assumption among science teachers. Teachers will find that, in using these strategies, students will gain scientific knowledge and become more intrinsically interested in learning science.

REFERENCES

Alexander, P. (1998). The nature of disciplinary and domain learning: The knowledge, interest, and strategic dimensions of learning from subject matter texts. In C. Hynd (Ed.), *Learning from text across conceptual domains* (pp. 263–287). Mahwah, NJ: Erlbaum.

Andre, T., & Windschitl, M. (2003). Interest, epistemological belief, and intentional conceptual change. In G. Sinatra & P.R. Pintrich (Eds.), *Intentional conceptual change* (pp. 173–198). Mahwah, NJ: Erlbaum.

Beck, I.L., & McKeown, M.G. (1991). Social studies texts are hard to understand: Mediating some of the difficulties. *Language Arts, 68*(6), 482–490.

Beck, I.L., McKeown, M.G., Hamilton, R.L., & Kucan, L. (1998). Getting at the meaning: How to help students unpack difficult text. *American Educator, 22*(1–2), 66–71, 85.

Britton, B.K., & Gulgoz, S. (1991). Using Kintsch's computational model to improve instructional text: Effects of repairing inference calls on recall and cognitive structures. *Journal of Educational Psychology, 83*(3), 329–345.

Chaiken, S., & Eagly, A.H. (1976). Communication modality as a determinant of message persuasiveness and message comprehensibility. *Journal of Personality and Social Psychology, 34,* 605–614.

Guzzetti, B., Hynd, C., Williams, W., & Skeels, S. (1995). What students have to say about their science texts. *Journal of Reading, 38,* 656–665.

Hand, B. (1999). A writing in science framework designed to enhance science literacy. *International Journal of Science Education, 21*(10), 1021–1035.

Hand, B., Prain, V., & Wallace, C. (2002). Influences of writing tasks on students' answers to recall and higher-level test questions. *Research in Science Education, 32*(1), 19–34.

Hewitt, P.G. (2001). *Conceptual physics* (9th ed.). Menlo Park, CA: Prentice-Hall.

Holliday, W.G. (2001, September). *Getting serious about reading instruction in science.* Paper presented at the Crossing Borders: Connecting Science and Literacy conference, Baltimore, MD.

Hynd, C.R., Guzzetti, B., Fowler, P., Williams, W., & Seward, A. (1997). *Text in physics class: The contribution of reading to learning counter-intuitive physics principles.* Technical report to the National Reading Research Center, Athens, GA.

Hynd, C., McNish, M., Qian, G., Keith, M., & Lay, K. (1994). *Learning counterintuitive physics principles: The effect of text and educational environment.* Technical report to the National Reading Research Center, Athens, GA.

Hynd, C., McWhorter, Y., Phares, V., & Suttles, W. (1994). The role of instructional variables in conceptual change in high school physics topics. *Journal of Research in Science Teaching, 31*(9), 933–946.

Illinois State Board of Education. (2002). Science—A common core of standards. In *Content area standards for educators* (2nd ed., pp. 145–154). Springfield, IL: Author. Available at http://www.isbe.net/profprep/CASCDvr/pdfs/27140_sciencecore.pdf

McKeown, M.G. (1985). Some effects of the nature and frequency of vocabulary instruction on the knowledge and use of words. *Reading Research Quarterly, 20*, 522–535.

National Institute of Child Health and Human Development (NICHD). (2000). *Report of the National Reading Panel. Teaching children to read: An evidence-based assessment of the scientific research literature on reading and its implications for reading instruction* (NIH Publication No. 00-4769). Washington, DC: U.S. Government Printing Office.

Towle, A. (2000). *Modern biology* (9th ed.). Austin, TX: Holt, Rinehart, & Winston.

CHAPTER 21

Choosing Science Textbooks:
Connecting Research to Common Sense

William G. Holliday

Science teachers selecting textbook-based programs need to consider many factors including content, comprehensibility, student and teacher support systems, motivational factors, adaptability to a target student population, and publisher's competence in providing after-purchase support. And teachers must base their decisions on a careful blend of research and practical concerns. Chambliss and Calfee offer research-based advice in *Textbooks for Learning* (1998). These researchers comprehensively reviewed how publishers' editorial, technical, and sales staffs coordinate the development and distribution of textbooks (i.e., textbook-based programs)—specifically science textbooks—to educators.

There are big changes afoot in the world of commercial textbook publishing that will serve to expand teachers' choices. The textbook publishing industry, similar to the publishing industry in general, is consolidated to an extent never before seen. Science teachers need to keep abreast of these developments, as current trends suggest that textbook publishers' corporate decisions probably will affect the way most students learn science in the coming years.

In this chapter, I point out recent improvements in science textbooks and then compare these improved textbooks with science-related trade books and government-funded textbook-based programs. I argue that teachers should incorporate the new generation of science textbooks into their classroom instruction. Finally, I propose six guidelines based in research and common sense for science teachers selecting textbook programs so that they can make better educated decisions.

Trade Books vs. Textbooks

Is it better to use trade books or textbooks in science class? (Trade books in contrast to textbooks cover limited content, seldom contain student support systems such as study objectives and questions, vary widely in quality and approach, but often express informational content situated in a wide variety of interesting contexts [Vacca & Vacca, 2002].) This important question does not ask which book is better because each medium serves a different purpose and, theoretically, is helpful to all students in reading, writing, discussing, and engaging in learning science. Teachers with a large assortment of trade books can accommodate students' individual needs, including their varied prior knowledge and conceptual interests. Such an instructional advantage also can provide teachers with increased opportunities to motivate students to read books of their own choosing, engaging them in authentic project-based activities directly supported by trade books covering highly specific domains and printed in language sometimes more familiar and appealing to some students. These important advantages suggest that trade books should be included in science programs whenever practical, especially at the elementary school level. Three experimental programs (Guthrie, Anderson, Alao, & Rinehart, 1999; McMahon, O'Hara, Holliday, McCormack, & Gibson, 2000; Romance & Vitale, 2001), which used trade books rather than textbooks alone as part of integrated reading and science programs, reportedly provided students with successful learning experiences in science and reading (Holliday, 2003a). Moreover, participating teachers were pleased with the effects of trade books as a means of having their students read about science.

On the other hand, Chall and Squire (1991), defending textbook use, remind us that some of the popular trade books touted as superior to textbooks are more similar to textbooks in one sense than is suggested by textbook critics (e.g., Vacca & Vacca, 2002). Authors of some trade books apparently have controlled, knowingly or unknowingly, the number and kinds of words used in trade book construction just as some textbook publishers have done in their products. In addition, these researchers hold that textbooks serve different purposes compared to trade books. For example, textbooks generally contain more densely written informational material including less-familiar vocabulary words and more complex sentence structures compared to popular trade books designed for K–12 students. Perhaps one advantage to students learning from these textbooks is that they may have an opportunity to learn how to read and comprehend demanding documents (Chambliss & Calfee, 1998; Holliday, 2002), which is essential in the preparation for later course work in secondary school, college, and technical schools.

An added advantage of textbook-based programs is availability. School districts are more likely to spend large sums of money on textbooks than on trade books. In addition, many teachers lack the science background, preparation time, and collegial support necessary when adopting a trade book-only approach, and they often lack experience at integrating reading and science instruction. State and local school district guidelines imposed on teachers also may militate toward the adoption of textbook- and not trade book-based programs, as textbooks often are designed with specific state standards and assessment instruments in mind. But counterarguments for using a good number of trade books, especially in elementary school science teaching, remain compelling (Chambliss & Calfee, 1998).

Recent Improvements in Science Textbooks

Many textbooks published more than a decade ago presented "needless comprehension challenges, exhibited...poor writing and...[were] difficult to understand," according to Chambliss and Calfee (1998, p. 13), who illustrate their point with analysis of a typical passage from a sixth-grade science textbook. But teachers and other educators need to inspect and compare textbooks produced today with ones published earlier; the current books still are far from perfect, but a lot has changed because of increased competition among sophisticated publishers for a greater share of the science textbook marketplace.

For example, errors in science textbooks remain a source of frustration for publishers and teachers (Galley, 2001), but current books contain only a fraction of the errors. The improved accuracy is because increased media, government, and citizen scrutiny of textbooks has forced publishers to employ many more expert reviewers to catch mistakes before the books are published. Some states, such as Texas, even impose penalties for errors, forcing publishers to work harder to locate errors before they run second printings destined for major markets. So, competition among publishers has forced them to take added care in providing products that are acceptable in the eyes of adoption committees at state and local levels.

The quality of the prose also is improved. In some past editions of science textbooks, some text passages were poorly written, failing to account for students' limited prior knowledge, presenting misleading information by using non-standard phrases such as "chemical paste," and using awkward wordings in need of heavy editing, as illustrated in the example below. This passage from a fifth-grade science textbook that was part of a best-selling series aimed at elementary school students is presented as an extreme example of this problem. The publisher removed the excerpt from subsequent editions. Apparently, none of the major publishers currently prints this type of prose. But, this aged textbook is probably still available in a few U.S. classrooms, as suggested by the Weiss study (2001).

> One type of electric cell is called a dry cell. A dry cell uses a chemical paste, carbon rod, and zinc case to produce a flow of electrons. Chemical reactions occur inside the dry cell. One reaction causes the wall of the zinc case to become negatively charged. Another reaction causes the carbon rod to become positively charged. The zinc case is called the negative pole. The carbon rod is called the positive pole. If the dry cell is connected to a circuit, electrons flow from the negative pole to the positive. This movement of electrons forms an electric current. (Mallinson, Mallinson, Smallwood, & Valentino, 1987, p. 170)

Another complaint by critics of textbooks reflects the apparent introduction of many new words into textbooks beyond students' readiness (Chambliss & Calfee, 1998; Vacca & Vacca, 2002). But, a comparative examination of past and present science textbooks suggests that some words have been deleted from earlier editions with the replacement of new words in current editions. Many books contain additional pages, but most of these pages present elaborated explanations of ideas with diagrams, line drawings, photographs, graphs, charts, and tables, which were used less frequently in earlier editions of the same textbooks. These enhanced visuals and the elimination of some scientific jargon have met with the approval of practicing science teachers who have some sense of what motivates and helps students learn science. Science teachers make most of the purchasing decisions regarding textbook adoptions (Chall & Squire, 1991), so publishers naturally listen to teachers when making developmental decisions. If teachers see unnecessary scientific words or other signs of textbook ineptness, they have a professional responsibility to complain to the publishers. For example, publishers' focus groups are used to assess teachers' preferences. Today's biology textbook publishers have reduced the number of unnecessary vocabulary words—for example, fungi-related terms such as *ostiole* and *perithecia* (see Otto & Towle, 1985, p. 292)—and have eliminated terms such as *Platyhelminthes* when the word *flatworm* would do (Towle, 1999, pp. 709–714). An examination of some popular textbooks targeting high school and college science students fails to reveal the fungi-related terms located even in the index of these modern texts. *Platyhelminthes* is not used in the high school textbooks and not located in the prose of two major general biology textbooks. However, *Platyhelminthes* is used in tables located in both popular college textbooks and as a subtitle in one of these textbooks. These terms apparently are considered relatively unimportant by editors of these textbooks.

The format, explanations, themes, and visuals contained in modern texts clearly are superior to those of earlier publications. Whether merely adding more colors to textbooks improves learning is questionable, although it seems self-evident that anyone reading a science textbook would prefer that the pictures and diagrams be in color. But textbook adoption committees are looking for more than splashes of color and large, fancy-looking visuals, and so publishers hoping to remain competitive must improve in more areas than page design and layout. One question that bears examination is whether or not colorful visuals distract students from other important textbook features. The answer to this question probably depends partly on the visuals' clarity and relevance to the presented science, although the research in this area is inconclusive (Carlson, Chandler, & Sweller, 2003; Holliday, 2001).

Recent science textbooks are more concerned with students' prior knowledge and their disposition toward learning science. For example, current authors assume more variance in students' abilities, as suggested by lengthened explanations of some important concepts and reduced coverage of seldom-used scientific terms. In addition, improved complex diagrams illustrating processes in the recent editions of science textbooks are more comprehensible. Science diagrams illustrate in an easy-to-understand fashion such principles as well-drawn stages of birth including dilation, expulsion, and the placental detachment (Bigg et al., 2004, p. 1013), and the clearly marked flow of blood through the human heart (Miller & Levine, 2004, p. 945). In chemistry, such complex diagrams with accompanying prose can be quite effective in illustrating complex ideas such as chemical bonding (Carlson, Chandler, & Sweller, 2003).

Publishers are getting better at presenting science in a way that seems relevant, interesting, and easier to comprehend than science presented in older textbooks. Clearly, there is still room for science textbook publishers to improve their products. There is every indication, however, that professionalism and market pressures will continue to influence them to do so.

Publishers' Influence

According to a recent analysis (Holliday, 2003b), major publishers increasingly are influencing science teaching and are likely to dominate what K–12 students read in future years as compared to a few years ago. Almost 90% of surveyed middle school science teachers (and 95% of high school teachers) ranked their science textbooks as "fair," "good," "very good" or "excellent," according to Weiss's (2001, p. 87) highly publicized survey of thousands of U.S. science teachers.

As Weiss (2001) states, "it is interesting to note that three publishers account for 70% of the textbook usage in grade K–4 science classes" (p. 82). Her data also reveal that two publishers account for 64% of textbook usage in grades 5–8, and three publishers account for 69% in grades 9–12. Four well-financed publishers in total now dominate the science textbook business, (1) providing needed capital to finance focus groups used to determine what science teachers are looking for in a textbook-based program, (2) developing elaborate textbook designs consistent with teachers' perceived needs, (3) providing expensive supplemental instructional materials including on-site training so teachers can devote their limited time to monitoring and fostering student learning, and (4) supporting online student instructional-assessment systems used to identify and ameliorate student learning problems. Some publishers are also offering the preservice training using online formats by matching their specific textbook-based programs directly to individual teachers' needs to learn specific content. In theory, school administrators in the future can keep precise track of their teachers' understanding of specific science content as it links to specific portions of an adopted textbook program. These latter developments are in direct competition with some government-funded developers of science curricular materials, often favored by academic and professional organizations (Holliday, 2003b).

Publishers vs. Government-Funded Developers

Other sources of science instruction materials are the various texts and curriculum packages produced under the auspices of the U.S. federal government. There are not very many of these, however, and their numbers are unlikely to increase under current funding schedules. Because these underfunded programs must compete with the extensively advertised products of commercial publishers, they never have made much of a dent in the market for science curriculum materials, according to data collected by Weiss (2001). An additional problem for government-funded programs is the need for extensive teacher inservice support because these programs usually are not designed for teachers with weak science backgrounds or who work in poorly funded school districts. In contrast, commercial publishers produce elaborate teacher's editions, user-friendly websites designed for teachers, and comprehensive ancillary materials often given to schools as inducements to purchase medium-to-large volumes of student edition textbooks (Holliday, 2002).

Whether the quality of publishers' products and services exceeds that of government-sponsored programs is a different question from who produces the superior programs because reasonable data-based studies of this issue are unavailable and very difficult to conduct (Kilpatrick, 2003). Yet, many academics seem critical or unsupportive of commercial publishers, although they have inadequate data to support some of their allegations (Holliday, 2003b). These criticisms often go unchallenged, which must leave some reading and science educators with poor impressions of the quality and practicality of today's science textbooks.

Six Guidelines for Textbook Selection

Because most science teachers select and use publishers' textbook-based programs (Weiss, 2001), they need to choose a book designed for a typical student population and want to base their decisions on research and common sense. Teachers should compare the following six factors with their own criteria:

1. Content
2. Comprehensibility
3. Student and teacher support systems
4. Motivational factors
5. Adaptability to a target student population
6. Publisher's competence in providing after-purchase support

Content

Teachers should ask, Will textbooks' content prepare students to succeed in subsequent science course work; on tests that assess student achievement; and toward my professional goals linked to literacy, students' independent use of learning strategies, and self-motivation toward science learning? Major publishers produce textbooks that are consistent with curricular standards adopted by most U.S. state departments of education, paying little attention to national guidelines. But this may be less important than it sounds: State guidelines usually are based on national standards, so textbooks aligned with state standards usually include national standards by default. In addition, many state and national guidelines lack specificity in recommended content, leaving science teachers with a good test of curricular flexibility. Textbook programs that cover content in exceptional depth, or in overpowering and unrealistic amounts, seldom succeed in the science teacher marketplace.

Comprehensibility

To test a book for comprehensibility, teachers should select sample chapters from textbooks under consideration, read various publishers' treatments of similar topics, and answer some analytical questions such as the following (Holliday, Yore, & Alvermann, 1994):

- What proportion or what kind of students will understand the explanations?
- What added instruction will be necessary to complement each textbook-based program's treatment of important content?
- Did the publishers' editors present clear explanations, visuals that go beyond fancy colors and confusing figures, analogies that work, recommended activities and long-term projects that complement other parts of the textbook, and questions and problems requiring mostly higher-order thinking?
- Does the textbook use an approach that makes students want to inquire more deeply into chapter concepts and issues, using principles of nature and science rather than providing some misleading description of "the scientific method"?
- Is the textbook's organization rational and consistent with that of other authorities such as local, state, and national guidelines?
- Does the textbook consider students' probable prior knowledge and their disposition toward school science?

Teachers with poor science backgrounds or little teaching experience who are assigned to judge textbooks' comprehensibility must receive support from experienced teachers familiar with the science content under consideration. Educators with little knowledge of science cannot judge independently the worth of a science textbook and should not try.

Student and Teacher Support Systems

Students need special help in learning science, unlike mature learners who have the needed learning strategies, reading fluency, background knowledge (including reasonable scientific vocabulary), and intrinsic motivation to want to inquire. So, teachers should ask the following questions when considering a book's support systems:

- Does the textbook provide students with adequate scaffolding to develop conceptual understanding and problem-solving strategies?
- Does the textbook provide a range of activities from which learners with varying backgrounds can make nontrivial decisions about which activities would be most productive?

- Does the textbook provide more than just good explanations for students with varying prior knowledge and dispositions?
- Does the textbook encourage students to read, write, speak, listen, and interact with other students?

Good textbooks provide devices to help students develop learning strategies they need in order to comprehend difficult content such as summaries, questions, visuals, problems, and activities that are realistic and interesting. Perhaps producers of textbooks and other learning materials will find ways to help additional students control their own learning rather than depending on the teacher or textbook to provide so much of the instructional support (Duffy, 2002).

Science teachers need a teacher's textbook edition that provides explanations concerning student study questions and worked problems. Science background information embedded in teacher's editions must go beyond the material presented in the student's edition. This is particularly important for practitioners with weak backgrounds in science and with little classroom experience. Sophisticated websites, videotaped exemplary lessons, and other supplementary materials provided by major publishers can support teachers' efforts. In the future, teachers should expect more of this kind of support from publishers.

Motivational Factors

Current textbooks are more likely to motivate students than earlier editions were. These newer textbooks contain real-life examples, more important science information, better visuals, more reasonable layouts and explanations, and prose that incorporates more active-voice verbs and improved analogies. Textbooks without these features should be avoided, as should radical approaches in which texts cover, for instance, a little content presented in extreme depth or overpowering and unrealistic amounts of content. Teachers also should be wary of textbooks with uninformative but flashy visuals, confusing layouts, incomplete and inadequate explanations, encyclopedic presentations of concepts, and boring prose full of unneeded modifiers and passive-voice verbs.

Newer books, with computer-based designs compared to yesteryear artist's hand drawings, logically engage more students in doing inquiry-oriented activities in which learners do more thinking rather than just following boring cookbook laboratory manuals. Textbook publishers must communicate to students that understanding science is neither so hard that it requires exceptional innate intelligence nor so easy that it is just a simple matter of engaging in mindless, fun-filled, nonthinking activities. With a proper balance, publishers are driving students toward understanding that learning science is engaging but also requires effort, persistence, patience, and flexibility. In this regard, all publishers and science editors need to focus more attention on research-based principles of motivation (see Alderman, 2004; Guthrie & Ozgungor, 2002).

Adaptability

Publishers must build books for large numbers of students with differing science backgrounds; academic abilities; dispositions toward schooling; and cultural, language, and numerical literacies. Textbook-based programs must have sophisticated ancillary materials, including websites that provide teachers with multiple ways of accommodating students' individual needs. For example, second-language learners often need prose presented in their first language or in some other way beyond reading the English-language student textbook. Teachers should seek textbook-based programs that incorporate ancillary materials for second-language learners or other student groups with particular needs.

Publisher Support

Teachers should ask themselves, Will the publisher be there after the textbooks are delivered to teach me how to use their science programs? Making purchases from sellers with unknown or questionable reputations can be costly and regrettable. Buying a textbook-based program means buying reasonable access to inservice support, sophisticated websites that are maintained over many years, and competent technical support. Some textbooks require more inservice support than others because of their complexity or novelty. Some of these high-maintenance textbook programs based in government-funded projects are quite good, but they can require added resources from organizations or publishers—resources often lacking in completeness because of inadequate government funding.

Conclusion

There is room for improvement in the development of publishers' science textbooks. Publishers are making changes to their products and services in reasonable ways that are consistent with some learning research and a great deal of common sense so they remain competitive.

Do trade books and other nontextbook materials represent critical resources to science teachers, essential materials not available in textbooks? Of course. Just assigning students to read science textbooks and engage in chapter activities described in student textbook editions makes little common or research-based sense. In their teacher's editions and ancillary materials, publishers recommend more reasonable suggestions to science teachers.

Should the government stop funding developers of federally supported learning materials because publishers can produce products and services cheaper and better in the eyes of practitioners, according to research related to sales and preferences of practicing science teachers? Of course not. The government must invest in educational research efforts; these produce valuable data and often produce products useful to some school districts. But whether these federally funded products are better than publishers' products remains a matter of opinion, not an established fact, in contrast to suggestions made in many practitioner outlets during the past few years (Holliday, 2003b).

Science teachers need to concentrate on more subtle questions about selecting components or selecting portions of entire programs that make sense for their unique situations. None of the makers of textbook-based programs, for instance, design materials with the assumption that teachers use the publisher's entire program. Fortunately, teachers are discriminating, using only what they deem appropriate for their particular classroom.

Selecting the best available science textbook challenges the most experienced practitioner. But thoughtful and reasonable selection procedures, knowledge of the industry and science teaching, alternative curricular materials, and the goal of choosing a textbook most likely to help students self-regulate their learning of science are ingredients consistent with research and common sense.

REFERENCES

Alderman, M.K. (2004). *Motivation for achievement: Possibilities for teaching and learning.* Mahwah, NJ: Erlbaum.

Bigg, A., Hagins, W.C., Kapicka, C., Lundgren, L., Rillero, P., Tallman, L.G., Zike, D., & National Geographic Society. (2004). *Biology: The dynamics of life.* New York: Glencoe/McGraw-Hill.

Carlson, R., Chandler, P., & Sweller, J. (2003). Learning and understanding science instructional material. *Journal of Educational Psychology, 95,* 629–640.

Chall, J.S., & Squire, J.R. (1991). The publishing industry and textbooks. In R. Barr, M. Kamil, P.B. Mosenthal, & P.D. Pearson (Eds.), *Handbook of reading research* (Vol. 2, pp. 120–146). White Plains, NY: Longman.

Chambliss, M.J., & Calfee, R.C. (1998). *Textbooks for learning.* Oxford, UK: Blackwell.

Duffy, G.G. (2002). The case for direct explanation of strategies. In C.C. Block & M. Pressley (Eds.), *Comprehension instruction: Research-based best practices* (pp. 28–41). New York: Guilford.

Galley, M. (2001, January 24). Middle school science texts full of errors, review finds. *Education Week*, p. 6.

Guthrie, J.T., Anderson, E., Alao, S., & Rinehart, J. (1999). Influence of concept-oriented reading instruction on strategy use and conceptual learning from text. *Elementary School Journal, 99*, 343–366.

Guthrie, J., & Ozgungor, S. (2002). Instructional contexts for reading engagement. In C.C. Block, & M. Pressley, (Eds.) *Comprehension instruction: Research-based best practices* (pp. 28–41). New York: Guilford Press.

Holliday, W.G. (2001). Assessing visuals in science textbooks and trade books. *Science Scope, 24*(4), 62–66.

Holliday, W.G. (2002). Selecting a science textbook. *Science Scope, 25*(4), 16–20.

Holliday, W.G. (2003a). Teaming up for science and reading success. *Science and Children, 40*(8), 38–40.

Holliday, W.G. (2003b). Methodological concerns about AAAS's project 2061 study of science textbooks. *Journal of Research in Science Teaching, 40*, 529–534.

Holliday, WG., Yore, L., & Alvermann, D.E. (1994). The reading-science learning-writing connection: Breakthroughs, barriers, and promises. *Journal of Research in Science Teaching, 31*(9), 877–893.

Kilpatrick, J. (2003). What works? In S.L. Senk & D.R. Thompson (Eds.), *Standards-based school mathematics curricula: What are they? What do students learn?* (pp. 471–488). Mahwah, NJ: Erlbaum.

Mallinson, G.G., Mallinson, J.B., Smallwood, W.L., & Valentino, C. (1987). Understanding electricity. In *The Silver Burdett elementary science program* (grade 5; pp. 154–179). Morristown, NJ: Silver Burdett.

McMahon, M.M., O'Hara, S.P., Holliday, W.G., McCormack, B.B., & Gibson, E.M. (2000). Curriculum with a common thread. *Science and Children, 37*, 30–35, 57.

Miller, K.R., & Levine, J. (2004). *Biology*. Upper Saddle River, NJ: Pearson/Prentice Hall.

Otto, J.H., & Towle, A. (1985). *Modern biology*. Austin, TX: Holt, Rinehart and Winston.

Romance, N.R., & Vitale, M.R. (2001). Implementing an in-depth expanded science model in elementary schools: Multi-year findings, research issues, and policy implications. *International Journal of Science Education, 23*(4), 373–404.

Towle, A. (1999). *Modern biology*. Austin, TX: Holt, Rinehart and Winston.

Vacca, R.T., & Vacca, J.L. (2002). *Content area reading: Literacy and learning across the curriculum*. Boston: Allyn & Bacon.

Weiss, I.R. (2001, November). *Report of the 2000 national survey of science and mathematics education*. Chapel Hill, NC: Horizon Research.

CHAPTER 22

Integrating Science and Literacy Instruction With a Common Goal of Learning Science Content

HAROLD PRATT AND NORBY PRATT

Any proposal for integrating two or more disciplines must be clear about the desired goals of the integration. Too often, the integration is presented as a goal in itself, in which the instructional strategies of the two disciplines—in this case science and literacy—simply are combined. Often, little or no thought is given to what it is the respective disciplines try to accomplish and how the methods of one discipline may advance the goals of the other.

The recent advent of standards-based accountability systems, combined with the research and lessons learned from successful schools, has taught the education community that a focus on the goals or outcomes of instruction is essential to making that instruction successful. Although there can be many desirable outcomes of the integration of two or more disciplines, including more efficient use of instructional time and increased student understanding of the connections between the disciplines, it is important not to lose sight of one overarching goal: the desired outcomes of both disciplines must be achieved, maintained, and enhanced.

The goal of science instruction is the achievement of what is generally known as scientific literacy. In describing scientific literacy, the U.S. National Science Education Standards (NSES) state:

> Scientific literacy means that a person can ask, find, or determine answers to questions derived from curiosity about everyday experiences. It means that a person has the ability to describe, explain, and predict natural phenomena. Scientific literacy entails being able to read with understanding articles about science in the popular press and to engage in social conversation about the validity about the conclusions. (National Research Council [NRC], 1996, p. 22)

Literacy instruction has a multitude of goals, but a major one is enhancing the student's comprehension of the content he or she is reading, writing, listening to, speaking, or viewing. This chapter will focus mainly on reading comprehension, which is considered to be a strategic process by which readers construct or assign meaning to a text by using the clues in the text and their own prior knowledge (Cooper, 2000). The commonality between the science and reading comprehension goals should be obvious; both place the understanding of subject matter content as the ultimate outcome.

Instruction in both disciplines often has additional supportive or subsidiary goals. In science, instruction often is designed to develop the skills of inquiry or understanding of the inquiry process. Literacy instruction, especially in the early grades, often focuses on the all-important goal of developing various literacy skills, in which reading dominates the instructional scene. In both disciplines, the subsidiary skills are a means to achieving the major goal of instruction—learning content. Distinguishing between the means and ends is critical to this discussion, as the role of skills in both disciplines often takes on the role of the ultimate rather than penultimate purpose of instruction. As an example, fluent word recognition is necessary to facilitate reading comprehension, but it is not sufficient. Additional strategies are needed to achieve comprehension of written text.

In science instruction, the process versus product debate has dragged on for far too long. It should be noted from the previous definition of scientific literacy that the goals of science instruction include developing the ability to inquire and gaining new knowledge through inquiry. The NSES (NRC, 1996) classify the role of inquiry as a means to the end of gaining new knowledge:

> a multifaceted activity that involves making observations; posing questions; examining books and other sources of information to see what is already known; planning investigations; reviewing what is already known in light of experimental evidence; using tools to gather, analyze and interpret data; proposing answers, explanations, and predictions; and communicating the results. (p. 23)

Again, note the role of the skills in helping reach explanations and answers. The importance of the literacy skills is explicit.

A number of researchers (e.g., Pearson, Roehler, Dole, & Duffy, 1992) point out the need for increasing the role of reading comprehension even in the primary grades. They blame the lack of attention to reading comprehension in the early grades for what is often called the fourth-grade slump. The phrase refers to a large number of students who master initial reading skills but are challenged by the more complex tasks required by subject area texts introduced in later grades (Manzo, 2002). In the same article, David Pearson states that "the fourth-grade slump" is becoming the "fourth-grade cliff" that kids are falling off because of an overemphasis on phonics and phonemic awareness. He goes on to say, "I don't see kids engaging with the big ideas...all those things that literature is all about" (p. 15).

The challenge of classrooms today is to bring the supportive skills from literacy and inquiry science together in a truly integrated way to support the goal of learning science content. In such a classroom, the integrated instruction would be an effective combination of learning from text, discussions, and encounters with the real world in laboratory investigations, field trips, and classroom projects. Although both strategies—literacy and inquiry—call for the construction of meaning from experience (Osborne & Whittrock, 1983), there is one major difference. The object or source of learning differs. In science, the object is physical phenomena in the natural world. In literacy, the object is the content described in the text or spoken word. Evidence from a variety of sources has demonstrated that hands-on science experiences increase student motivation and achievement in literacy skills (Guthrie & Wigfield, 1999; Klentschy, 2001). However, there is evidence that difficult scientific concepts are understood better by students who are taught scientific content using literature (Moore & Moore, 1989).

What We Know About How Students Learn Science

Although there is ample empirical evidence to support the integration of literacy skills and science inquiry skills, it is critical to know the fundamental reasons for these results by examining the recent research on how students learn science. Under the sponsorship of the National Research Council, an expert panel headed by John Bransford produced a seminal work, *How People Learn: Brain, Mind, Experience, and School* (Bransford, Brown, & Cocking, 1999). The new science of learning documented in this work places a heavy emphasis on learning with deep understanding, in contrast to learning that emphasizes memory from a behaviorist's perspective in which the recall of simple information dominates the goal of instruction. Deep understanding in science requires an individual to integrate the complex structure of many types of knowledge, including facts and information, the ideas of science, relationships between ideas, reasons for these relationships, and ways to apply these ideas. Bransford et al. (1999) gleaned a number of important principles about the learning process from the research, which were summarized by the National Research Council (2000).

1. Students build new knowledge and understanding on what they already know and believe. A student's prior knowledge (often called world knowledge in the comprehension literature) has been well established as the most important factor in his or her ability to comprehend new ideas, whether they be encountered in direct experience with phenomena or based on the comprehension of text material. The prior knowledge is derived from the learner's earlier learning experience, which may create preconceptions (sometimes called misconceptions) that work in a limited context but are often applied in situations in which they do not work. The notion that the sun revolves around the Earth is a classic example of an idea derived from experience that is useful in a limited context to know when it will rise, when it will set, and where it will be in the sky at any time of day on any day of the year, but ultimately leads to misunderstandings about the solar system if left unaltered.

Because the preconceptions are anchored in everyday experiences that young children encounter repeatedly, these ideas often are held tenaciously and are resistant to change. Conversations, reading, and adult explanations rarely affect the preconceptions.

2. Students formulate new knowledge by modifying and refining their current concepts and adding new concepts to what they already know. If traditional discourse and instructional methods are unable to change the preconceptions, what will? What is required is to find an experience in which the original preconception is no longer satisfactory to the student. This encounter with what might be called a discrepant event at first will unsettle or confuse a student, but if additional experiences and explanations are provided, the student may begin to change his or her view based on the evidence. As an example, students may believe that the weight of an object determines whether it sinks or floats, until they encounter two objects of the same weight with one floating and the other sinking. At this point, additional experience, not explanations, is in order. By spending time with a variety of objects of varying weights and volumes, students begin to see that a combination of the two properties seems to affect sinking or floating. Reshaping a ball of clay that originally sank so that it now floats also adds to the repertoire of experience, which slowly grows into a new way of viewing sinking and floating.

3. Understanding science is more than knowing facts; it involves placing and retrieving them in a conceptual framework. Much of science starts with observations that lead to facts and bits of information, but this knowledge is rather useless until it is organized in some way. The big ideas or concepts in science only provide the framework in which to place the facts, observations, and tidbits of knowledge. For example, the wild array of animals that students encounter by direct observation or through films and other media may seem to be unrelated until students learn that all the animals have the same basic survival needs. This also allows students to place themselves in the same framework and to see how similar they are to other animals.

4. Learning is mediated by the social environment in which learners interact with others. There is ample evidence that students learn best when they are interacting with others during the learning process. Their social engagement with the teacher and with other students during activities, discussions, and reading groups is a critical part of the learning process. Although the social engagement is important, it must be focused on a second dimension—the knowledge, outcomes, and goals determined to be important for these students. The third dimension of the environment is the use of assessment—both formative and summative—by the teacher and the students themselves. It is the mix and orchestration of these three dimensions—social interaction, knowledge, and assessment—that produces the greatest outcome.

5. The ability to apply knowledge to novel situations (transfer of learning) is affected by the degree to which students learn with understanding in a variety of contexts. In many respects, learning for deep understanding is synonymous with the ability to transfer the learning to novel situations. The ability of a student who has learned to classify one set of objects based upon their properties to apply this skill to a totally new set of objects is an example of the transfer of learning. Can the system of classifying plants be transferred to the classification of rocks and minerals? Expert learners are those who grasp the structure of the knowledge to such an extent that they can apply what they know in a wide range of situations. Transfer of learning can be enhanced by providing a variety of contexts in which students can use and practice using their knowledge. Transfer also is a function of how deeply the idea is understood.

6. Effective learning requires that students take control of their own learning. When students take control of their own learning, they recognize their role in interpreting information, both written and direct experience, and the way they use the information to generate new knowledge for themselves. They can reflect on their role in the learning process and the degree to which they are successful in reaching the learning outcome. This critical skill must be developed with the help of the teacher through the frequent use of explicitly explained formative assessment procedures. The teacher may ask the students to note what it is they have learned and what it is they still do not understand. The all-important part of this comprehensive strategy is assisting students with what they should do to reach the desired outcomes. In other words, if they are missing some key ideas or understandings, what do they do about it?

A Research-Based Instructional Model for Learning Science: Integrating Inquiry and Literacy Strategies

Research on learning science and reading comprehension holds great potential if it can guide classroom instruction in broad but nonprescriptive ways. The challenge is to select the strategies from both disciplines, based on the research on learning, then weave them together in a way that is synergistic with the goal of learning science content. A number of similar models have been proposed for inquiry-based science instruction that capitalize on students' prior knowledge, provide direct encounters with the phenomena as a means of constructing new concepts, and provide a wealth of opportunities for the use of literacy (Bybee, 1997).

Phase One: Engagement

Although each instructional model has its own language, they all start with an introductory or engagement phase designed to access the students' prior knowledge, raise questions, and motivate interest in a new topic. Such activities also allow the teacher to informally assess student interests, prior experience, and their vocabulary related to the topic. The experience at this point need not be long or complex, but it can be designed from a number of dimensions. It can involve allowing the students to ask questions, participate in shared reading experiences, engage in the initial phase of Carr and Ogle's (1987) K-W-L Plus strategy (What I know, what I want to learn, what I have learned), observe a discrepant event, and write in their journals.

Early in the first phase of science instruction, it will be important to determine the words or phrases that will ultimately be critical to understanding and communicating the desired outcome(s). What words are necessary in order to understand and communicate the concepts in the topic? What words will students read in written material? What words might some students know through previous experiences? To begin vocabulary instruction in the first and second phase of science instruction, it is helpful to record words as students use them during discussions. In addition to recording the technical words, record the common words that support the understanding of the topic. A word wall is a helpful strategy in all age-level classrooms to assist students in seeing written vocabulary words that are significant to a particular topic. The teacher records words as students engage in discussions and during any shared book experience. Then, the word wall or list becomes a visual reference for writing in journals and similar assignments.

During these phases, it is helpful to record a word the students use if it means the same as the associated scientific word. For example, students may use *sticky* instead of *cohesive* at this point. Later, the teacher will write the word *cohesive* next to *sticky* so students can begin to use the more technical vocabulary. The initial stages of K-W-L Plus also are an excellent written visual for all students to see the vocabulary words they are using or will encounter while studying a topic.

Phase Two: Exploration

The second phase is designed to allow the students to explore their current ideas through new experiences and to provide activities so that all students have common concrete experiences they and the teacher can use later to introduce new ideas formally. This phase of instruction often serves as an equalizer by providing common experiences and background world knowledge that is a critical element in improving reading comprehension in subsequent reading activities. Some students may have encountered the material earlier in school or in family activities, but the classroom instruction reinforces it and brings it into the present so that it can be used as the instruction progresses. For some students, the exploration will allow them to build on their prior concepts; for others, their preconceptions may be challenged by the activities or experiences in this phase. In either case, the beginning of generating new concepts should start to emerge.

The activities in the second phase should include as much direct experience with the phenomena, objects, materials, or organisms as possible. Well-illustrated text material, photographs, video, and other means to enrich and expand direct experience can also be provided. Eldredge, Reutzel, and Hollingsworth (1996) demonstrated that students involved in shared book experiences enhanced their reading comprehension development, oral reading, fluency, and vocabulary development and that shared book experiences were more effective than round-robin practices. The shared book experience provides the same information to all students at the same time. With the wide range of experiences that students bring to the classroom, the shared book experience can narrow the gap of known information and begin to build a common base of information and vocabulary.

Care should be taken at this phase of using reading material and other media not to preempt or over-guide the thinking of students, but rather to provide a rich array of firsthand and indirect encounters with phenomena.

The teacher should encourage students to interact, raise questions and propose answers, discuss, and even argue in a constructive manner their interpretation of their observations and experiences.

During this phase, new words will be encountered and should be added to the vocabulary list. The vocabulary should not be comprehensive but simply a recognition of words students are using. Minimal vocabulary instruction will improve students' chances of understanding these words in context (Jenkins, Stein, & Wysocki, 1984). As students move through the topic and begin to form opinions, their word knowledge in reading and writing will be strengthened by the casual reference to important words placed on a word wall. In addition, as students write in journals during the first two phases, they will use the words on the word wall in their writing and note taking.

Phase Three: Explanation

In some ways, the third phase is a seamless extension of the exploration in which students have been engaging for several days. In this phase, with support and facilitation of the teacher, students continue to create new ideas and explanations based on their exploration activities. In the early part of this phase, student explanations should dominate the discussion. Then, the teacher will find ways to introduce accepted scientific explanations and vocabulary. Explanations, whether they are from the student or the teacher, should be connected to the experiences, observations, and evidence in the earlier phases of instruction. In the third phase, the information and ideas that emerge should be connected when possible to some larger framework that allows students to begin to see the new ideas as related to other experiences and concepts.

The third phase is the anchor stage of the instructional model. The objective or desired outcome of the instructional sequence should begin to take shape in this phase. When planning a series of lessons or activities following this instructional model, it is often useful in this phase to begin the development of the outcome and clarify the major idea or skill to be learned. The phases that precede it are designed to support the development of the outcome; the phases that follow should reinforce it.

This is the time to add scientific terms on the word wall, in addition to the informal words used by students during phases one and two. For example, write *cohesive* beside *sticky*. This is an excellent time to begin to add to the "What have I learned" portion of the K-W-L Plus if this strategy was used in phase one or two. Direct instruction on word meaning also is given during this phase. Stahl and Fairbanks (1986) found that teaching vocabulary directly increased student comprehension of new material. Powell (1980) found that the use of imagery produced achievement gains in word knowledge and reading comprehension. As an example, if the students have experienced several examples of what habitat means to plants, animals, people (children and teacher), and things, students can be asked to draw or graphically represent their observations and ideas. This activity can be revisited in the next phase, and new insights can be added. In phase five, the visualization activity could be used as part of the student's presentation and as an informal assessment for the teacher.

Phase Four: Elaboration

In the fourth phase of the instructional model, students have an opportunity to use what they have learned up to this point in a new situation. This allows them to reinforce correct ideas, transfer them to new situations, and continue to develop their understanding or explanations if they had difficulties in the previous phase. A multitude of resources and strategies are possible in this phase, as students are now ready to elaborate on their own learning and discover what others have written. It may be useful for them to use their ideas in short stories, presentations to others, or other means of communicating to other audiences.

In phase four, students begin to organize their thinking and formulate plans for a final product. More reorganizing of information can be done by extending the learning process using the *plus* in K-W-L Plus and by making a semantic map or graphic organizer. All these activities give students practice in applying vocabulary words from the word wall and from K-W-L Plus for their final product.

In this phase, reading comprehension ability can be enhanced by finding opportunities to challenge students with text tasks that require more than simple recall. How can the ideas in the text be used in their world?

Phase Five: Evaluation

In this last phase, both teacher and students will devise one or more means to evaluate how well students understand, communicate, and defend their thinking and explanations. A formal presentation, using a combination of methods—written, spoken, graphic presentation—should provide the teacher with enough examples to be able to assess students' levels of knowledge and their use of critical words.

The assessment at this point is essentially summative for ideas or skills developed in the previous four phases. Best practice suggests, and the research on learning confirms, that teachers should help students by using a variety of formative (often embedded) assessments and help them develop self-assessment procedures throughout all phases of the instructional model. Students need to develop the skill and procedure of asking questions of each other, presenting explanations and listening to critiques, and a variety of other strategies that help students take control of assessing their own learning. When students have an opportunity to reflect on what they have done and learned through writing and discussion, they are developing the metacognitive and reflective practices that have proven to be effective in the learning process.

Advantages of the Instructional Model

The instructional model proposed here has a number of strengths and advantages that are worth noting:

1. The model is based on principles derived from the research into how people learn. Although the research does not suggest a specific order in which the principles should be applied, common sense suggests that some principles come before others.

2. The model is similar to those used by virtually every elementary and middle school standards-based science curriculum project funded by the National Science Foundation.

3. The model follows the inductive process generally associated with actual science research. Students are engaged with questions and investigative activities before they are called on to create their own explanations or understand explanations from the teacher or text.

4. The model provides an example of how reading and other literacy skills used in concert with science inquiry skills can support students' learning of science content. A variety of supportive skills from both disciplines were carefully placed in the model to enhance the goal of learning content.

5. The combination of inquiry and reading skills in the model should improve students' comprehension of science text material. One of the main determinants of whether a student can comprehend text is the knowledge of the world—also called prior knowledge—that the student brings to the text. The research from Vacca and Vacca (1999) indicates that a student's prior knowledge is "the single most important resource in learning with texts" (p. 25) The reading com-

prehension literature does not address whether schools have a responsibility for providing this world knowledge, but the science activities suggested in this model are designed specifically to meet this need in order to increase the students' abilities to comprehend science text material.

REFERENCES

Bransford, J.D., Brown, A.L., & Cocking, R.R. (Eds.), & Committee on Developments in the Science of Learning. (1999). *How people learn: Brain, mind, experience, and school.* Washington, DC: National Academy Press.

Bybee, R. (1997). *Achieving scientific literacy: From purpose to practice.* Portsmouth, NH: Heinemann.

Carr, E., & Ogle, D. (1987). K-W-L Plus: A strategy for comprehension and summarization. *Journal of Reading, 30,* 626–631.

Cooper, J.D. (2000). *Literacy: Helping children construct meaning.* Boston: Houghton Mifflin.

Eldredge, J.L., Reutzel, D.R., & Hollingsworth, P.M. (1996). Comparing the effectiveness of two oral reading practices: Round-robin reading and the shared book experience. *Journal of Literacy Research, 28*(2), 201–225.

Guthrie, J.T., & Wigfield, A. (1999). How motivation fits into a science of reading. *Scientific Studies of Reading, 3*(3), 199–205.

Jenkins, J.R., Stein, M.L., & Wysocki, K. (1984). Learning vocabulary through reading. *American Educational Research Journal, 21*(4), 767–787.

Klentschy, M.P. (2001, August). *Science-Literacy Connections: A case study of the Valle Imperial Project in Science, 1995–1999.* Paper presented at the Crossing Borders: Connecting Science and Literacy conference, Baltimore, MD.

Manzo, K.K. (2002, March 6). RAND: Don't let basics obstruct comprehension strategies. *Education Week,* p. 15.

Moore, S.A., & Moore, D.W. (1989). Literacy through content: Content through literacy. *The Reading Teacher, 41,* 170–171.

National Research Council (NRC). (1996). *National science education standards.* Washington, DC: National Academy Press.

National Research Council (NRC). (2000). *Inquiry and the national science education standards: A guide for teaching and learning.* Washington, DC: National Academy Press.

Osborne, R.J., & Whittrock, M.C. (1983). Learning science: A generative process. *Science Education, 67*(4), 489–508.

Pearson, P.D., Roehler, L.R., Dole, J., & Duffy, G. (1992). Developing expertise in reading comprehension. In S.J. Samuels & A.E. Farstrup (Eds.), *What research has to say about reading instruction* (2nd edition, pp. 145–199). Newark, DE: International Reading Association.

Powell, G. (1980, December). *A meta-analysis of the effects of "imposed" and "induced" imagery upon word recall.* Paper presented at the annual meeting of the National Reading Conference, San Diego, CA. (ERIC Document Reproduction Service No. ED199644)

Stahl, S.A., & Fairbanks, M.M. (1986). The effects of vocabulary instruction: A model-based meta-analysis. *Review of Educational Research, 56*(1), 72–110.

Vacca, R.T., & Vacca, J.L. (1999). *Content area reading: Literacy and learning across the curriculum* (6th ed.). Menlo Park, CA: Longman.

REACHING TEACHERS

I n this section, three master teacher educators describe the importance of engaging teachers in the inquiry process. In chapter 23, "Mind Engagement: What Is Not Typically Accomplished in Typical Science Instruction," Robert E. Yager elaborates on the principles underlying his notion of inquiry and then discusses the habits of mind as well as the classroom practices that support that vision. Community and world problems become the site for authentic and personalized investigations. Yager wants teachers to invite student thinking by engaging young people in real issues that matter to them. Only then, he believes, can students learn to evaluate and trust their thinking, or later, to explain their thinking. Yager offers the Iowa Chautauqua Model as one successful example of such integration.

In chapter 24, "'Reading the World Before Reading the Word': Implications for Professional Development of Teachers of Science," Hubert M. Dyasi and Rebecca E. Dyasi use their experience as science educators to discuss the role of literacy in science education for both children and teachers. Because the physical world is accessible to and shared by all human beings, situating language development in the study of that world makes sense for young people of various backgrounds, the authors note. The chapter provides a theoretical overview of the ways in which language study and science study are consonant and, in fact, support one another. The authors then detail the activities and insights gained from their own programs at the City College Workshop Center at City University of New York and at Long Island University, Brooklyn—hands-on, inquiry-based programs that call on teachers to embed literacy skills such as data collection, data recording, discussion, and presentation into their studies of the world.

Professional development that seeks to link literacy and science instruction presents special challenges for school systems. The goal here is to create opportunities that support inquiry in both domains.

CHAPTER 23

Mind Engagement: What Is Not Typically Accomplished in Typical Science Instruction

ROBERT E. YAGER

Too many science teachers view their mission as conveying what they know about science to students who will need this knowledge in order to achieve later academic and professional goals. But many students put up with the science they are exposed to because they have been convinced that they need to memorize the skills and concepts in the curriculum, textbook, or teacher's repertoire. Students rarely get a taste of what science really is. Simpson (1963) has described science as five activities:

1. asking questions about the natural universe, i.e., being curious about the objects and events in nature;

2. trying to answer one's own questions, i.e., proposing possible explanations;

3. designing experiments to determine the validity of the explanation offered;

4. collecting evidence from observations of nature, mathematics calculations, and whenever possible, experiments carried out to establish the validity of the original explanations; and

5. communicating the evidence to others who must agree with the interpretation of the evidence in order for the explanation to become accepted by the broader community of scientists. (p. 3)

Instead of gaining experience with any aspect of science as a human activity, students are merely told what they need to remember to pass tests and to get good grades. This is, of course, a far cry from real science—a far cry, as well, from an instructional environment that produces what could be described as "mind engagement."

True mind engagement requires student involvement in defining the content. Students need to question, to wonder, to pursue their own interests. In order to give students genuinely scientific experiences, science study needs to be like a mystery, an evaluation of guesses concerning interpretations of nature. Activities in science classrooms should include student inventions. Original products should be created by students to permit them to be "experts." But this is not what usually happens. Instead, typical instruction usually leads most students to feel inadequate rather than empowered. (See chapter 5 of this book for more discussion of how to enrich students' experience with science.)

The fact that most science instruction does not yet strive for, much less achieve, this level of engagement indicates that many adults, teachers, and other stakeholders remain ignorant of the nature of science and scientific thinking. But my call for mind engagement and for science instruction that more closely resembles the work that real scientists do is neither radical nor particularly new. The U.S. National Science Education Standards (NSES), published in 1996 by the National Research Council (NRC), synthesize the best thinking and practices of hundreds of leading scientists and science educators. The student-centered, investigational model previously mentioned is central to the NSES's vision of ideal science instruction.

The type of instruction outlined in the NSES is not just the latest instructional fad. The NSES reforms directly address the gravest failings of traditional science instruction, and at the same time make use of what we know about how and why people learn (and do not learn). The fact is that much of what continues to pass for science education is counterproductive: Founded on misconceptions not only about science but about the educational needs of students, traditional science instruction simply does not help students achieve what the American Association for the Advancement of Science calls *scientific literacy* (Rutherford & Ahlgren, 1990).

Carl Sagan stated, "Everybody starts out as a scientist. Every child has the scientist's sense of wonder and awe" (NRC, 1998, p. 1). But sustaining this wonder and awe in traditional science study rarely occurs. Teachers, parents, and school and community leaders all must accept responsibility for finding ways to ensure that children's inherent interest in science is nurtured rather than destroyed. In a rapidly changing, increasingly technological world, everyone needs to understand science and technology. Teachers and administrators increasingly need parents and others in the community to become partners in an attempt to make sure all students in schools know what they need to know. Students need to be able to ask questions, construct explanations, test those explanations with currently held explanations, and communicate their ideas to others.

One of the biggest obstacles to improved science instruction and to fostering mind engagement in our students is the reluctance of many educators and students to cross the traditional boundaries between academic disciplines. This reluctance is problematic, if for no other reason than that the world and its problems cannot be divided into such neatly defined categories. But this is not the only reason for a cross-curricular approach: Put simply, working on real-world problems the same way real-world problem solvers do will vastly increase students' interest in and mind engagement with their studies. In order to achieve this, improved preservice programs and staff development efforts certainly need to be offered to accomplish the goals.

This chapter looks at mind engagement and the benefits of teaching for mind engagement from several angles. First, it is important to contextualize mind engagement within cognitive theories of thinking and learning. Second, I consider how best to prepare teachers to make these improvements in their own classrooms. I describe a successful instructional model in which cross-curricular connections—including, most prominently, science—help foster a more dynamic and motivating learning environment for students as well as teachers. Finally, I connect mind engagement in the classroom to the inquiry and investigation work that is the real essence of science.

Gaining Mind Engagement

Basic to mind engagement are the workings of the human brain. How can we get the brain focused on the problems that plague modern society? How can science (and technology) help? Certainly, science will never be seen as vital in school programs until its broader meaning and its uses in resolving current problems are firmly established.

Many such as J.T. Bruer (1997, 1999), Wolfe and Brandt (1998), and Sousa (1995) now see the potential in reforming education of understanding the human brain and how it functions. There is the inherent belief that if the human brain were better understood, more could be done to gain mind engagement. Mind engagement is seen as the first step necessary if learning is to occur (Starnes & Paris, 2000).

Smith (1986) has captured the problem with gaining mind engagement in typical K–12 and college science classrooms. He writes, "We under-rate our brain and our intelligence—reluctance to learn cannot be attributed to the brain. Learning is the brain's primary function, its constant concern, and we become restless and frustrated if there is no learning to be done" (p. 6).

It is apparent that it is not science, technology, or both that fail to gain mind engagement. All people learn; they cannot stop their brains from operating. The problem is that most of what is taught in the guise of science is not interesting, relevant, or a stimulus to the brain. If we are to succeed as a society in improving children's learning, changes are needed in how we involve and include learners in classrooms, and maybe more important, beyond the school itself. Too often, learners do not learn what teachers teach.

A major goal—sometimes unstated—is to gain mind engagement prior to assigning work, providing information, or testing to see if information can be recalled accurately and completely. Perhaps better goals are to try to get students to think, then get them to trust their thinking, and finally to get them to explain their thinking. This sequence rarely occurs in most classrooms; most teachers see their role as assigning and getting through material as defined in the curriculum and/or the textbooks. They feel that if students seem to understand, and if they remember and repeat the information and skills directly taught to them, that minds have been engaged and learning has occurred.

Too often, a true dialogue between teachers and students or, more important, among students, does not occur. The purpose of dialogue in a learning situation is fulfilled through mutual respect and when certain preconditions are achieved. Examples of preconditions for teachers could include the following:

- Make a commitment to be fully present—bring yourself to the game or moment
- Adopt a collaborative role rather than an advocacy role
- Allow everything
- Be open to learning from one another
- Allow for silence—be patient
- Recognize assumptions of self and others
- Be willing to embrace risk
- Ask questions for clarification
- Always notice and acknowledge what seems to be a surprise

The teachings of Tao illustrate the power of teacher-student dialogue. In a sense, a teacher's actions are more important than verbal instructions. According to the philosophy of Tao, "The Master doesn't talk, he acts. When his work is done, the people say, 'Amazing: we did it, all by ourselves!'" (Mitchell, 1988).

The opposing situation suggests a more typical classroom. Silberman (1996) illustrates what happens when teachers teach directly:

You can tell people what they need to know very fast. But, they will forget what you tell them even faster. People are more likely to understand what they figure out for themselves than what you figure out for them. (p. 21)

Hullfish and Smith (1961) summarized what is needed to gain mind engagement, which in turn can result in learning and some growth in terms of scientific literacy: "Knowledge is constructed and continuously reconstructed...we must operate on experience to produce knowledge—as a result knowledge has a personal quality and is unique for each individual" (p. 43).

Gaining mind engagement is a requisite across the curriculum. Achieving it is still another example of crossing the borders that seems so difficult to cross in many schools and colleges.

The Value of a Relevant Curriculum

Mind engagement occurs easily and readily if the curriculum is seen by students as relevant. Usually, standard textbooks in science—and even trade books on science topics—interest few students. Most of these books make science seem impersonal, not useful, and unrelated to daily living.

Dewey (1938) often mentioned the value of a relevant curriculum—the necessity for real learning to come from actual involvement. The arbitrary division of the curriculum and the school day into subjects or courses may be detrimental to real learning. We may be missing every opportunity to involve students directly in real learning, and missing the chance of offering a program that is preparatory for students who will live and operate in a future not totally unlike the present. Instead of isolating students and forcing them to learn information solely from books and teachers—information that often seems unrelated to the world today—perhaps a focus on the world today (i.e., current issues and problems) will provide the missing ingredient that is necessary for real learning to occur. Such efforts will likely provide the needed bridges to cross borders between science and the humanities.

Cognitive psychologists (Bransford, Brown, & Cocking, 1999; Champagne & Klopfer, 1984; Halpern, 1992) are united in their observations that most high school graduates (college students and adults as well) have many naïve theories or misconceptions about the real world. They seem to retain these views even when they complete and succeed in advanced courses dealing with scientific concepts and theories. Apparently, the science learned in school is not internalized. The best students perform well on tests and advance to the next level; however, they internalize and believe interpretations of the real world based on real experiences they have had.

There is often a discrepancy between school science and real-world experiences. Real-world experiences with science are remembered more than experiences with the science of textbooks in classrooms and laboratories. There is every reason to believe that similar discrepancies exist between school experiences and personal experiences for students in other subjects as well. This suggests reasons and pathways (e.g., staff development efforts) to cross the borders that divide the curriculum, prevent learning, and create competitive situations across the curriculum.

There is certainly no shortage of real-world issues that could inform classroom instruction. Some like Shamos (1995) and Piel (1993) fear that more issues—and more complicated ones—arise than can be dealt with. There are problems of energy depletion, population explosion, food supplies, toxic wastes, nuclear proliferation, nutrition, disease, warfare, communications, transportation, agricultural production, synthetics, computerization, and space exploration. It is difficult to conceive of any newsworthy current event that is not a science- or technology-related issue. Appropriate issues will provide a need for mathematics and a point of departure for social studies. As for language arts, why not use current problems and issues to practice good communication and to develop better writing, reading, and speaking skills? It would seem that an issue focus in a school would have advantages for all students, such as helping them view school as preparation for living. Further, most curriculum areas could meet their objectives more easily because students would be more motivated to learn once they could see the real-life uses and connections of the material under discussion. Teachers would not have to insist that their students "need to know" and yet find it difficult to justify the need. But, such changes will require different and more effective staff development programs as well as preparatory programs at the 1,600 colleges and universities that currently offer such programs.

Some schools, such as those in Chariton, Iowa, involve students and teachers in selecting an annual issue. For two years, an aspect of space technology has been chosen as a focus in middle school science. Every department in the school gets involved with the issue. Many aspects of space exploration are rooted in basic physical science. Industrial technology is directly involved with communication systems, principles of flight, and design and construction. There are economic, psychological, government, and sociological aspects—they make up the social science focus. The need for communication is great—letter writing, public forums, debate, and journalism. The art department of the school is intimately involved; there also are direct ties to foreign language. Mathematics is used in a variety of ways—always because of the need, not because there is another important skill to teach.

The Iowa Chautauqua Model, started in 1983, is a staff development program that supports teachers for a full year in learning about and considering science in the context of society and the world. From the outset, the program has sought to help teachers change in terms of the teaching strategies they use and with regard to the place of curriculum in defining what they do. The program was one of the first to be validated by the National Diffusion Network. Information concerning the model and evidence of its successes with teachers has been reported widely (Blunck, 1993; Blunck & Yager, 1996).

Greeno (1992) has reported,

> If we view the ability to think as a natural endowment, we will expect that its growth will depend mainly on opportunities to think. The ability grows through a progression of activities that increase their difficulty, but they involve thinking from the beginning, rather than having the opportunity to think withheld until an inventory of alleged materials for thinking has been stockpiled. According to this view, we should try to change education in science and mathematics so that mathematical and scientific thinking are the main focus of activities in situations of learning, enabling students to develop their capabilities of scientific and mathematical thinking through elaboration, refinement, and modification of capabilities that they bring. (p. 40)

Instead of arguing about the breadth and depth of content to include in science courses, the contexts provided and the thinking they induce will lead to content (and process skills) because they are needed. The usual situation is to teach content and process skills because teachers and curriculum developers feel they are important and will be the basis for evaluating student success (and learning?). Greeno (1992) has synthesized the cognitive science research, which suggests that

> the task of school learning should primarily be to strengthen and refine student capabilities to think, rather than primarily providing knowledge of terms and procedures that are thought to be the materials on which thinking has to be based. (p. 41)

Many projects for the Chautauqua teachers start with a common situation—and at times a comical one. Some have included clogged toilets, a dripping faucet, a disaster caused by severe weather, an automobile accident, or a current event reported in the local news. It is often amazing to see the connections students can make to basic science, and to the basic content of a variety of school disciplines, when they are encouraged to do so. When content is introduced by the teacher, textbook, or course of study, it is rare for the students (or teacher) to see or to identify any connections to their daily lives.

In every instance, staff development projects such as the Iowa Chautauqua Model stimulate effective programs that affect teachers and learners more than science alone. The focus on community and world problems becomes something with which all can identify. The community becomes the laboratory, not just a place called a science laboratory, where laboratory guides give directions geared toward results and answers already known to the students. The activities are designed to verify what teachers and textbooks proclaim. The amount of communication among the faculty as a whole increases by 50%. There is need to work with other educators; the learning occurs in more than one classroom or department. There is more community involvement, including parents, business leaders, and service organizations. The teaching model is the major ingredient leading to the change. Administrators—central office level as well as building level— become involved. In some instances, administrators are directly involved with establishing the new programs. In all instances, community leaders become directly involved with school programs. New alliances are created and new partnerships are formed; in several schools, community members initiate new organizations to support school efforts. Teacher inservice training becomes much more important: Teachers are quick to realize that they must continue to grow, and that the best teachers are involved learners. In all cases, teachers become much more involved with each other, with students, with school officials, with community leaders, and with persons across the nation and world.

Although real societal issues may provide a significant organizing force for the school program, expertise with developing needed communication skills is another vital link in developing an exemplary school program. Skills with interviewing, writing, speaking, reading, and debating are needed if teachers and students are to become involved in resolving school, community, state, national, and international problems. Many science teachers may not have enough skills in teaching about societal issues (traditionally viewed as the realm of the social sciences), applications of science (traditionally handled in applied areas such as agriculture, industrial arts, and homemaking), and effective communication (seen as the primary responsibility of educators in language arts). A focus on local issues can help schoolwork to be seen as more relevant as teachers and students work together on one or more problems. Such cooperative efforts serve as a better model for future citizens who must work together to resolve problems and to advance a society's common culture. And, such efforts accomplish the needed changes in producing a more universal definition for literacy itself.

Active Learning Results in Mind Engagement

According to the 1993 National Survey of Science and Mathematics Education, approximately three of four teachers surveyed in all grades said that hands-on activities should be part of science instruction. However, the same survey reported that in half the elementary science classes studied and in nearly two thirds of the middle school and high school classes studied, terms and facts were emphasized, and the largest proportion of class time was devoted to lecture and discussion (Smith et al., 2002).

Parents, teachers, and psychologists know that children learn best through concrete experiences. Young children often need to have a particular experience first before they are ready to read about or discuss an underlying concept. Older students also benefit from engaging in scientific investigations to learn important science concepts (Bransford et al., 1999).

An instructional approach patterned after the way scientists study the natural world, called *inquiry*, can achieve several important results. Through a combination of hands-on and minds-on learning, inquiry engages students in a process through which they learn science (and other) content best. By carrying out investigations, students learn how to make observations, pose questions, plan investigations, use tools to gather information, make predictions, propose explanations, communicate results, and reflect on the processes they have used. As students engage in these processes, they develop the ability to think critically and to learn how to learn. Students learn to use inquiry to acquire ideas and information on their own (NRC, 1996).

In addition, students learn that what they are doing is similar to the way scientists develop hypotheses, test their ideas, and discover new ideas or create new products. The uniqueness of science and a major reason it has made a large contribution to civilization is its basis in observations and experimentation. Scientists learn by starting with what is already known and then asking questions about what they do not know. These questions often lead to hypotheses about what the answers might be. The most useful hypotheses are those that can be tested experimentally. When the experimental results appear to agree with those predicted by hypothesis, a scientific theory begins to emerge. If the results are confirmed by others and no evidence to the contrary is found, scientists become more and more confident in the theory, and it becomes treated as an accurate and usable explanation that is then often summarized and used in general textbooks and science courses (Simpson, 1963; Ziman, 1984).

This ability to learn how to learn through inquiry also should be a crucial component of exemplary science teaching and learning. Knowing how to learn means that young people can locate new information and data, answer their own questions about the natural world, and solve problems with new technologies. It is a process not always used in other subjects and is one of the reasons science should be a part of all students' education from the beginning (Bransford et al., 1999). This may be another border to cross in education. Once it is crossed, the border will no longer exist. Staff development efforts such as the Iowa Chautauqua Model can help—perhaps because the model calls for college-school partnerships in which professionals work together for at least three years to accomplish the new goals and the reform conditions together. When such collaborative efforts occur, the borders become easy to cross.

REFERENCES

Blunck, S.M. (1993). *Evaluating the effectiveness of the Iowa Chautauqua Program: Changing the reculturing behaviors of science teachers K–12.* Unpublished doctoral dissertation, University of Iowa, Iowa City, Iowa.

Blunck, S.M., & Yager, R.E. (1996). The Iowa Chautauqua Program: A proven in-service model for introducing STS in K–12 classrooms. In R.E. Yager (Ed.), Science/technology/society as reform in science education (pp. 298–305). Albany, NY: State University of New York Press.

Bransford, J.D., Brown, A.L., & Cocking, R.R. (Eds.). (1999). *How people learn: Brain, mind, experience, and school.* Washington, DC: National Academy Press.

Bruer, J.T. (1997). Education and the brain: A bridge too far. *Educational Researcher, 26*(8), 4–16.

Bruer, J.T. (1999). In search of brain-based education. *Phi Delta Kappan, 80*(9), 648–654, 656–657.

Champagne, A.B., & Klopfer, L.E. (1984). Research in science education: The cognitive psychology perspective. In D. Holdzkom & P.B. Lutz (Eds.), *Research within reach: Science education* (pp. 171–189). Charleston, WV: Research and Development Interpretation Service, Appalachia Educational Laboratory.

Dewey, J. (1938). *Experience and education.* New York: Macmillan.

Greeno, J.G. (1992). Mathematical and scientific thinking in classrooms and other situations. In D.F. Halpern (Ed.), *Enhancing thinking skills in the sciences and mathematics* (pp. 39–61). Hillsdale, NJ: Erlbaum.

Halpern, D.F. (Ed.). (1992). *Enhancing thinking skills in the sciences and mathematics.* Hillsdale, NJ: Erlbaum.

Hullfish, H.G., & Smith, P.G. (1961). *Reflective thinking: The method of education.* New York: Greenwood.

Mitchell, S. (Trans.). (1988). *Tao Te Ching.* New York: Harper & Row.

National Research Council (NRC). (1996). *National science education standards*. Washington, DC: National Academy Press.

National Research Council (NRC). (1998). *Every child a scientist: Achieving scientific literacy for all*. Washington, DC: National Academy Press.

Piel, E.J. (1993). Decision-making: A goal of STS. In R.E. Yager (Ed.), *What research says to the science teacher* (Vol. 7, pp. 147–152). Washington, DC: National Science Teachers Association.

Rutherford, F.J., & Ahlgren, A. (1990). *Science for all Americans* (American Association for the Advancement of Science Project 2061). New York: Oxford University Press.

Shamos, M.H. (1995). *The myth of scientific literacy*. New Brunswick, NJ: Rutgers University Press.

Silberman, M. (1996). *Active learning: 101 strategies to teach any subject*. Boston: Allyn & Bacon.

Simpson, G.G. (1963). Biology and the nature of science. *Science, 139*(3550), 81–88.

Smith, F. (1986). *Insult to intelligence: On bureaucratic invasion of our classrooms*. New York: Arbor House.

Smith, P.S., Banilower, E.R., McMahon, K.C., & Weiss, I.R. (2002). *The national survey of science and mathematics education: Trends from 1977 to 2000*. Retrieved October 21, 2003, from http://www.horizon-research.com/reports/2002/2000survey/trends.php

Sousa, D.A. (1995). *How the brain learns: A classroom teacher's guide*. Reston, VA: National Association of Secondary School Principals.

Starnes, B.A., & Paris, C. (2000). Choosing to learn. *Phi Delta Kappan, 81*, 392–397.

Wolfe, P., & Brandt, R. (1998). What do you know from brain research? *Educational Leadership, 56*(3), 8-13.

Ziman, J. (1984). *An introduction to science studies: The philosophical and social aspects of science and technology*. Cambridge, UK: Cambridge University Press.

RECOMMENDED RESOURCES

Educational Testing Service. (1988). *The science report card: Trends and achievement based on the 1986 national assessment* (Report No. 17-S-01). Princeton, NJ: National Assessment of Educational Progress.

Gardner, H.E. (1993). *Frames of mind: The theory of multiple intelligences*. New York: Basic.

Gardner, H.E. (1995). Reflections on multiple intelligences: Myths and messages. *Phi Delta Kappan, 77*(3), 200–203, 206–209.

Gardner, M., Greeno, J.G., Reif, F., Schoenfeld, A.H., diSessa, A.A., & Stage, E. (Eds.). (1990). *Toward a scientific practice of science education*. Hillsdale, NJ: Erlbaum.

Hueftle, S.J., Rakow, S.J., & Welch, W.W. (1983). *Images of science: A summary of results from the 1981–1982 national assessment in science*. Minneapolis, MN: Minnesota Research and Evaluation Center, University of Minnesota.

Mestre, J.P., & Lochhead, J. (1990). *Academic preparation in science: Teaching for transition from high school to college*. New York: College Entrance Examination Board.

Miller, J. (1989, April). *Scientific literacy*. Paper presented at the meeting of the American Association for the Advancement of Science, San Francisco.

Miller, J.D., Suchner, R.W., & Voelker, A.M. (1980). *Citizenship in an age of science: Changing attitudes among young adults*. New York: Permagon.

National Assessment of Educational Progress. (1978). *The third assessment of science, 1976–1977*. Denver, CO: Author.

National Science Teachers Association. (2000). Science/technology/society: A new effort for providing appropriate science for all. In *NSTA Handbook 2000–2001* (p. 237). Arlington, VA: Author.

Weiss, I.R., Banilower, E.R., McMahon, K.C., & Smith, P.S. (2001, December). Instructional resources. In *Report of the 2000 national survey of science and mathematics* (Status report, chap. 6, NSF grant REC-9814246). Retrieved April 5, 2002, from http://2000survey. horizon-research.com/reports/status/chapter6.pdf

Yager, R.E. (1996). History of science/technology/society as reform in the United States. In R.E. Yager (Ed.), *Science/technology/society as reform in science education* (pp. 3–15). Albany, NY: State University of New York Press.

Yager, R.E., & Penick, J.E. (1986). Perceptions of four age groups toward science classes, teachers, and the value of science. *Science Education, 70*(4), 355–363.

Zuga, K.F. (1996). STS promotes the rejoining of technology and science. In R.E. Yager (Ed.), *Science/technology/society as reform in science education* (pp. 227–238). Albany, NY: State University of New York Press.

CHAPTER 24

"Reading the World Before Reading the Word": Implications for Professional Development of Teachers of Science

HUBERT M. DYASI AND REBECCA E. DYASI

Learners' direct experiences with the physical world are legitimate starting points for elementary school science. By the time children enter school, they already have considerable firsthand experience and knowledge of many aspects of the physical world; they also have developed their language in relation to the physical world and can readily talk and think about their knowledge and experiences. A science education that focuses on the physical world, therefore, continues their learning trajectories. An elementary school science curriculum that focuses on the physical world also is justifiable because major goals of all scientific endeavors are to understand, explain, and predict events in that world; it follows, therefore, that direct familiarity with that world is an integral part of scientific knowledge. Like all scientists, children engaged in learning about their world need to read and write about it. Teachers who are able to ensure a close fit between the physical world of their students and the science reading and writing that goes on in the classroom will best help their students develop facility as readers, writers, and scientists.

To be successful at ensuring this fit, it is not enough for teachers of elementary school science to concern themselves merely with becoming skilled practitioners and connoisseurs of the science content of the ordinary world while acquiring useful ways of guiding students to learn. Teachers also must be good at reading and writing about science, and they must continually work to enhance these skills. Just as with student learning, continuing science education for teachers must center on firsthand experience with the ordinary physical world.

The ideal teacher education framework includes an articulated belief system, a clear rationale and strategies, careful implementation, and ample resources; partnerships among school district professionals and students, university science educators, scientists, educational evaluators, and support agencies such as the National Science Foundation also are vital. When considering the effectiveness of a particular teacher education program, it is important to look at its impact on individual achievements and not just at statistical descriptions. This chapter considers the continued science education of teachers at the City College Workshop Center at City University of New York (CUNY).

Why Start With Reading the World

The physical world with its living and nonliving things is generally accessible to, and is shared by, all humans irrespective of time and place. It is, therefore, a convenient context for the development of language and many other valuable human activities (including science) in all cultures, and when used as a focus of study in schools it can give an advantageous starting point for all children:

> A child's inquiry takes place in a world of people and things. In the process of his questioning he accumulates answers that are the "facts" of science. He focuses on this or other thing, and his focusing is concrete: He asks what the thing can do and what it means. Long before and even after he has acquired words, his asking can be observed in his actions, and his tentative solutions in his adaptations of his actions. (Weber, 1973, p. 4)

Weber's statement was based on experience she had gained from many years of teaching young children in New York City, on her study of early childhood education in England, and on the findings of Susan Isaacs's (1966) research. Isaacs had written,

> words are only tokens of experience, and are either empty or confusing to children until they have had enough immediate experience to give the words content. With young children, words are valueless unless they are backed by the true coin of things and doings. They have their own place as aids to experience, and to clear thought about experience. (as cited in Weber, 1971, p. 179)

Authentic exploration of language, therefore, resides most properly in direct experiences in the world.

After working closely for many years with nonliterate adults in different countries in Latin America and in Africa, Paulo Freire came to the following realization:

> The act of learning to read and write has to start from a very comprehensive understanding of the act of reading the world, something which humans do before reading the words. Even historically, human beings first changed the

world, secondly proclaimed the world and then wrote the words. (as cited in Berthoff, 1987, p. xi)

This is not to gainsay the idea that adults who comprehend the written word learn a great deal from doing so. They do, but in order to acquire scientific skill and connoisseurship in reading the world, they must have firsthand experiences with the physical substance from which scientific knowledge is derived. The large amount of time spent by students of chemistry, biology, and medicine in their practical courses "shows how greatly these sciences rely on the transmission of skill and connoisseurship from master to apprentice" (Polanyi, 1962, p. 55). In other words, literate adults can obtain information about the world by reading text, but a direct, generative experience of the world is a *sine qua non* of personal knowledge. Thus the world is a suitable forum not just for the development of language, but also of the written word, science inquiry, and other aspects of scientific knowledge. And because all people share it, the world also is an excellent medium for the realization of the educational and social goal of inclusion of all people in these spheres of human activity.

Reading the World

Acts of reading the world are many and varied. Examples include an infant distinguishing between familiar and unfamiliar faces; fishermen navigating correctly by using stars; a person predicting weather based on observations of air masses, temperature, humidity, and clouds; and a farmer engaging in selected agricultural activities in light of seasonal changes. These acts can be learned successfully without reading the word; a combination of direct participation and the spoken word can suffice.

Other examples include many artists, designers, potters, and mechanics in many parts of the world who can neither read nor write the word, but who manage their complex tasks skillfully. These specialists owe their ability to manage these tasks not to knowledge of the written word but to an insightful understanding of the portion of the world they have selected to read and write (Morrison & Morrison, 1984). All of these people—the parent, the farmer, the nonliterate weather reader, the fishermen, and the artisans—decipher and translate signs in their worlds; they are, therefore, readers of the world. They read the world through lenses ground by personal knowledge. A fisher and a surfer, for example, read waves differently because each has a distinct personal knowledge of waves shaped by different goals and experiences.

Scientific Ways of Writing the World

Reading the world is inextricably bound with acting on the world. When a person engages in physical and intellectual manipulations of a phenomenon, noticing it and asking questions that lead to touching it, arranging and re-arranging it for a closer look or to see what happens as a result, represent-ing it in symbols, and making sense of it, he or she is coloring it from his or her own perspective; that is, "writing" it. A scientific writing of the world has deep, real, and repeated connections with the physical world itself and with scientific ways of making those connections. A few of the scientific ways or epistemologies used in gathering reliable science facts and in the develop-ment and verification of scientific laws and theories include science inquiry; experiments; science processes (e.g., observation, measurement, recording, etc.); and use of science tools and equipment, discussion, and documenta-tion. "The ability to conduct an investigation where they [students] keep everything else constant while changing a single variable" is one of the most important science inquiry skills because it "provides a powerful general strat-egy for solving problems encountered in the workplace and in everyday life" (Alberts, 2000, p. xiii).

In her suggested guide for elementary school science, Harlen (2001) expanded the process of writing the world to include exploration of a general problem leading to formulation of an investigable question. To answer the in-vestigable question, one decides ahead of time what to change, what to keep the same, what to observe, and what the result will mean. In some cases, however, it is not possible to manipulate the phenomenon freely, for example in the question, Is the wood at the top of a tree the same as the wood at the bottom? In such cases, instead of deciding what to change, an investigator decides what to look at (e.g., hardness of the wood), the differ-ences between the things looked at (e.g., different parts of the trunk from where the wood was taken), what must be the same (e.g., "the position of the block in relation to the bark and the heart of the wood" [Harlen, 2001, p. 75]), and how the results will be used to answer the question. In practi-cally all situations, the crucial aspect is deciding on suitable tests and how to conduct them. The U.S. National Science Education Standards (NSES) (National Research Council [NRC], 1996) address inquiry as a very impor-tant scientific epistemology and discusses its facets as a content standard.

Scientific epistemologies are a vital aspect of scientific knowledge be-cause they are the basis for judging whether a major goal of science is being achieved; that is, the creation of tested, valid models that can be used to ex-plain and to accurately predict events in the world.

There are two important points to note: First, an infusion of language in these processes generates a symbiotic development of a comprehensive understanding of the acts of reading and writing the world on the one hand and of the requisite language for their communication on the other. Rosen (1981) said, "the use of language...is the making of meaning and language development is the process of learning how to mean" (p. 20). More recently, James Britton (as cited in Rivard & Straw, 2000) stated,

> We come to an understanding in the course of communicating it. That is to say, we set out by offering an understanding and that understanding takes shape as we work on it to share it. And finally we may arrive co-operatively at a joint understanding as we talk or in some other way interact with someone else. (p. 568)

For both child and adult, therefore, it is not experience alone that has significance in making sense of the world; it is experience aided and amplified by language. In their preliminary research findings on this notion, Rivard and Straw (2000) suggest that "peer discussion combined with analytical writing enhances the retention of science knowledge by students over time, but appears to have little effect on immediate learning" (p. 578). In the case of science, it is experience and language modulated by use of scientific epistemologies that helps in making sense of the world.

Second, the acts of reading and writing the world emanate from, and remain closely associated with, a person's curiosity—a desire to know, to make sense, and to communicate—and with his or her perceptions of a potential readability and writing of the selected portion of the world. These points are relevant considerations in classroom applications.

Reading the Word

Reading the word demands a capacity to read and interpret man-made symbols that combine to form words and sentences. Reading the word has attributes found in reading the world; for example, inasmuch as reading the world imposes meaning on nature, reading the word imposes meaning on text. According to Resnick (1987), in the process of understanding a written text, a reader constructs

> a plausible representation of what the author presumably had in mind.... The mental representation constructed by the reader does not match the text itself...except under special circumstances.... The reader's representation omits details that do not seem central to the message. It also *adds* information needed to make the message coherent and sensible. (p. 8)

In the reading of the world, however, the "mental representation constructed by the reader" needs to be a faithful representation of that world.

Resnick (1987) also highlighted four attributes shared by successful readers of the word:

> The first is linguistic knowledge: knowledge about how sentences are formed, rules of forward and backward reference, and the like. This knowledge is often only implicit, but readers depend on it to find common referents, to link agent to action to object, and to otherwise construct a representation of a coherent set of events and relationships. The second kind of knowledge is topical knowledge, that is, knowledge about the text's subject matter. Like linguistic knowledge, topical knowledge is often used so automatically that readers are unaware of its contribution. Third, readers invoke knowledge about rules of inference. This knowledge, too, is likely to be implicit for the skilled reader. Finally, knowledge of conventional rhetorical structures often aids the process of text interpretation. (p. 9)

By the time they begin school, children have acquired linguistic knowledge in their mother tongue and can form and connect sentences—as is evident in their conversations—thus meeting the first criterion for success in reading text. At that time, however, they are not accomplished readers of the word, but they have considerable topical knowledge of matters from their life experience. Although they are not fully aware of conventional rhetorical structures or of rules of inference, they make inferences. Very early in their lives, therefore, children possess important prerequisites for success in the reading of text.

Writing the Word

Successful nonfiction writers of the word share the four attributes with successful readers of the word: namely, linguistic knowledge, topical knowledge, and knowledge of rules of inference and of rhetorical structures. In general, linguistic and topical knowledge have a "real connectedness to life situation and experience" (Rosen, 1981, p. 20). Speaking in praise of English teachers in inner-city London, England, for their commitment to the use of their students' life situation and experience as starting points in literary writing, Harold Rosen (1981) commented,

> If teachers have turned to their pupils' experience, it is not because they believe in some modern version of the Noble Savage, nor all that needed to happen was that experience should be verbalized and they could stand back and admire it in middle-class humility. (p. 20)

It is because, he maintained, life experience is an essential building block in literary writing.

Just as is the case in the learning of science, the road to mastery of writing the word is long and winding and is often untidy. Rosen found it necessary to urge literary scholars to

> acknowledge the deep and prolonged pre-analytic *immersion* in all kinds of literature, an immersion which alone makes their [the literary scholars'] activities possible or conceivable, which occurred during all those long years which finally led them to the conviction that the making and receiving of literature was indeed an essential and significant activity of human beings. It is precisely with those years and with that kind of reader that schools have to be concerned. (1981, p. 10)

There is a connection between reading and writing the world and reading and writing the word. In both areas, the world provides the substance of experience, and the reader makes meaning from it. The learning of science and its epistemologies and the learning of writing and reading the word in the milieu of the everyday world are not one-off activities, nor do they initially follow a straight, smooth road to significant knowledge. In science, especially, much messing about, untidiness, doing and redoing, extensive talk and discussion, writing and rewriting, and reading are accepted and recognizable points on the paths to acquisition of important knowledge and to fluency in meeting standards of design and evidence and standards of relating evidence to explanations.

There is, however, a major difference between science writing and literary writing. Analytical scientific writing uses special linguistic features. Aldridge (1992) drew attention to some of them:

> When one uses a scientific name, such as that of a plant or an element, the name has more generality. It means that every plant or element with these names is identical in some way. The name is agreed upon so that we can communicate about the plant or the element. But the name is still arbitrary, and by itself has no meaning. It has meaning only to those who understand which characteristics of the plant or element are inherent in the names we have agreed upon. And understanding those characteristics requires experience with the plant and element and with the characteristics used to categorize the plant or element. (p. 14)

Aldridge further stated that some terms in science are not just names of things; they represent concepts, some of which are derived from other concepts. For example, *pressure* and *acceleration* are not names; they are concepts derived from other concepts. The fact that some scientific terms do not represent concepts but phenomena further increases the complexity of science text. For example, *melting* and *dissolving* are not concepts or things; they are different phenomena or events. Even science facts are not all one thing; some facts are measurements (both direct and indirect) and others are empirical laws or summaries of observations. This high degree of lexical complexity can create serious comprehension problems for readers of science text.

The Worlds of School Science

The worlds of school science grow out of, and are connected to, the world we all experience. They include light and shadows; day and night and seasons; plants and animals; soil and rocks; the moon and stars and planets; rockets; rainbows; the weather; batteries, bulbs, and wires; simple machines; many different measuring devices; tools and instruments that extend our senses; and many other phenomena. In these worlds, students have opportunities for direct participation in scientific acts of reading and writing the world that lead to making scientific meaning, for experience in the use of language to enhance the making and communication of meaning, and for writing and reading the word and other symbols to clarify and communicate thought and meaning. (The scholastic benefits of children's science notebooks and journals have been documented by Klentschy, Garrison, and Amaral [2001] and by Shepardson and Britsch [2001].) The worlds of elementary and middle school science, therefore, bring together acts of reading and writing the world (science and science inquiry as portrayed, for example, in the NSES), language (talk, discussion, argument), and writing and reading the word (written records, science notebooks and journals, and print materials such as case studies and suitable books). This view of science education has profound implications for the goals of science teacher education and for the teaching and learning of science in schools.

Educating Teachers in the Scientific Ways of Reading the World and the Associated Word: A Case Study

Weber and Dyasi (1985) wrote, among other things, the following about the City College Workshop Center:

> Some years ago, at the inception of our work, we could have described ourselves as working to further develop children's language by maximizing language use.... At the same time we were also described as focusing on classroom organization, as assisting teachers on-site with classroom changes.... We continue to relate to how teachers can make their classrooms better contexts for active

learning and to respond to teachers' questions on the fitting of science into their classrooms. Our help with classroom organization is now in the service of primary-school science but most of the work we do with teachers...centers on how they, the teachers themselves, understand the common everyday phenomena that engage children. (p. 566)

Weber and Dyasi also commented on the fact that the center operates in the Harlem area of New York City, and that

both the children we work with and those whom they [visitors from other places] work with have been analyzed as lacking understanding, even sometimes the capability of developing understanding...we refuse to accept this analysis and assert the capacity for active and further development of all children. (p. 566)

They drew this assertion

from what we know from the real-life history of almost all children who acquired their first language, their mother tongue, in interaction concerning meaning with their home life, and in interaction with the life experiences in the surrounding community environment. (p. 567)

Descriptions of the work of the center are a record of what staff members actually do to support the nonacceptance of the inability of some children and of any of their teachers to learn science. It is a record of building the teachers' understanding and acceptance that difference does not mean incapacity and of educating teachers to acquire a deep understanding, through their own experiences, of the process of science inquiry in the context of common phenomena of the world—ordinary things that are part of the ordinary environment.

Although much remains to be done, many gains have been made. At the national level, excellent science education support materials, developed with the help of the National Science Foundation, now are widely available in some school districts. In addition, several excellent video-based exemplars of inquiry-based science teaching and learning have been published and are broadcast regularly. In New York City, individual schools and community school districts have devoted some of their financial and human resources to the support of their teachers' enrollment and participation in the Workshop Center's science education programs and to the purchase of support science teaching materials. As a result, categorical statements are possible about the frameworks, strategies, and impacts of the Workshop Center's programs.

The Workshop Center's Framework for Action

A suitable continuing science education for middle and elementary school teachers must be a medium through which teachers become successful, confident scientific readers and writers of the worlds of school science in the context of everyday life experiences. The science education must enable teachers to be accomplished science inquirers and possessors and interpreters of significant science content, as well as adept users of the spoken and written language. In other words, teachers should experience success in the ways they wish their students to be successful and in developing abilities to guide their students. The Workshop Center's teacher education practice is based on four principles: primary or firsthand experiential inquiry, representation, abstraction, and science research council conference.

Primary or firsthand experiential inquiry involves noticing and exploring phenomena and raising questions that can be answered through scientific investigations. It also incorporates designing and carrying out investigations, collecting and organizing data in scientifically reliable ways, and formulation of testable scientific conclusions based on evidence.

Representation, although a distinct principle in itself, plays a part in the other three principles. For example, teachers communicate their activities and perceptions among themselves and with staff, verbally and through written records. Depending on the kinds of investigations carried out, teachers also use pictures (e.g., charts, diagrams, graphs, equations), numbers (e.g., measurements), and other suitable mechanisms. Firsthand investigation and representation are necessary but not sufficient; teachers also must make scientific abstractions from data—that is, they should see patterns and generate possible scientific explanations consistent with evidence.

In a science research council conference, science inquiry teams or individual inquirers present comprehensive oral and written reports on their investigations to a critical but friendly community of peers. Reports include investigation question(s) raised and how they arose, designs followed (including equipment used, observations made, and the number of tests conducted), modifications made to the design and why they were made, data collected and the scientific ideas they suggest, and unresolved questions. A peer or a City College Workshop Center staff member serves as a moderator. After each report, the moderator highlights the report's scientific achievements, unresolved issues, and possible next steps. (Hubert M. Dyasi first presented this elemental model at the San Francisco Exploratorium in 1987. It was later published in Dyasi, 1990.)

Acts of writing and reading suitable text by participants are integral experiences in all four principles. Participants' writings may be science notes, records, and narratives. These writings portray teachers' levels of understanding of science inquiry and their capacity to speak and write using science discourse. Initially, however, staff pay attention mostly to the enhancement of the former rather than to mastery of the technicalities of the latter, because they believe that a quick concern with technicalities of scientific writing might interfere with acquisition of scientific concepts and processes. Nevertheless, teachers read and write reviews of carefully selected science and science education texts that represent good science writing.

After extensive, successful experience reading science texts on phenomena that they have investigated firsthand, teachers also can be successful readers of science writings on phenomena that they have wondered about but not previously investigated. Combining science inquiry experiences, oral and written language, and reading and reviewing good science and science education literature helps teachers to improve their knowledge and communication of science.

The Workshop Center's Science Education Strategies

The City College Workshop Center gives teachers rich, varied opportunities to live the experiences in which their students will participate. The center uses eight science education strategies: group inquiries, scientists' inquiries, extended self-selected individual inquiries, readings and written reviews and journals, discussion groups, specialized sessions with a scientist, teachers and staff working as coprofessionals guiding students' inquiries, and classroom applications by teachers.

Group Inquiries. Group inquiries provide a shared base of experience. Working in small groups, teachers experience the processes of noticing, exploring, talking, and writing about phenomena. Carefully selected materials and guiding questions ensure positive and rewarding experiences, leading to improvements in abilities to generate investigable questions, design investigations, collect and organize data, use scientific tools and techniques, and formulate data-based, testable conclusions and generalizations. Group discussions also introduce teachers to scientific demonstration and to formal scientific discourse and writing.

The Workshop Center staff select phenomena from teachers' life experiences. For example, for inquiry-based scientific study of liquids, the staff selects mystery liquids such as clear water, mineral oil, vinegar, a saturated saline solution, a solution of baking soda (sodium bicarbonate), clear liquid detergent, water colored with red cabbage, etc. (all are labeled only with a letter—A, B, C, etc.). Teachers first talk about their experiences related to liquids they know, circumstances in which they use them, significance of the liquids, and so on. Then, they divide into small groups and work on tasks such as answering the following questions about the liquids:

- What are observable characteristics of each liquid (without changing the liquid)?
- How do the masses of the liquids compare?
- What happens when you put A and B together?
- What happens when you put B and C together?
- How does each liquid react with the substance labeled X (water colored with red cabbage)?
- What is the reaction of the paper strip (pH paper) with each liquid?
- Based on your observations and measurements, what general scientific statements can you make about this group of liquids?

The tasks require teachers to use scientific tools and techniques and to focus on important physical and chemical properties, for example, color, texture, viscosity, measurements of mass and volume, ratios, pH values, and chemical reactions and their products. Teachers learn to design fair tests as a basis for making comparisons among different substances. On that basis, they engage in data recording and organization, in making logical inferences from data, and in developing operational definitions of density, acidity, alkalinity, neutralization, and indicators. At the conclusion of the tasks, each group discusses its work and prepares a report; then pairs of groups discuss and critique their reports and produce a single report for presentation to the whole group. As they discuss, write, and discuss again in small groups and later with the whole group, they sharpen their language for expressing their scientific inquiry activities and the resulting scientific knowledge. Later, they are allowed sufficient time to reflect upon and to write about their science inquiry and perceived staff roles, before staff tease out the science content and pedagogical components of the inquiry activities.

Teachers' written reflections provide glimpses into their thinking and ideas. In a draft version of her reflective journal, Donna Smith, a teacher in a summer institute, wrote,

> We were then asked to share our results with another group of 5 students that had worked together. Their list of characteristics were [sic] similar to ours.

When examining the weight of the liquids the other group did not measure a specific amount of fluid but rather a random amount of each liquid (or an eye-balled amount). They had similar mixing data as we did. They had a much more detailed examination of pH, where they commented upon how the liquid reacted with the pH paper when it entered the liquid, how quickly the liquid dryed [sic] on the pH paper. How quickly the liquid rose up dry pH paper. They noticed that color from the pH paper moved into one of the liquids. They also matched the colors of the pH paper strips to a color chart determining a pH value for each liquid.

Ms. Smith chose to comment on others' failure to carry out scientific measurement and to apply the concept of fair testing in their science inquiries, and on an inability to distinguish between important and trivial observations. The staff's immediate interest, however, was in whether she had acquired scientific practice and ideas. She had, as shown here:

The whole class came back together so that groups could make summaries of what they had done. It was apparent that other groups had approached some of the questions very differently. For instance, one group added 2 drops of liquid X [the indicator] to a cup of each liquid A, B, C, D, & E. One group discussed very different results from measuring 1 oz. vs. 5 ml of the liquids. Noting the larger sample showed variations between liquids masses that were indistinguishable in small samples.... I think one drop of a substance in a container full of a different substance allows one to notice different behavior than one notices with more equal amounts.... I think these two experimental methods support the same concept about the materials, one floats on top of the other with different technique and therefore different observational data. Similarly different quantities of the substance provide the groups with different data, but in looking at the ratio of wt. to volume roughly the same concept will be apparent (=/- experimental error).

Ms. Smith understood the components of a systematic, scientific approach to working with liquids. She knew, for example, that when testing one liquid against another, it is better to add one drop of one liquid at a time into a fixed amount of the other. Although she thought that the ratio of mass to volume (i.e., density) of a liquid should remain the same at room temperature regardless of amounts used, she did not yet trust the thought, and she also thought about the reliability of the equipment she would use. Her thoughts were evident in her questions:

What difference in density would I get if I measured the mass of 100 ml of each liquid?

What is the error in the triple beam balance (or what difference would I see in weighing the same item several times on the triple beam?)?

The following excerpt shows how Ms. Smith's language of discourse about the natural world underwent necessary changes.

> After lunch Prof. D. asked us "what was the phenomena [of study in the morning]?" I had not thought of "phenomena" in the way he began encouraging us to think about it. To me characteristic and phenomena I would have interchanged. But from this dialog it was apparent that:
>
> A phenomena
>
> Catches our attention
>
> It's not expected
>
> It's worth noticing and recording
>
> It's tangible and concrete

She concluded with significant reflections that show her progress toward understanding aspects of science inquiry:

> In inquiry we need to plan our work and therefore need some experience with the materials we will be using, in order to plan. We may need to initially get experience in a haphazard fashion. Once we have the experience we can then refine the experience (or plan).... Using our plan, we collect information about our materials. If we collect reliable information that we can repeat, it's data. Other information might as well be considered gossip.... I think most of my odor and color descriptions on previous pages count as gossip.

When asked what she meant by "gossip" in descriptions, she responded, "Because it's a vague comparison and I haven't considered that a *reliable* way of measuring because it's not very repeatable."

It is clear that Ms. Smith knows the acts of reading and writing the world; she needs to use them repeatedly so that they become second nature in her investigations and in her work with students. She also knows she needs to pay more attention to how she uses words during discussions and in writing; for example, in her final paper, she wrote, "I found that I was being imprecise with much of my language.... This made me think about being more articulate with my language." She has grasped an important characteristic of growth in reading the world and in writing the word: "Once we have the experience we can then refine the experience."

In the early stages of the program, many participants do not display an acquisition of scientific ways of reading the world as readily as Ms. Smith. They need more opportunities in loosely structured exploration before they can appreciate and feel comfortable with focused scientific investigations. David Hawkins (1965) has characterized the early preplanning activities in science learning as "messing about in science" (p. 5). Similarly, before becoming good writers, people go through a long nontechnical immersion in writing. Flexible early experiences are valuable because a person does not ordinarily pay equal attention to processes of inquiry and writing simultaneously; Polanyi (1962) would say that when one is in "focal awareness," the other is in "subsidiary awareness" (p. 55). Over time, however, most people attain proficiency in scientific ways of reading and writing portions of the worlds of school science, as well as in reading and writing about them. The quality and density of investigative opportunities and a sensitive familiarity with, and support of, each teacher's learning trajectory at the Workshop Center are critical factors in the attainment of proficiency. To classify learners according to a statistical distribution in these cases, therefore, does not add value to their learning of science. It is the different inquiries that should constitute a sample, rather than the teachers.

Scientists' Inquiries. The study of scientists' inquiries introduces teachers directly to models of authentic practice in the conduct of scientific investigations. Teachers study and analyze an "amateur scientist's" investigations carried out informally by Feynman (1990), Redi's systematic inquiries on whether living things come from other living things or arise spontaneously (see Nuffield Junior Science, 1967), and Morrison and Morrison's (1987) videotaped measurements of conservation of energy. In addition to these demonstrations, teachers learn about planning scientific ways of inquiry from specific readings, such as Harlen (2001).

Individual Inquiries. Through extended, in-depth, independent individual inquiries, teachers apply lessons learned from small-group and scientists' inquiries and from assigned readings. Each teacher selects a phenomenon of interest for investigation. Some selections are predictable, such as light, sound, ants, plants, mealworms, and rates of evaporation; but others are unexpected, for example, feathers, chewing gum, and cracking sidewalks.

Julia Henke, a second-time participating teacher in one of the Workshop Center's intensive institutes, wrote a reflective account of her experiences that sheds light on her growth as an inquirer. Following are selected parts of what she wrote:

> I was in a small group following a general introduction to the staff and the center feeling great anxiety about what I was to choose as my subject of inquiry....
> I decided to verbalize this feeling to the group and found that each person was experiencing the same anxiety. Although I intellectually understood the philosophy of the Workshop Center, part of me felt that since I had attended the Institute before I had to make some new discovery about the world or I would

be a failure. Hubert reminded me that little investigations in nature are not unimportant.... What may appear to be a "little investigation" is actually a demonstration of one's ability to come to an understanding of an aspect of nature, and that will in turn lead to other "little" discoveries and a deeper understanding of the world we live in.

Ms. Henke captured some of the struggles that a teacher may have in a quest to understand and implement scientific acts of reading the world. She also has shown that she is aware, although hesitantly, of how to break away from initial anxiety:

> It was made clear to us, however, that the investigation we were to do was not a duplication of someone else's efforts.... In our investigations we were to focus on actual phenomena, each phenomenon had to be closely observed and fully described, notes had to be made of observations (particularly discoveries about the phenomenon), and then "research" could be done to further one's inquiry.

For her individual investigation, she inquired into down feathers. First, she examined texture, using a magnifier and then a microscope, always noting the magnifications she used. After making many drawings of what she saw under the microscope and getting exhausted in the process, she wished to photograph what she saw but did not know how. Consequently, she therefore learned about microphotography and the entire photographic process—she developed her own photos, taught others in the Workshop Center how to develop and print their photos, and built a bank of documented data. Later in her investigation, she wondered what happens to birds' feathers during oil spills and carried out investigations that revealed oil's dramatic deleterious effects on feathers.

Near the end of her reflective journal, she wrote,

> I was hurrying to the darkroom with a completed role of film when I noticed some leaf prints on a table. The main veins of the leaf had the exact same structure as the limbs of my down feather. I stopped rushing. I realized that by rushing so much over the past two years, I had gradually stopped observing and questioning. Here I was doing it again. I stopped next to a container on the floor which held a patchwork quilt. The different pieces of the fabric had different weaves to them. The tight weave of one piece of fabric seemed very familiar to the weave of the down feather with water on it. Feathers apparently have some natural oils and I began to wonder about the tightness of the weave in waterproof raincoats, and what type of oils might be used to bring out waterproofing. Does the weave tighten as it did with my feathers when I put water on it? Here was a thread! Seeing how things in the world around us are interrelated. I felt excitement all over again.

At the end of her individual investigation, Ms. Henke had progressed considerably in her ability to scientifically read and write the world of feathers. By talking to her peers and to the staff, by drawing ideas from others and from supportive readings, and by using scientific epistemologies, she deepened her scientific knowledge of feathers and of the effects of environmental conditions. She also fell in love once again with science ways of knowing, and explained why she had decided to be in the Workshop Center for a second time.

> The Summer Institute in 1985 had changed the way I looked at the world and at myself. I wanted to re-experience the excitement and feeling of self-confidence that resulted from those weeks at the Workshop Center.... I remembered tears at having to leave fellow teachers/students and the Workshop Center staff, the joy of personal and shared discoveries that made sensuous that fact that the world was knowable by actively and reflectively looking into nature.

Readings, Written Reviews, and Journals. In the Workshop Center, teachers also study, write reviews and critiques, and reflect on applicable professional literature. Some readings explain the educational approach of the Workshop Center, and others provide scholarly and research rationale for inquiry-based learning and science. Readings include the following:

- *Project scope, sequence, and coordination: A new synthesis for improving science education* (Aldridge, 1992)
- *Lillian Weber: An ample view of teaching* (Alberty, 1995)
- *Critical barriers phenomenon in elementary science* (Apelman, Hawkins, & Morrison, 1985)
- *Doing what scientists do: Children learn to investigate their world* (Doris, 1991)
- *The pupil as scientist?* (Driver, 1983)
- *The dynamics of pluralism and education that is multicultural* (Grant, 1987)
- *Primary science: Taking the plunge* (Harlen, 2001)
- *Respecting children's own ideas* (Harlen, 2000)
- *Inquiry and the national science education standards: A guide for teaching and learning* (NRC, 2000)
- *Foundations: Vol. 2. Inquiry: Thoughts, views, and strategies for the K–5 classroom* (National Science Foundation, n.d.)
- *Inquiring children and their teachers* (Rose, 1987)

- *Beyond the science kit* (Saul & Reardon, 1996)
- *Patterns in nature* (Stevens, 1974)
- *A scientist at the seashore* (Trefil, 1984)
- *The English infant school and informal education* (Weber, 1971)
- *Language development and observation of the local environment: First steps in providing primary-school science education for non-dominant groups* (Weber & Dyasi, 1985)
- *Placing children at the center of science education reform* (Worth, 1996)

Teachers also relate the readings to possibilities of engaging children in practical science inquiry in their classes.

Through science notebooks and narrative journals, teachers develop skills in the science genres of communication and comprehensive narrative, respectively. Journals include notes and reflections on the teachers' experiences in the program and facilitate the recall of, and reflection on, participants' experiences and special moments that illuminate and further the teachers' investigative efforts. Journals also serve as a means of communication between each participant and the staff and allow staff to revisit and highlight for the teacher specific instances that illustrate evolving understandings. As the staff learns directly from the journals what the teachers choose to recapitulate and what meanings they attach to events, they are better able to confirm insights into what each teacher might use to further his or her efforts. Through this process, staff also are increasingly able to identify problems that might impede growth.

Discussion Groups. Each participating teacher is assigned to a discussion or consultative group of seven or eight teachers, led by a staff member. In a four-week intensive program the group meets twice each week for two hours to allow for each teacher to present a progress report on his or her investigation and for the group to discuss the report and make suggestions before writing takes place. Each group of peers, therefore, provides a community for each participant to practice public expression of thoughts and reflections, and to plan next steps in both the investigation and the narrative journal.

Sessions With a Scientist. Teachers interact directly with a research scientist who focuses primarily on the scientific ideas and epistemologies embedded in the teachers' investigations of nature (e.g., in the study of liquids) and only secondarily on her or his own research interests. This practice helps many participating teachers who have not associated the study of science with the ordinary phenomena of nature but with formulae, abstract ideas, and unfamiliar language—all found in books—to see scientific knowledge potentials in their investigations. For example, in her narrative journal about our summer institute on science education, Sheila Evans wrote,

> As the staff talked about getting first-hand experience, I thought about the farm and all the things I had been fortunate enough to try first-hand...Whenever we went to the farm my cousins and I...captured frogs and tried to keep them alive, we looked at the minnows in the fish pond along with dragon flies. For inner city kids this was heaven! Little did I know that this was related to science.

Usually, following teachers' reports on their investigations, a scientist responds to teachers' questions, highlights significant scientific epistemology and knowledge elements evident in their work, and discusses the historical development and current status of related scientific ideas and foci of related current scientific research. The scientist's descriptions and explanations introduce teachers to "live" science discourse. One teacher's narrative journal, for example, describes a session in which Dr. Anthony DePass, a scientist at Long Island University, New York, USA, linked teachers' activities in the investigation of citrus fruit to graphing, density, and the meaning of the pH scale. They also learned that pie graphs are used to show percentage breakdowns of data rather than continuous data such as acidity levels of different fruit juices. The pH scale is based on abstract knowledge of ionization and powers of ten and is very hard for some people to conceptualize, yet when the scientist related it to the teachers' own data, it made sense to them. In that session, teachers also learned why it is important to study acids and bases, for example their critical importance in digestive processes, medicine, and pharmacology (they affect bacterial levels), in addition to their roles in chemical reactions generally. Dr. DePass deliberately did not address early notions in chemistry that associated acidity with oxygen (rather than with the hydrogen ion concentration), because his aim was to demystify scientific acts of reading and making meaning of the natural world. The sequence of events here is noteworthy: First, the teachers read the world of citrus fruits, next they talked and wrote about their experiences with citrus fruits and resulting understandings of the properties of the fruits, and finally they received supplementary input from a scientist. The usual sequence includes receiving the word first, then doing scripted experiences designed to confirm the given word, and finally submission of students' notebooks for correction.

Teachers and Workshop Center Staff Working as Coprofessionals. In specially arranged three-hour Saturday sessions, six groups of five participant teachers each guide a group of ten elementary school students in science inquiries, emulating Workshop Center staff pedagogical practice. In these sessions, teachers gain practical experience in teaching science inquiry and in relating children's ways of inquiring into nature and to teachers' ways. Staff attend all sessions, functioning unobtrusively as coprofessionals and helpers.

Following each session, staff and teachers discuss their roles and their observations of students' work. Very often, teachers express great surprise at the children's immense capacity to inquire with meaning and to communicate clearly. Teachers who might have been previously skeptical of children's motivation and abilities to engage in serious science inquiry change their viewpoints on the basis of their own observations, reinforced after learning from parents that it is the children who push their parents to bring them to the Workshop Center for these Saturday sessions, instead of the other way round. By the end of the Saturday series, teachers have learned to guide and accurately read relevant science in students' inquiries, to orchestrate students' discussions, and to coach students in the preparation and use of science notebooks and in writing narratives of their learning. When teachers implement in their classrooms what they learned at the Workshop Center, staff make classroom visits upon invitation and coteach with the class teacher.

Classroom Applications. Alicia Diez, a graduate of the Workshop Center's programs, teaches sixth-grade science. In her pedagogical practice, she gives students time to select, plan, and carry out scientific investigations in groups and individually to discuss their work with one another; to make public presentations; to draft analytic reports for review by peers; and to write final reports. She wrote,

> In my class, I incorporate writing throughout the curriculum. Students write scientific reports every week after each experiment. The scientific reports include an abstract, review of the literature, problem, hypothesis, materials and methods, results, discussion and references. In the discussion, they include their reflections in addition to their analysis of their results. Students edit each other's papers for clearness, understanding and content. Revisions are made and new editing is done again by a different student and then by me, the teacher. Having students participate as tutors not only increases the tutors' learning experience but also the students' who are getting help. (Diez, 2001, p. 2)

To introduce her sixth-grade students to a study of physical and chemical changes, Ms. Diez asked her students to conduct inquiries into interactions between seashells and selected household liquids. Lisa, one of the students, began her report, "An Experiment on a Seashell," with a story:

> It all started like this. Before I got out of school for summer vacation my father was trying to get airplane flight tickets for him, my grandmother and me. When school ended I had my airplane flight ticket already, I was so excited.
>
> Over the summer I went to the Dominican Republic. I went to the beach a lot so I ended up collecting seashells and rocks. A week before I came to New York I had a collection of rocks and seashells. On my way here I was counting my seashells and rocks and all together I had more than 15 rocks and shells in all. When I got to New York I couldn't wait to go to school.
>
> When I got to school I had to do an experiment on a seashell. What a coincident [sic] I had collected rocks and seashells over the summer. When I found this I was sad because I had to give up one of my shells but on the other side I was happy because I didn't have to look for a shell. Overall, I had a good time doing this experiment. Everything has gone well so far.

Lisa's story shows that seashells are part of her life experiences. As stated earlier, life experiences are important factors in learning science inquiry and in reading and writing. Her report continues with a table of contents, question and hypothesis, list of materials, materials and method to test for base or acid, results, and discussion. Her good writing skills are evident in the following excerpts:

Materials and Method to Test for Base or Acid

> To test if my mixture was an acid or a base, I had to get cabbage and liquefy it. After I did this, I had to pour in a container and pour my mixture and if the color turned blue it was a base, if the color didn't change then it was neutral. When I tested my mixture the result was red, acid.

Lisa examined the mixture and recorded her observations daily for seven days. She used a chart to organize the observation by days. In her analysis, she wrote,

Discussion

> My shell went through chemical and physical change. It went through physical change when it's [sic] color changed. When it peeled and when it chipped. This also happened because of the strong acid. It went through chemical change when it peeled and it chipped because it turned into powder. Also because $Ca+CO_2+H_2O$.
>
> My hypothesis was that the shell will dissolve quickly and it'll get thinner but I was wrong. Also, I thought that it's [sic] color was going to fade and that it was going to get softer and smoother, in this part I was correct. Therefore, 70% of my hypothesis was correct.

We can improve the experiment by pouring different kinds of chemicals. For example place a seashell in an acid, place one in a base and place one in a neutral liquid. After this you can compare and contrast whatever happens to the seashell.

In my opinion, another experiment that we can do is to plant a plant and check what is going to happen if, instead of pouring water you pour any type of acid, base or neutral. What'll be the difference in plants?

Lisa concludes her report with the following personal reactions:

While doing this project I had ambivalent feelings. I felt excited and I also felt bored. I felt excited because I like to deal with different chemicals. On the other hand, I felt bored because I had to sit and explore the difference in the shell day by day. Overall, it was an extremely fun project.

The report shows careful experimental design, data collection and organization (e.g., use of charts), and careful linking of evidence to conclusions. Significantly, it illustrates thoughtful reflection, critical evaluation of the strengths and limitations of the evidence, and knowledge of how to obtain further evidence to corroborate her initial conclusions. The good quality of writing is testimony to the effectiveness of the class's practice of reading and editing peers' analytical writing. A more elaborate analysis would show evidence of topical knowledge (initial and final states of the seashell); factual material (characteristics of the seashell); observational data (daily records); methodological issues (observations made day by day); and inferential (turned red, acid), observational-inferential (70% of my hypothesis was correct), and affective aspects (ambivalent feelings).

At the completion of investigations and report preparation, Ms. Diez's class often convenes as a science research council conference.

Students prepare PowerPoint presentations for some of their experiments. They present their work in front of the class. Their writing must be correct, well thought out, clear, and understandable. During their presentation, the students are not only improving in their writing but in their speech skills, social interaction and the ability to explain their work. (Diez, 2001, p. 2)

The students also write for a wider audience. For example, Ms. Diez writes that

Along with their reports and presentations, students are asked to create Websites about their project that others can view through the Internet. Websites need to be legible, well-written, creative, and should to [sic] include related links to their project. In this way, students expand their knowledge in science and writing. (Diez, 2001, p. 3)

Ms. Diez believed that as a result of these experiences, her students saw themselves as science inquirers, as articulate speakers, as readers and writers, and as one another's teachers. Elizabeth, one of her students, confirms this belief.

> During this school year, science class has been very exciting. We do many interactive activities. We had a chance to tutor each other. It is very interesting because you go home to study the material. It is like a teacher "one on one" to the student. So it is easier to understand the material, when it comes from a classmate rather than coming from the teacher. We also do a lot of writing in science. We conduct experiments and write our reflections through reports, PowerPoint presentations and anything else that we can use to reflect the experiment. We ask each other for help in checking our grammar. All these science activities not only makes us better scientist [sic] but better writers. (Diez, 2001, p. 3)

Other teachers use different phenomena. Sandra Jenouré and her bilingual third graders, for example, made a videotape of their science explorations of flashlight batteries, bulbs, and wire to facilitate use of English in conversation, reading, and writing. Betty Marolla's third-grade class took advantage of Central Park's proximity to their school and studied butterfly habitats. As a result, they acquired science substance around which to cultivate communication skills, appreciation of nature's art, and knowledge of social studies, and with which to use computer technologies. In Brooklyn, New York, George Theodore's students carried out scientific studies of snails. For all the teachers, the goal is the same: to provide a high-quality education for all their students by faithfully translating the pedagogical practice they learn at the Workshop Center, supplemented by complementary programs and resources, into gainful science education and into reading and writing classroom experiences for students.

Effects of Workshop Center Programs on Participant Teachers

As a result of participating in the Workshop Center's science education programs, elementary school teachers feel confident in their abilities to provide experiential science learning activities in their classrooms. Repeatedly in their journals, teachers made statements indicating that their experiences in the program had taught and changed their way of looking at the world to seeing the world as a rich resource for teaching and learning science. Significantly, they also changed from viewing themselves as inadequate to the task of teaching science to seeing themselves as empowered teachers who are themselves learners of inquiry-based science. For example, at the completion of the 1990 Summer Institute, Martha Greenawalt (a participant) wrote in her journal,

> I caught the vision that real insight and learning about the natural world comes out of a combination of inspiration and technique. I saw how much more meaningful and helpful secondary sources are when they are used to support firsthand learning. I learned about myself and my own learning style.... And perhaps more importantly, I learned how much more there is to learn, and...how capable I am of pursuing new knowledge.

Teachers have also written not only about how their experiencing of ups and downs of active learning gave them a more solid sense of confidence in their own ability to learn, but also about how they began to see that language learning can be integrated in science learning. They referred to the significant amount of discussions they had conducted in small groups and also during presentations of their science investigations to the whole class, and how those discussions had sharpened their use of language. The extensive writing involved in their journals and in their written reviews of published science and science education articles further cultivated a sense that discussion and writing are integral parts of science.

Most of the teachers who completed the Workshop Center program have incorporated into their science teaching the requirement that their own students maintain fully documented written journals and science notebooks. Their students, therefore, first collect science data from natural phenomena, discuss and then write out their science learning activities in journals, and review and revise their ideas and writings before submitting the written work to the teacher.

Although our evidence that reading and writing the world can fruitfully precede and then be integrated with reading and writing the word is anecdotal, we see signs that combining the world and the word in children's learning of science can advance both their science and their literacy education.

Concluding Thoughts

This chapter has drawn similarities and distinctions between scientific ways of reading and writing the world on the one hand, and acts of reading and writing the word. We also have suggested that students' and teachers' firsthand experiences in the physical world around them may make the best platform for engaging students in verbal and written communication. After conceptual knowledge has been acquired this way, teachers can begin to require that students use scientific terminology as they talk about and write about science. Keys (1999) asked the following question:

> For children to become proficient in science writing, reading, and communication, should the emphasis be on enhancing children's knowledge bases, or should science writing structures be taught along with science concepts and thinking skills? (p. 1045)

We believe that emphasizing technical science-writing skills at the same time that students are first being exposed to scientific inquiry, facts, and tools could slow students' learning in all of these areas. Students might even end up simply parroting scientific language that they do not understand.

What mechanisms should be used to connect students' informal expressions of their knowledge of the world with more formal, scientific ways of expressing it? A research report by Moje, Collazo, Carillo, and Marx (2001)—focusing on bilingual students—makes these guarded suggestions:

> four characteristics of classroom interaction seem necessary: (a) drawing from students' everyday Discourses and knowledges, (b) developing students' awareness of those various Discourses and knowledges..., (c) connecting these everyday knowledges and Discourses with the science discourse genre of science classrooms and of the science community, and (d) negotiating understanding of both Discourses and knowledges so that they not only inform the other, but also merge to construct a new kind of discourse and knowledge. (p. 489)

Many school districts appear to be going in the opposite direction, however. There is an increasing emphasis on basic reading and arithmetic skills in elementary and middle school grades, accompanied by calls for high-stakes, standardized test-based accountability. Three results of this reemergence of an over-emphasis on reading and arithmetic are specific, timed curriculum prescriptions, a reduction in children's hands-on science investigations, and the imposition of constraints on the degree to which teachers can respond to children's own questions and ideas.

An important underlying belief in this chapter is the educability of all people. The implication of this belief is that in cases of failure to learn, there may not be a good match between the learner, and the quality, density, and relevance of those portions of the world that have been used as vehicles to enhance learning. Is this belief tenable? If so, how can it be honored in the face of the above-stated external pressures facing schools and their staffs?

REFERENCES

Alberts, B. (2000). A scientist's perspective on inquiry. In S. Olson & S. Loucks-Horsley (Eds.), *Inquiry and the science education standards: A guide for teaching and learning* (foreword). Washington, DC: National Academy Press.

Alberty, B. (1995). *Lillian Weber: An ample view of teaching.* New York: City College Workshop Center.

Aldridge, B. (1992). Project scope, sequence, and coordination: A new synthesis for improving science education. *Journal of Science Education and Technology, 1*(1), 13–21.

Apelman, M., Hawkins, D., & Morrison, P. (1985). *Critical barriers phenomenon in elementary science.* Grand Forks, ND: Center for Teaching and Learning, University of North Dakota.

Berthoff, A.E. (1987). Foreword. In P. Freire & D. Marcedo, *Literacy: Reading the word and the world* (p. xi). South Hadley, MA: Bergin & Garvey.

Diez, A.M. (2001). *Peer tutoring: Students tutoring each other help them succeed academically and become better writers.* Unpublished manuscript, Mott Hall School, New York.

Doris, E. (1991). *Doing what scientists do: Children learn to investigate their world.* Portsmouth, NH: Heinemann.

Driver, R. (1983). *The pupil as scientist?* Milton Keynes, UK: Open University Press.

Dyasi, H. (1991). Assessing imperfect conceptions. In K. Jervis & C. Montag (Eds.), *Progressive education for the 1990s: Transforming practice* (pp. 101–110) New York: Teachers College Press.

Feynman, R. (1990). *"Surely, you're joking, Mr. Feynman": Adventures of a curious character.* New York: Bantam.

Grant, C.A. (1987). *The dynamics of pluralism and education that is multicultural.* New York: City College Workshop Center.

Harlen, W. (2000). *Respecting children's own ideas.* New York: City College Workshop Center.

Harlen, W. (2001). *Primary science: Taking the plunge.* Portsmouth, NH: Heinemann.

Hawkins, D. (1965). Messing about in science. *Science and Children, 2*(5), 5–9.

Isaacs, S. (1966). *Intellectual growth in young children.* New York: Shoken Books.

Keys, C.W. (1999). Language as an indicator of meaning generation: An analysis of middle school students' written discourse about scientific investigations. *Journal of Research in Science Teaching, 36*(9), 1044–1061.

Klentschy, M., Garrison, L., & Amaral, O.M. (2001). *Valle imperial project in science (VIPS) four-year comparison of student achievement data 1995–1999.* Unpublished manuscript.

Moje, E.B., Collazo, T., Carillo, R., & Marx, R.W. (2001). "Maestro, what is quality?" Language, literacy, and discourse in project-based science. *Journal of Research in Science Teaching, 38*(4), 469–498.

Morrison, P., & Morrison, P. (1984). *Primary science: Symbol or substance?* New York: City College Workshop Center.

Morrison, P., & Morrison, P. (1987). Change [Video series episode 2]. In *The ring of truth: An inquiry into how we know what we know.* Alexandria, VA: Public Broadcasting Associates.

National Research Council (NRC). (1996). *National science education standards.* Washington, DC: National Academy Press.

National Research Council (NRC). (2000). *Inquiry and the national science education standards: A guide for teaching and learning.* Washington, DC: National Academy Press.

National Science Foundation. (n.d.). *Foundations: Vol. 2. Inquiry: Thoughts, views, and strategies for the K–5 classroom.* Arlington, VA: Author.

Nuffield Junior Science. (1967). *Science and history: Teacher's background booklet.* London: William Collins.

Polanyi, M. (1962). *Personal knowledge: Towards a post-critical philosophy.* London: Routledge & Kegan Paul.

Resnick, L.B. (1987). *Education and learning to think*. Washington, DC: National Academy Press.

Rivard, L.P., & Straw, S.B. (2000). The effect of talk and writing on learning science: An exploratory study. *Science Education, 84*(5), pp. 566–593.

Rose, A.J. (1987). *Inquiring children and their teachers*. New York: City College Workshop Center.

Rosen, H. (1981, April). *Neither Bleak House nor Liberty Hall: English in the curriculum*. Inaugural lecture delivered at the University of London Institute of Education, London, United Kingdom.

Saul, W., & Reardon, J. (Eds.). (1996). *Beyond the science kit: Inquiry in action*. Portsmouth, NH: Heinemann.

Shepardson, D.P., & Britsch, S.J. (2001). The role of children's journals in elementary school science activities. *Journal of Research in Science Teaching, 38*(1), pp. 43–69.

Stevens, P. (1974). *Patterns in nature*. Boston: Little, Brown.

Trefil, J.S. (1984). *A scientist at the seashore*. New York: Scribner.

Weber, L. (1971). *The English infant school and informal education*. Englewood Cliffs, NJ: Prentice Hall.

Weber, L. (1973). But is it science? In L. Weber (Ed.), *Science in the open classroom* (pp. 3–10). New York: Workshop Center for Open Education.

Weber, L., & Dyasi, H. (1985). Language development and observation of the local environment: First steps in providing primary-school science education for non-dominant groups. *Prospects: Quarterly Review of Education, 15*(4), pp. 565–576.

Worth, K. (1996). *Placing children at the center of science education reform*. New York: City College Workshop Center.

What's Next? A View From the Editor's Perch

Academic disciplines might be differentiated by thinking about the gifts and possibilities each offers. In his book *The Hedgehog, the Fox, and the Magister's Pox: Ending the False War Between Science and the Humanities* (2003), Stephen Jay Gould uses a metaphor from a proverb from the seventh century B.C. to explain different ways of being in the world. The fox develops innovative and context-responsive approaches, one after the other, to ensure his survival, whereas the hedgehog relies on only one tried-and-true method—he rolls into a prickly and odoriferous ball and plays dead. Each of us as teachers—and the academic approaches we represent—have much to learn from both the fox and the hedgehog, Gould tells us. As I read through this volume, I asked myself what we were doing in schools to mend or exacerbate the gap between science and the humanities.

For me, in seeking to bridge this gap, it is important to differentiate between narrowly defined instrumental associations—that is, those links directly targeted to teach specific skills and knowledge—and those connections that reach to the heart of what it means to do science or to communicate in such a way that what one knows or values is made available and inviting to others. My argument here may have as much to do with beliefs and philosophy as it does with outcomes.

For example, a review of reading test scores shows that students have been doing well with what test makers refer to as reading for global understanding, but considerably less well on expository and procedural reading and writing. That is, U.S. students seem to be fairly adept at reading stories, but far less successful in reading expository or procedural texts (i.e., what we now call nonfiction). And, as one might guess, the primary subject matter for nonfiction reading is science and social studies. Given the urge to devote as much instructional time as possible to improving reading, and given the realization that science topics, in some form, might be addressed by reading science-related nonfiction, schools could efficiently address both reading requirements and science deficiencies by introducing science-related reading. And in many school systems, this is currently the practice. In fact, some schools have relegated hands-on science programs to an after-school or enrichment program, ensuring that struggling readers or children in high-needs schools get little but text-based science. And if test scores improve, educators pat themselves on their collective backs and move to the next crisis.

A noninstrumental approach invites a different kind of thinking. In this case we would begin by seeking the essential—or "hedgehog"—elements of both literacy and science knowledge. What is it that we do not wish to lose under any circumstances as we seek to engage students in these subjects?

The Gifts of Science

About 30 years ago, I married a scientist and have since joined him in various places where science takes place, including national laboratories, universities, and meetings of various high-level boards. In each of these settings, as well as in my work with science educators and science-enthused students, my goal is the same—to gain some insight into what it is that scientists view as central to their work. Questions—not the kind of questions that can be answered by a quick check in a reference book, but the kind that require the gathering and interpretation of data—are absolutely central to the enterprise we call science. Succinctly stated, decent science instruction must embrace inquiry; without inquiry, the activity called science is not really science at all.

Of course, there are many ways in which inquiry finds its way into science. If a reader has a specific curiosity or is intrigued by the questions the author addresses in an article or book, an otherwise dry, informational text can become exciting and captivating. Conversely, what may be an engaged interaction with a book for one reader may turn out to be a terrible or boring experience for a reader whose sole purpose is to reproduce the knowledge the text presents in order to get a good grade.

Inquiry also may have to do with a predisposition toward the material in hand, what Donna Alvermann refers to in chapter 12 of this book as self-questioning. How much of one's ability to question the text has to do with background information, I wonder? If I know a lot about the dangers of certain chemicals, my reading on the subject will be much different than for someone who knows nothing about the topic and is scared of toxicity or someone who believes the dangers of so-called hazardous chemicals are exaggerated and reads with a dismissive stance. Which takes us to another hedgehog value of science—science is built on evidence; to work within a scientific paradigm, one must continually evaluate rather than simply accept information. People who read and write and talk science with understanding are aware not only of the value of evidence but also of the value of revision. What other evidence might someone wish to collect? How does what I know about X compare to what this text is saying about Y? Reading science or engaging in science has much to do with putting together bits of information and using this information to confirm beliefs or to create doubts. It is a gift of the discipline.

The Gifts of Literacy

Do we use reading, writing, and talking in order to learn, as a means of knowing, or must we first understand something before we can read, write, and talk effectively? Surely, all of us in literacy education are aware of a salient connection between literacy and knowledge acquisition, critique and development in various intellectual domains. The hedgehog values of literacy then have to do with communication, with communication in context. To study literacy is fundamentally to study the act of meaning-making, the act of interpretation. Sometimes science-related communication becomes bogged down in content issues or vocabulary load. We may not be clear about what we are trying to say, and we may get lost or hide in language. At other times, we may want for an appropriate vocabulary or a convincing rhetoric. Sometimes scientific information is coded in tables or graphs and labeled in unfamiliar ways. Without the experience or referents, these codings seem inaccessible and frustrating (see chapter 2 for more on this topic).

How are those hedgehog values of science confounded by or helped along by language? In a huge gym-turned-exhibit hall, middle school students shift nervously in front of their science fair trifolds. I stop to talk with one student about his project on the feeding habits of birds. Unlike most of his peers, this young man exudes confidence. He points with assurance to his hypothesis and chats comfortably about dependent and independent variables. But as I listen, I realize that most of what he prattles on about makes little or no sense, though his seventh-grade colleagues listen enviously, with respect. A student who lives on a farm stands nearby, confident that her knowledge of butchering will stave off anyone likely to criticize her award-winning project on bacteria growth in organ meat. Other students appear to talk reluctantly, almost painfully.

Looking back on my observations of students who view themselves and who are viewed by others as good or bad at science, I think about what James Paul Gee calls the discourse/Discourse of science (see chapter 1). How do students learn to talk science, to write science, to read science? How do students learn to see themselves as fit to play on the science field? Now considerable effort is being expended to identify specific literacy strategies that students who are good in science have mastered, but perhaps not enough attention has been dedicated to the understanding of how those literacy strategies serve or even connect to a student's ability to inquire. How does such work—specific instruction in using headings, indexes, or tables of contents, and lessons on recognizing main ideas and details—aid students in their ability to ask and recognize meaningful questions?

Exchanging Gifts

Ten years ago, the program of the annual convention of the National Science Teachers Association included only a handful of sessions devoted to science-related reading and writing. In 2003, more than 10% of the offerings addressed literacy instruction. Similarly, at the International Reading Association's 2003 Annual Convention, nonfiction—much of it focused on science—reigned on the exhibit floor, and many of the sessions devoted to strategies for comprehending science text had filled to capacity and disappointed crowds were turned away 30 minutes before the sessions began.

Although this interest in literacy–science connections may appear promising to those concerned with science-related discourse, a closer look at the practices being promulgated under this heading is needed. As foxes, educators run from session to session and from book to book, seeking answers that make sense at this particular moment and in this current climate, but educators must, I believe, keep alive those hedgehog values. Before becoming excited about the latest interdisciplinary methods, it may be time to stop and ask questions:

- Is the connection natural and authentic? Does the connection distort either discipline? Is it intellectually honest?

- Does the connection foster understandings useful in interpreting the world; that is, does it provide a strong and useful light for interpreting experience and information, or is it the intellectual equivalent of a momentary spark?

- Does the connection, even if it allows a teacher to check off boxes on a curricular rubric, take away from time that may better be spent in other ways?

- Who/what benefits from promoting (or not promoting) this particular notion of connections?

In attending various conference sessions and reading articles and books devoted to linking literacy and science, I use my queries to check out various approaches. If science is essentially about inquiry and evidence, for example, what do I make of a strategy that asks students to look through books to see if what they report "knowing" is, in fact, true? Is this how information is confirmed in science—by checking in a book? Surely, this is not the message science educators wish to send.

What about a question board (Pearce, 2003) on which students make public, and then try to sort through and organize, their questions—which ones are testable, which require sustained observation, which are best developed through further reading? This involves writing and reading for authentic purposes, fosters and amplifies current understandings, and addresses the goals of both the reading and science communities as well as the classroom community.

The point here is that linking literacy and science study is not the time-saving and efficient measure many had hoped. To substitute science vocabulary lessons for inquiry and exploration shortchanges both vocabulary and science instruction. Put another way, the student who has worked with a thermometer will have a much richer understanding of words such as *measurement*, *estimation*, *temperature*, *Celsius*, and *Fahrenheit* than a student who has simply learned these words for a vocabulary test. The potential rewards of linking literacy and science growth also go far beyond those associated with "learn the definition" vocabulary instruction. And the ability to answer formulaic questions based on reading selections should be seen neither as a marker of scientific skill nor as an indication of a student's potential interest in science.

In order to extrapolate students' perceptions of what it means to be a scientist, science educators typically ask children to draw a picture of a scientist. Often the resulting drawing—man in a lab coat—is viewed as a measure or indicator of the student's perception of his or her ability to do science. But perhaps it is time for a more nuanced understanding of science identity. There are strategies or gifts to borrow from literacy educators that may be of help here. What if, for instance, we modified the questions used by Goodman, Watson, and Burke (1987) to understand better the issue of a literacy identity and used this interview schedule to think about students' perceptions of themselves as scientists? A conversation about science competence might include the following questions:

- Do you ever come across questions in science that you cannot answer? What do you do?
- If that doesn't work, what might you try next?
- Who do you know who is really good at science?
- What makes (person X) really good at science?
- Do you think (person X) ever finds questions he or she cannot answer?
- What do you think he or she does to figure things out?
- If you knew someone was having trouble with a science problem, how would you help that person?
- How did you learn to do science?
- What do you do well as a scientist?
- What would you like to do better?
- Do you think you are good at science right now? Why or why not?

We seem to be at a point in history when funders, curriculum developers, and school personnel are looking to educational researchers for material from which research-based instruction readily can be built. If only it were that easy. At best, researchers offer statistical likelihoods or enable us to ask better, more probing questions. But a classroom teacher's obligation is to all the children in his or her charge. Any programs, activities, or strategies that seek to circumvent the teacher (that, in the parlance of the 1960s, are "teacher-proof") are, I believe, doomed to failure. Although this book includes data, explanations, and interpretations designed to help practitioners and policymakers as they seek to develop better science and literacy curricula, it is not a prefabricated house ready for easy assembly.

At present, I am working to fit two seemingly unrelated ideas into place. The first is that school curricula are written largely in response to social and political demands. Problems or challenges are identified, and educators—problem-solvers by nature and profession—seek to find solutions. At this point in history, schools show a definite preference for clearly defined elements that can be taught and measured.

The second idea has to do with the definitions or the lenses we use to recognize what is to be learned and what, in fact, is worth knowing. Current attention is directed to the distinction between fiction and nonfiction. We divide classroom libraries into fiction and nonfiction. We ask if boys seem to like nonfiction better than fiction. We tell students that they will need to look for the table of contents and glossary in certain books, and these books contain information that is true. Or conversely, we tell students that certain books are fiction; they need no glossary and are not true.

I wonder about these distinctions, about their usefulness and about their truth and value. At one time teachers talked about texts differently; there were literary and nonliterary texts. Thomas Jefferson, for instance, wrote literary texts, and potboiler fiction was viewed as nonliterary. Perhaps the question is not whether boys or girls particularly like nonfiction but whether they like science. Perhaps we need to ask if there is truth in a given work of fiction and how we know it is true. And what about this work of nonfiction—this book itself? What in it makes you doubt? On what basis do you doubt?

Presently, in the primary grades, reading programs emphasize the decoding of text; in the upper grades, instruction centers around formulaic writing and the delivery of information through which mastery can be assessed comfortably (easy-to-score, multiple-choice questions or clearly explained rubrics). Is this the best use of student time? Might young children benefit more from less simple texts? Do educators' current attempts to present students with only materials that they can read independently make sense? Are these the texts that best serve students' literacy and scientific interests? Does the diminution or obliteration of inquiry-based science programs actually help or hinder students' ability to think critically and creatively about what they read and write?

This afterword is a kind of personal reflection—my own attempt to identify some of the issues that remain, if not unexplored, at least underdeveloped. Stephen Jay Gould leaves us with this thought:

> We can enjoy our fusion of intentions, motives and several aspects of creative practice (the hedgehog's one great way), but also respect our discreteness and separation as guardians of distinct magesteria charged with the exploration of logically different kinds of questions (the fox's many effective but separate ways). (2003, p. 155)

Finally, what matters most may be our ability to recognize and distinguish between that which should remain discrete and that which benefits from being connected and united.

REFERENCES

Gould, S.J. (2003). *The hedgehog, the fox, and the magister's pox: Ending the false war between science and the humanities.* Prospect, KY: Harmony.

Goodman, Y., Watson, D., & Burke, C. (1987). *Reading miscue inventory: Alternative procedures.* Katonah, NY: Richard C. Owen.

Pearce, C. (2003). The question board. *Thinking Classroom/Peremena, 4,* 43–44.

E

EAGLY, A.H., 373
EARLE, A., 263
EDMUNDS, J., 230
EDWARDS, M., 248
EGAN-ROBERTSON, A., 164
ELDREDGE, J.L., 401
ELLENBOGEN, E., 86
ELLEY, W.B., 261
ENGESTRÖM, Y., 20
EYLON, B.-S., 241, 246, 254

F

FAIRBANKS, M.M., 318, 402
FARRIS, P.J., 319
FELDMAN, A., 142, 144, 152
FELLOWS, N., 345
FENSTERMACHER, G., 143
FEYNMAN, R.P., 102, 434
FINN, P.J., 230
FISHER, C.W., 260
FLAVELL, J.H., 239
FLEVARES, L.M., 48
FLODEN, R.E., 85
FLORENCE, M.K., 72, 74, 77, 79, 81, 355
FORD, C., 83
FORD, D.J., 277–278, 285, 288, 330
FOUNTAS, I.C., 266
FOWLER, A., 161, 165, 169–170, 174, 180
FOWLER, P., 370–371
FRACTOR, J.S., 262
FREEMAN, S.H., 260
FREIRE, P., 421–422
FYFE, L.M., 120

G

GALLAS, K., 111, 116–117, 141
GALLEY, M., 385
GAMAS, W.S., 293
GARRISON, L., 344, 347, 351–352, 427
GATES, A., 190
GAVELEK, J.R., 228
GEE, J.P., 13–14, 17–18, 20, 25, 27, 143,
   145, 148, 180, 187
GEHRINGER, M., 74
GEORGI, M.C., 317
GIBBONS, G., 190–192, 197–207, 291
GIBSON, E.M., 384
GILBERT, J., 118–119
GLASS, G.V., 293, 322

GLENBERG, A.M., 19–21
GLENN, C.G., 129
GOLDIN-MEADOW, S., 48, 54, 59, 63
GOLDMAN, S.R., 126–127, 163, 317
GONZALEZ, N., 179
GOOD, R.G., 79, 163, 316, 319
GOODMAN, Y., 451
GOODWIN, C., 53, 60
GORE, J.M., 116
GOULD, G., 234
GOULD, S.J., 447, 453
GRANT, C.A., 436
GRAY, S., 268
GREEN, J.L., 133
GREENE, M., 146–148
GREENLEAF, C., 236
GREENO, J.G., 414
GRIFFIN, P., 14, 240, 261
GRITSAVAGE, M.M., 120
GUIGNON, C.B., 145
GULGOZ, S., 370
GUNSTONE, R.F., 233, 241
GUTHRIE, J.T., 243, 251, 384, 392, 397
GUZZETTI, B.J., 111–117, 120, 234, 293,
   322, 370–371

H

HADAR, U., 61
HAGINS, W.C., 387
HALLIDAY, M.A.K., 16, 163, 192
HALPERN, D.F., 412
HAMILTON, R.L., 245, 370
HANCOCK, G.R., 251
HAND, B.M., 72, 74, 77, 79, 81–83, 85–86,
   88–90, 241, 246, 253, 355–357, 371
HANKS, W.F., 23, 57, 64
HANRAHAN, M., 349
HAPGOOD, S., 332
HARAWAY, D., 141
HARDENBROOK, M., 120
HARLEN, W., 341, 346–347, 423, 434, 436
HARLEY, B., 132
HARMS, N.C., 105
HARTLEY, K., 269–270, 272
HARTMANN, D., 317
HARWELL, S.H., 111, 113
HASAN, R., 192, 196
HAVENS, L.T., 253, 349
HAVILAND, J., 53
HAWKINS, D., 434, 436
HAYES, D.A., 231

164–165, 165*t*–168*t*; within unit, 169–179, 170*t*–171*t*

INVESTIGATION: benefits of, 210–211; examples of, 211–216; with notebook text, 323; in student notebooks, 347–348

IOWA CHAUTAUQUA MODEL, 414–415

IRE DISCOURSE STRUCTURES, 164

I-THOU RELATIONSHIP, 151

J–K

JOURNALS: City College Workshop Center and, 436–437; model, 316–339. *See also* logs; notebooks

KNOWING: in science, 140–157

KNOWLEDGE: definition of, 123; development of, 123–124; transferring, high-science read-alouds and, 310

KNOWLEDGE CLAIMS: evaluation of, Science Writing Heuristic and, 355–368

K-W-L PLUS STRATEGY, 400–403

L

LANGUAGE: acquisition of, and perspective taking, 22–25; expanded, 28–31; in science classroom, 13–32; and science process, 342

LANGUAGE ARTS: study by future scientists, rationale for, 71–94

LANGUAGE-ORIENTED TASKS: in science instruction, 83–90

LANGUAGES OF SCIENCE, 11–67; development of, 36–38; as hybrid, 33–34; versus lifeworld language, 25–28; Yore on, 71–72

LANGUAGE USERS: scientists as, 73–82

LEADERSHIP AND ASSISTANCE FOR SCIENCE EDUCATIONAL REFORM (LASER) MODEL: National Science Resources Center, 344

LEARNING: active, and mind engagement, 416–417; as natural, 410–411. *See also* science learning

LECTURES: teacher gestures in, 61–64

LESSON ORGANIZATION: common, in science and reading, 247–248

LEXICOGRAMMAR, 200–201

LIBRARIES, CLASSROOM: informational books for, 261–265; inventorying, 265, 266*t*

LIFEWORLD LANGUAGE, 15–18; and science, 25–28

LINGUISTICS: systemic functional, in informational books, 190–208

LISTENING: and explanation development, 58–59; scientists and, 77–79

LITERACY(IES): development of, gestures and, 48–67; gifts of, 449–450; multimodal,

38–41; multiple forms of, and science learning, 226–238; school-based: academic social languages as heart of, 13–32; of science, 33–47; science instruction for understanding and, 316–339; and science learning, 372–374

LITERACY INSTRUCTION: goals of, 395–396; role in science, 69–107; and science instruction, 42–43, 374–376, 375*f*; and science learning, 127–130. *See also* literacy–science connections

LITERACY–SCIENCE CONNECTIONS, 1–9; collaboration areas for, 45–46; curricular integration and, 43, 251–252; definition of, 6; future of, 447–453; goals in, 395–405; nuances in, 1; questions on, 2, 450; reciprocal skills in, 340–343, 342*t*; recommendations for, 130–131; young learners' reasoning and, 209–223. *See also* literacy instruction

LOGS: exploration, 211; learning, 253. *See also* journals; notebooks

M

THE MAGIC SCHOOL BUS SERIES, 291–313; creation of, 296; recommendations for, 312

MATERIAL RESOURCES, 5–6; limitations of, 105–106

MEANING: by degree, 34–38; by kind, 34–38; situated, in social language, 18–22

METACOGNITION, 239–257; definition of, 239; focus on, 239–240; notebook text and, 331; and reciprocal skills, 342–343; recommendations on, 243–248; in science writing, 252–254; social origins of, 240–242; student notebooks and, 348–351

METACOGNITIVE AWARENESS READING STRATEGIES INVENTORY, 249

METAFUNCTIONS: in trade books, 201–204

METHODOLOGICAL MODEL: of science, 328

MIND: as computer, 142–144

MIND ENGAGEMENT, 408–419; active learning and, 416–417; brain and, 410–412; in instructional model, 400–401; NSES on, 366–367; strategies for, 102–103

MISCONCEPTIONS ON SCIENCE: refutational text and, 293–294

MIXED TEXTS, 264–265

MODE: definition of, 193

MOTIVATIONAL FACTORS: and textbook selection, 391–392

MULTILITERACIES: definition of, 227; and science learning, 226–238; and social constructionist learning theory, 227–229
MULTIMODAL LITERACY, 38–41; in science inquiry, 277–278
MULTIMODAL TEXTS: informational, 190–208; nature of, 190–194

N

NAMING: students on, 1
NARRATIVE INFORMATION BOOKS, 195, 264; generic structure in, 197–200, 199f; lexicogrammar of, 200–201; as read-alouds, 291–313; refutational, concerns with, 293–294; visual communication in, 202
NATIONAL COUNCIL FOR TEACHERS OF ENGLISH, 1, 6
NATIONAL SCIENCE EDUCATION STANDARDS (NSES), 99–101, 409; on activities of science, 243; on engagement, 366–367; on goals, 395; on inquiry, 423; and metacognition, 240; on scientific literacy, 99, 101f
NATIONAL SCIENCE RESOURCES CENTER: Leadership and Assistance for Science Educational Reform (LASER) Model, 344
NATIONAL SCIENCE TEACHERS ASSOCIATION, 1; on scientific literacy, 97; and teachers, 6; on trade books, 292
NATURAL LANGUAGE: limitations of, 33–34; meaning by degree in, 35–36
NONFICTION. See informational text
NONNARRATIVE INFORMATION BOOKS, 195; generic structure in, 197, 198f; lexicogrammar of, 200–201; visual communication in, 202–204
NOTEBOOKS: design of, 319–321; sample, 334–339; student, and inquiry process, 340–354; student evaluations of, 330–331; use of, investigation of, 321–330. See also journals; logs
NSES. See National Science Education Standards

O–P

OBSERVATION: overemphasis on, 287–288
ORACY, 86
PEERS: discouragement of girls by, 115–116; and metacognition, 241
PERSPECTIVE TAKING: and language acquisition, 22–25
PIAGET, JEAN, 241
PODENDORF, ILLA, 1
PREWRITING: in science, 89–90

PRIMARY GRADES: choosing informational books for, 260–276
PROBLEMS: and students' reasoning, 217–218
PROSE: in textbooks, 385–386
PUBLISHERS: versus government-funded developers, 388–389; influence on science instruction, 387–388; support by, and textbook selection, 392

Q–R

QUESTION BOARD, 451
QUESTIONS: information-bearing structures and, 307–308; with read-alouds, 301–307; as science activity, 408; on science-literacy connections, 2, 450; for student notebooks, 346; and students' reasoning, 217–218; types of, 232
READ-ALOUDS: high science content, 291–313; informational, promotion of dialogic inquiry with, 161–189; recommendations for, 312
READERS: as scientists, 209–223; successful, attributes of, 425
READING: of science, 123–125; in science inquiry, 250; science of, 125–126; scientists and, 79–82; textbook selection and, 370–382; the word, 424–427; the world, 420–446
READING ACHIEVEMENT: strategies for, 379
READING COMPREHENSION: and learning from scientific inquiry, 317–319; and science content, 395–405; and science inquiry, metacognition and, 239–257; strategies, and reading achievement, 379
READING SKILLS: prerequisite, for science, 123–139
REAL-WORLD ISSUES: and classroom instruction, 413–414
REASONING: community-stimulated, 222–223; notebook text and, 325–330; writing and, 223; of young learners, 209–223
REFUTATIONAL TEXTS: benefits of, 371, 377, 378f; concerns with, 293–294
RELEVANCE: and mind engagement, 412–416
REORGANIZING: in instructional model, 403
REVIEWS: City College Workshop Center and, 436–437
RHETORICAL ARGUMENTS, 87

S

SAGAN, CARL, 409
SALIENCE, 202
SCHOOL-BASED LITERACY: academic social languages as heart of, 13–32

SCIENCE: access to, 4, 109–157; across the curriculum, 43; activities of, 408; definition of, 123; gestures in, 48–67; knowing and being in, 140–157; language arts in, role of, 71–94; models of, 328; myths on, 73–74; navigating, 3–4; outside school, 43; of reading, 125–126; reading of, 123–125; reading skills for, prerequisite, 123–139; school, worlds of, 427; and technology, 98–99; versus written materials, 95–107

SCIENCE INQUIRY: City College Workshop Center and, 430–436; highly recommended trade books and, 277–290; metacognition and, 239–257; reading comprehension and, 317–319; student notebooks and, 340–354; text model for, 316–339. *See also* inquiry

SCIENCE INSTRUCTION: context and, 102–107; current status of, 340; as dialogic process, 159–223; eras of, 97–98; gender bias in, 111–122; goals for, 104–105, 395; informational books and, 190–208; language-oriented tasks in, 83–90; literacy instruction and, 42–43, 374–376, 375*f*; metacognition and, 239–240; mind engagement in, 408–419; reform goals in, 84; strategies for, 430–442; time frame of, 324*f*; two-dimensional view of, 100; for understanding, and literacy, 316–339

SCIENCE LEARNING: as change in way of being, 144–145; context and, 102–107; definition of, 140–145; informational text and, 185–187; literacy and, 372–374; literacy instruction and, 127–130; reading comprehension and, 126–127; research on, 397–400. *See also* learning

SCIENCE (SCIENTIFIC) LITERACY: definition of, 6, 95–99; elements of, 83–84, 355; gender and, 111–122; versus reading science materials, 95–107; strategies for, 88–89

SCIENCE STORIES: creation of, 4

SCIENCE WRITING HEURISTIC (SWH), 253, 355–368; student template, 356, 357*f*; teacher template, 356–357, 357*f*

SCIENTIFIC ACTIVITY: nature of, highly recommended trade books on, 283–285, 284*t*

SCIENTIFIC TERMS: high-science read-alouds and, 310–311

SCIENTIFIC THINKING: text model for, 316–339

SCIENTISTS: inquiries, City College Workshop Center and, 434; as language users, 73–82; readers as, 209–223; on science,

74–75; sessions with, City College Workshop Center and, 437–439

SECOND-LANGUAGE LEARNERS: exploration and, 210; and prerequisite reading skills for science, 132–137, 135*t*–136*t*

SELF: self-construction of, 147

SELF-QUESTIONING, 229–234; and science learning, 226–238

SELF-REGULATION: fostering, 240–242

SENSE MAKING: in science, young urban children's ways of, 161–189

SITUATED MEANING: in social language, 18–22

SITUATION: existentialism and, 145–146

SMALL-GROUP INTERACTIONS: gender and, 113–114, 117–118; inquiries, 430–434; teacher gestures in, 59–61

SOCIAL CONSTRUCTIONIST LEARNING THEORY: multiliteracies and, 227–229

SOCIAL ENVIRONMENT: and science learning, 399

SOCIAL LANGUAGE CODE, 14–15

SPECIALIST WORLDS: language of, 15–18

SPEECH: scientists and, 77–79; and writing, 55–59

STORIES: student exposure to, versus informational text, 128

STRUCTURED ANALYTICAL IMAGES, 203

STRUCTURED CONTROVERSY, 87–88

STUDENT(S): control of own learning, 399–400; on naming, 1; on readers as scientists, 210–214, 223; and Science Writing Heuristic, 356, 357*f*; support systems for, and textbook selection, 390–391; term, 140

SUBGENRES: in trade books, 201–204

SUPPORT SYSTEMS: and textbook selection, 390–391

SWH. *See* Science Writing Heuristic

T

TALK. *See* speech

TAOISM: and mind engagement, 411

TEACHER(S), 407–446; and City College Workshop Center, 439; existentialist, 149–156; and gender bias, 112–114, 120; gestures by, 59–65; and metacognition, 248; and mind engagement, 408–419; and notebook text, 330; professional development of, 420–446; and read-alouds, 291–313, 302*t*–306*t*; and reform, 106; role of, 6–7; and Science Writing Heuristic, 356–357, 357*f*; standards for, 375*f*; and student notebook use, 350–351; and student self-questioning,

233; and student self-regulation, 241; support systems for, and textbook selection, 390–391

TEACHER-PROOF MATERIALS, 6, 151, 452

TEACHERS' GUIDES, 377–379

TECHNOLOGY: and science, 98–99

TENOR: definition of, 192

TEXTBOOKS: comprehension of, 126–127; difficulties with, 370–371; evaluation of, 369–405; gender bias in, 114–115, 118–119; guidelines for selection of, 389–392; improvements in, 385–387; reading, strategies for, 88–89; recommendations for, 376–380; versus science, 95–107; selection of, factors affecting, 383–394; versus trade books, 383–385

TIME: for instruction, 4–5

TRADE BOOKS: alternative, 287; comprehension of, 126–127; and curricular integration, 251; evaluation of, 267–274, 270t–271t; gender bias in, 114–115, 118–119; highly recommended, in inquiry science, 277–290; multimodal literacy and, 190–208; as read-alouds, 291–313; reading, strategies for, 88–89; versus science, 95–107; in science instruction, 292–295; selection of, 259–313; versus textbooks, 383–385

TRANSFER OF LEARNING, 399

TRIPTYCH, 203

TRUTH: nature of, 234–235

TRUTH VALUES: critical stance on, 246–247; of informational text, 129

U–V

UNDERSTANDINGS: social construction of, 222–223

URBAN CHILDREN: City College Workshop Center and, 427–443; ways of making sense in science, 161–189

VALLE IMPERIAL PROJECT IN SCIENCE (VIPS), 343–351

VERB: science as, 73

VERBAL COMMUNICATION: relation to visual communication, 203–207; in trade books, 192–193, 196–201

VERIFICATION: in science, 124

VIDEOTAPES, MENTAL, 20, 143–144

VIPS. See Valle Imperial Project in Science

VISUAL COMMUNICATION: in read-alouds, 301; relation to verbal communication, 203–207; in trade books, 193–194, 201–204; Vygotsky on, 347

VOCABULARY: controlled, in trade and textbooks, 384

VOICE: in model notebook, 320–321; in student notebooks, 344–345, 348–351

W

WHOLE-CLASS DISCUSSIONS: gender in, 113, 117–118

WONDER: high-science read-alouds and, 310

WONDERMENT QUESTIONS, 232

WORLD, READING, 422–424; importance of, 421–422; and professional development, 420–446

WRAPPED TEXT: instruction on, 272–273

WRITING, 315–368; evaluation of, 271t, 273; explanations for, 219–220; instruction, current status of, 340; investigation of, 216; metacognition and, 252–254; and reasoning, 223; in science, 89–90; science versus literary, 426; Science Writing Heuristic, 253, 355–368; scientists and, 79–82, 81t; speech and, 55–59; student notebooks, and inquiry process, 340–354; textbook selection and, 370–382; the word, 425–427; the world, 423–424